3RD EDITION

ADVERTISING CREATIVE

3RD EDITION

ADVERTISING CREATIVE

STRATEGY, COPY, DESIGN

Tom Altstiel
PKA Marketing

Jean Grow
Marquette University

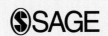

Los Angeles | London | New Delhi
Singapore | Washington DC

Los Angeles | London | New Delhi
Singapore | Washington DC

FOR INFORMATION:

SAGE Publications, Inc.
2455 Teller Road
Thousand Oaks, California 91320
E-mail: order@sagepub.com

SAGE Publications Ltd.
1 Oliver's Yard
55 City Road
London EC1Y 1SP
United Kingdom

SAGE Publications India Pvt. Ltd.
B 1/I 1 Mohan Cooperative Industrial Area
Mathura Road, New Delhi 110 044
India

SAGE Publications Asia-Pacific Pte. Ltd.
3 Church Street
#10-04 Samsung Hub
Singapore 049483

Acquisitions Editor: Matthew Byrnie
Associate Editor: Nathan Davidson
Editorial Assistant: Stephanie Palermini
Production Editor: Laura Stewart
Copy Editor: Melinda Masson
Typesetter: C&M Digitals, Ltd.
Proofreader: Joyce Li
Indexer: Teddy Diggs
Cover Designer: Dan Augustine
Marketing Manager: Liz Thorton
Permissions Editor: Karen Ehrmann

Copyright © 2013 by SAGE Publications, Inc.

Photo credits: 4, completelyseriouscomics.com; 13, Steve Ohler; 31, © Juan Herrera/istockphoto; 73, © Can Stock Photo Inc./monkeybusiness

Printed in Canada

Library of Congress Cataloging-in-Publication Data

Altstiel, Tom.
ADVERTISING CREATIVE : Strategy, Copy, and Design / Tom

Altstiel, PKA Marketing, Jean Grow, Marquette University.—Third Edition.

pages cm

Includes bibliographical references and index.

ISBN 978-1-4522-0363-8 (pbk.)

1. Advertising. I. Grow, Jean. II. Title.

HF5823.A758 2013
659.1—dc23   2012026844

This book is printed on acid-free paper.

12 13 14 15 16 10 9 8 7 6 5 4 3 2 1

Brief Contents

Detailed Contents

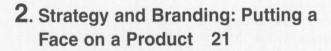

3. Legal and Ethical Issues: Doing the Right Thing   49

6. Concepting: What's the Big Idea?   110

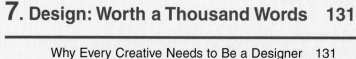

7. Design: Worth a Thousand Words   131

8. Campaigns: Synergy and Integration   155

9. Headlines and Taglines: First Get Their Attention   171

10. Body Copy: Writing for Readers   192

11. Print: Writing for Reading   211

12. Radio and Television: Interruptions That Sell   227

16. Beyond Media: Everybody Out of the Box   317

17. Business-to-Business: Selling Along the Supply Chain 343

18. Survival Guide: Landing Your First Job and Thriving 359

Appendix   383

Why a Third Edition of This Book?

When we penned the second edition, our book got a new name. With the third edition, we've taken a deeper dive into digital technology.

Of course, we still provide practical, how-to advice. We still discuss the strategic blending of copy, design, and technology. We still feature case histories, checklists, contemporary examples, and profiles of inspirational people in our business, including young rising stars too. We thought it might be inspiring for students to see stories from recent grads on their way to the top.

However, this time around our exploration into digital technology exposes pervasive changes across the global advertising landscape. Theses changes go far beyond technology yet are driven by it. Brands now cut across geographic and cultural boundaries with lightning speed. The interplay of technology and culture, both local and global, is fast creating a marketplace that knows no boundaries. And where there are boundaries, technology often shatters the barriers. As cultural, geographic, and economic boundaries shift under our feet, three things will define the future leaders of our industry—and how we edited our third edition:

- Be a risk taker.

- Understand technology.

- Live for ideas.

Being a Risk Taker

We spend a lot of time on strategy, with the overarching theme that people don't buy things. Rather, they buy satisfaction of wants and needs. Selling satisfaction often means taking risks. We discuss how technology is changing consumer behavior and how to develop strategies that take the risks to meet the challenges of our time.

Being a risk taker also means that you had better understand that legal and ethical considerations are more important than ever and ever more complicated. With issues more than a little blurred in this digital world and brands rapidly crossing global and cultural boundaries, companies often face issues framed by corporate social responsibility. We added stand-alone chapters on ethics and law and international issues, each dedicated to these discussions. After all, students need to decide not only how to do things right, but also how to do the right thing.

Those who take risks will stand out. Those who stand out rise to the top.

Understanding Technology

Rapidly accelerating technology continues to blur the lines between marketing communication tactics. Even the definition of "traditional" and "nontraditional" media has become pointless. The seamless integration of word of mouth, mobile, social media, cause marketing, public relations, viral, guerrilla, and sales promotion makes it difficult to divide a text into discrete chapters for a segregated lesson plan. Chapter by chapter we strive to help you sort out the right tool for the right result.

However, knowing the importance of social media, we've added a stand-alone chapter addressing the changing social landscape. Of course, we know nearly all we've written is already out of date as soon as we go on press. So, we framed our discussion around using creative ideas to build and sustain brand-building communities. That never goes out of date.

We wanted to walk the walk and not just talk the talk with this book. So, Sage is hosting a new website allowing flexibility to update content and help connect our community. It is a resource for instructors and students, and over time will showcase for student work. Most of all, we hope it becomes a place to initiate and continue ongoing conversations.

Understanding technology will increase your value. The higher your value, the greater your success.

Living for Ideas

From Leo Burnett to Alex Bogusky, it's always been about having big ideas. Copywriter, designer, web developer, account planner, sales promotion specialist, blogger—it doesn't matter where students land in the creative side of our business; they all need big ideas with the potential for big results. While we have a separate chapter on concepting, the development of big ideas is woven throughout the book.

The third edition is structured to help students develop visual and verbal approaches that best fit each of the various technologies, but always with the idea in the lead. Far from being a dying art, copywriting skills are even more important today for online marketing. In addition, copywriters still need a solid understanding of design, whether their work appears in a magazine or on an iPad screen. Those who can express their ideas will be the future leaders.

As technology expands, the world gets smaller, and brands increasingly must communicate global messages. This time around we explore ethnography and how it can be a tool to help advertisers develop ideas that build and sustain global branding. We've introduced a new chapter on international advertising with tips and techniques to help students develop a global point of view. And, you'll see work from around the world throughout the book.

Ideas can come from anyone, anywhere. We hope to inspire the future leaders of our business, not so much by telling them what to do, but rather by showing them what others are already doing. We showcase outstanding student work along with the most contemporary examples available in a printed textbook. Over 90% of the examples are new to this edition. And because ideas can be found anywhere, we've also included a lot of new people in Who's Who, with more women and young people who have made and are still making a difference. We've also added our new Rising Star feature with profiles in each chapter.

We scoured a lot of websites, blogs, social media sites, books, and industry trade publications, in addition to conducting quite a few personal interviews, to provide insights for this book. One of the books we discovered was *The Handbook of Advertising*, written in 1938. In discussing the potential of television, the authors stated, "Its commercial development is still in the future, and any arbitrary statement at this date as to the shape of that course, would be patently absurd."[1] Sounds silly today, but didn't we feel that way about the Internet in 1994 and social media in 2006? Who knows where our business is heading? We can only agree with the *Handbook of Advertising* authors when they stated, "Advertising, like all businesses, does not stand still. Its principles and practices are in a constant state of flux."[2] So we focus on creative principles that have stood the test of time and report trends that we trust will continue— and know full well that too much guesswork about the future is as "patently absurd" now as it was in 1938.

We hope you like what we've done with this new edition. If you have ideas about how to improve it, we'd love to hear from you.

In praise of ideas—here's to the risk takers who understand technology and are willing to step boldly onto the world stage.

Ancillaries

The password-protected Instructor Teaching Site at www.sagepub.com/altstiel3e gives instructors access to a full complement of resources to support and enhance their course. The following assets are available on the site:

Test Bank: This Word test bank offers a diverse set of test questions and answers for each chapter of the book. Multiple-choice and true/false short-answer, and essay questions for every chapter help instructors assess students' progress and understanding.

Discussion Questions: Chapter-specific questions help launch discussion by prompting students to engage with the material and by reinforcing important content.

PowerPoint® Slides: Chapter-specific slide presentations offer assistance with lecture and review preparation by highlighting essential content, features, and artwork from the book.

Chapter Exercises and Activities: These lively and stimulating ideas for use in and out of class reinforce active learning. The activities apply to individual or group projects.

Video Links: Carefully selected, web-based video resources feature relevant interviews, lectures, personal stories, inquiries, and other content for use in independent or classroom-based explorations of key topics.

Web Resources: These links to relevant websites direct both instructors and students to additional resources for further research on important chapter topics.

The open-access Student Study Site available at www.sagepub.com/altstiel3e is designed to maximize student comprehension of the material and to promote critical thinking and application. The following resources and study tools are available on the student portion of the book's website:

Video Links: Carefully selected, web-based video resources feature relevant interviews, lectures, personal stories, inquiries, and other content for use in independent or classroom-based explorations of key topics.

Web Resources: These links to relevant websites direct both instructors and students to additional resources for further research on important chapter topics.

E-flashcards: These study tools reinforce students' understanding of key terms and concepts that have been outlined in the chapters.

Web Quizzes: Flexible self-quizzes allow students to independently assess their progress in learning course material.

You may also want to see what we are doing outside of the classroom. We invite you to follow us. Find Tom at LinkedIn. Find Jean at Grow Cultural Geography (growculturalgeography.wordpress.com/) and @jeangrow. And, of course, we want to hear your ideas. So, don't hesitate to share them with us through the *Contact the Authors* link on the Sage site.

Acknowledgments

We'd never have completed this third edition without the help of some amazing folks. First, you wouldn't be reading this if our previous editions had not been so well accepted. Thanks to teachers and advertising professionals from around the world who have purchased past editions and adopted them for classes. We hope you like this one even more. Thanks to the creative practitioners who have shared their wisdom by contributing new War Stories. Your views of the inner workings of our business are invaluable. Thanks also to the young people who shared their personal stories in the new Rising Stars sections. Your voices brought an insightful new dimension to this edition.

Once again, our former student, good friend, and colleague Dan Augustine has helped make this book come to life with a new cover design, infographics, and a Rising Star story. Student worker Bryan Miguel helped research material and find examples, and provided a few of his own excellent ad concepts. We're grateful to the students from around the world who provided incredible creative samples no other book can feature. We are very appreciative of the entire Sage team who helped guide this book to completion: Matt Byrnie, Nathan Davidson, Melanie Birdsall, Elizabeth Borders, and especially Stephanie Palermini, Melinda Masson, and Laura Stewart. It's been a pleasure to work with such a helpful and personable group of professionals.

We would like to thank the following reviewers for their thoughtful contributions: Roberta G. Steinberg, Mount Ida College; Dick Fox, Belmont Abbey College; Joni A. Koegel, Cazenovia College; Tricia M. Farwell, Middle Tennessee State University; Ginger Rosenkrans, Pepperdine University; Kenneth C. C. Yang, The University of Texas at El Paso; Mark J. Brand, St. Ambrose University; Ronald Spielberger, University of Memphis; Tim Chandler, Hardin-Simmons University; Roger Saunders, University of Worcester; Christin Walth, Emerson College; Linda B. Gretton, High Point University; Laurence Minsky, Columbia College Chicago; Anthony Patino, Loyola Marymount; J. Mark Rokfalusi, Savannah College of Art and Design, Atlanta Campus; Cindy J. Price, University of Wyoming; Art Halperin, Savannah College of Art and Design; Rod Carveth, Fitchburg State University; Kathleen S. Micken, Roger Williams University; Jim Clark, University of Idaho; Bridgette Colaco, Troy University; Alexandra Hutto, Metropolitan State College of Denver; Mohammed Ibahrine, American University of Sharjah; Michael F. Johanyak, The University of Akron; Kris Kranenburg, University of Wisconsin-Whitewater; Stan McKinney, Campbellsville University; Peter Oehlkers, Salem State University; Lane Last, University of Tennessee Martin; Marvin G. Lovett, University of Texas at Brownsville; Dorothy Pisarski, Drake University; John Durham, University of San Francisco; Teresa L. Simmons, Western Illinois University; Susan Seymour, Webster University; Billy Bai, University of Nevada Las Vegas; Dora Fitzgerald, University of the Incarnate Word; Joe Bob Hester, University of North Carolina at Chapel Hill; and Barbara Czarnecka, University of Bedfordshire. You can't imagine how many ways your insights and kind words have encouraged us.

We'd also like to acknowledge the support of our coworkers, both on the academic and on the professional side, who allowed our passion for this book to encroach into our real jobs.

Finally, we thank our loved ones, who tolerated our late nights and weekends sitting at the keyboard instead of by their sides. Mary, I promise you will see more of me than the back of my head in front of a monitor. Cesare, I promise to be a bit less obsessed about advertising, but never less obsessed about life's adventures. And to our children, thank you for making us better people.

Chapter 1

Copy, Design, and Creativity: The Nature of Our Business

No one can teach you to be creative. But you may be surprised how creative you really are. You may not have been an A+ English student. But you may find you're an excellent copywriter. You may not be a great sketch artist. But you may discover you have a talent for logo design or ad layouts. You may not know much about advertising. But you may have a knack for building communities online through social media. If you're lucky, you'll take classes that allow you to discover a lot about creative strategy and tactics, and probably a lot about yourself. At the very least you should learn:

- The correct format for writing copy for traditional and new media.

- The basic rules of copywriting and when to break them.

- How to put more sell into your copy.

- Design basics that apply to all media.

- Sensitivity of issues that affect consumers.

- Awareness of ethical and legal issues.

- How to connect the reader or viewer with the advertiser.

- How to keep continuity throughout a campaign.

- The importance of presenting your work.

Words of Wisdom

"Properly practiced creativity can make one ad do the work of ten."[1]

Bill Bernbach, copywriter and founding partner, Doyle Dane Bernbach

Who Wants to Be a Creative?

At the beginning of each semester we ask students, "Who wants to be a copywriter?" We get a halfhearted response from about two or three at the beginning of the class. "Who wants to be an art director or designer?" Usually we get a few more people raising their hands. The truth is most students don't want to commit to any specific career path in the creative field. These are the most common reasons:

The French anti-AIDS organization AIDES created a series of ads showing superheroes such as Superman and Wonder Woman infected with HIV/AIDS. When translated, the French version reads, "We should all be worried about AIDS." The English version says, "AIDS makes us equal." Which headline do you think is more powerful?

- "I think I want to be an account exec."
- "I might want to be an account planner."
- "I want to be a media director."
- "I want to work in social media."
- "Words are boring. I'm more of a picture person."
- "I'm not sure I can write."
- "I'm not sure I even want to be in advertising."

Those are legitimate reasons, but we can make a case for learning about creative strategy and tactics to answer every one of them.

Account executives need to know how to evaluate creative work. Does it meet the objectives? What's the strategy? Why is it great or not so great? When account executives and account managers understand the creative process, they become more valuable to the client and their agency.

Account planners have to understand consumers, their clients' products, market conditions, and many other factors that influence a brand preference or purchase. In essence they function as the voice of the consumer in strategy sessions. The skills required to develop creative strategy are key components in account planning.

Media folks need to recognize the creative possibilities of each medium. They need to understand tone, positioning, resonance, and the other basics pounded into copywriters.

Bloggers and social media specialists have to be able to merge their mastery of digital media with creative skills. Someone has to write all those blog posts and build those online communities with a few well-chosen words—even if they are limited to 140 characters.

Designers, art directors, producers, and graphic artists should know how to write or at least how to defend their work. Why does it meet the strategies? Do the words and visuals work together? Does the font match the tone of the ad? Is the body copy too long? (It's *always* too long for art directors.) As we'll stress repeatedly throughout this book, writers also need to understand the basics of design. Design can't be separate from the concept.

There is English, and there is advertising copy. You're not writing the Great American Novel. Or even a term paper. You are selling products and services with your ideas, which may or may not include your deathless prose. What you say is more important than how you write it. Ideas come first. Writing with style can follow.

Creativity outside of advertising. You can put the skills learned through developing creative strategy and tactics to work in more fields than advertising. The ability to gather information, process it, prioritize the most important facts, and develop a persuasive message is useful in almost every occupation.

Even if you don't aspire to be the next David Ogilvy, you might learn something about marketing, advertising, basic writing skills, and presenting your work. Who knows? You might even like it.

The Golden Age of Creativity

Every generation seems to have a Golden Age of something. Many people who built their careers in the post–*Mad Men* era look back to the 1950s through the early 1970s as the Golden Age of Advertising. This so-called Creative Revolution was one of many uprisings during turbulent times. Unlike any other era before or since, the focus was on youth, freedom, antiestablishment thinking, and—let's face it—sex, drugs, and rock 'n' roll. So it's not surprising that some of the world's most recognized ads (some of which are included in this book) were created during this time.

What made these ads revolutionary?

Think small.

- First, they began to shift focus to the brand, rather than the product. They developed a look, introduced memorable characters, and kept a consistent theme throughout years of long-running campaigns. All of these factors built brand awareness and acceptance.

- Second, they twisted conventional thinking. When most cars touted tail fins and chrome, VW told us to "Think Small." When Hertz was bragging about being top dog, Avis said they tried harder because they were number two. When Levy's advertised their Jewish rye bread, they used an Irish cop and a Native American as models.

- Third, they created new looks, using white space, asymmetrical layouts, minimal copy, and unique typography—all design elements that we take for granted in today's ads.

The driving forces of this revolution included such giants as Leo Burnett, David Ogilvy, Mary Wells Lawrence, Howard Gossage, and Bill Bernbach, who are mentioned prominently in this

When other automakers were crowing about being bigger, faster, and more luxurious, VW took the opposite position. VW's innovative campaigns not only established a very successful brand; they also ushered in a new age in creative advertising.

text. First and foremost, they were copywriters. But they were also creative partners with some of the most influential designers of their era, such as George Lois, Helmut Krone, and Paul Rand. Even though these top creative talents went on to lead mega agencies, their first love was writing and design.

Today we look to creative inspiration in the digital space from visionaries such as the late Steve Jobs, Mark Zuckerberg, and Biz Stone. In this brave new world where the "third screen" is rapidly becoming our primary communication, news, and entertainment source, we may be entering a new Golden Age. Who knows? Maybe *you* could become a leader in the next creative revolution.

The Creative Team

Most copywriters do a lot more than just write ads. In fact, writing may only be a small part of their jobs. Although this section focuses on the copywriter, designers and art directors also handle many of these functions.

Co-captain of the Creative Team

Traditionally a creative team has comprised a copywriter and an art director, with participation by web developers and broadcast producers. This team usually answers to a coach—the creative director.

Every player has his or her role, but in many cases the copywriter drives the creative process. However, once the art director understands the creative problem, he or she may become the idea leader. No matter who drives the process, the creative team needs to know the product frontward and backward, inside and out. They have to understand who uses the product, how it compares to the competition, what's important to the consumer, and a million other facts. No one does it all. Sometimes art directors write the best headlines. Or writers come up with a killer visual. Sometimes the inspiration comes from a comment on Facebook or a tweet. However, the creative leaders need to be able to sift that nugget of an idea from all the white noise that surrounds it.

So, What Else Does a Writer Do?

In small shops, the writers wear so many hats, it's no wonder they develop big heads. Some of the responsibilities besides writing copy include:

- **Research**—primary and secondary.
- **Client contact**—getting the facts direct from the source rather than filtered through

This little sketch says it all. In this case, direct marketing makes a big impact in addressing a consumer's needs.

an account executive, presenting those ideas, and defending the work.

- **Broadcast producer**—finding the right director, talent, music, and postproduction house to make your vision come to life.

- **New business**—gathering data, organizing the creative, working on the pitch, and presenting the work.

- **Public relations**—some copywriters also write the news releases, plan promotional events, and even contact editors.

- **Internet/interactive content**—the Internet has become an integral part of a total marketing communication effort. A lot of "traditional" media writers are now writing websites, blogs, and social media content.

- **Creative management**—much has been written about whether copywriters or art directors make the best creative directors. The answer: yes.

Controlling the Creative Process

Step 1: Getting the facts. If you have a research department and/or account planners, take advantage of their knowledge. But don't settle for someone else's opinion. Talk to people who use the product, as well as those who don't or won't even consider it. Talk to retailers who sell the product. Look at competitive advertising: What's good, and where is it vulnerable? In short, know as much as you can about the product, the competition, the market, and the people who buy it. Try to make the product part of your life.

Step 2: Brainstorming with a purpose. If you've done your homework, you should know the wants and needs of the target audience and how your product meets those needs. From that base, you can direct the free flow of creative ideas. Thanks to your knowledge, you can concentrate on finding a killer creative idea rather than floundering in a sea of pointless questions. But you must also be open to new ideas and independent thinking from your creative team members.

Step 3: Picking up a pencil before you reach for the mouse. This is critical, because it's all about the creative concept. Even if you can only draw stick people, that's OK. Where does the headline go? How much copy do you think you'll need? What's the main visual? How should the elements be arranged? Even though artists may ridicule your design, they will appreciate having the raw elements they can massage into a great-looking ad.

Step 4: Finding the reference/visuals. You may have a clear vision of the creative concept. Can you communicate that to your art director, creative director, account exec, or client? You can help your art director by finding photos, artwork, or design elements, not to rip off but to help you make your point. The finished piece may not look anything like your original vision, but at least you can start with a point of reference. Browse the web, stock photo books, and awards annuals. We can't emphasize this enough, especially for beginning writers—if you can't find what you want, it might trigger a new idea. The visual selection is a starting point, not the end game.

Step 5: Working with the rest of the team. For most creatives, the happiest and most productive years of their career are spent collaborating with others. When two creative minds click, the whole really is greater than the sum of the parts. A great creative partnership, like any relationship, needs to be nurtured and will have its ups and downs. While one person may want to drive the whole process, it's best not to run over other teammates. They may come up with some ideas that will make you look like a genius.

Step 6: Preselling the creative director and account executive. Chances are you will not be working directly with the client, and even if you are, you probably won't be the sole contact. That's why you need the people who interface with the client to buy into your ideas. Maintaining a good relationship with the creative director not only protects your job; it also gives you an ally when you pitch your idea to the account executive and client. In many cases, the account executive represents the client in these discussions. He or she may try to poke holes in your logic or question your creative choices. That's why every creative choice must be backed with sound reasons. In the end, if the account executive is sold, you have a much better chance of convincing the client.

Step 7: Selling the client. As the person who developed the idea, you have to be prepared to defend your work, using logic rather than emotion. Many times your brilliant reasoning will fail since clients usually think with their wallets. Over time you'll know how far you can push a client. The trick is to know when to retreat so you can fight another day. Most clients don't mind being challenged creatively, as long as there are sound reasons for taking chances.

The three things you *never* want to hear from a client:

- "That looks just like the competitor's ads. I want our ads to stand out."

- "I was looking for something a lot more creative. Take some risks."

- "You obviously don't understand our product or our market."

You won't hear those things if you take care of Steps 1–6.

Step 8: Getting it right. OK, you've sold the client. Now what? You have to hand your creation to the production team, but your responsibilities don't end. Does the copy fit the way it should? If not, can you cut it? Can you change a word here and there to make it even better? Are the graphics what you envisioned? Your involvement is even more critical for broadcast. Did you have a specific talent in mind for voice or on-camera roles? Does the director understand and share your vision? Does the music fit?

If you remember nothing else, keep the following quote from the great Leo Burnett in mind and follow it through Step 10: "Nothing takes the guts out of a great idea like bad execution."

Step 9: Maintaining continuity. Almost everyone can come up with a great idea. Once. The hard part is extending that great idea in other media and repeating it, only differently, in a campaign. Over time, elements of a campaign tend to drift away from the original idea. Clients usually get tired of a look before the consumer. Art directors may want to "enhance" the campaign with new elements. Someone on the creative team needs to continually monitor the elements of an ongoing campaign to make sure they are true to the original idea.

Fifty years after its groundbreaking introduction of the original Beetle, VW continues to lead with innovative concepts that resonate with buyers. This Super Bowl favorite enjoyed widespread viral popularity as well.

Step 10: Discover what worked and why. If the ads in a campaign achieve their objectives, great! If they win awards, but the client loses market share, look out. Keep monitoring the efficacy of the campaign. What are the readership scores? What do the client's salespeople and retailers think? How are sales? If you had to make any midcourse corrections, what would you do? If you never stop learning, you'll never miss an opportunity to make the next project or campaign even better.

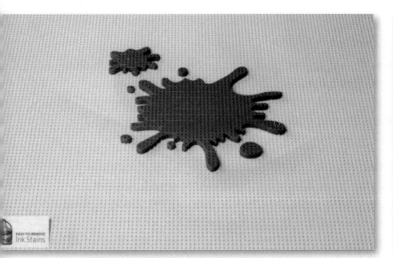
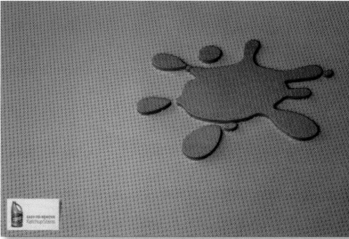

It's really very simple: Clorox makes it easy to lift out ink and wine stains—almost as easy as removing a LEGO® piece from its base. This Dubai agency found a dramatic way to depict the simplest of ideas.

Where Do I Go From Here?

A lot of entry-level copywriters and art directors set lofty career goals—most often the coveted title of creative director. However, many junior writers or designers don't consider the other exciting possibilities. We've listed a few to consider. You may actually take several of these paths in your career.

Chick-fil-A's cows have waged a long-term guerrilla war against burger joints. The antibeef campaign has been extended across all media, but it really made its mark in out-of-home media.

Copywriter/art director for life: It could happen. Many people are happy to hone their creative talents throughout their whole career. You can do it if you continue to improve and never stop growing.

Management/creative director: A great job with great responsibilities. It often involves more personnel management than creative talent, requiring the skills of a head coach, sales manager, and kindergarten teacher.

Account manager: Many writers are drawn to the "dark side." It makes sense, especially if you like working with clients and thoroughly understand the product, market, and consumers. In some small shops, the copy-contact system gives account execs an opportunity to create and creative types a reason to wear a suit. Art directors also work directly with clients, and in many cases are the primary agency contact.

Account planner: A natural for many writers who like research and enjoy being the conduit between the account manager, the creative team, and the consumer. It involves thorough knowledge of research, marketing, creative, and media, as well as a lot of intuition. Most successful advertising copywriters already possess those skills.

Promotion director: Writers and art directors are idea people. So it makes sense to use that creativity to develop sales promotions, special events, sponsorships, specialty marketing programs, displays, and all the other marketing communication tools not included in "traditional advertising." This is a rapidly growing area with a lot of potential for creative people.

Public relations writer: Although most PR people won't admit it, it's easier to write a news release than an ad. Most advertising writers won't admit that editorial writing is usually more persuasive than advertising. PR writing involves much more than news releases, though. You may become an editor for a newsletter or an in-house magazine. You may produce video news releases or schedule events, press conferences, and any number of creative PR efforts.

Internal advertising department rep: So far, we've outlined agency jobs, but other companies need talented creative people. In small companies, you may handle brochure writing or design, PR, trade shows, and media relations, in addition to advertising. In larger companies, you may handle promotional activities not covered by your ad agency. You may even write speeches for your CEO.

Web/interactive expert: The web is so integrated into most marketing communication programs it seems ridiculous to consider it nontraditional media. Any writer or designer today should be web savvy. You should

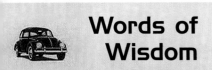

Words of Wisdom

In the ad game, the days are tough, the nights are long, and the work is emotionally demanding. But it's worth it, because the rewards are shallow, transparent and meaningless."

Unknown copywriter[3]

know the terminology and capabilities of the Internet—just as well as you understand magazines or television. You don't have to be a whiz at HTML, but having some technical expertise is a huge plus. As with any phase of advertising, creativity, not technology, is the most precious commodity.

Social media specialist: This job usually involves daily monitoring, posting, and content development. It can also mean developing social media advertising and creating brand awareness online. You could moderate chats as well as initiate conversation through forums, Twitter, and postings. Writing skills, creativity, and knowing when social media is *not* the solution are keys to success.

Freelance writer/designer: A lot of people like a flexible schedule and a variety of clients. Being a successful freelancer requires tremendous discipline and endless self-promotion, plus the mental toughness to endure the constant rejection, short deadlines, and long stretches between assignments.

Video and broadcast producer/ director: Like to write video or radio commercials? Maybe you have the knack for writing scripts, selecting talent, editing, and other elements of audio and video production. As for web/interactive experts, creative talent and a logical mind are the keys. Technological expertise can be learned on the job.

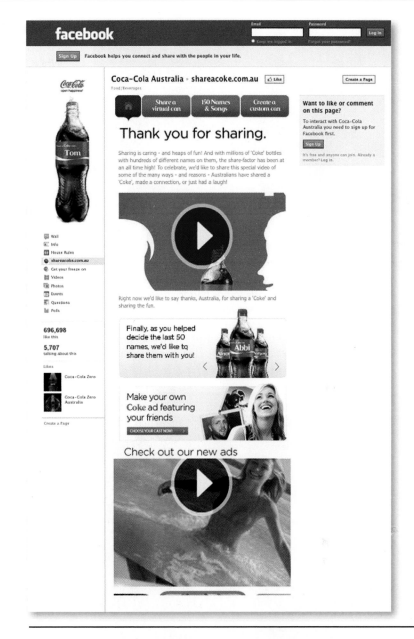

Coca-Cola Australia launched their version of the "Share a Coke" campaign by offering to put one of 50 common first names on their bottle (in place of the Coke brand). Friends were invited to share the customized Coke with their friends and to make their own commercials. Companies have to be really confident in their brand equity to alter their packaging this way.

Consultant: Too often it's another word for unemployed. A select few actually make a living as creative consultants. Sometimes they are no more than repackaged freelancers. Sometimes they are "rainmakers" who help with a new business pitch. Still, a number of downsized companies and agencies will pay consultants for skills and contacts they don't have in-house. Keeping current and connected is the key to success.

In this web video for a Norwegian bank, a woman wakes up from a blackout and finds to her horror she was married the night before. Then she discovers her new husband is George Clooney. The moral: "Some people are born lucky. The rest of us have to save." Not all hangovers have such happy results.

Sunglasses aren't about shielding your eyes. They're about fashion and expressing yourself. The active model wearing stylish Oakleys and the headline "Perform Beautifully" says it all.

Creativity and Online Media

While traditional media advertising usually rides up and down on the waves of economic conditions, many advertisers have shifted more money into social media and mobile. According to the MagnaGlobal Advertising Forecast,[4] mobile advertising grew by 32% and online video advertising grew by 40% in 2011, while more traditional advertising experienced modest gains and losses.

So what does this mean for the future of creative advertising? Many marketers will shift their emphasis to such "middle of the funnel" approaches as social media, in addition to paid search and e-mail marketing. Creatives will have to understand how to do business in the digital space and anticipate an increasingly faster pace to changes in technology, pop culture, and online viewing trends. That means you will have to know more than how to create a banner ad. You may have to develop entire online communities for very specific target audiences and find ways to keep them engaged . . . and oh, by the way, you still have to sell something.

What's in It for Me?

You might have discussed the role of advertising in society and explored ethical issues. You have probably reviewed theories of communication and might have even read about the greatest creative people of all time. That's all good, but let's be honest—if you want a creative career, you're only interested in three things: fame, fortune, and fun. Not necessarily in that order. Let's look at each one in a little more detail.

Fame: Everyone wants recognition. Since advertising is unsigned, there are only two ways to get recognized—awards and having people say, "You're *really* the person who did that?" If they're judged good enough, writers and art directors are immortalized in *Communication Arts* annuals. Last time we looked, there are no books showcasing account execs and media buyers.

Fortune: Depending on experience, the economy, the results they generate, and a million other factors, creative people can make as much or more than any other people in advertising. Recent salary surveys show salaries for top creatives and top account supervisors are pretty much the same. But as a writer or an art director, you get to wear jeans, have a tattoo, pierce your nose, and spike your hair. But only if you want to.

Fun: You can be famous and rich and still be unhappy in any business. Even if you're not well known or a millionaire, you can still get a kick out of solving problems for clients. It's still a treat to work with other creatives, interact with musicians and actors, win presentations, and travel to exotic locales. No matter how much you're earning, when it stops being fun or if you lose your edge, you should probably consider getting out.

Knowing the Rules and When to Break Them

We will not dwell on too many of the rules of advertising writing and design, but we will look at some accepted practices. These are the tips and techniques that have proven successful over time.

One "rule" will always be true. Advertising is a business. A business populated by a lot of crazy people, but still a business. Although the slogan "It's not creative unless it sells" has lost its impact, we still have to persuade someone to buy something. This reality leads to something we call "creative schizophrenia"—the internal conflict between the stuff you want to do and the stuff clients make you do. For example, if you want to get a job, you need really cool, cutting-edge stuff in your portfolio, which is usually not usable in the real world. When you land that job, you'll probably be forced to do a lot of boring stuff that sells products but looks terrible in your book. That's the nature of this business, and unless you can live with a split personality, it's hard to survive.

one child dies from **water-related disease EVERY 15 SECONDS.**

Nearly 3.6 million people die every year from water-related disease, and 84% of them are children. Four will die in the next minute alone. Most of these deaths occur in the developing world, but we cannot ignore the fact that one in eight people worldwide lack access to safe water supplies. Water is the main ingredient in supporting life on earth. We must ensure its protection to ensure our survival.

WHY WATER?

Can advertising change the world? We keep hoping. This student-created ad was designed to raise awareness of waterborne diseases around the world.

You Don't Have to Be Crazy, but It Helps

Psychologists have spent years studying creativity. We know that creativity is not an isolated right-brained activity. Rather, it "reflects originality and

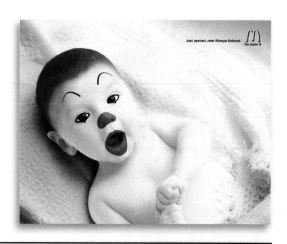

How would you announce the opening of a new McDonald's restaurant? In India they used a newborn version of Mickey D's iconic symbol. Still think clowns aren't creepy?

appropriateness, intuition and logic. It requires both hemispheres."[5] The left side likes words, logic, and reasons. The right side likes pictures, emotions, and feelings. Bringing both hemispheres together in a mediated form is what Mihaly Csikszentmihalyi calls "flow . . . a phenomenon constructed through an interaction between producers and audience."[6] Flow requires flexibility and "the capacity to adapt to the advances, opportunities, technologies, and changes that are a part of day-to-day living."[7] Advertising creativity is the end product of balancing logic with irrationality, artistic freedom with the constraints of the creative problem, and divergent thinking with convergent thinking.[8] It's about making strategy come to life. What does that mean for you?

Daniel Pink, in his groundbreaking book *A Whole New Mind: Why Right-Brainers Will Rule the Future,* argues that we are moving away from left-brain leadership toward the attributes associated with the right brain. Pink describes right-brain thinking as holistic, big picture, intuitive, and nonlinear. He states, "The Information Age we all prepared for is ending. Rising in its place is what I call the Conceptual Age, an era in which mastery of abilities that we've often overlooked and undervalued marks the fault line between who gets ahead and who falls behind."[9] So we are moving from high tech to high concept and high touch. The Information Age was about knowledge workers. *The Conceptual Age is about creators and empathizers—in other words, right-brain thinking.*

Before You Get Started

Most texts will tell you that you just can't start creating an ad from scratch. Of course you can. And you just might get lucky the first time. But can you repeat that success? That's why we need to discuss the foundations of marketing communications. First, a few definitions.

Advertising, MarCom, IMC, or What?

Everyone knows what advertising is, right? George Orwell said it was "the rattling of a stick inside a swill bucket."[11] H. G. Wells claimed, "Advertising is legalized lying.[12] For a less cynical take, Professor Jef Richards of the University of Texas says, "Advertising is the 'wonder' in Wonder Bread."[13] You've probably learned that advertising is paid communication to promote a product, service, brand, or cause through the media. Is direct mail advertising? Well, if you consider mail a medium, yes. How about a brochure? Probably not; however, it can be mailed or inserted into a magazine as an ad. The Internet? Yes and no. A website by itself is not really advertising although a banner ad on that site is.

Birth of a Network

Verizon Wireless had been running the "Can you hear me now?" guy (or Test Man as we called him) for about four years. He had quickly become an icon and had helped reinforce the perception that Verizon had a better network. While it was true that Verizon's network was in fact better, AT&T had begun attacking that perception with their "Fewest Dropped Calls" campaign. And the effects of that were showing in tracking results.

We were faced with two problems: After four years Test Man was beginning to wear thin (there are only so many times you can hear "Can you hear me now? Good" before you never want to hear it again), and AT&T's offensive was gaining ground. Verizon wanted a new idea that upped the perception of their network difference, convinced consumers of the value of that difference, and, hopefully, didn't abandon the equity they had built with Test Man.

Trying to convince consumers about the value of an intangible telecommunications network is a tough thing. It's a little like trying to convince diners of the value of a brilliantly efficient kitchen when all they care about is the food on the plate. We had to make it clear that the brilliant efficiency of the kitchen is directly connected to the deliciousness of the food.

In a couple of weeks we had come up with about a half-dozen ways of doing this, including one simple executional idea of literalizing the network as an infinite army of technicians, equipment, and high-tech gizmos with one person leading it all—Test Man.

It honestly took us a little while to appreciate how smart it was. It took an abstract concept and made it real, it gave our consumers a feeling of personal strength by giving them an army behind them, it had an unintended consequence of implying better customer service, and, of course, it created a new role for Test Man.

Over time, it too wore thin. And it was expensive to produce (we became experts in the digital art of cloning). But for four years and dozens and dozens of spots and ads, it did its job wonderfully. Verizon's network superiority perception gap over AT&T began increasing once again and stayed there.

And it worked not only as a brand idea but also as a retail deal breaker—if Verizon and AT&T had the same phone on sale for the same price, well, the one that comes with the network suddenly looks like a better deal.[14]

Steve Ohler, executive creative director, McCann Worldgroup, New York, mccann.com.

Social networks? They can be a vehicle for ads, but they are even more effective when they influence consumer behavior without obvious advertising. Public relations? No, because the advertiser is not paying the editor to publish an article (at least not directly). Confused? Don't feel alone. Many marketing professionals can't make the distinction between advertising and other forms of promotion.

MarCom (Marketing Communications)

That's where the term *MarCom* arose. MarCom to some people takes in every form of marketing communication. Others describe MarCom as every form of promotion that's not traditional advertising. Traditional advertising usually covers print (newspapers, magazines), television, radio, and some forms of outdoor advertising. "Nontraditional" promotion includes direct marketing, sales promotion, point of sale, public relations, e-mail, online advertising, search

Creative people tend to care about much more than promoting products. Whether the projects are for paying clients or pro bono, many important causes benefit from the talents of concerned professionals.

engine marketing, mobile, social networks, guerrilla marketing, viral/buzz, word of mouth, and everything else you can attach a logo, slogan, or message to. These divisions evolved as large agencies discovered that they could make money beyond earning media commissions for "traditional" advertising. So they created MarCom units or separate interactive, direct, and sales promotion divisions. Sometimes these are set up as separate entities under the corporate umbrella of a large agency.

IMC (Integrated Marketing Communications)

IMC (integrated marketing communications) unites the MarCom elements into a single campaign. IMC has become a buzzword, especially for agencies that recently set up MarCom divisions. Actually, IMC is nothing new. Smaller full-service agencies and in-house ad departments have been doing it for years under the banner of "doing whatever it takes to get the job done." With limited budgets, companies need to get the most mileage from their promotional dollar with a variety of tools, including advertising.

Advertising's Role in the Marketing Process

The buying process for some products may take a couple seconds, such as picking out a sandwich at the drive-through, or it may take years, as with buying a multimillion-dollar piece of industrial equipment. No matter the time frame, there is a process that starts with awareness and ends with the sale. One of the best ways to describe the process is using the acronym AIDA. It's not the opera, but rather it stands for *attention, interest, desire,* and *action.* Understanding AIDA helps you as a creative person to guide a consumer from just recognizing your brand to demanding it. Here's how AIDA works in advertising:

1. **Attention:** How do you get someone who is bombarded with hundreds if not thousands of messages a day to look at your ad or commercial? If you're a writer, one way is to use powerful words, or if you're an art director you need a picture that will catch a person's eye.

2. **Interest:** Once you capture a person's attention, he or she will give you a little more time to make your point, but you must stay focused on the reader or viewer's wants and needs. This means helping that person to quickly sort out the relevant messages. In some cases, you might use bullets and subheadings to make your points stand out.

3. **Desire:** The interest and desire parts of AIDA work together. Once people are interested, they need to really want the product. As you're building the readers' interest, you also need to help them understand how what you're offering can help them in a real way. The main way of doing this is by appealing to their personal needs and wants. Another component of desire is conviction—the willingness to buy when the opportunity is right. So even if your message does not result in an immediate sale, keeping your messages on track and on time could eventually trigger a sale.

4. **Action:** OK, they're hooked. Now what do you want them to do? Visit a website? Take a test drive? Call for information? Plunk down some cash now? You should be very clear about what action you want your readers or viewers to take.

Knowing What Makes the Consumer Tick

Consumer behavior is the study of how people buy, what they buy, when they buy, and why they buy. It blends elements from psychology, sociology, and marketing, and quite a bit of insight. Marketers attempt to dissect the buyers' decision-making process, both for individuals and for groups. They study demographics, psychographics, and lifestyles to understand what people want and how they want to get it. Billions of dollars are spent on research to test new products and the consumer's willingness to buy. But many times the most successful marketing concepts spring from some crazy idea no research could predict. Can you say Google? Steve Jobs relied on his intuition instead of focus groups. He and his talented team developed products consumers didn't even know they wanted—the Macintosh, iMac, iTunes, iPod, iPhone, and iPad—and in the process created the most valuable technology company in the world. We'll discuss some of the tools you can use to gauge consumer attitudes and opinions later in this book. However, at this point, suffice it to say a successful creative practitioner writes and designs materials that appeal to a consumer's wants and needs. Unless you're the next Steve Jobs, you may need some research to guide you.

Creating From the Consumer's Point of View

If you remember nothing else from this chapter, remember this:

People do not buy things.
They buy satisfaction of their wants and needs.

In an integrated marketing communications program, all elements work individually and cumulatively.

Source: Created by Dan Augustine.

Words of Wisdom

"Creativity without strategy is art. Creativity with strategy is advertising."[15]

Jef Richards, PhD, professor,
Universityof Texas

Rising Star

Gut Instinct

I have shaped my career based mostly on gut instinct. In a pre-journalism class my freshman year at the University of Colorado at Boulder, my professor talked for 20 minutes about advertising. It was in those 20 minutes, of all the minutes I sat in class that semester, that my life truly changed. I knew I wanted to get into advertising.

After graduate school, it was that same gut instinct that told me to move to Los Angeles and take a freelance job at a shop that most people had never heard of, Goodness Mfg., rather than a full-time job at a bigger, more established agency. A year later it happened again, resulting in a move to New York City, and ultimately a job at a smaller, less known agency, Johannes Leonardo. When I took the position, I was one of eight people at the agency and the only person in the creative department, a big risk but one I knew was right.

It is that same gut instinct that has driven me creatively to do work that in my wildest dreams I never thought I could do, or be a part of. I just knew what felt right and went for it. Without my gut instinct I know my creative output would have suffered, and I would not have made the same impact on the world that I have currently made.

In short, never be scared of what you feel is right. If I have learned anything, it is that the voice inside you, your gut instinct, will take you on the wildest, most exciting, best ride of your life if you let it.[16]

Emmie Nostitz, art director, Johannes Leonardo, New York, @emmienostitz.

Tapping into the self-perception of their loyal users, Apple ran a four-year TV campaign that personified the Mac and the PC. Mac was young, hip, and unassuming, but confident. PC was frumpy, jealous, and clueless. Who would you rather be? We thought so.

You may have studied Abraham Maslow's theory of the hierarchy of needs. This model is usually depicted as a pyramid, ranging from the most basic needs to the most complex and sophisticated.

According to Maslow, the needs at each level must be met before one can progress to the next level. Maslow considered less than 1% of the population to be truly self-actualized.[17] Some communication theorists have expanded on Maslow's list. Some texts list more than 30 needs. To simplify matters, we can probably sum up wants and needs from a marketing communication standpoint as follows:

- Comfort (convenience, avoid pain and discomfort)
- Security (physical, financial)
- Stimulation (aesthetic, physical)
- Affiliation (esteem, respect)
- Fulfillment (self-satisfaction, status)

So how does all this talk about Maslow and wants and needs play in the ad business today? That's where account planning comes into play. The account planner is the connection between the business side and the creative side of a marketing campaign. The planner works with the account manager to understand what the client is looking for and then relate that to what the consumer wants. The planner also helps the creative team develop a more focused creative brief to lead them to that One Thing. Planners want to know what makes people tick—to bring the consumers' voice into the strategic process. They use that information to develop branding strategy for the campaign. It is the planner's job to take all this information, insight, and nuance and condense it into a form that the creative

A handy person doesn't just buy a can of oil. He or she wants and needs something that helps make jobs around the house and workshop easier.

Green is part of the dream.

It gives our kids courage to leap.

Cushions their falls. Softens the edges of our lives.

Welcomes our visitors with open arms.

Green says we're committed to something.

Something the whole neighborhood believes in. Something good.

Something the world, even on its best days,

Could use more of.

For 75 years, Scotts® Turf Builder® has helped make millions of lawns greener. Because, better than any other fertilizer, Scotts Turf Builder feeds with the perfect blend of nutrients grass needs to flourish. And American dreams need to grow.

For help building your dream, go to scotts.com

Green is part of the dream.

Don't tell me about your grass seed; talk to me about my lawn. Here's a classic example. The copy almost reads like poetry: "Green says we're committed to something. Something the whole neighborhood believes in. Something good. Something the world, even in its best days, could use more of." While this ad isn't for grass seed, it's about a lot more than fertilizer.

team can understand (preferably short sentences for the writers and pictures for the art directors). We provide more detail about account planning in Chapter 2.

But what exactly do we do with all this? Once you have discovered the consumers' sweet spot, you have to communicate in a way that convinces them your brand can satisfy their wants and needs. One of the best explanations of a consumer's wants and needs can be found in this simple declarative sentence: *Don't tell me about your grass seed; talk to me about my lawn.*

Think about that. People aren't really looking for seed. They need a play area for their kids. They want a calm green space for relaxing or a yard the neighbors will envy. Security. Comfort. Fulfillment. Wants and needs. A $30 Timex will probably tell the time just as well as a $3,000 Rolex. (Well, close enough for most folks.) Which wants and needs are satisfied by spending 1000% more? Hint: It's really not about telling time.

Who's Who?

In this and future chapters, you'll see some Words of Wisdom floating around. Who are these wise guys and gals? At the end of most chapters we'll provide a very brief bio on some of the best-known voices in advertising, as well as other innovators whom we have cited in Words of Wisdom and Ad Stories.

Leo Burnett—Founder of the agency that still bears his name, he established a new creative style of advertising, along with many memorable characters that are still working today, including Tony the Tiger, the Jolly Green Giant, the Keebler Elves, the Marlboro Man, and the Pillsbury Doughboy. Leo Burnett believed that creativity made an advertisement effective but, at the same time, that creativity required believability.

Steve Jobs—This legendary force drove Apple Computer and Pixar to the top of their games. Complex, difficult to work and live with, impatient, and always outspoken, Steve Jobs controlled everything related to his products, including the copywriting for his ads. Biographer Walter Isaacson describes Jobs as "a creative entrepreneur whose passion for perfection and ferocious drive revolutionized six industries: personal computers, animated movies, music, phones, tablet computing and digital publishing."[20]

Mary Wells Lawrence—While CEO, chair, and president of the legendary Wells Rich Greene agency, Mary Wells was the highest-paid, most well-known woman in American business. She was also the first female CEO of a *Fortune* 500 company. Her innovative campaigns for Braniff, Alka-Seltzer, Benson & Hedges, and American Motors brought a fresh new look to established brands. At age 40, she became the youngest person ever inducted into the Copywriters Hall of Fame.

Jon Steel—One of the early leaders in account planning, Jon Steel is well known for his innovative approach to focus groups, in which he elicits opinions from people where they live, work, and shop, rather than in sterile interview rooms. As head of Goodby, Silverstein & Partners' planning department, Steel was named "West Coast Executive of the Year" by *Adweek* in 2000. He also finds time to share his depth of knowledge in the world of academia at Stanford University's Graduate School of Business as a regular lecturer. His first book, *Truth, Lies, and Advertising: The Art of Account Planning,* has become a must-read for anyone interested in account planning.

Exercises

1. No More Wonder® Bread

Wonder® Bread is bland, white bread. Sorry to insult any Wonder® Bread lovers, but in advertising you can't be bland. You have to have flavor. Back in the 1940s Wonder® Bread made the claim that it "built strong bodies in 12 ways." That's where we begin.

Below are 12 ways to build strong insights.

- Feel free to add and subtract as you see fit, making these experiences relevant to your environment. By semester break you must have experienced all 12.

- Keep a journal with an entry for each experience: who (alone or with friends), what (use brief detail, for instance, the title of a foreign film or name of a club), where (a no-brainer), when (another no-brainer), and why (your reaction, how it made you *feel*). Use your six senses as you describe how each experience made you feel. That's where you'll find the insights.

    1. Go to the local public market, where "slow" food is sold.

    2. Watch a subtitled foreign film.

    3. Hit the Latin dance floor.

    4. Catch the week's news on BBC online: www.bbc.co.uk.

    5. Check out live jazz or blues at a neighborhood club.

    6. Attend an event sponsored by the Gay-Straight Alliance Network, the Muslim Students Association, the Black Student Council, or an international student organization—one for which you don't fit the demographics.

    7. Attend a local Rotary function.

    8. Dine on tofu.

    9. Settle in for an afternoon of NASCAR racing or WWE (World Wrestling Entertainment) viewing.

    10. Experience a meeting of the college Republican/Democratic student association—and it has to be the opposite of your political point of view.

    11. Join in the fun at a bingo gathering.

    12. Visit the local art museum and check out the current special exhibits.

2. Personal Branding Timeline

- Create a map moving across your life at 5-year increments. Begin with birth and end with your current age (which might be less than a 5-year gap). For each 5-year stage generate a list of the brands you associate with that time of your life.

- After each brand write a single sentence about what that brand meant to you at that time.

- Now extend this map out by 10-year increments, 30, 40, 50, 60, and 70. List brands you think will be a part of your life. Again write a single sentence about why you believe each brand will be relevant to you at that time.

- Now discuss what factors are influencing your choices: familiarity, aspiration, current usage, personal or family associations, trends, and so on.

- Next see if there are any brands that were constant over a long period of time. Discuss what makes those brands have traction over time. What inherited qualities and brand messages enable brand loyalty?

3. AIDA in Action

Consider the buying process for the following product categories using the AIDA steps: hybrid cars, microbrews, running shoes, frozen vegetables, and cosmetics. Or create your own categories.

- Make a list based on the following questions: What gets your *attention*? What part of the brand messages within this category captures your *interest?* At what point and due to what circumstances do consumers feel a compelling *desire* for the product? What are common intended *actions* that might be relevant to this product category?

- Now find an ad for each category and discuss how the AIDA process works for that brand. How much influence do advertising and promotion have on the buying decision for that brand?

Visit www.sagepub.com/altstiel3e to access these additional learning tools

- Video Links
- Web Resources

- eFlashcards
- Web Quizzes

Chapter 2

Strategy and Branding

Putting a Face on a Product

Creative Strategy in the Marketing Mix

Congratulations! Your agency's request for proposal (RFP) has been selected, and you've been invited to pitch the Garlowe Gizmo account to introduce their new line of gizmos. Your job is to develop a creative strategy and build a marketing communication campaign that will knock the socks off the Garlowe management. You really need this account, because if you don't win, half of your agency will be laid off, including you. Right now, you know nothing about the company, their products, their customers, their competition, or their market. By the way, you've got two weeks until the presentation. Once again, congratulations!

The above scenario happens every day somewhere. The good news is you're invited to the dance. But there are very few "gimmes" when it comes to new business, and if you're lucky enough to win an account, the euphoria quickly dissolves into the daily grind of keeping the business.

Mad Men Versus Reality

In *Mad Men,* the award-winning TV program about 1960s advertising, Don Draper, the creative director at the fictional Sterling Cooper Draper Pryce agency, usually saves the day by (a) ignoring all research, (b) threatening to resign the account, and (c) delivering brilliant insight just as the client gets up to leave. His coworkers are envious, the client is impressed, he gets another big raise, and everybody meets back in his office for martinis and cigarettes. It's great fun to watch, but it doesn't happen that way in today's advertising game . . . if it ever did. So, at the risk of destroying the myths of the Golden Age of Advertising, the following sections deal with the hard work of looking brilliant.

Objectives, Strategies, and Tactics

The difference between strategy and tactics stumps a lot of clients and their agencies. They usually mix them up and throw in a few goals and objectives for

TOOLS & TIPS

SITUATION ANALYSIS

Assemble the facts, including competitive analysis, brand history, consumer's point of view, SWOT analysis.

OBJECTIVES

Marketing communications objectives establish what you need to accomplish to achieve the marketing/sales objectives. Should be (a) specific (b) challenging (c) achievable and (d) measurable.

STRATEGY

How are you going to achieve your objectives? What's your position, who are you targeting, how will you segment markets? What's your brand strategy? Creative strategy? Media strategy?

TACTICS

What is your big creative idea? Who will you show it to, how will you show it and when will you show it? If strategies are the blueprints, tactics are the tools.

Source: Created by Dan Augustine.

good measure. Typically the net result is a rather random laundry list of what they'd like to happen—about as specific and realistic as wishing for world peace. Other than drafting a mission statement by committee, listing strategy and tactics can be the most confusing and worthless task in marketing.

Don't get us wrong. A creative person needs to follow a strategy. Otherwise you're working for the sake of creativity rather than solving a problem. Your objective is to visit mid-America. Think of strategy development as picking the destination, such as "I want to go to Cleveland." The strategy is to make the trip. The tactics are how you get there. If I drive, which roads do I take? Should I fly? If so, which airlines have the best rates? Where will I stay? How long will I be there? And a bunch of other questions that deal with specific actions you must take to get to Cleveland and back. Another analogy comes from the military. (There are a lot of other masculine analogies in creative departments, but that's another story.) The objective speaks to the big picture, like winning the war. Strategies deal with achieving objectives, like capturing specific cities, blocking their ports, and hacking into their power grid. Tactics are the means to achieve the strategy. In the case of taking a city, it might be tactics such as using a combination of close air support, flanking maneuvers from infantry, frontal assaults by tanks, and constant bombardment of artillery. So, it's objective, strategy, and tactics. Got it: one, two, and three.

Account Planning—Solving the Client's Problem

Strategy often deals in long-term solutions such as building brand share. Strategy is concerned with continuity, growth, and return on investment. It's very specific and almost always measurable, and it begins with account planning.

If you were working on the Garlowe Gizmo account, where would *you* start? The first thing to do is ask, "What's their problem?" Every client has a problem.

Otherwise they wouldn't need to promote their products. Some clients state the problem as a broad objective, such as sell more Gizmos in the next fiscal year. That's not the problem. The problem is: What's going to make it difficult to sell more Gizmos, and how can we overcome those difficulties? The client may tell you, but these may not be the only problems. Often the client doesn't have an in-depth understanding of their target audience. An even more challenging situation emerges when the client can't even identify the problem.

Account planning is how agencies come up with the solutions that solve a client's problem. So, even before you get to the strategies and tactics, account planning lays the foundation. All strategy documents and the subsequent strategies and tactics emerge from account planning.

Here's a little background on planning. It developed in Britain in the late 1960s and was based on the desire to create an environment where creativity flourished, but where the consumer's voice was a key part of strategic development. Coming into existence on the heels of the Creative Revolution of the 1960s, it's not surprising that planning also sought a modern, creative approach to research replacing irrelevant, inappropriate, and outmoded methodologies. Prior to the introduction of account planning, advertising research was highly marketing-oriented, often detached from both the creative team and the consumer. At the heart of account planning is the need to understand consumers—to bring their voice into the strategic process—to find the key insight.

Stanley Pollitt, of London's Boase Massimi Pollitt, is credited with developing account planning. His goal was to put a trained researcher, representing the voice of the consumer, alongside every account person. In the 1980s Jay Chiat, of the original Chiat\Day in Los Angeles, brought account planning to North America. Jon Steel, of Goodby, Silverstein & Partners in San Francisco and a noted author on account planning, calls account planning an essential strategy tool. By the mid-1990s account planning was common practice in many ad agencies across North America.

Get the Facts

The first step in planning for any type of research is gathering and organizing information. You have to answer the basic questions listed in Table 2.1.

TABLE 2.1   Defining Marketing Tasks

Marketing Tasks	What They Mean
Define the target audience	Who are we talking to?
Identify features and benefits	What makes this product better?
Clarify the current position	What do people think about the product?
Align wants and needs with the product	Why should people buy it?
Determine call to action	What do we want people to do?

Notice the above creative development questions include some of the basic journalism questions, such as who, what, and why. Where and when are media questions, which may also influence your creative strategy. For example, an ad in the *Sports Illustrated* swimsuit edition may inspire a far different look than an ad in the regular edition.

Where to Look for Information

Research can be divided into two basic categories: primary, where you gather the facts directly, and secondary, where you assemble research done by others. We'll look at secondary research first, because that's usually more accessible.

Secondary Research

You can find a wealth of information about markets, products, and consumers. A lot of it is available for free on the Internet. However, most of the really good stuff comes from subscription services. Most university libraries offer the same information that costs companies thousands of dollars, although it is usually slightly out of date. Buying current data is often prohibitively expensive. Simmons Market Research Bureau and Mediamark Research and Intelligence are good places to begin. Many universities will have one or the other as they are commonly used by the industry. Learning how to navigate these databases will give you a leg up when you interview.

Primary Research

Most people think of formal types of research such as focus groups or mail surveys, but primary research can be very informal and personal. Ethnography and projective techniques are hot. And they're hot for a good reason. With ethnography you'll find yourself immersed in the consumers' world. With projective techniques you'll use psychological tools to find out how people feel about or perceive your product. Start thinking like an anthropologist or a psychologist, and you'll quickly learn how to identify consumers' sweet spot—the One Thing that links your consumers' desire with your product. As you might imagine, these kinds of techniques pose some ethical considerations. Not the least of which is, how far is too far? So before you begin your research take the time to know exactly how far is too far—and don't cross that line.

- Check out the competition. Review ads and other promotional material for your product. Study their visual structure and symbolism. Study their claims. Where are they weaker or stronger compared to your product?

- Read the publications your media department is considering. Watch the TV shows they recommend for your product.

- Talk to the people who buy, or might buy, your product. Why did they buy it or not buy it? Would they buy it again? If not, why not?

- Talk to people who considered, but did not buy, your product. Why didn't they? What would make them change their mind?

Ethnography—Immerse Yourself in Their World

- Visit a store and check how your product and its competitors are displayed. How does the shelf appeal of your product compare? While you're there, spend some time watching consumers interact with your brand and its competitors.

- Observe the salespeople who sell your product. Eavesdrop. What do they tell customers about it, and how do consumers respond?

- Sometimes it's helpful to take a factory tour. Observe with all your senses. Is there a key insight waiting to be shared with consumers?

- Hang out with the consumers. Go to their homes. Explore the rooms in which they will use your product. What do you observe that can help you successfully pitch this product?

Projective Techniques—Eliciting Inner Feelings

- Provide some images or words related to the product and ask consumers to make associations.

- Ask them to draw pictures or create collages that remind them of something related to your product or something you're trying to find out.

- Give them sentences to complete based on what you want to find out.

- Show them a storyboard or cartoon about the product and ask them to tell you what they think about the main character (the consumer) within the story.

You can find subjects to observe or interview in a number of places—stores, malls, sporting events, trade shows, basically anyplace where members of your target audience may gather. You might even consider conducting more formal research with focus groups of members of the target audience. These groups, professionally moderated, can explore attitudes and opinions in depth. And of course, there are always surveys. Whatever you decide on, the goal is to find the sweet spot—without crossing ethical boundaries.

Interpreting Research Findings

Funny thing about research—if it confirms the client's opinions, it wasn't really needed; if it contradicts the client's opinions, it's flawed. While the "facts" may be gathered and presented objectively, the interpretation is highly subjective.

Sometimes research reveals information about something you're not even measuring. For example, a survey for a business-to-business client revealed a strong negative opinion of the brand in the Southeast. Why did they love them in Ohio but hate them in

it could happen to everyone   don't discriminate

When is nudity a gratuitous attention grabber . . . and when can it be used to raise awareness about a serious social issue? This poster certainly stops viewers, but will they read the message "It could happen to everyone. Don't discriminate"?

Georgia? The client considered running some image ads in the South to build a more favorable opinion. Further investigation revealed the problem was not with the brand, but with the person selling it. In this case, no amount of brilliant advertising could solve the problem. A quick realignment of the sales force did. Another observation we've seen from years of gathering information and testing concepts: Clients focus on verbatim comments rather than numbers. They pay attention to a few video interviews rather than a mountain of statistics. Clients, like consumers, want to see and hear real people. They may analyze all the facts and figures, but a few memorable quotes usually help them form an opinion. Knowing how clients respond to research can put the agency in the driver's seat.

No matter how much research you gather, always remember . . .

Research does not replace insight.

- Facts are not always true.

- Objective research is evaluated subjectively.

- Data are perishable commodities.

Who Is the Target Audience?

Who are you talking to? Your client may tell you. Your account planner should tell you. Your secondary and primary research will tell you. If you're lucky, marketing objectives will be very specific, such as 35- to 65-year-old married men, living in the top 10 markets, earning $100,000 or more. Usually, though, a client tells the creative team about the product. Period. It's up to the agency to find out who is most likely to buy it and why. Unless you know who's buying the product and why, your creative strategy will be a classic example of "ready-fire-aim" planning.

- Who's buying the product now and why?

- Who's not buying the product now and why?

Features and Benefits

The object of your effort may not be a tangible product at all. It may be something you can't hold in your hand, like the local bus company, an art museum, or a government agency. It may be about corporate image—a campaign that promotes the integrity or strength of a company, but doesn't highlight products. Good examples are utility and telephone companies and multinational megafirms like General Electric. You could also develop creative

WD-40 knows their audience: no-nonsense guys who get it done. So they embrace that blue-collar sentiment in both copy and design.

for an organization such as the American Cancer Society or Amnesty International. For the sake of simplicity, we will call the object of promotion the "product" no matter what it may really be.

From the Inside: Features

Products have characteristics and personality traits just like people. By themselves these features are not good or bad. They're just there. That's why listing product features without putting them in the context of a benefit to the customer usually wastes time and space. Sometimes the benefit is so obvious the reader or viewer will make an instant connection. But other times, writers just include a list of features and hope someone will figure out why they're important. On a luxury car, for example, features can be technical, like a GPS navigation device; functional, like side curtain air bags; or aesthetic, like brushed aluminum console trim. In most cases, the more technical and abstract the feature, the greater the need to tie it to a benefit to the consumer.

From the Outside: Benefits

Not all products have features you can promote, but all have benefits. A benefit leads to the satisfaction of a consumer's wants and needs. "Cool, crisp flavor" is a benefit (it quenches thirst and tastes good). "Firm, smooth ride" is a benefit (it pleases the senses, and gives peace of mind). "Kills 99.9% of household germs" is a benefit (you're protecting your family).

Anyone can write a feature ad. All you need is a spec list. As a writer, you have to translate those features into benefits that resonate within the customer. Sometimes it's as simple as listing a feature and lining up a benefit. That's the old FAB (features-advantage-benefits) approach used for years in industrial brochures. However, we encourage you to think of more subtle and clever ways to promote the benefits. Edward de Bono, a cognitive expert, suggests that marketers pay close attention to the UBS, or unique buying state of consumers. So, when you're thinking about how to leverage a benefit, consider the UBS. Another approach came from a client. He uses the formula SW²C (So what? Who cares?). If you can answer those questions, you're halfway there. Table 2.2 gives some examples of features, benefits, and how they satisfy a consumer's wants and needs.

As we'll discuss shortly, you should think in terms of an overriding benefit. Remember the adjective you need to tack onto the brand name. If that adjective is positive, such as *economical, stylish, effective, safe,* or *powerful,* you've established an overall benefit. And, don't be afraid to work with the account planners to connect your key benefit to the UBS. You might also consider the fact that many of the choices

Not much doubt here—this ad from Israel is about chest hair removal, with before and after images in the same photo.

TABLE 2.2   Features and Benefits

Feature	Benefit	Wants and Needs
Contains fluoride	Prevents tooth decay	Saves money, saves time
Automatic shutoff	Shuts off unit if you forget	Safety, saves money, convenience
Electronic ignition	Easier starts in cold weather	Convenience
Slow nutrients release	Greener plants, more flowers	Aesthetically pleasing, convenient

consumers make today are based on symbolic product attributes. So don't discount the intangible. Finally, when spinning your benefits, think back to your brand—to its promise. Can your benefit engender trust? If so, you have leveraged the feature to its maximum potential, creating great strategic advantage. Now let's get to work.

Assembling the Facts

You've gathered a lot of information. Now it's time to organize it into something you can use. The following are three basic ways to organize information.

Copy Platform

The Copy Platform is also known as a Creative Strategy Statement and several other names. It can be as simple or as detailed as you'd like. No matter what you call it and how complicated it can be, a good Copy Platform should cover the product features and benefits, competitive advantages and weaknesses, information about the target audience, the tone of the message, and a simple, overriding statement about the product. We call this the One Thing. It can also be called the Central Truth, the Big Idea, or the Positioning Statement.

The best way to develop that connection is to ask this question:

"If you could say just One Thing about this product, it would be
_____."

It's not an easy sentence to complete. When we begin working with new clients, we sometimes ask them to complete that statement. You'd be surprised how many times they struggle with an answer. The most common response is "Gee. Nobody really asked that before. It's really so many things. I can't think of just one." Then they provide a laundry list of features. No wonder they needed a new agency!

You'll find an example Copy Platform in the Appendix. It's a compilation of several forms used by different agencies. Each firm will have its own way to organize information, but this one will do a pretty good job most of the time.

To summarize, we use Copy Platforms for the following reasons:

- **Provide a framework for your ad:** You have all the basic facts about the target, the product, the competition, and the marketplace. If you have some blank lines, you know you need more information.

- **Identify the One Thing that's most important:** You could use a position statement. Or the single adjective to attach to the brand. Or it could be a long sentence that describes what you want the consumer to believe about this product.

- **Support that One Thing with believable information:** This could be features and benefits that support product claims. In the case of a copy-free ad, only the visual supports that overriding image of the product.

- **Connect people with the product:** In your Copy Platform you should ask: What do you want the reader/viewer/listener to do? What is the desired conviction and action step? Do you want the consumer to take a test drive? Ask for more information? Visit a website? Or do nothing?

- **Organize the client's thoughts:** A good Copy Platform is a collaborative effort between client and agency. The client can provide a lot of information, and together you can clarify and prioritize it. This should not be done by a large committee—at least not by a committee larger than one or two people per client and agency. When completed, both the agency and the client have the same road map for creative strategy.

- **Justify your creative decisions:** If the client signed off on the Copy Platform, they will be less likely to criticize your creative efforts if you can prove you're on strategy. If the client says you're off target, you can ask where and why, based on your collaboration on the Copy Platform.

The One Thing about Axe fragrances is that they are so irresistible it takes extraordinary effort to resist temptation. Some critics would also hold their noses when reviewing such overtly sexist imagery in advertising.

Creative Brief

Creative Briefs may be prepared from a Copy Platform, or directly from the assembled information. The Creative Brief is a more linear progression from where we are to where we want to be and how we will get there. The strategy is more clearly defined than in most Copy Platforms. One of the best Creative Brief formats we've seen is used by the Virginia Commonwealth University Brandcenter. The questions are very simple, but if they are answered correctly, you've got just about everything you need to know to start concepting an ad.

- What do we want to accomplish? (objective)
- Who are we talking to? (target audience)
- What do they think now? (current position)
- What do we want them to think? (reinforce position or reposition)
- Why should they think this? (features/benefits)
- What is our message? (the One Thing and how you say it and show it—the tone)

  The following is a sample Creative Brief written by a student for Q-tips:

What do we want to accomplish?

The main objective of my campaign will be to introduce Q-tip cotton swabs to the next generation of adults, showing them the many uses as well as the quality that distinguishes Q-tip cotton swabs over the generic competition.

Who are we talking to?

We are speaking to people who value a good product and want the best. More importantly, we are targeting the emerging twentysomething crowd to sway their future buying habits.

What do they think now?

The majority of our new audience is indifferent to Q-tips cotton swabs. They consider this a very menial purchase and usually pick the cheapest package on the rack. They have always depended on others to pick up this item, so this will be a brand-new purchase for them.

What do we want them to think?

We want to instill a brand image into their minds, when they walk into a grocery store for personal care products; we want them to think Q-tips. We want them to pass over the generic products and choose Q-tips because Q-tips are a personal product as well as a practical one.

Why should they think this?

Because Q-tips will be presented in a very edgy and fun way, we will be able to connect to our audience. This will carry over to the point of purchase and influence their buying habits. We want them to realize the importance of taking care of themselves with the highest quality of cotton swabs.

What is our message?

Q-tips cotton swabs are a personal item with practical applications.

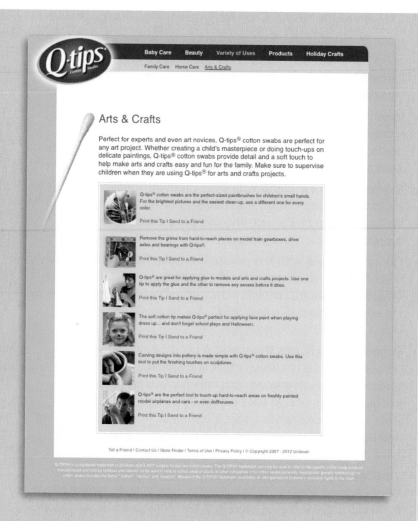

Consumer Profile

The Consumer Profile takes the Copy Platform and Creative Brief a step further by putting a human face on the target audience. Think of journalism's Five *W*s in terms of the consumers: Who are they? What are their wants and needs; their buying intentions; their attitudes toward the product and competitors? What do they do for a living? What are their hobbies? Where do they live and work, and how does that affect their buying patterns? When are they planning to buy? When do they watch TV or use other types of media? Why should they consider your product or competitors? Based on the demographic, psychographic, lifestyles and values, and other research, a Consumer Profile puts some flesh on the bare bones of the Copy Platform. You might consider summarizing the demographics in the first paragraph and include the psychographics in the second paragraph, while you weave the lifestyles and values through the whole profile.

The list below should help you develop some basic information about the product and potential customers:

- *Who* is the prospect?
- *What* does she do, and *what* does she want?
- *Where* does she live?
- *When* does she buy?
- *Why* would she be interested?
- *How* does she want to buy?

Meet Maria

Maria Sanchez is a modern 35-year-old working mom with a husband and two children, aged 10 and 3. She graduated from the University of Illinois with a degree in management, which helped her get a job in the human resource department of a large insurance company in Chicago. She has steadily advanced to become assistant department manager. She earns $65,000 and expects to continue moving up the corporate ladder. Her husband Carlos is a sales representative for a large manufacturing firm. His income varies greatly from year to year, so Maria's large and stable income is extremely important to their family. Maria and Carlos live in a four-bedroom home in Hoffman Estates, which is a 45-minute commute one way (when traffic is moving). Maria loves her job, but the stresses of caring for a family, commuting, and the usual pressures of a human resources department can sometimes trigger a migraine headache. With her busy schedule, Maria can't take time off from work and family when she has a migraine. The increased frequency of her migraines creates even more stress, but she doesn't have time to visit a doctor or make an extra trip to the pharmacy.

In her spare time, Maria likes to ride her bicycle, play tennis, and shop. She and Carlos enjoy traveling, with and without the kids. They try to set aside at least one weekend a month as "date night" to recharge their marriage. After work and dinner at home with the family, Maria usually reads the mail and watches her favorite TV programs—*CSI, Dancing With the Stars,* and old movies on TCM. Occasionally, she will watch telenovelas on Univision when her mother visits. When her iPod isn't plugged into her car stereo, she surfs SiriusXM and almost never tunes into a local radio station. She rarely has time to read the newspaper, except on weekends when she relaxes with the Sunday *Chicago Tribune.*

Migraine sufferers aren't looking for advertising claims. They're looking for answers to understand and relieve their symptoms. This website provides a lot of useful information for managing migraine pain . . . and, yes, a little something about the sponsor's product.

The previous example was written by a student to describe the ideal prospect for Excedrin Migraine.

You can see how by focusing on demographics and psychographics you can create a personal portrait of the ideal person within the target audience. From this profile, thanks to attention to her media habits, we know that an advertiser can reach Maria through radio (drive time), billboards (along her commute), direct mail, television, and, in a more limited way, newspapers and magazines. Through demographics and psychographics we know our approach must be intelligent (she's smart and successful) and to the point (she doesn't have a lot of spare time). The benefit of a nonprescription remedy that could relieve her symptoms without taking time out for a doctor's visit may be the main selling point.

In the end, you have to use judgment. The ad will not write itself based on a compilation of facts. Sometimes a great creative idea stems from a minor benefit and blooms into a powerful image that drives a whole campaign. Our advice: Get the facts and use them, but don't be a slave to data.

When you see a feature or even a rather vague benefit, be sure to ask this question:

SO WHAT?

What does that feature do for the consumer? Keep asking "So what?" until you get to the benefit that satisfies a basic want or need. Think about the questions you'd ask if you were buying something. You may not always get something you'd include in the body copy, but if you keep probing, you might get an idea for a whole campaign.

For example:

Dove soap is one-quarter cleansing cream.

So what?

It's creamier, less harsh to the skin.

So what?

Your skin looks younger, less dry.

So what?

You feel better about yourself.

Now you've got a hook. Don't tell her about your soap, talk to her about feeling young, beautiful, free, and sexy.

Put yourself in the target customer's shoes. Luke Sullivan says, "Ask yourself what would make you want to buy the product? Find the central truth about the product . . . hair coloring isn't about looking younger. It's about self-esteem. Cameras aren't about pictures. They're about stopping time and holding life as the sands run out."[8]

This student-created ad compared a pet adoption service with human dating sites. The One Thing is unrequited love. It resonates because no pet owner can resist love at first lick.

Tone: Finding Your Voice

You know what you want to say; now you have to figure out how to say it. Whether you create a formal tone statement or just think about it, you really do need to define the tone of your creative effort. Another way to think about it is finding your voice: Is it loud and obnoxious, soft and sexy, logical and persuasive, fun and carefree, melodramatic and sensational, or some other characteristic? For example, if you did ads for a hospital, you wouldn't make jokes about kids with cancer. You'd be hopeful, respectful, empathetic, and maybe emotional. On the other hand, if you advertised an amusement park, you wouldn't feature a serious discussion about the benefits of a given ride. You'd be wild and screaming with excitement.

The tone or voice of an ad or a commercial is more than the concept. It's reflected in the selection of talent, music, editing, art direction, and voice inflection. For example, a TV commercial for Cheerios features baby boomers "lamenting" the fact they have to eat healthy food to reduce their cholesterol. The words are serious, but their facial expressions and the fact they are actually enjoying their Cheerios provide a totally different voice than if you just looked at the script.

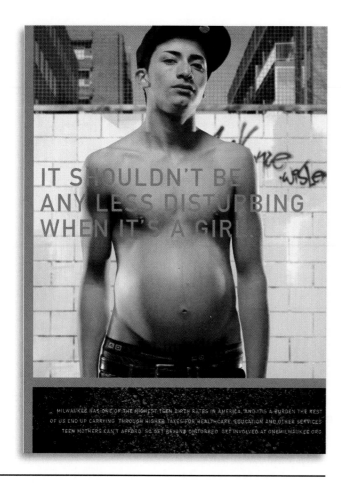

Making a serious point sometimes takes a little gender bending. This public service announcement concept, originally done in the United Kingdom, tries to shock the reader into taking action to reduce teen pregnancies.

As with everything else, know the target audience. Then find the right tone to communicate your message.

What Do You Want Them to Do?

Remember AIDA? The *action* component is the finish line of your advertising. If you can get the reader or viewer to contact the advertiser, most of your work is done. Although you will continue to reinforce the brand and encourage future sales to consumers who take action, your primary job is to connect buyers to sellers. It's up to them to close the deal.

The main idea is to connect the reader, viewer, or listener with the advertiser. Make it easy to get more information if it's needed. If personal selling is critical to a purchase, find a way to connect the prospect with the salesperson. These connections can take the following forms:

- Easy-to-remember and meaningful URL
- Outbound e-mail (that doesn't look like spam)
- Mobile apps encouraging continued interactivity
- Meaningful engagement with Facebook
- Maximizing Twitter, sometimes employing hash tags
- Onsite engagement from test drives to taste tests
- Prepaid reply cards to request more information or an appointment
- QR codes leading to mobile sites
- Toll-free phone number in ads to connect to a live person

Think about the many ways customers can take action, and then make it easy to connect them with the advertiser.

Putting It All Together

You've done your homework on the audience, the product, and the competition. Now you're ready to talk to a prospective customer. You're ready to be an account planner—or at least rely on one. It's your job to give voice to the consumer. Imagine you're talking to a neighbor over the fence, instead of writing an ad or a TV spot. Could you tell him or her the One Thing to know about your product? Could you give reasons to support that One Thing? Do you have answers to objections or misconceptions about your product? Could you convince that neighbor to seek more information, or visit a store to compare or just buy the product? It's all about making a personal connection.

Think Like a Planner, but Write Like a Creative

Here are a few samples:

Objective: Introduce new hybrid crossover utility vehicle

Type of Product: Considered purchase, high-involvement durable good

Target Audience: 20- to 30-year-old women in top 25 markets, $45K–$70K income

Possible Creative Strategy: Lots of pictures to show features, styling, captions to explain benefits (environmentally friendly, dependable, lots of space, mileage)

Tone: Convey fun, independence, adventure, and social responsibility

Objective: Encourage contributions to animal rights group

Type of Product: Emotional issue, high involvement for select few

Target Audience: 18- to 64-year-old women

Possible Creative Strategy: Show animal suffering in lab tests, long copy tells story of animal and how you can help

Tone: Emotional, urgent, call to action (send money)

Objective: Introduce new style of brace for arthritic knees

Type of Product: Considered purchase, high involvement

Target Audience: 45- to 80-year-old men and women with arthritis

We don't think there's any doubt this ad is about mobile marketing. But just in case the readers don't scan the QR code, they can call the toll-free number or visit the website listed in the ad.

Words of Wisdom

"Making the simple complicated is commonplace. Making the complicated simple, awesomely simple, that's creativity."[10]

Charles Mingus, jazz musician

Possible Creative Strategy: Position as alternative to surgery and drugs, show active seniors, possible testimonials or before/after photos

Tone: Create peace of mind (postpone surgery, relieve pain, resume active lifestyle)

Branding

It seems we are firmly entrenched in the age of the brand, or, as marketing guru Scott Bedbury called it, "a new brand world." Today more than ever consumers' interactions with a brand are critical. And managing those interactions is at the heart of branding. With the explosion of peer-to-peer sites, branding involves a lot more than communicating the advertiser's point of view. Social media and word of mouth can make or break a brand, no matter how much the advertiser spends.

Before you start supporting a brand, you first have to understand what a brand is and what it does. Many authors have their own ideas about brands, and they're all good. We've summarized them into two main thoughts:

What it is: A brand is a promise. It's shorthand for all the product's attributes, good and bad.

What it does: A brand makes the promise personal by conveying the product's personality, which reflects on the people who buy the product. It's really all about relationships.

Luke Sullivan expands those thoughts when he says, "A brand isn't just a name on the box. It isn't the thing in the box either. A brand is the sum total of all the emotions, thoughts, images, history, possibilities and gossip that exist in the marketplace about a certain company."[11] If you think he's exaggerating a bit, consider the fact that brands (at least those with positive images) are assets, sometimes worth billions of dollars to a company. Some companies protect their brands like a momma bear guarding her cubs. Put yellow arches on a taco stand or an unlicensed Harley-Davidson logo on a T-shirt, and you'll quickly find out how sharp those claws can be.

Brand Image

Companies spend millions to establish and nurture a brand image. Brand image advertising (and promotion) sells the personality, the mystique, and the aura surrounding or emanating from the product, not the product itself. Think of the old cliché "Sell the sizzle, not the steak."

Every product has a brand image. Some are stronger than others. Think of the brand image or brand character of well-known products. How does the

Nothing exemplified Steve Jobs's philosophy more than this branding campaign for Apple shortly after his return as CEO. This campaign was designed to buy time, keeping the Apple brand promise alive until exciting new products could be launched that would ultimately save the company.

brand image of BMW differ from that of Cadillac or Lexus? They all cost about the same, but have different characters, as do their customers. How did Apple differentiate itself from Microsoft? Not as a technically superior and more expensive computer, but rather as a computer with an easy-to-use operating system favored by right-brain types. IBM told people to "Think." Apple said, "Think Different." Luke Sullivan states, "Most of the time we're talking about going into a customer's brain and tacking on one adjective onto a client's brand. That's all. DeWalt tools are tough. Apple computers are easy to use . . . Volvos are safe. Porsches are fast. Jeeps are rugged. Boom. Where's the rocket science here?"[12] To support a brand's image, advertisers use simple, unique, and easily recognized visuals. Over time, the brand (and all its attributes, good and bad) comes to mind when a consumer catches even a glimpse of these visuals.

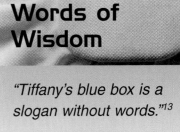

Words of Wisdom

"Tiffany's blue box is a slogan without words."[13]

Seth Godin, author of
Purple Cow and several
other marketing books

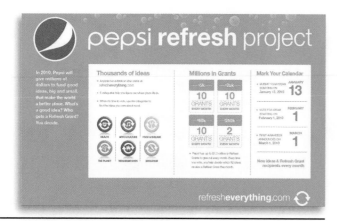

The Pepsi Refresh Project replaced traditional Super Bowl advertising with sustained crowdsourced philanthropy, saving millions of promotional dollars and building goodwill for the brand in the key youth target audience.

This classic ad from Mexico says "Just Do It" without any words . . . in any language.

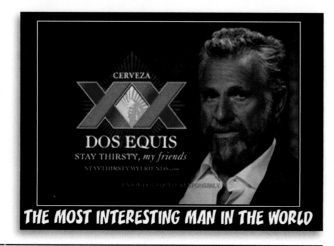

"The most interesting man in the world" is probably even more fascinating after a few Dos Equis, but you can't dispute what he did to propel the brand to leadership in its category.

Branded Storytelling

Every brand has a story behind it. A marketer's job is to make sure it's a good story, one that can be told over and over again by satisfied customers. In the past, advertisers developed the Unique Selling Proposition. Today they're searching to create their Unique Story Proposition. Alain Thys writes, "Great brand stories stem from the reason a brand exists. Apple wanted to free creative spirits while slaying the Microsoft dragon. Coco Chanel set out to reinvent fashion and liberate women from tradition. Pepsi wants to be a catalyst for change for every generation. Dig into the history, people and promises of your brand to uncover its Unique Story Proposition (USP). Make this the anchor for every story you tell."[14]

Self-described marketing heretic Mark Di Somma states, "Stories are the backbones of powerful brands. Every strong brand is backed by a powerful brand story that weaves together all the brand elements into a single and compelling tale packed with truth, insights and compelling ideas."[15] Stories are driven by emotions, and consumers are expressing these emotions through their consumption choices. Think of how Nike has managed to direct all its communications toward one underlying message—the will to win. They have to do this through telling the story of individual athletic success, but always in the context of the athletic community—the Nike community. In the process consumers see themselves within these stories and thus within the Nike community. They too dream of winning, and Nike's stories represent their stories—or at least their mythological possibility. Nike's advertising provides the context for this mythology to grow. It also demonstrates how branding and the USP shape consumers' experiences.

Perhaps no brand was a greater reflection of its CEO than Apple. Steve Jobs's fanatical control over everything, including advertising, resulted in some of the greatest campaigns of all time. As a struggling upstart and later as a market leader, Apple's brand story was consistent: Create simple, easy-to-use, elegant products that make the user a better person and, as a result, the world a better place. Jobs's brand message of technology as a humanizing force was eloquently stated in the introduction of the iPad 2, his last big product launch.

> *This is what we believe. Technology alone is not enough. Faster. Thinner. Lighter. Those are all good things. But when technology gets out of the way, everything becomes more delightful, even magical. That's when you leap forward. That's when you end up with something like this.*[16]

Brand Agents

Consider the power of Martha Stewart, Phil Knight, and Richard Branson to shape their brands. It is their personal stories that provide the mythology that shapes and sustains their brands. Thought of in this way, myths give a brand an emotional context, which provides the platform from which consumers find a sense of identity and belonging. Remember Maslow? Think of brands as "the narrative of mankind. It's a story told with a collective voice and a shared point of view."[17] When brands are conceived in this manner, you can see how the brand story articulates the brand promise.

Traditional branding strategy dictates that to be effective, a brand must be used consistently and must invoke meaning. However, a 2011 survey published in *Adweek* suggests that opinion may be changing. Based on data from agencies and clients, only 27% said it's critical to ensure that all of a brand's various messages are strategically consistent. On the other hand, 73% said the days of strategic consistency are over: It's all about inspiration and engagement.[18]

How do you establish a relevant brand? Some people would say saturate every advertising medium and slap it on anything that won't move. However, advertising funds are limited, even for huge companies, so a more sophisticated approach is required to make that brand stick in the minds of consumers. Two concepts, which started as theories, are now considered crucial to establishing a strong brand. These are positioning and resonance.

Assume the Position

Jack Trout and Al Ries revolutionized marketing in the late '70s and early '80s with their theory of positioning. Their book, *Positioning: The Battle for Your Mind*, introduced a new way of thinking about products and how they fit into the marketplace. This is the best definition of positioning we've found: *Simply stated, positioning is the perception consumers have of your product, not unto itself, but relative to the competition.*[20]

The key to understanding and using positioning lies in the consumer's mind. The consumer files product considerations in two broad categories: garbage ("nothing there for me") and maybe-I'm-interested. In the second category, consumers use subcategories for different products, often aligning those positions with heavily promoted brand images. For example, BMWs are fast. Volvos are safe. Jeeps are rugged. And so on. So if you asked most consumers to "position" or rank those brands in various categories, you'd probably find some resistance to the idea that a BMW is as safe as a Volvo,

Chrysler repositioned their ailing brand with the slogan "Imported From Detroit." They embraced the gritty, hardworking image of the city in their TV ads as they showcased their redesigned cars. They extended that theme with the "Halftime in America" pep talk by Clint Eastwood a year later.

Words of Wisdom

"Briefs will try to put it together for you, analyze it and tell you what it means. But I already know the idea isn't in the brief . . . [it's] in my head. Somewhere."[21]

Kate Lummus, senior copywriter, McCann Erickson

or a Jeep can be as fast as a BMW, or a Volvo can be as rugged as a Jeep. All true in some cases, but not universally believed. Once a position is established, it takes a lot of effort to change it.

Before you develop the position of your client's product, you have to ask:

- What is the current position?

- What is the competitor's position?

- Where do you want to be?

- How are you going to get there? (That's strategy.)

Repositioning and Rebranding

If you don't like your product's position, you may want to change it from what you have to what you want. Here are three examples:

Dove's landmark "Real Beauty" campaign encouraged women who were less than perfect to feel good about themselves. But they only reached half the population, so Dove chose to extend their brand to men's skin care products. In 2010, Dove Men+Care was launched to make men "feel comfortable in their own skin"—a not-so-subtle appeal to real men who are not afraid of losing their masculinity if they use Dove products. Supported by a Super Bowl ad, public relations, promotions, and mobile, digital, and social media, the campaign appealed to men in places where they live and play using language that resonated with them. Although men needed to feel OK with using Dove products, it's important to note that women make most of the personal grooming purchases for men. So having a brand they know and love for their men was a definite advantage.

Rolling Stone magazine gained wide acceptance as the first mass-market counterculture publication. The Woodstock Nation grew up in the 1980s, cleaned up, and found that Wall Street was cooler than Haight-Ashbury. Yet they still read *Rolling Stone.* However, advertisers were still stuck in the '60s. *RS* needed mainstream advertisers, not smoke shops and Earth Shoes. Fallon McElligott Rice (the precursor of today's Fallon) did the trick with their famous "Perception/Reality" campaign. By using icons for the perceived image of *RS* readers next to a symbol of the real readers, *RS* attracted big-bucks advertisers. This not only kept the magazine in business; it helped make it slicker and ultimately pushed it into the mainstream.

Corona beer was discovered in the 1980s by college kids on spring break who were looking for a light and inexpensive yet slightly exotic brew (at least more exotic than Milwaukee's Best). Corona soon became a cult brand, known as the tropical party beer, especially when guzzled with a slice of lime. But as the spring breakers grew up, they moved on to more sophisticated beers, and Corona sales suffered . . . until a new ad agency repositioned the brand as the one to relax with. Ads invoked images of lazy days in a hammock rather than wet T-shirt contests. The "Change Your Latitude" and "Find Your Beach" campaigns put Corona back on the map, and sales soared. After all, no matter how hard you partied in college, you can always dream about relaxing on the beach.

Corona repositioned their brand from a cheap spring break staple to the preferred beer of laid-back people looking to find their inner beach.

Positioning Redux

While Trout and Ries opened a lot of minds to a new way of thinking, a lot of writers take issue with their premise that creativity makes no difference. Sometimes it's the only difference. Creativity can create the position or reposition the product. Another caveat is that Trout and Ries analyzed successful campaigns from the past and made them fit their theory. Did the 7Up creative team really think about positioning when they launched the "Uncola" campaign, or did they just want to do great advertising? Often the creative is the only thing that makes a brand memorable. Remember that a brand's position usually happens over time.

Resonance: Did You Just Feel Something?

When you achieve resonance, your external message connects with internal values and feelings. Tony Schwartz notes, "Resonance takes place when the stimuli put into our communication evoke meaning in a listener or viewer . . . the meaning of our communication is what a listener or viewer gets out of his experience with the communicator's stimuli."[23]

Resonance requires a connection with feelings that are inside the consumer's mind. You don't have to put in a new emotion—just find a way to tap what's already there. In other words, to get your idea to resonate in the consumer's mind, your communication must trigger some internal

War Story

Eva Luna—A Nontraditional Approach to Engagement

Since T-Mobile's 2004 launch in the Hispanic market, young Latinos had embraced the carrier as a hip, trendy brand with products they loved. By mid-2010, however, business began to slow. While the brand was doing well with single lines, T-Mobile wasn't winning with family lines—the fastest-growing chunk of the overall wireless market and, thus, subscriber acquisitions. To capture this lucrative segment, T-Mobile needed to connect with Latino families without losing its existing youth customer base.

The task wasn't an easy one. T-Mobile occupies a unique space among the major U.S. carriers—greatly outspent from above by its much larger competitors and fending off from below a variety of local and regional carriers trying to wrest away market share. In order to maximize media investment, we knew we would have to up the emotional ante with our audience.

We analyzed family-targeted advertising and spoke to Hispanic families about the things that drive conversations at home. It became clear that *novelas* (soap operas) were more than a pastime for many people; they were an obsession. People would constantly call and text friends and family on their cell phones to discuss major plot twists played out on the serial television shows. Research showed that the one thing that limited these conversations was the concern of exceeding phone and data plans. People loved to share but were afraid of the costs.

Using this insight, we developed a partnership with *Eva Luna*, a brand-new *novela* that was set to debut on Univision. The sponsorship centered on unique broadcast integrations that opened and closed each episode. The idea was based on family members who were so connected that they stayed on their cell phones throughout the entire *novela*. The show would start with a woman discussing the opening moments, which faded into the action. The episode would conclude with the same woman talking about the ending—giving the impression that she spent the entire hour telling the story. The campaign's tagline "Ahora las familias van a estar más juntas que nunca" ("Families will now be closer than ever") was brought to life thanks to T-Mobile's unlimited family plan.

Eva Luna was a hit, and rated as the sixth most successful prime-time *novela* of all time, with 3.5 million Latinos watching its finale. The T-Mobile custom-branded site attracted 3.4 million visitors, and the campaign's smart and innovative television engagement strategy made T-Mobile synonymous with Hispanic family values whilst embodying the brand's "cool, fun, genuine, and daring" personality.[24]

Mario Granatur, vice president/creative director, Conill, Miami, FL, conill.com

---

experience and connect it with your message. Your brand story must be relevant. Relevance leads to resonance, which will strengthen awareness, begin building comprehension, and lead to conviction and possibly action. How's that for connecting multiple streams of psychobabble?

Want an even simpler explanation?

$$1 + 1 = 3$$

Resonance is connected to branding because a brand can make a consumer feel something—sometime it's something good, and sometimes it's bad. A harried vacationer with a carload of hungry kids sees those Golden Arches and thinks, "At last—familiar food, Happy Meals for the kids, and

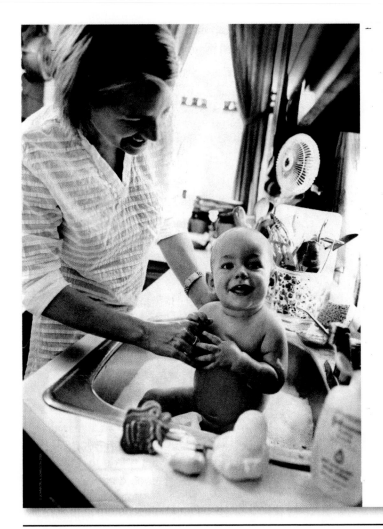

Who'd have ever thought the love of your life would be short and bald?

You always went for the tall, dark, mysterious types. You fell in love with one, married him and started a family. Then when the baby was born, an amazing new feeling hit you. And now, as much as you'll always love your husband, this new little man just takes your breath away. Having a baby changes everything.

Johnson & Johnson

What's more appealing than a little baby? Johnson & Johnson knew that making the baby the star of this ad would resonate much stronger with moms than featuring the package. The tagline "Having a baby changes everything" also makes a strong connection with any parent.

clean restrooms." The next driver turns up her nose and thinks, "Ugh—greasy food, indifferent service, and a restaurant full of kids demanding Happy Meals." There's resonance, but for the mom looking for Happy Meals and clean bathrooms, there's also relevance.

The convergence of brand strategy and resonance theory succeeds best in brands that make consumers happy. Marketing professor Pierre Chandon states, "People align themselves with a brand that reflects what they see when they look in the mirror."[25]

According to Meghan Casserly at Forbes.com, here are the world's "happiest brands" and our take on why:

- Apple—"I belong to a special group of creative nonconformists."

- Campbell's Soup—"It brings back warm feelings after coming in on a cold day."

Apple positioned their brand for folks who wanted other people to think they were cool. Samsung turned that around to position Apple fans as "iSheep" who were so loyal they ignored superior technology and design. In the last installment in the ad series, the smug hipsters are liberated from their slavish devotion to Apple.

- Coca-Cola—"I remember all the good times when a Coke was the ultimate refreshment."
- Facebook—"I'm in control of my own brand story."
- Fruit of the Loom—"My mom bought this for me when I was a kid."
- J.Crew—"Classic quality for a reasonable price."
- Johnson's Baby—"My mom used it on me; I use it on my kids."
- Kraft Macaroni & Cheese—"It's easy, cheesy, and sometimes still the perfect food."[26]

Sometimes playing off consumers' slavish loyalty to another brand pays off. Samsung created a series of ads featuring bored but smug "iSheep" waiting in line for the next big thing. While they are trapped in line, they notice other people walking freely with really cool Samsung phones that offer features their iPhones lack. One of these hipsters comments, "I could never have a Samsung. I'm creative," to which his friend says, "Dude. You're a barista." The last spot in the series was a 90-second Super Bowl spectacular showing the weary Apple aficionados breaking free to enjoy their new Samsung phones. Some would say this is a modern twist on Apple's antiestablishment "1984" spot. In terms of resonance, Apple fans wondered, "Are we really like that?" and everyone else said, "Yes, you are."

Extending Your Brand

David Aaker, brand consultant and author of more than 14 books, suggests that the value of a brand is often rooted in the parent brand. Sub-brands are the value brands. Marriott is the parent brand, while Courtyard by Marriott is a value-based sub-brand. Aaker suggests there are three types of relationships between parent brands and sub-brands: endorser, codriver, and driver brands. Let's use Nike to walk you through. Nearly every extension of the Nike brand, from Nike Golf to NIKEiD to Livestrong (its philanthropic venture with Lance Armstrong), carries with it the cachet of the parent brand. Now let's see how it plays out.

Rising Star

I Hate Advertising

A few weeks ago I listened as a recent college graduate enthusiastically recounted his lifelong love of advertising. Midway through his declaration of advertising love, he abruptly shifted the conversation toward me. "What made you go into advertising?"

I knew my answer. After his passionate discourse, it felt a bit cynical. I answered. "Growing up I didn't like advertising. I hated it. I thought it was intrusive, lowbrow, and annoying." He looked confused. "Then, why did you go into it?" He asked. I laughed and replied, "It just kind of happened. After changing my major five times, it was the only other major that my built-up credits would transfer into."

With that answer he thought he understood. "OK. So, then you found a love for advertising." I shook my head. "Nope. I still don't really like it. But, I love making it."

That realization has been one of the biggest surprises of my adult life. I found that I love how fast-moving advertising is. How the assignments, clients, and deliverables are always changing and that, at the end of the day, it's creative problem solving at its most fun.

After graduating, I started as a copywriter at a small shop in Salt Lake City. I mostly did long-format copywriting for brochures, books, and webpages. Nothing glamorous. But it forced me to hone my writing skills. Which is why the work I did there is probably the most important I've ever done. Without developing those skills, I would not have been able to create a fraction of the work I have since then.

Not all my creative work is good. Not all the times are great. Not all the people are nice. But for the most part, I love creating work. Maybe one day, I'll even start liking advertising.

I don't consider myself experienced enough to give advice, but if I were to pretend I am, I'd say: Hone your skills and let life lead you. You never know where you're going to go, but if you're prepared, you'll be able to make something of it.[27]

Matt Miller, Leo Burnett, Chicago, leoburnett.com

- **Endorser brand:** This brand is endorsed by the Nike parent brand—Nike+ (running gadgets).

- **Codriver:** This brand is equal to the parent brand in terms of its influence with consumers and sometimes appears as a competitor—Adidas.

- **Driver brands:** With this brand the parent maintains primary influence as driver and the sub-brand acts as a descriptor, telling consumers that the parent company is offering a slight variation on the product or service they have come to know and trust—Nike Women.

Next come **line extensions.** Robert Sprung, partner of a major branding services company, says, "A good line extension takes a brand with a solid core of values and applies it to an area where the brand has permission to go."[28] Staying with Nike, think of the various sports as line extensions: Nike basketball, Nike running, and so on. Marketers for strong brands naturally want to leverage that strength whenever possible.

The Branding Strategy Insider website lists some guidelines for successful brand extension:

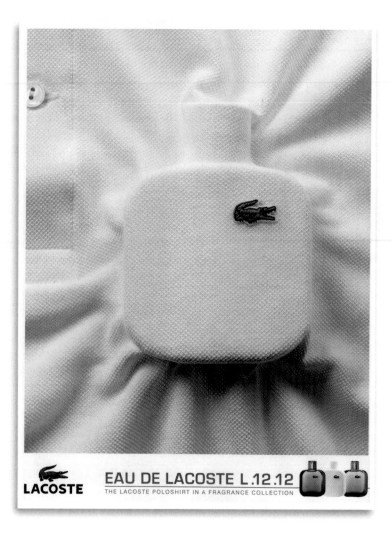

Could Lacoste charge just as much for a shirt without the little alligator? Probably not. Neither could Lacoste cologne. A strong symbol is essential for extending a brand to new products.

- Have you identified what your brand owns in the consumer's mind? [In other words, what is your brand's position?]

- Have you identified all the areas in which the consumer gives your brand position to operate?

- Have you identified all the ways your brand and others in its category have made compromises with the consumer?

- Have you found ways to redefine your business to break those compromises?

- Have you explored ways to make your brand more relevant to the next generation of consumers?

- Do you have a way to screen all new brand extension proposals for their congruence with the brand promise and impact on brand equity? [A fancy way of asking if you've done your homework.][29]

Who's Who?

David Aaker—Brand consultant and CEO of Prophet Consultancy David Aaker is the author of more than 14 books, including *Managing Brand Equity, Building Strong Brands, Brand Leadership, Brand Portfolio Strategy*, and *Spanning Silos: The New CMO Imperative*. Professor Emeritus at the Haas School of Business, University of California, Berkeley, he has been awarded four career awards including the 1996 Paul D. Converse Award for outstanding contributions to the development of marketing.

William Bernbach—Although he was the third name in Doyle Dane Bernbach, there was no doubt who was in charge of the creative process. Bill Bernbach revolutionized advertising from the late 1950s and through the 1970s, suggesting advertising was an art and not a science, with groundbreaking campaigns for Volkswagen, Alka-Seltzer, Polaroid, Avis, Ohrbach's, and many others. His simple yet sophisticated commercials generated huge sales for his clients as they wove their way firmly into the popular culture. Doyle Dane Bernbach not only changed advertising forever; it also spawned many of the creative superstars of the 1970s, '80s, and '90s who formed their own shops.

Marty Neumeier—Before launching and becoming president of Neutron LLC, a San Francisco-based firm specializing in brand collaboration, in 2002, Marty Neumeier was editor and publisher of *Critique*, the "magazine of graphic design thinking," which had quickly become the leading forum for improving design effectiveness. In editing *Critique*, Neumeier joined the conversation about how to bridge the gap between strategy and design, which led directly to the formation of Neutron and the ideas in his book, *The Brand Gap*.

Rebecca Van Dyck—As chief marketing officer of Levi's, Rebecca Van Dyck was challenged to make the old brand relevant to a new generation of fickle and skeptical consumers. One winning strategy was promoting the Levi's Curve ID line for women. She also expanded the iconic "Go Forth" campaign to 24 countries and debuted the "Now Is Our Time" campaign to an audience of 325 million people on Facebook, telling them they have the power to change the world. Regarding her global strategy, she said, "Initially, America was our canvas. Now, our canvas is the world." The world is buying it—resulting in significant increases in sales and profits for this venerable brand. *Adweek* named Van Dyck as a 2011 Brand Genius.[30]

Exercises

1. What's the Big Idea, Buddy?

(Contributed by Kimberly Selber, PhD, associate professor, University of Texas–Pan American)

This exercise is all about finding the Big Idea or the One Thing and linking it to strategy.

- Find several campaigns with at least three ads. (Try using archive magazine for this assignment; the online version—http://www.luerzersarchive.net—is great, because you can easily grab all the ads together.)

- Write a Copy Platform or Creative Brief for each campaign. End with one sentence describing the overarching concept in the campaign—the One Thing.

- Compare how other students or groups interpreted your message. If the messaging is tight, the briefs should be similar. This works great as an in-class exercise or as homework in teams or solo.

2. Brand Stretching

- As a class, generate a list of five brands, from five different product categories. Now, individually generate a list of brand extensions for each product. Consider what areas the parent brand already owns and in which areas of the brand you find growth opportunities.

- Now pick one brand. Post your brand and list of potential brand extensions. Explain the rationale for each brand extension choice.

- Then, as a class, generate other possible brand extensions.

3. Tagging the Heart of a Brand

- Choose four brands. As a class, brainstorm a list of words that personify the heart of each brand.

- Break into four groups, one brand per group. Based on the words generated, write a positioning statement.

- Visit brandtags.net. Click on "Tag Brands" and "Explore Brands" to find brands to analyze.

- Next click on "Guess Brands" and see how many of the first 10 brands that pop up your group can guess correctly. If you guess the brand, you can be pretty sure the brand positioning is strongly articulated and maintained.

- Share your results with the class and learn which brands have strong positioning and why.

Visit www.sagepub.com/altstiel3e to access these additional learning tools

- Video Links
- Web Resources
- eFlashcards
- Web Quizzes

Chapter 3

Legal and Ethical Issues

Doing the Right Thing

As you'll see in later chapters, the perception of ad messages can vary widely depending on the audience. You may find it's worth taking a creative risk to persuade one small group, knowing full well it will turn off most everyone else. You have to weigh the risks (which may include loss of overall sales, adverse publicity, and even lawsuits) against the benefits (higher sales to a select group, publicity, and creative recognition). We do not advocate doing anything creatively for the sake of shock value. Nor do we recommend using sexist, racist, or homophobic messages; sleazy gimmicks; or gutter humor to gain attention. Some of the examples in this book may go beyond the threshold of acceptable taste for some people. They are what they are, and even if we don't always agree with their content, they are part of the real world.

Legal issues are often black-and-white and, in most cases, backed by years of established precedents. However, digital marketing has opened up new challenges that lawmakers are still trying to wrap their brains around, such as what constitutes privacy in social media and what defines intellectual property on the web. We will try to address some of these issues, knowing that new ones will emerge as technology continues to evolve.

Ethical issues fall into that vast gray area between black-and-white legality. And sometimes things that are legal might not be ethical. In some cases what you are asked to do may be legal, but it may not be the right thing to do. That's where it gets really tough. We will do our best to offer guidance, but realize that ethical behavior is difficult to define. The one thing we can recommend is that you take some time to define your own individual ethical boundaries before you get into this business. Having given ethics serious consideration in advance will help you when you get mired in the vast sea of gray.

The American Association of Advertising Agencies provides this creative code of ethics for its members. Even if you're not a 4A member, it's good advice:

Industry Codes of Conduct

We the members of the American Association of Advertising Agencies (AAAA), in addition to supporting and obeying the laws and legal regulations pertaining to advertising, undertake to extend and broaden the application of high ethical standards. Specifically, we will not knowingly create advertising that contains:

a. False or misleading statements or exaggerations, visual or verbal.

b. Testimonials that do not reflect the real opinion of the individual(s) involved.

c. Price claims that are misleading.

d. Claims insufficiently supported or that distort the true meaning or practicable application of statements made by professional or scientific authority.

e. Statements, suggestions or pictures offensive to public decency or minority segments of the population.

We recognize that there are areas that are subject to honestly different interpretations and judgment. Nevertheless, we agree not to recommend to any advertiser, and to discourage the use of, advertising that is in poor or questionable taste or that is deliberately irritating through aural or visual content or presentation.[1]

The American Marketing Association (AMA) also has a strong statement of ethics.[2] We've highlighted the key points because they serve as a great guide for everyone in our business.

Ethical Norms

1. Do no harm.

2. Foster trust in the marketing system.

3. Embrace ethical values.

Ethical Values

- Honesty

- Responsibility

- Fairness

- Respect

- Transparency

- Citizenship

In today's political climate we cannot help but wonder if some of the ethical values espoused by the AMA have been tossed aside in the partisanship of

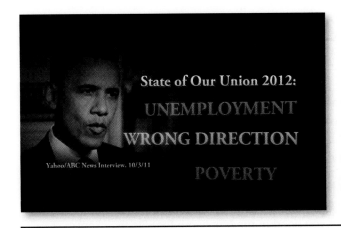

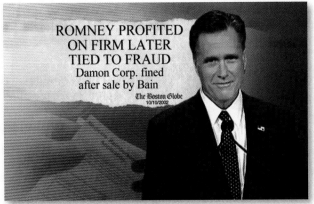

The AMA, or any other, code of ethics does not apply to most political attack advertising. First Amendment rights don't prevent broadcasting half-truths, innuendo, slander, and even the most blatant lies. Unfortunately, negative advertising has proven effective, no matter how questionable its ethics may be.

postmodern American politics. You might argue that many of the ads are partially true. However, almost everyone can agree that they often do not represent the values of fairness and respect, which certainly calls into question whether they are responsible. Throw into the mix that corporations, labor unions, and political action committees (PACs) now have the same legal status as individuals, in terms of free speech. We have to wonder about transparency and the ethical values of citizenship when it comes to ads from PACs and special-interest groups. From the presidential race down to a local aldermanic district, it's gotten increasingly toxic. No matter which side you're on, it's fair to say that most political advertising does not foster trust in the marketing system, nor does it embrace ethical values. As for doing no harm—the damage is already being done to our political system, the marketing industry, and ultimately our country if we blindly accept unfair attack campaigns.

Corporate Social Responsibility

With the ruling by the U.S. Supreme Court giving corporations, unions, and other organizations such as PACs equal status with individuals in terms of free speech, it is incumbent upon marketing practitioners to be even more ethically vigilant. Yet, even prior to this ruling, corporations here and abroad were moving toward showcasing their socially responsible initiatives. Thus, today many companies have formal corporate social responsibility programs. When done correctly, it is part of a company's business model and should be proactive, not a response to negative publicity. One simple way to wrap it up is to consider the "triple bottom line"—people, planet, and profits. In other words, a company can do well by doing good.

Somewhere between total irresponsibility and strict legal conformity that may never be enforced are several steps that provide a checklist for ethical advertising and promotion.

1. **Your personal moral code.** Do you know right from wrong, and, more importantly, do you care? And have you taken the time to think about how your personal ethical codes will translate into your professional ethical codes?

2. **Are you conforming with your company guidelines?** Do they expect you to follow these rules, and will they hold you accountable? And what is your responsibility if they don't hold others to the company guidelines?

3. **Are you conforming to your client's guidelines?** If you're a freelancer or an agency, you need to make the effort to find out what these guidelines are. And you need to produce work that fits the client's corporate culture.

4. **Are you conforming to industry guidelines?** Many companies are part of trade associations and other organizations that have firm rules for advertising and promotion. You need to make the effort to find out what these guidelines are and adhere to them. Industry guidelines are instituted mainly to prevent unfair competition between association members, but can also be in place to promote a positive image for the entire industry. This can also mean network or station standards. For example, ads that are not accepted for prime-time broadcast may be allowed on late-night cable.

5. **Can you risk negative reaction from the media and potential customers?** Will you win a creative battle but lose in the court of public opinion? With YouTube and social media, bad news travels a lot faster. The decisions you make at the front end can have significant impact all the way down the line.

6. **Are you aware of local, state, and federal regulations?** We'll get into that in much more detail, but remember: Not knowing the law is no excuse! It's your job to make the effort to find out what these regulations are and to adhere to them.

When creating advertising, knowing what *not* to do does not absolve you of responsibility. While you might not be able to change the world through advertising, you can certainly avoid adding to the current problems. We encourage you to find ways to include positive images of minorities and marginalized groups in mainstream advertising. We hope you will not be forced to make misleading claims. If you can encourage a strategy that promotes truth and sustainability, make your voice heard. Easier said than done when clients are looking for good, fast, and cheap rather than long-term customer goodwill. Overall, the philosophy of "enlightened self-interest" works best.

Ethics becomes even more complex when you consider the diverse and ever-changing world in which we live. Much of the work you do will influence or touch consumers with sensibilities significantly different from your own. Whether these consumers hold different religious values or live on the other side of the globe, it is incumbent upon you to remain sensitive to the impact your work has beyond its obvious or intended audiences. The consumers you may intentionally or unintentionally touch may have very different cultural perspectives than you do, and those perspectives often pose tangled ethical challenges. We'll talk more about this in Chapters 4 and 5. However, we encourage you to think about this as you reflect on some of the issues we have discussed in this chapter.

Ethical Challenges Within the Advertising Industry

The advertising industry faces a few ethical dilemmas within its own ranks. While this is not a book on ethics, we know that most of you will one day enter this industry. Candidly addressing, albeit briefly, a few of the challenges the industry faces is the right thing to do.

Advertising has long seen itself as a meritocracy—a place where the best and brightest compete to make it to the top. It is an industry that gave women opportunities when other businesses shut them out. Today those opportunities remain vibrant across all departments except creative. Across the United States, Canada, and much of Europe, women make up only about 20% of those working within creative departments. This poses a twofold ethical issue. First, with women making upwards of 80% of all consumption choices, don't agencies have an ethical obligation to have more women on their creative teams? Wouldn't women provide relevant and salient perspectives? Some argue, absolutely. Others argue that a good creative can and should be able to climb into the skin of their target audience and create resonant and effective work. Regardless of where you fall on this issue, the disparity is striking. Second, what does the lack of women in creative suggest about environmental circumstances and subsequent employment opportunities for women? The numbers alone suggest a masculine world within creative departments. How that impacts the creative work or the environment in which the work is produced is open to debate—and undoubtedly changes from agency to agency. One thing is for sure: It certainly poses challenges for young women entering creative.

A second challenge our industry faces is that of racial equity. The numbers of African Americans and Hispanics within advertising, and most certainly within creative, do not even come close to representing the marketplace. Complicating matters, the industry has traditionally segmented work for multicultural audiences to separate multicultural agencies. The lack of minority representation in advertising was so extreme that the city of New York filed suit against the industry in the 1990s. In the end, the suit did little to change the numbers. For racial minorities, employment equity, in advertising, remains elusive.

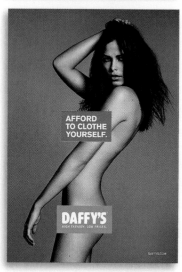

Just because you can, doesn't mean you should. Several brands have ignored good taste to shock customers into noticing them. Does the relentless drive to attract attention to a brand justify the objectification of young women?

These industry-specific issues do not even touch on the issues inherent in advertising brands that target sensitive or at-risk demographics from children to the elderly. Nor do they address the ethical implications of globalization. Frankly that's the topic of another book—a long one. However, this chapter provides a framework for discussions, and throughout the book we try to weave in discussions on ethics where we see it relevant.

We know many good people working hard to make changes that address these issues. Yet, still today, the embrace of diversity within the creative workforce remains a challenge for the industry. Whatever the specifics of these issues, for young people choosing a life in creative, we have an ethical obligation to talk about the challenges our industry faces.

Making a Difference

Beyond the work they do for their clients, advertisers have long made use of their skills to raise awareness of social and economic issues. Many agencies keep a small roster of pro bono clients. In the midst of World War II, these contributions became formalized as an industry endeavor with the foundation of the Ad Council in 1942. The genesis of this was a passionate 1941 speech given by New York advertising executive James Webb Young.

The mission of the Ad Council is to identify a select number of significant public issues and work collaboratively with members to stimulate action on those issues through communications programs. The Ad Council's goal is to make measurable differences in society. Volunteer talent from the advertising and broader communications fields work with media to facilitate messaging using the resources of the business and nonprofit communities. In the end, the Ad Council's mission is to create awareness, foster understanding, and motivate action to make positive changes in our society.

Since its inception the Ad Council has done hundreds of campaigns. The inaugural campaign was "Rosie the Riveter," which helped sell war bonds during World War II. In 1944, working with Foote, Cone & Belding, the Ad Council introduced "Smokey Bear." In 1957, and for many years following, it created fund-raising campaigns for the American Red Cross. The Ad Council helped launch the 30-year Peace Corps campaign in 1961 with the tagline "The Toughest Job You'll Ever Love." The "Crying Indian" ad from 1973 won two Clios while promoting an antilittering message. The reason 99% of you wear your seat belts is in large part due to work the Ad Council began in 1985. In 1988, the Ad Council began its first of many AIDS awareness campaigns. Publically addressing

Images of some of the Ad Council's work that has made a positive difference in society. What will your contribution be?

childhood obesity began with a campaign launched by the Ad Council in 2005. In celebration of the Ad Council's 70th birthday, in 2012 it launched a campaign encouraging consumers to "Rosify Yourself" with a Facebook app.

We hope we've got you thinking about some of the ethical issues involved in what you as a creative person actually do and what you as a practitioner may encounter. We also hope we've inspired you to work toward making a positive difference in the world. How you make a difference for you, for your client, and for society is up to you. Just remember it really does matter how you frame an issue, highlight a benefit, select an image, take on the competitor, or choose your words. Your work impacts not just your client but also the consumers you touch and the world in which you live, work, and play. In the end, it's about ethics, but it's also about legality because the law kicks in where ethics ends.

You don't have to be perfect to be a perfect parent.
There are thousands of teens in foster care who would love to put up with you.

1 888 200 4005 · adoptuskids.org

Adoption From Foster Care

The "Adoption" campaign has been one of the Ad Council's biggest success stories in the past decade, even though we faced long odds. We led social marketing campaigns on dozens of social issues, but can you imagine an ask that is more daunting than taking a child from foster care permanently into your home?

There are more than 408,000 children in the foster care system in the United States; 107,000 of them are available for adoption.[3] The majority of these children are not infants—they are older (age 8+)—and many have special needs, or are in sibling groups. Their stories can be heartbreaking.

Several ingredients for success came together when we planned and launched the initial campaign. First, we had a pro bono agency team from Kirshenbaum Bond Senecal + Partners who delivered a single-minded and unique strategy, and who then executed consistently excellent work against it. We also had clients—the Children's Bureau and AdoptUSKids—who were willing to back the strategy even though at the time some saw it as risky.

Most foster care and adoption advertising—what little there was of it—focused on the need of a child waiting to be adopted. Everyone involved in the campaign agreed that we really needed to shift the focus to the mind-set of the prospective adoptive parents. They are a wide-ranging group, and they don't fit into a neat demographic category. What they have in common is that they are highly compassionate people who want to make a positive difference in the lives of others. They've thought about adoption, and they've had many of the concerns and questions that you'd expect. But their deepest worries are about themselves. Their main concern is "Can I do this?" They are afraid of failing a child who has been let down many times before.

This insight has been the key driver of this campaign since Day 1. Prospective parents needed to be "given permission" to take the next steps toward adopting a child. They needed to know that "you don't have to be perfect to be a perfect parent." There are thousands of kids in foster care who would take them just as they are. The tone of the advertising was sweet, funny, and playful. It wasn't heavy. We launch new work every year, all staying true to the core strategy. People have really responded.

Ad Council campaigns run on donated media, and the media community has embraced the "Adoption" campaign, to the tune of more than $300 million in free media support across platforms since 2004. We've seen steep increases in inquiries to AdoptUSKids, with more than 24.6 million visits to the website, 160,000 phone inquiries, and 54,000 e-mail inquiries. Most important, since the launch of the campaign in July 2004, more than 20,000 families have registered with AdoptUSKids, and more than 14,000 children who were once photo listed on adoptuskids.org have been placed with a permanent family. It's real proof of the impact that a public service advertising campaign can have on the life of a child.[4]

Peggy Conlon, president and CEO, Ad Council, New York, adcouncil.org

Note: Source of information: HitsLink and Google Analytics. Each analytics tool calculates a "visit" using different methods. The campaign advertising is not solely responsible for the number of inquiries; there are multiple drivers to phone and web.

Legal Concepts That Really Matter

Whole books have been written on the subject of the law and advertising. However, for this text we'd like to very briefly focus on two aspects that we think really matter to copywriters: claims and copyright.

Stake Your Claim

Copywriters make all kinds of claims, and most of them are perfectly legal. Yet, it's worth briefly talking about what *legal* really means. All fact claims are viewed very seriously under the law. There can be no deception. However, advertisers have a fair amount of wiggle room found in the nonfact claims that advertisers routinely use. Most of us write claims that fall into one of two categories—puffery and lifestyle claims—and thus we escape the scrutiny of the law.

Commercial free speech, while not as "free" as noncommercial speech, is protected under the First Amendment. For example, the government can regulate advertising products that are illegal, such as prostitution or street drugs, as well as products whose manufacture is regulated, such as prescription drugs, alcohol, tobacco, and some food products. As we discussed in the previous section, corporate First Amendment rights have been vastly expanded, and that will impact the work you do.

Puffery is using superlatives or obvious falsity to tout the greatness of your brand—so consumers are bound to know it's an exaggeration. As one judge said, "The bigger the lie, the bigger the protection." The Uniform Commercial Code of 1996 states that exaggerated claims are acceptable, even if they are lies, unless someone can prove the claim was meant to be a fact. The government believes that most consumers are smart enough to see through the boasting and not take it seriously. Sometimes the puffery can be incorporated into a slogan, which blurs the intent. For example, Walmart used to use the tagline "Always the low price. Always." The Better Business Bureau (instead of the Federal Trade Commission) said this went beyond puffery to claim that the store always had the lowest prices of all retailers. Walmart lost the challenge and decided to change the slogan to "Always low prices. Always Walmart." A subtle change but not as misleading.[5]

Lifestyle claims indicate a product or service will make the user's life better with such benefits as cleaner shirts, delicious food, a car that is fun to drive, social acceptance, finding the love of your life, and even a better sex life. The claims may be direct or implied. Contrast the in-your-face product demonstrations

Stir up something good for your

Just add water and enjoy *Campbell's® Healthy Request®* condensed soups. 98% fat free, low in cholesterol, no MSG® and heart-healthy levels of sodium. 10 delicious flavors. M'm! M'm! Good!® For you.

Health claims, especially for processed foods, are watched very closely. Campbell's claims their Healthy Request soups are heart healthy and provides the data to back it up.

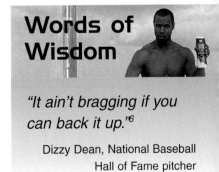

Words of Wisdom

"It ain't bragging if you can back it up."[6]

Dizzy Dean, National Baseball Hall of Fame pitcher

Thank you for suing us.

Here's the truth about our seasoned beef.

The claims made against Taco Bell and our seasoned beef are absolutely false.

Our beef is 100% USDA inspected, just like the quality beef you buy in a supermarket and prepare in your home. It is then slow-cooked and simmered in our unique recipe of seasonings, spices, water, and other ingredients to provide Taco Bell's signature taste and texture.

REAL•BEEF
QUALITY GUARANTEED

Plain ground beef tastes boring.

The only reason we add anything to our beef is to give the meat flavor and quality. Otherwise we'd end up with nothing more than the bland flavor of ground beef, and that doesn't make for great-tasting tacos.

So here are the REAL percentages.

88% Beef and 12% Secret Recipe.

In case you're curious, here's our not-so-secret recipe.

We start with USDA-inspected quality beef (88%). Then add water to keep it juicy and moist (3%). Mix in Mexican spices and flavors, including salt, chili pepper, onion powder, tomato powder, sugar, garlic powder, and cocoa powder (4%). Combine a little oats, caramelized sugar, yeast, citric acid, and other ingredients that contribute to the flavor, moisture, consistency, and quality of our seasoned beef (5%).

We stand behind the quality of our seasoned beef 100% and we are proud to serve it in all our restaurants. We take any claims to the contrary very seriously and plan to take legal action against those who have made false claims against our seasoned beef.

Greg Creed

Greg Creed
President, Taco Bell

TacoBell.com
Facebook.com/TacoBell

TACO BELL

Taco Bell was sued for selling "seasoned beef" that plaintiffs claimed was only about 35% real beef and 65% something else. Their "Thank you for suing us" ad set the record straight: They stated the product is actually 88% real beef and only 12% "secret recipe." Sounds delicious.

of OxiClean with the symbolic imagery found in Cialis commercials. Both of them make lifestyle claims that focus on the benefit rather than features. Since the benefit is more subjective, actually addressing the wants and needs of the consumer, the interpretation of the claim is usually given more latitude.

Too often some advertisers go over the line and commit fraud. The most obvious form of fraudulent advertising is to promote counterfeit goods—knockoffs of well-known high-quality brands. Promoting something that's fake is not only unethical but also highly illegal. Another less blatant kind of fraud is bait-and-switch advertising—when you promote a low price for a product that's not available with the intent to sell the customer a more expensive product. If supplies of the low-priced product are very limited, the store is obligated to tell shoppers. Even so, thousands of shoppers wait in line for Black Friday specials when they know they might not get that special deal.

Substantiation is a fancy word that says you can prove what you claim. This is especially important when you're comparing your product to the competition or when you're making an exclusive claim. Keep in mind that if the substantiation has not been obtained *before* a claim is made, the advertiser may be subject to legal action. Get the facts first, not just when you're forced to.

Figure 3.1 shows some highly exaggerated illustrations of misleading claims, substantiation, puffery, and corrective advertising.

The Old Spice guy (Isaiah Mustafa) told women that if their men could not look like him, at least they could smell like him. A series of commercials, print ads, and online videos showed increasing outrageous situations that made him even more desirable. No reasonable person believed this blatant puffery, but it sure sold a lot of Old Spice.

FIGURE 3.1   Claims Infographics

Misleading claim: If part of the ad is false, all of it is false. You should not make claims that can't be substantiated or that you know are false. Your competitors are watching.

Substantiated claim: If it's true and you can prove it, you can claim it. You don't always have to cite your source of proof, but you should be prepared to if you are challenged.

Puffery: The more outrageous the claim, the better.

Corrective advertising: Sort of admitting guilt. Regulatory agencies or the courts usually determine the magnitude of the mea culpa.

Note: Oscar Mayer advertising samples are used only for educational purposes, and none of the ads shown above were ever authorized or produced by that company. As far as we know, Oscar Mayer sells high-quality products and follows the highest ethical standards for advertising and promotion.

Rising Stars

It's Never Too Late

As a team, we took a fairly traditional route into the ad business. We met on a postgrad course, teamed up shortly afterward, and, just two years, a few placements, and a lot of hard work later, we had a job. It's another two years after that, and, thankfully, we're still working.

However, we did start late. We are both in our 30s now and feel like we're just getting started. Not that this is a bad thing. It means that we were committed to becoming creatives. We really had no other options by then. If there's one thing you need when you're starting out, it is commitment, as there is normally a long road ahead.

We also felt it important to decide what sort of team we wanted to be early on. Of course you need to show you can work across everything, but if you want to work in a digital agency, then balance your book with more integrated ideas than press and TV. The important thing is to agree on your direction and make sure your book reflects this. Once you've started in an agency, it may not be so easy to change paths.

We wish there was a secret to getting a job. You will hear the same advice over and over again—work super hard, be nice, get contacts in the industry, and so on. Unfortunately it is all true, and it applies to everyone. It's the teams that get along with people, while they put in the hours, that get hired. And it's the ones that maintain that energy and enthusiasm that stay hired. If we find a shortcut, we will let you know.[7]

Mike Insley, art director, and Harry Stanford, copywriter, Euro RSCG, London, eurorscglondon.co.uk

Copyrights and Copywriting

A copyright is the exclusive right granted to authors, artists, and composers to protect their original work from being plagiarized, sold, or used without their permission. It's very important to understand and respect copyright law. Legal protection is extended to the work without the need to register it with the U.S. Copyright Office. A work must be registered, however, before a copyright owner may bring suit for infringement.

You can't copyright an idea. The work must be produced or published. For example, you can't reproduce Picasso's paintings and sell them without permission. But you can create new works of art that mimic his style. This could explain why there are so few original ideas in marketing, movies, and television. Or as one cynic put it, "Imitation is the sincerest form of advertising." This is something to keep in mind when you're showing your portfolio around. Until you actually have your work produced, your ideas are fair game. An unethical person could steal your potential award-winning concept, and there's not much you can do about it. Fortunately, people in our business belong to a pretty tight fraternity, so sleazy idea stealers don't get away with it for very long.

A published work remains protected by a copyrighter for the lifetime of its creator plus 70 years. If the work is created anonymously or under a pseudonym or as work-for-hire, it's protected for 95 years from the first date of publication or 120 years from the date of its creation, whichever is less. So if an advertisement, a tagline, ad copy, music, a photo, a commercial, a website, a video clip, or any portion of an advertisement or other marketing communication is produced or published, no one can legally use or modify it without permission for a long, long time.

As the Internet grew, it became imperative to protect copyrighted material online. The Digital Millennium Copyright Act (DMCA) extends existing copyright laws to the Internet, while limiting the liability of the providers of online services for copyright infringement by their users. As scrapbooking sites like Pinterest gain popularity, users may risk violation of the DMCA if they post copyrighted images without permission. Bottom line: When in doubt, never display copyrighted text and images on the Internet without permission.

Work-for-hire describes the creators of a work signing their rights away for a given work to an employer. This may happen when a freelance writer or designer creates work for an agency, when a company for a specific assignment hires a photographer, or when an agency creates work for a client.

If the copyrighted work is used without permission, it's considered copyright infringement. Even something as simple as making photocopies or scanning another person's work is an infringement.

There is an exception to copyright protection, which is called fair use. In general, fair use includes the work in news reporting, teaching, scholarship, or research. The publisher of this book has determined that the images used here for education fall under fair use, and so we do not need specific permission from the agency, client, copywriter, or designer. In this book we are using these examples as teaching aids, with comments that relate to the accompanying text—although we do have to document the origin of these materials and we do our best to give credit where it is due.

Since the advent of the computer and the massive expansion of the Internet, art directors and copywriters have been borrowing images and pasting them into layouts. Actually they are using the images to illustrate concepts for their clients. The fact that they are not reproducing them for profit is what allows them the wiggle room. That's where fair use ends. After that they must either buy the image or re-create it in a manner that is substantially different so as not to be construed as copying the likeness of the image.

Use of Archive Photos

The issue of copyright infringement takes many twists and turns in our business. For example, years ago we wanted to do a series of ads for tool safety using some stills from *Three Stooges* films. Our target audience fit the demo for *Stooges* fans, and the images showing Curly's head in a vice and Larry's nose being pulled by pliers certainly made the point. Only one problem—these images, even though they were over 70 years old, were still not in the public domain. They are owned by the estate of Moe Howard, who controls their use, and at the time were prohibitively expensive. We ran into the same issue when we wanted to use a photo of Albert Einstein for another client. Advertisers quickly find out that estates, publications, or photo agencies own most of the great iconic images of famous people. The more famous the image, the more it will cost.

Words of Wisdom

"Only one thing is impossible for God: To find any sense in any copyright law on this planet."[8]

Mark Twain,
great American author

Photography-for-Hire

Typically the images taken by a professional photographer for a client or agency belong to the photographer. If the images are to be used in advertising or other commercial purposes, the client or agency pays the photographer for their use. Rates vary depending on how they are used, where they are used, and how often they are used. Sometimes a photographer or videographer will agree to a flat rate called a buyout. In this case, the agency or client can use those images just about any way they see fit.

Voice Talent

Announcers for television or radio commercials can work under union rules, which cover the session fee, pension and welfare payments, and residual use of the work. Or they can accept a buyout, which may be more or less than the costs dictated by the union. We won't discuss the pluses and minuses of hiring union or nonunion talent; however, no matter which system is in place, you usually can't use that voice track forever without permission. For example, a radio spot is scheduled to run in a small market for 13 weeks, so the talent fee is negotiated for that situation. However, if the spot starts running on a national network for a whole year, the talent fee is renegotiated, unless the talent signs off on a complete buyout. Every announcer sets his or her own payment system, but suffice it to say law protects his or her voice.

Music

The good news is you found the perfect song for your next TV commercial. The bad news is you can't get the rights. And even if you could, your budget doesn't allow it. Music licensing is the licensed use of copyrighted music. A purchaser of recorded music owns the media, not the music itself, and has limited rights to use it. Licensing could involve a flat fee or royalty payments based on time and/ or units sold.

Now, if you think that any old song over 70 years old is fair game, think again. The world's best-known song "Happy Birthday to You" was written in 1893. It's now owned by Time Warner and generates over $2 million a year in royalties. It's protected by copyright extensions until 2030.[9]

Copyrights in the Digital Age

Rapid development in digital technologies has prompted reinterpretation of copyright protection. Copyrights are harder to protect, and there are more challenges to the entire philosophy of intellectual property. The legal system is constantly scrambling to catch up with technology.

Using Celebrities

Public figures are protected from commercial use of their name or likeness without their permission. They can't be used in ads or other materials unless they sign off. That includes dead celebrities. The cost will depend on how and where they are used. You might wonder how paparazzi shots of celebrities can be plastered all over the tabloids. In this case, public figures have less protection than the general public because they are considered newsworthy. So you can see Kim Kardashian on every magazine cover in the checkout line, but you won't see her in an ad without her permission.

Even dead celebrities have their rights. Making the bold assumption that deceased punk rocker Sid Vicious is in a better place, Dr. Martens used this visual puzzle to pay off their "Forever" tagline.

Libel

Competitors and sometimes government watchdogs watch product claims closely. But what happens when a false or misleading statement is made about a person? The legal term is *libel* and has some very specific tests that must be passed before a lawyer will even touch a case.

You must prove:

1. A false statement was communicated to the media. The definition of what is "false" becomes tricky in a "he said/she said" scenario.

2. The libeled person must be identified or identifiable. The person's name and/or image must be involved or some reference made where there is no reasonable doubt that the person is being portrayed in an unflattering way.

3. Actual injury or financial loss must result. This injury or loss could be a hit to a person's reputation or mental suffering, which can be very difficult to prove.

4. The person accused of libel is proven to be willfully negligent or to have malicious intent. In other words, there's a motive to smear someone.

After reading the above you're probably saying, "I see this happening every day in the news, entertainment, and politics. How can people get away with saying all these nasty things about each other?" Public figures, entertainers, politicians, and government officials are treated differently. So a movie reviewer can lie about a leading lady's personal life, pan the actors and director, drive people away from the box office, and be negligent or malicious with no consequence. In fact, it's expected. Politics keeps getting uglier because negative advertising works, no matter how many lies and half-truths are told. When critics demand accountability and substantiation in political advertising, the First Amendment is waved in their faces. It's freedom of speech—which does

Words of Wisdom

"Every product has its own truth, its own believability zone. Stray and your readers will know. Oh yes, they'll know."[10]

Jim Durfee, copywriter and founding partner, Ally & Gargano

not apply to phony product claims, but certainly has helped elect a lot of phonies who make the rules.

Trademarks

Most slogans and taglines are considered protected. So are brand names. A trademark, designated by ™ or ®, means the brand or slogan is registered with the federal government. When you are applying for a trademark, you will have a better chance of success if your brand has a unique spelling. For example EZ Duzzit would be easier to register than Easy Does It. Even if you pick a brand name that is already in use, you may be able to register it when it is used in a different market. For example, both Microsoft and Volunteers in Service to America used the Vista brand.

If you really want to protect a brand, you'll need to keep a few things in mind. David Weinstein, an intellectual property lawyer, states the easiest brand or product name to protect is a "word, picture, or symbol that conveys little or no information about the nature . . . of the products."[11] Case in point: Apple. Apple Corps was The Beatles' business holding company and, as a name, had nothing directly to do with the band. For years Apple Corps disputed the use of the Apple Computer name, which by itself had nothing to do directly with computer products. Apple Computer paid Apple Corps $80,000 in 1991 to use the name, and promised to never get into the music business. Of course, with the Mac able to play music and with the introduction of iTunes and the iPod, the surviving ex-Beatles claimed the computer company reneged on their promise and sued again . . . and again. In 2007 Apple Computer agreed to pay Apple Corps $500 million for the name.[12] How about them Apples?

Another consideration when coining a brand name and protecting it is to include a descriptor. While Kleenex has become a generic name with consumers, it is still protected because the word *tissue* always follows it. Aspirin was a brand but over time became a generic product. The world *cola* became generic when Coca-Cola originally placed the ® between the words, thus protecting *Coca* but setting *Cola* free. When you look closely, you'll see everything related to Coca-Cola from the bottle shape to the contour design to the word *Coke* is trademarked and rigorously protected.

Using someone else's slogan or tagline will get you into legal trouble, and it won't do much for your career either. You need to do your homework in order to be sure that the brilliant tagline you just thought up is not already being used by another brand somewhere, somehow. When in doubt, run it by a colleague or do a word search and check online government resources such as TESS (Trademark Electronic Search System). If you're still in doubt, contact legal counsel. In short, don't make assumptions, and do your homework.

Who's Who?

Alex Bogusky—After joining Crispin and Porter Advertising in 1989 as an art director, Alex Bogusky became creative director five years later and a partner in 1997. In 2008, he became cochairman of Crispin Porter + Bogusky (CP+B), the same year he was inducted into the Art Directors Club Hall of Fame. While at CP+B, he created the "Truth" campaign and helped Al Gore debunk the notion of "Clean Coal." In 2010, he left CP+B to create the FearLess Revolution, a consortium of entrepreneurial creatives dedicated to educating and empowering consumers.

Nancy Hill—The first-ever CEO of the American Association of Advertising Agencies (AAAA), Nancy Hill began her career in 1983 at the Doner agency in Baltimore and advanced with increased responsibilities. Prior to accepting the AAAA position, she served as CEO of Lowe Worldwide in New York. Her personal and professional interests have long focused on the high-tech sector, serving such clients as AOL, Cisco Systems, Sony, Motorola, and Verizon, among others. As CEO of the AAAA she is firmly committed to the "business case for diversity . . . whether we are talking about race/ethnicity, points of view/life experience, and skill sets."[13]

Jean Kilbourne—Recognized globally for her critical work exploring images of women in advertising, Jean Kilbourne was named by *The New York Times Magazine* as one of the three most popular speakers on college campuses. She is an award-winning author and filmmaker. Her films include *Killing Us Softly*, *Spin the Bottle*, and *Slim Hopes*. Her books include *Can't Buy My Love: How Advertising Changes the Way We Think and Feel* and *So Sexy So Soon: The New Sexualized Childhood*.

Ivan Preston—Ivan Preston was professor emeritus at the University of Wisconsin–Madison and expert on consumer ethics and fraud. In 1975, he published *The Great American Blow-Up: Puffery in Advertising and Selling,* which catapulted him into prominence. Preston frequently served as an expert witness in advertising litigation cases for both government agencies and advertisers. Although he had a brief tenure with the Federal Trade Commission's Division of Advertising Practices, he never shied away from condemning the relaxation of regulations and the commission's lack of consumer behavior expertise. Preston died in 2011.

Exercises

1. Supporting Your Claim

Analyze the following product claims, decide which would be legal, and explain your opinion. If you feel the claim is not supportable, how would you change it?

- Nobody makes a beer colder than Coors Light.
- With adult education classes at Bridgestone University, one night a week can change your life.
- The new Hyundai Genesis offers the luxury and performance of a BMW 5 Series for about half the sticker price.
- You can't survive in this climate without a Trane air-conditioning system.
- Mr. Coffee is the most dependable, reliable, and energy efficient coffeemaker ever made.

2. Whose Ethics?

(Contributed by Kimberly Selber, PhD, associate professor, University of Texas–Pan American)
Find six print ads you feel are "ethically questionable."

- Write up a one-page critique of each ad. Explain why you feel it is ethically questionable—focusing on the ad and not the product itself (i.e., not drinking is bad and shouldn't be advertised, but ads promoting alcohol should not target minors). Focus your comments on the target, placement, the content, and so on.
- Next write a short survey. Poll 10 people from various backgrounds on the ads they found ethically questionable. Add in several neutral ads when polling your audience.
- Finally, write up the results, along with a comments section considering the following questions: Do your friends think like you do? What did you find that was surprising? End with a short reflection section. Ask yourself, what kind of socially responsible person do I want to be? What is the advertising industry's responsibility? What would I do if I was asked to work on something I felt was ethically wrong or simply bad for society at large?

3. (Dis)abled

This exercise is designed to help you think about your perceptions of people not like yourself, in this case people with disabilities.

- Your instructor will provide you with a brief and a storyboard based on that brief.
- Once you've had a chance to look it over, think about how you could insert a person with an obvious disability into the commercial. Challenge yourself to do it in a way that naturally integrates the person into the story line. The challenge will be for the new addition to feel seamless, as if that person was part of the original spot.
- Share revised storyboards.

In Britain, legal stipulations now require advertisers to include people with disabilities in a small percentage of all advertising. Discuss how this changes people's perception of people with disabilities and how it can have a positive impact on brands.

Visit www.sagepub.com/altstiel3e to access these additional learning tools

- Video Links
- Web Resources
- eFlashcards
- Web Quizzes

Issues

The Times They Are A-Changin'

A little over 50 years ago, Bob Dylan wrote the lyrics to this song. He could have written it today. Look around. Does everyone look like you? Until the 1960s, advertisers must have thought everyone in the United States was a straight, uptight, well-dressed, married, White suburbanite, which sometimes still seems to define the general market. For years, that's what advertisers showed in their ads. However, the past 50 years have seen social, cultural, and economic forces that have dramatically changed the way we portray the "average" consumer. Along the way, marketers finally discovered that African Americans own homes. Women buy cars. Gays and lesbians like vacations. Arab Americans are not terrorists. Seniors can have an active lifestyle. People whose primary language is not English still spend money. And, today, a lot of people prefer to live alone. Our social landscape has fundamentally shifted since Dylan penned his lyrical prophecy. Creating advertising that reflects our ever-changing society is not only the right thing; it is the smart thing.

Just around the time Dylan was writing his first songs, demographers were also examining people's perceptions on marriage and family. Back then 80% of Americans thought it was sick, even immoral, to prefer being single. Today only 51% of adults are married, and 28% of households consist of one person. In major metro markets like Atlanta, Minneapolis, San Francisco, Washington, Seattle, and Manhattan, the numbers are over 40%.[1] Travel outside the United States, and the numbers climb even higher. We'll talk more about that in the next chapter. These new singletons are also fueling the economy. Their average spending in 2010 was $34,471 compared with $28,017 for married individuals. For individuals with children, that number drops even lower.[2] The majority of singletons are between 35 and 64.[2] These solo dwellers have come together, via well-tended social networks, to create "urban tribes" that in many ways have become a substitute for the traditional family.[3] So showing the "typical" nuclear family of mom, dad, and 2.3 kids in your ads may not resonate with your target audience these days.

This ad appeared about the same time Dylan's song was popular. Yes, "the times they are a-changin'."

Until the late 1960s, the best African Americans could expect from mainstream advertising was to be portrayed as happy servants.

As the singleton demographic has grown, so too have many ethnic groups. Today, one in every three Americans is a person of color, and that's a trend that will only increase. In the last U.S. census, more than half of the people who identified themselves as "black in combination with at least one other race" were under 18 years old."[4] This points to shifting ethnic identities. Age-related demographics are also changing as Americans are aging in huge numbers. The generation that grew up with Bob Dylan is now entering retirement, but their version of it is a lot different from their parents'. Ways of viewing gender and sexual orientation are also changing. Equality was once only a dream for gays and lesbians. Now, it's a topic of mainstream discussions, with gays and lesbians no longer willing to be second-class citizens. Women make up nearly 51% of the total population, and continue to demonstrate formidable spending power. Single moms are on the rise, and women 40 to 64 years old represent the single largest U.S. market segment. Women have money to spend.[5] Even when they are not the end user, they influence over 80% of the consumption decisions. Together these niche markets (African Americans, Hispanics, Asians, and women) make up 84% of the total population.[6] No, your eyes did not deceive you—it did say 84%! Trust us; this chapter is worth reading.

Love and romance are changing the demographic landscape in other ways too. In 2010, more than 15% of new marriages were interracial, and the majority of Americans don't have a problem with that.[7] These changing attitudes are reflected in the choices of spokespersons and models, which indicate a fluidity of cultural definition, as well as a desire for cross-cultural immersion. Some of the hottest models today have an indefinable ethnic look. We suggest that despite his fall from grace, Tiger Woods's resistance to a narrow definition of ethnic identity opened the doors to an embrace of multiracial or bicultural identification. Another change is the acceptance of openly gay or lesbian spokespeople, who often have huge appeal within the general market. Ellen DeGeneres, a married lesbian, is the spokesperson for the mainstream J. C. Penney brand. The lines they are a blurrin'.

Today, it's not a question of whether to appeal to multicultural, often known as specialty, audiences. It's more a question of how to do it. How do we show people of color and other specialty markets in our ads without using stereotypes? If we avoid the obvious, do we deny their identities? Can we keep it real without alienating other audiences? Creating ads for today's marketplace presents a multiplicity of unique challenges. Advertisers need to be responsive to the social and cultural shifts that suggest many people see themselves as having multiple and fluid identities. Maybe as these trends take root, the work of multicultural and general market agencies will also begin to blend. Maybe not. Regardless of the structure of agencies, to work in the industry you'll need to be on the cutting edge of trends, with sensitivity toward the shifting lines of social and cultural identity.

It's All There in Black and White

When advertising began to focus on the African American market in the early 1970s, the trend was to make African Americans look like "dark-skinned white people."[8] While some African Americans were happy to finally be represented in mainstream advertising, others resented the lack of realistic models and situations as well as the limited media placements.

Before minority-owned agencies existed, the industry lacked messages that reflected cultural experiences beyond a White world. People like Thomas Burrell, founder of Burrell Communications, now part of Publicis, and Caroline Jones, founder of Mingo, Jones, Guilmenot, now Chisholm-Mingo, were advertising pioneers. As the lines defining race and ethnicity blur, the work of reaching bicultural people becomes more challenging. Al Anderson, another early leader in multicultural advertising, suggests that the *multi* in multicultural marketing has gotten a bit blurred: "Last time I checked, all marketing is targeted at somebody. Now how you construct this young, black, Latino, Asian person, I don't know. I've never met one of these folks."[10] That blurring is not likely to go away anytime soon, with marketers stretching for cultural crossover, at the same time that more and more people define themselves as bicultural.

However, when you do need to reach a multicultural target, you'll need to leverage cultural knowledge with cultural sensitivity and respect. For Burrell and Jones, success came by tapping into the unique cultural experiences of African Americans with specified sensitivity. They also knew the importance of media placement, and leveraged channels that resonated with their audience. But the focus on ethnicity-specific advertising agencies also highlights the fact that general market agencies seem to be unable or unwilling to give voice to multicultural consumers. As agencies attempt to grapple with the dilemma of separate agencies, there is a tendency for the big multinationals to buy smaller multicultural agencies to have under their corporate umbrella.

Can You Hear Me Now?

Brands like Verizon and American Airlines have long demonstrated a commitment to the African American community. And African Americans have heard their call. Within mainstream media, African Americans have the highest representation of any ethic group. How African Americans use media is truly interesting. They have higher recall scores than any other group for magazine readership. Further, their preference for magazines is striking and driven by the medium's ability to provide

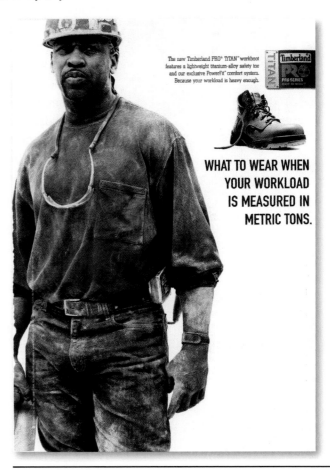

The new Timberland PRO® TITAN™ workboot features a lightweight titanium-alloy safety toe and our exclusive PowerFit™ comfort system. Because your workload is heavy enough.

WHAT TO WEAR WHEN YOUR WORKLOAD IS MEASURED IN METRIC TONS.

To some people this ad might represent a stereotype of African Americans as blue-collar laborers. To others, it's just another hardworking guy who needs a good pair of work boots. What do you think?

Coke celebrated diversity as well as their 125th anniversary. Coca-Cola's early commitment to advertising to African Americans has paid off with strong brand loyalty.

information, offer a good value, and share stories of interest.[11] That may be because stories have a long cultural history within the African American community. Many brands put significant efforts into courting African Americans. Coca-Cola has a dedicated African American marketing group, which puts a huge emphasis on moms and teens. The Coca-Cola marketing group views teens at the trendsetters and moms as the gatekeepers. Cosmetic and weight reduction brands, along with auto, fast-food, and travel brands, all put a huge emphasis on this market segment.

African American celebrities are an important part of the advertising mix. A decade ago, African American endorsements went mainly to athletes. Today we see African Americans endorsing a wide range of products. Queen Latifah remains a staple in CoverGirl collections with the "Queen Collection." Beyoncé racked up early deals with Pepsi and Walmart and later with L'Oréal for the "True Match" collection. Today she pitches House of Dereon perfume. Dasani enlisted R&B star Chilli to deliver its story-based message of health and hydration to African American moms on Mother's Day. African American celebrities made the A-list for weight-loss promotion, playing into consumers' desire to emulate stars and embrace a multicultural world. Jennifer Hudson and Charles Barkley sing the praises of Weight Watchers, while Janet Jackson promotes Nutrisystem. Multiracial Mariah Carey adds her star power to Jenny Craig.

Tapping Into the African American Market

It's sometimes hard to talk about a target market without sounding stereotypical. However, there are some cultural commonalities, and for an advertiser they are worth paying attention to. Community involvement is a huge part of African American life, and women play a very prominent role in family life. Don't underestimate African American women's influence or their buying power. They have the highest spending power among women of color. Storytelling and by extension music play huge roles in the everyday lives of African Americans. Personal expression is also crucial within African American culture. Knowing these cultural nuances is essential when trying to reach this target with resonance messages. At the same time, African Americans' preferences, habits, and attitudes reflect a broad range of sensibilities. When it comes to writing, in most cases, it's best to avoid using slang. If you aren't really part of the culture, trying to use slang can be embarrassing at best and often insulting. We also know that media matters. Finding African Americans where they live, work, and play is essential. So it's no surprise to see music as the thread that crosses ethic boundaries, moving easily across multiple media.

Jennifer Hudson and Charles Barkley, each of them playing to their strengths, sing the praises of Weight Watchers, "because it works."

Music Is the Rhythm of Life

Music is a defining part of African American cultural life, with its roots being an essential ingredient in communal storytelling. But don't assume that it's all about hip-hop. The use of pop music in advertising got a big boost with Michael Jackson's 1984 "Billy Jean" Pepsi commercial. Spike Lee and Nike's early collaborations soon followed. That collaboration continues today, including a video narrated by Lee about his son, soccer, and Black culture. Ultimately the industry came to embrace hip-hop as the crossover sound. Beyond contemporary urban music, you'll find jazz all over advertising. While hip-hop may have made the biggest impact, relying on it as "the" African American music is a dangerous move.

Music is a staple in African American culture. The key is to marry the right brand with the right sound.

Spike Lee has long been able to create messages that celebrate African American culture while crossing over seamlessly to the mainstream market. Brands like Nike figured that out quickly and have never looked back.

¿Cómo Se Dice *Diversity* en Español?

Today over 50 million Hispanics live in the United States. They live in communities all across the nation, but the three biggest media markets are Los Angeles, New York, and Miami.[12] The Hispanic population is expected to keep growing—fast. In fact, in the next 40 years the Hispanic population is projected to double, and since 2007 Latinos have outnumbered African Americans. Plus, they're young. The median age of Latinos is 27, and 23% of Latinos are under

The California Milk Processors asked Latinos to "Toma Leche" (drink milk) using television commercials to drive them to this whimsical yet informative site.

The language of love transcends cultures, and so do these ads for Docol showerheads. The benefit is visually merged with the product with words of a classic love song strategically pouring from the showerhead. ¡Bésame mucho!

18.[13] According to Leo Olper, chief operating officer at Tonality in New York, if we think about American Hispanics as a world economy, they would be number 13.[14]

Hispanic life centers strongly on family. However, if you think Hispanics are all the same, think again. Even among themselves, Hispanics have differing preferences for what to be called. According to Ileana Aléman-Rickenbach, chief creative officer at BVK/MEKA in Miami, 65% prefer to call themselves Hispanic.[15] However, age can be a big influence in preference. *Hispanic* is generally preferred by older, established residents while younger people prefer *Latino* or *Latina*, which they feel is more personal. In this text we'll use *Hispanic* and *Latino* or *Latina* interchangeably, just to keep everyone happy or annoyed. This debate is only the tip of the cultural iceberg.

Let's begin by taking a deeper look at language. Nearly 90% of Hispanics learned Spanish before they learned English.[16] Today 76% of Latinos still speak Spanish at home.[17] American Hispanics have multiple countries of origin including Mexico, Cuba, and Puerto Rico, and come from every country in Central and South America, with 63% of the Latinos being of Mexican decent.[18] What's really interesting, and what marketers need to pay attention to, is the trend

Hispanic Hyperreality

Ileana Alémán-Rickenbach at BVK/
MEKA, a Hispanic advertising agency
in Miami, explains that there is no
single Hispanic culture but rather a
"hyperreality" that blurs the difference
between the symbolic and the real:

"*Hispanic* is really just a marketing term coined by the advertising industry in the U.S. This hyperreal market lumps together people of Latin American and Spanish heritage under one 'ethnic' classification, when in fact the 19 Latin groups under the Hispanic umbrella can be drastically different from one another.

"One of our clients, a top telecom, was launching a new international calling plan for mobile phones. Another opportunity to practice those hyperreal Hispanic Spanish skills, right?

"I started by asking Sandra, a Mexican coworker, 'How do you answer the phone?' We say, '*¿Bueno?* (by the way, *bueno* literally means 'good'). Nereyda said Cubans answer '*Oigo*' ('I hear'). The Venezuelans told me they say, '*Aló*' (which has no meaning). Puerto Ricans say, 'Hello' (pronounced '*jel-ó*'). The Argentine said she had the only legitimate, polite, correct, and perfect phone greeting: '*Hola.*' From there on everyone had a say; visiting clients opined . . . '*Buenas,*' '*Dígame,*' '*Sí.*' It was Babel.

"A little later, the client called to 'remind' us that we should use the proper Mexican 'dialect' for the West Coast and 'generic' Spanish for the rest. That's exactly what we did. We created a pun for the West Coast version where one character answered the phone by saying '*¿Bueno?* ('Good') and the caller replied, '*Bueno no, buenísimo*' ('Not only good, but very good'). We sent a creative rationale explaining that literally *bueno* means good, but that in context it really means hello. That it was a play on words to introduce the retail message (great prices), etc., etc. . . . of course. She never got it. The cultural divide was insurmountable. On the other hand, we never found a Pan-Latin way of saying hello. The hyperreal had turned surreal.

"We ended up creating a funny, clever, and very effective campaign where people call their countries of origin, but no one answers the phone by saying hello. We just started the spots midway through the calls. In the world of Hispanic Hyperreality, definitely less is more."[20]

*Ileana Alémán-Rickenbach, Chief Creative Officer, BVK-MEKA, Miami,
www.bvkmeka.com*

toward people preferring to identify themselves by their country of origin. They are more likely to be a proud *Chicano* or *Argentino* or *Cubana*.[19] Toyota's award-winning "Somos Muchos" campaign leveraged Hispanics' passion for their country of origin to reinforce Toyota brand loyalty and won back Latinos in huge numbers.

Now, let's consider how language works, or doesn't, across cultures. An exterminator in Mexico will remove your *bichos* (bugs), but the same word in Puerto Rico refers to a man's private parts. You have to do more than just find the right slang. You have to understand the culture. Here are some examples:[21]

- A Coca-Cola ad may use the slogan "y su comida favorita" ("and your favorite food"), but for Miami Cubans the ad shows pork loin, for South Texas Mexicans it's tacos, and for New York Puerto Ricans they use chicken and rice.

This witty ad reads, "Your clothes were not there." Memorable images drive home the benefit of Gain with Febreze.

- When McDonald's first developed a series of "Hispanic ads," they considered all Hispanics the same until they received complaints from Puerto Rico that the ads were "too Mexican."

- A telephone company tried to market its products to Latinos by showing a commercial in which a Latina wife tells her husband to call a friend and tell her they would be late for dinner. The commercial bombed since Latina women generally do not give orders to their husbands, and their cultural concept of time would not require a call about being late.

So what does all this mean for advertisers? For one, we know that bilingual Latinos are more influenced by advertising in Spanish than by advertising in English.[22] Needless to say, when it comes to Latinos' private lives, Spanish-language media are *caliente*. However, when they head to work, that changes dramatically. In the workplace, two thirds of Latinos speak English.[23] Many Hispanics prefer to consider themselves "bicultural," as they see themselves embracing both cultures. The key take-away: Most Latinos are not interested in picking their country-of-origin culture over American culture or vice versa. They want both.

Spanglish: The Blending of Cultures

Of all the Hispanic market segments, Millennials have their feet firmly planted in both cultures. Most were born in the United States and have been immersed in American pop culture through the media and in school, as well as their Latino heritage at home and with friends. This seamless melding of cultures and languages makes Millennials the most "American" of all Hispanic segments.[24] Their identity is generational as much as ethnic. In fact, Greg Knipp of Dieste, a consulting firm for multicultural, urban, and youth marketing, states, "What we're seeing is that a 24-year old Hispanic may have more in common with a 24-year old African-American or Asian-American than with his 45-year old uncle."[25] Living online is one of the primary reasons this age group has more in common with their peers of all colors than older people from their own community. This is evident in a study that showed U.S. Hispanics overwhelmingly preferred English or a mix of English and Spanish online versus Spanish only.[26] So while we should never ignore Hispanic sensibilities in marketing materials, we also need to

No matter the culture, taking on sensitive issues can be a challenge. This ad reaches out to Hispanic men who may want to get HIV testing but are afraid of deportation. It reads, "In American clinics the test for HIV is confidential." The use of the typography certainly enhances the message.

look at how generational differences change that perspective.

Dígame Más (Tell Me More)

Let's get back to the business of advertising for a moment. Advertising to Hispanics tends to be done through multicultural ad agencies, just as with advertising to African Americans. Agency folks may argue that to reach Latinos, Hispanic agencies have a better handle on the intricacies of speaking to this complicated target. When it comes to creativity, Special K and its agency Lápiz are big winners. Why? Because Special K found a way to reach across the cultural divide and share a consistent brand message with Hispanic women in a culturally resonant way. Conill, named *Advertising Age*'s Multicultural Agency of the Year in 2010, also understands cultural resonance, producing needle-moving work for Toyota, T-Mobile, and Sony.

Dominion Energy demonstrated their respect for Hispanic consumers with a headline that read, "For Danny Segura, Spanish is not a second language. It's a cultural heritage."

Latinos are huge consumers of television and radio, and most of it is in Spanish. Hispanics are also big mobile media users, and nearly 50% are on smartphones,[27] in part because many have limited access to home computers. Their embrace of mobile also makes them strong social media consumers. We also know that Latinos, even among English-dominant speakers, prefer Hispanic-themed advertising even though many consider English their primary language.[28] Brands that take the time to understand them, such as Verizon, Toyota, McDonald's, General Motors, Walmart, Coca-Cola, and State Farm, are well rewarded.

Tapping Into the Latino Market

As with other groups, you need to check stereotypes against cultural understanding. Yet it's fair to say some things are common across Hispanic cultures and tend to transcend country of origin. Family-focused activities are a central element of Latino life, and it's not uncommon for multiple generations to share the same household. For Latinos, familial concerns often trump individual needs. Family-centered obligations often supersede outside commitments. Compared to other cultures, everyday life can be a bit slower paced within the Latino community. Music is also a big part of Latino life, and is a venue that often blends mainstream American culture with a multitude of Latino sensibilities. Just

This playfully mysterious spot for Mazola pokes fun at the occasional tensions within multigenerational Hispanic families. Though the plot implies death may be imminent, the hero does not kill her mother-in-law. She only changes her recipe.

It's not surprising to see that Procter & Gamble, the biggest consumer packaged goods manufacturer in the world, has devoted a website to boomers. Life Goes Strong taps into boomers with an information-rich site focusing on health, family, technology, and play.

consider the fact that *American Idol* continues to be the top English-language TV program among Hispanics.[30] Finally, don't forget that the majority of Hispanic television originates in Mexico, including the beloved telenovelas (soap operas). This may speak volumes about Latinos' passion for family life and love of romantic adventure.

You're Never Too Old to Buy Something

If it's true that mature Americans tend to think of themselves as 10 years younger than they really are, does it make sense to turn off a huge potential market by showing a bunch of wacky geezers in your ads? So how do you address this growing market? You begin by understanding that there are two distinct groups within this market. One is the *matures*. They are 65-plus and generally have a strong work ethic, and are self-sacrificing, tolerant of authority, comfortable with conformity, loyal, and patriotic. They'll happily spend what they've earned and appreciate a good value. Then there are the *boomers*. This group is 50–64 and generally focused on self-improvement, a bit hedonistic, nonconformist, educated, and way more tech-savvy than you might imagine. They believe work should be fulfilling, feel a sense of entitlement, tend to tolerate differences, and seek adventure and new experiences. Despite their differences, people nearing or in retirement have a lot in common.

Boomer and mature consumers are a more dynamic group than you might think. They've also got a lot of money to spend and skew female. According to Stephanie Holland, executive creative director at Holland+Holland, senior women age 50 and older control a net worth of $19 trillion and own more than three fourths of the nation's financial wealth.[31] Most boomers and matures own their own homes, and most are mortgage-free.[32] While boomers represent about 25% of the population, they spend 39% of all dollars spent on consumer packaged goods.

Connecting With Boomers and Matures

When it comes to media, boomers and matures are big users, especially boomers. The old marketing adage that 18- to 49-year-olds are the bread-and-butter target of television advertising could not be more outdated. Today the median age of prime-time television viewers is 51.[33] To remain relevant, advertisers are going to have to rethink television messaging. This is a demographic group that reads a lot. So magazines and direct marketing will remain a big part of the media equation.

Despite their reliance on traditional media, this group is quietly becoming a major technological demographic. While you are digital natives, boomers are digital immigrants. But they are learning to assimilate quickly. Consider this: Boomers now spend more money on technology than any other demographic. That includes fees, gadgets, and online purchases.[31] Today 70% of boomers are online every day as matures are gaining confidence in the online world.[35] As boomers age into matures, they will take technology with them. Social media is also a big part of boomers' lives. Their use of social media grew by 88% in 2010. Don't expect that to slow down anytime soon. If you think you are the only ones texting, think again. In all, 66% of boomers sent texts, putting them far ahead of matures with only 28%.[36] The bottom line with technology and boomers is this: Technology to them is a way to get something done. For you, technology is a way of life: a way to connect. That difference is the key take away. So when you need to reach the senior consumer, the prudent approach is to include online ads, social media, mobile, e-mail—the whole digital toolbox—in an integrated marketing communications campaign.

When it comes to crafting messages, never make assumptions. Get to know the mature market, just as you would any other audience. This group tends to respond very positively to relationships—so build them. Consider using life-stage marketing because the mature market responds strongly to the life-changing events, especially those that are personal. Make these events the defining moments of your campaign. Consider testimonials and use research and

Found.MyReclaimed.com, an online antiques retailer, is a brand that understands the emotional connections matures and boomers have with the past. The brand also knows that this target has money to spend and is not afraid to play in the digital world.

endorsements to back up your claims. Give them facts. Be clear and straightforward. Let them know the benefits; consider demonstrating your credibility. Education will engender loyalty. From a tonal perspective, celebrate the joys of retirement, and by all means avoid scare tactics. Above all, don't pressure them. They will take their time to make their decision. Once they've decided your brand is the one, they will be very loyal. The bottom line: Don't call them names. If there's one word they hate, it's *senior*. *Old* and *elderly* won't get you very far either. The single word that seems to have the most positive benefits is *grandparent*.

Tapping Into the Boomer and Mature Market

Now that you have an overview of your grandparents, and perhaps parents, here are a few specific things to consider related to various media. But first, here are a few tips about design that apply across most media. Make your ads visually accessible. Keep them simple, avoid clutter, and use plenty of white space. Don't forget to make type legible and a bit larger.

- *Print:* Give them information because they tend to read more. Use bold headlines and clear subheads, and break your copy into columns to deliver that information. Avoid glossy stock because it glares.

- *Radio:* Keep background music to a minimum, and remember they are heavy early-morning listeners.

- *Television:* Nobody watches the news like they do. However, don't forget boomers are happy to DVR programs, so product placement and sponsorships might be good alternatives. Watch the background music, and keep titles on the screen just a bit longer.

- *Digital:* Don't waste their time. Make your message meaningful and information rich, and they will come, stay, and return. Give them a reason to trust you.

- *Mobile:* Make your message meaningful. They're on the move with over 80% of boomers and 67% of matures packing their mobile wherever they go.

- *Direct:* They don't mind getting mail; in fact matures look forward to it. Many, especially boomers, are happy to engage with you online, as long as you make it worth their while.

- *Promotion:* If something can save them money and the offer doesn't expire too soon, they'll participate.

Don't buy into the old marketing adage that 18- to 49-year-olds are the Holy Grail, and it's best to cut off serious engagement after age 50.[37] Levi's was the brand that saw boomers through the 1960s, and they rewarded the brand by taking Dockers to work. Nobody loves a Harley-Davidson more than a boomer guy, and his biker gal either is riding on back or has her own bike. Pepsi sang to this demographic with voices that resonated from Michael Jackson to Madonna, from Ray Charles to Tina Turner. This is the Pepsi generation. But it's not just these traditional brands that have secured a spot in the hearts and wallets of boomers. Remember they bought 41% of all Apple computers[38] (they actually remember the "1984" ad), and they're logging onto Facebook with their new computers. The fastest-growing Facebook user group is women 55 and over, and growing at a 175% clip. Men 55 and over aren't far behind with 138% growth.[39]

Don't Ask. Don't Tell. Just Sell.

Depending on the survey, anywhere from 6% to 10% of the American population identifies as gay, lesbian, or bisexual. Smart marketers know they can't ignore 20 million to 32 million people. Aside from the sheer numbers, the gay and lesbian segment offers marketers other advantages. They tend to have more money than other Americans, and they spend it. They look fondly on products and services advertised in gay, lesbian, bisexual, and transgender (GLBT) media. Generally, GLBT households tend to be brand-loyal and seek out product upgrades at higher rates than their nongay counterparts.[40]

Hook this target with a bit of humor, then pass along the information they covet. They will reward you.

Just Do It

Back in the mid-1990s Nike Women ran an ad, "Canoeists," featuring two lesbians. Ironically, no one at Nike knew they were lesbians. That fact was not lost on the creative team, who consciously chose the two women because they felt they epitomized the empowerment theme and spoke to an often-ignored audience.[41] Some brands such as Absolut, American Express, Eclipse, J. C. Penney, Pepsi, Subaru, Aetna, and IKEA benefit greatly from their gay-friendly positioning. It's all about knowing your target, mainstream and GLBT, and their tolerance threshold. If you understand this target and show them respect, they will return the favor with brand loyalty.

Years ago, American Express began courting the gay and lesbian target when it highlighted Ellen DeGeneres as a cardholder in its "My Life. My Card" campaign. It worked well because the campaign's One Thing originally focused on celebrities, so DeGeneres fit perfectly and slipped under the radar—but not to this community. Members of this group notice brands that speak to them, and they reward them. Just remember that backlash is always a possibility.

J. C. Penney debuted their first four commercials with Ellen DeGeneres during the 2012 Academy Awards, turning a controversy into an opportunity. The new tagline, "That's fair and square," reflects the brand's focus on low prices and, not so subtly, their choice of spokesperson.

Tapping Into the Gay and Lesbian Market

If your assignment is to reinforce brand preference among gays and lesbians, you have several options, but one of them is not stereotyping. While gays and lesbians may identify themselves by sexual preference, they also tend to strongly identify as mainstream consumers. You might run your general market campaigns in mainstream media that also have a high gay/lesbian concentration. You don't change the creative, but the media selection indicates that you're interested in their business. Running in straight and gay media demonstrates your commitment to their community. They will notice and thank you at the checkout. Then, using visuals, copy, or both, incorporate gay themes and run those in gay publications. Reviewing gay and lesbian media, you'll notice that they tend to have the ability to laugh at themselves and the world; just be careful not to fall victim to stereotypical images.

The strength of this ad is that it simply shows a couple enjoying life. The same ad was produced for the mainstream market. It was shot in exactly the same way, identical except for the couple. "Period. Finished. End of story"—to quote the art director. That's the power of the campaign.

Absolut demonstrated its support of the GLBT community by running this ad, boldly speaking of their support for GLADD—the Gay & Lesbian Alliance Against Defamation.

Another approach is to integrate gay-themed ads across the entire campaign. IKEA, for example, has used gay themes in television commercials that also reach the straight market. This demonstrates that you believe your brand is for all consumers, and you're willing to risk a possible backlash. You might also consider keeping your mass-media advertising mainstream, or gender neutral, and focus on promotional and public relations programs that target gays and lesbians, such as sponsorship of an AIDS benefit or movie trailers at movies that appeal to this demographic. Just remember that it's all about context, and respect rules the day.

Children: Walking a Fine Line

Targeting children is fraught with ethical dilemmas. Should marketers even be talking to children? Maybe, maybe not. However, if we could stop advertising to children, Alex Bogusky, former chief creative officer at Crispin Porter + Bogusky, now founder and principal of FearLess Revolution, suggests, "A lot of things would happen, and almost all seem to be for the good of society."[42] In this spirit we challenge you to consider a few questions before you read on. When and where do media placements cross a line? We know brands engage young children on Saturday mornings. But they are also reaching into schools and appealing to adolescents online and on their increasingly present mobile phones. It seems no place is advertising free, and the consequences of this are not insignificant. There are two crucial considerations that should guide you. First, use media and messages that are age appropriate. Second, consider the

Airheads reaches out to adolescents with a rich digital experience offering games, tours, and contests while linking them to branded experiences on Facebook or television. Invitations to meet "Big Time Rush" or "like us" on Facebook encourage young consumers to share information, setting up a lifelong habit of opting in.

OK, pick your issue. Using toys to get kids to eat junk food. Using Barbie as the role model for young girls. Using cars and dolls to reinforce gender stereotypes. Or putting the responsibility on parents to help their kids make the right choices.

This ad from Singapore strikes just the right note that appeals to a kid's imagination and a parent's concern about safety.

concerns of parents, especially for younger children. These two considerations are not only the right thing to do, but they may save you from having to engage in damage control after the fact. Is advertising to children an invasion of privacy that dilutes parental influence? Advertisers have long claimed that advertising is informational, and that they simply use entertainment to engage the target. However, young children do not have the cogitative facilities to discern information from entertainment. Even if and when they do, most parents want to be the decision makers. They may also have values or expectations that differ from those that brands might promote. Parents, especially in these challenging economic times, have limited financial resources and, no doubt, feel undue pressure from brands. Finally, moms, as you will soon find out, are the big decision makers, and they prefer brands they can trust. Advertisers know that children influence a lot of parental spending—up to $1.12 trillion by some estimates.[43] Media are a powerful tool and can have a huge impact on long-term brand equity and short-term sales among children. In fact, the "nag factor" can influence up to 21% of purchases.[44] Consider that 2- and 3-year-olds can easily name fast-food and snack brands.[45] Children 5 to 8 years old respond strongly to television commercials, while adolescents are engaging with brands across social media, mobile, and gaming platforms.

Engaging Kids

Reaching children requires engagement that is culturally embedded and repetitive. Characters have proven to be highly effective and not new. The Pillsbury Doughboy and Charlie the Tuna have been used successfully for decades. Today Nickelodeon's SpongeBob SquarePants has cobranding licensing agreements with a range of brands.[46] Characters offer brands a chance to emotionally engage with children with a message ensuring strong recall.

Not surprisingly, fast food, soda, and toys are product categories that have the highest recall among children. Among all these brands, McDonald's has the highest recall.[47] Recall that McDonald's is a brand that has strong loyalty among Latinos, and that community has a lot of children under 18. These two factors are not mutually exclusive. Coca-Cola is another brand that reaches out to children. In fact, Coca-Cola's classic accounted for three quarters of all branded messages targeting children in 2010.[48] With evidence of an obesity epidemic in America, is this the right thing to be doing?

Advertising to children is controversial and justifiably so. The fact is, advertising is invasive and persuasive, and it permeates an ever-expanding part of children's lives. However, advertising to children is not going away even if we want it to. What is the right thing for advertisers to do? What will *you* do?

Women in Advertising: Have We Really Come a Long Way, Baby?

Women hold 53% of the jobs within the advertising industry, yet they account for only 28% of the top management positions.[49] In creative departments, the place where messages are created, women hold about 20% of the jobs.[50] And women make up only 3% at the top in creative management positions.[51] However, women make 85% of all—all—consumption decisions. What's wrong with this picture?

Hey, Big Spender, Spend a Little Time With Me

The idea that women are a "niche" market appears even more odd when you consider that women:[53]

- Spend close to $7 trillion annually.

- Purchase 50% of the products marketed to men.

- Represent the majority of the online market.

- Buy 68% of the new cars and influence up to 80% of all car purchases.

- Make 80% of all health care decisions.

- Influence 91% of all new home purchases.

- Buy 92% of all vacations.

- Open 89% of all bank accounts.

- Purchase 66% of all computers.

- Buy 93% of all food.

- Hold 60% of all personal wealth in the United States.

But here's the real kicker: 91% of women think advertisers do not understand them.[54] "Advertising is missing its mark with women."[55] Maybe that's because advertisers still consider women a "niche" market.

Besides wielding an immense amount of economic power, women are also considered the leading indicators of social change. To engage women, a brand must demonstrate that it understands the meaning, significance, and direction of large social changes and how it impacts women's lives. Think of how that plays

Words of Wisdom

"Trust is a crucial element in building your relationship with women to a level of loyalist."[52]

Tom Jordan, cofounder, T-J Communications, and former chairman and chief creative officer, HY Connect

This ad speaks volumes about women's commitment to social change. And it leverages a voice that echoes across generations.

out in the work world. Women have a high preference for personal networking, and they prefer dispersed or shared authority. This makes them strong mentors. They thrive on conceptual thinking, consensus building, and flexible work and lifestyles. Now, think about how that plays out in women's personal lives. Women talk whether it's one-on-one, word of mouth, or sailing across the social networking landscape from mom blogs to Facebook. They will sing a brand's praises or take it down with lightning speed. Women use brands to add ease and joy to their lives, and they use media to gather and share information.

Tapping Into This Influential "Niche" Market

The andHow Marketing group suggests seven insights for marketing to women.[56] First, identify unique segments based on lifestyle. Nike does this well. Second, "brand lite" isn't the answer. Don't make the mistake of creating a softer women's brand. Apple is a great example of a brand that women love—just the way it is. Third, communicate product values instead of listing features. Volvo does that well. Women know it stands for safety and dependability. Fourth, understand that she's always watching. If you don't speak the truth, she will know. When Motrin called the slings mothers use to carry their babies "fashion accessories," it nearly brought down the brand. Fifth, respect her. McDonald's is great at this. In 2002 they introduced salads, and in 2011 they invited mommy bloggers to the press conference that introduced the new Happy Meal with fresh fruit. Sixth, embrace high standards. Women demand quality and reward brands that serve it up. Whole Foods is a brand that can charge more in exchange for strong community engagement and high standards. Finally, be willing to commit. If you want her to commit to you, you'd better commit to her. Dove is a brand that is committed to women, with its game-changing "Campaign for Real Beauty," and years later women are still returning the commitment.

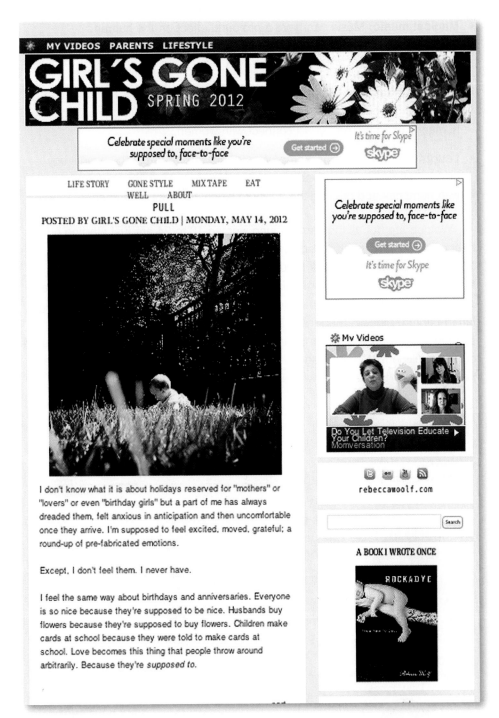

Now that you understand what makes women tick and what doesn't, let's talk about crafting messages they will respond to. The vast majority of women see advertising as a source of information as compared to entertainment.[57] But how you give then that information is based on "four emotive pathways," according to *PurseStrings* by Amanda Stevens and Tom Jordan:[58]

- **Storytelling:** Tell a story that feels real and can be told across multiple platforms. They will embrace it and share it.

- **Magical music:** Music can have a profound effect on the human body. Find out what motivates your women, and use music to tap into their emotions.

- **Embrace humanity:** Studies have documented how infants respond to faces, baby girls more than baby boys. As adults that difference remains. Add humanity to an ad, and you'll connect with women.

- **Laughter is the best medicine:** We are not talking about the typical boy humor that dominates advertising today. We are talking about merging humor with humanity and offering the ability to laugh with, not at, someone.

Women are not all the same. Young women 18 to 24 are just starting out on their own and very much reflect Gen Y. They are a lot different from 20- to 30-year-old women who work hard and play hard, and are often highly focused on their careers. Women in their 30s and 40s bear little resemblance to career-focused 20- and 30-year-olds. They are often moms with a burgeoning family-centered focus. Then there are women over 50. These boomers are starting a new phase of life and tend to have an adventurous streak that focuses on self-fulfillment. Women's age and life experiences make a huge difference in how you speak to them and where you'll find them. Do your homework.

Dove's "Campaign for Real Beauty" is no longer new, but it has staying power. Its revolutionary way of speaking to women has earned it a following that lives on with perfectly targeted partners, moving the needle year after year.

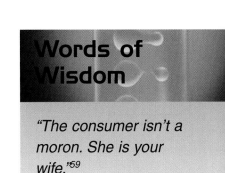

These ads demonstrate humanity through storytelling. Athleta speaks of taking action to take care of yourself and offers "Power to the She" while Johnson's Baby Lotion visually connects mother and daughter as the copy provides tangible, emotive information. These are human stories that sing with resonance.

Respect Women. Reap Rewards.

In the end, reaching women requires that you do your homework and make no assumptions. Women view the world through a unique lens. Before you start talking to a woman, listen to her.

Did We Miss Anyone?

You'd better believe it.

What about Asian Americans? While there are some cultural similarities, you can't use the same tactics for Chinese, Japanese, Korean, Indian, Pakistani, Thai, and the dozens of other Asian American ethnicities. And remember, Asian Americans may be a small market segment, but in general they are also a well-educated and highly affluent segment. Jeremy Lin, the Harvard-educated basketball sensation, demonstrates immense potential as a spokesperson representing this niche, but, more importantly, he has huge crossover. That fact was not lost on Nike, which signed him long before he burst onto the national media stage in winter 2012.

Rising Star

Hungry for Work

When I first graduated, I was e-mailing the CEO of a small agency in Chicago. Every Tuesday before lunch, I would attempt to make his mouth water with decadent descriptions of filet mignon and garlic mashed potatoes. And when I felt like I'd really hooked him, I would remind him that while he was salivating over a gourmet lunch, I wasn't hungry in the traditional sense. I didn't want a steak. I wanted a job.

He never e-mailed me back.

One thing I know for certain is that you can't take things personally in advertising. Just like that guy, people are not always going to like what you're putting out there. Who knows why? In this case, I like to think it's because he's a vegetarian.

After a few other failed attempts to get noticed through online portfolios, professionally printed books, and internship applications, I took the closest thing I could get to a job in advertising—working as a receptionist at Designkitchen, a digital agency in Chicago's meatpacking district. And now I'm a writer there.

I think my best advice would be to take whatever job you can get, as long as it gets you close to the work. Getting in is by far the hardest part. But once you're there, surround yourself with creative people who inspire you and ask them questions. Let your interests and your strengths steer your career. And when in doubt, just ask more questions.[60]

Sarah Kell, copywriter, Designkitchen, Chicago, @sekell

What about Arab Americans? Not all Arabs are Muslim. Not all Muslims are Arabs. How do we address them while not alienating other groups of Americans? American Muslims have $170 billion in purchasing power.[61] Brands such as Lowe's, Walmart, and McDonald's began courting Muslim Americans, but ran scared when in December 2011 a conservative group targeted the show *American Muslim* accusing these brands of supporting extremist views. Brands need to act ethically and proactively, always prepared for consumer responses. Brands that react to extremist groups often reduce their credibility across multiple consumer groups.

What about people with disabilities? Every disability presents different wants and needs. Like African Americans before the 1970s, people with disabilities are nearly invisible in today's advertising. In the United Kingdom, the VisABLE Campaign works to bring disabled people into advertising. One2OneNetwork, a mobile brand, used a man in a wheelchair as part of a slice-of-life story. They got it right, naturally. There are three reasons to switch on to people with disabilities in advertising. It's the right thing to do. It's commercially viable. And, at least in the United Kingdom, it's a legal obligation.

There just isn't enough time or space. In the spirit of relevance and respect, we offer a few tips that apply to most situations:

- Don't make assumptions.
- Do your homework.

- Always remember that even within a market segment there can be huge variation.

- Market segments, like subcultures, are culturally bound.

- Social context matters.

- We'll steal an old slogan: "Act globally and think locally."

- Humility goes a long way.

- Above all, be respectful.

This last point—respect—needs some more discussion. John Kuraoka, a freelance copywriter, offers some great advice:

> Racism, sexism, and other us-against-them motifs are not funny. It is no more acceptable to poke fun at a middle-aged white man than it is to poke fun at a young black lesbian. It makes no difference that you, personally, are either a middle-aged white man or a young black lesbian. On reflection, it's questionable whether poking fun at anybody helps sell anything.[62]

On the other hand, don't let political correctness overrule common sense. Kuraoka has some good advice on this, too: "*There is a difference between race and racism, sex and sexism. It is pointless to make a pantyhose ad gender-neutral, just as it is foolish to craft political messages about birth control without fully bringing women into the deliberation. Be aware of cases and causes in which neutering the tone of your message will degrade its effectiveness.*"[63]

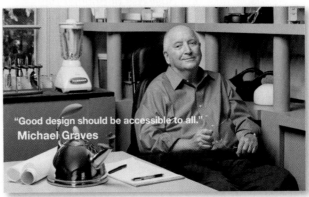

"Good design should be accessible to all."
Michael Graves

UK marketers have taken the lead in mainstreaming people with disabilities in their ads. Debenhams, a British department store, was the first to use a disabled model. While disabled people are not as prominently featured in the United States, they are not invisible. In the above case, designer and architect Michael Graves (who is also disabled) promotes a teapot design from OXO that works for everyone.

A Humble Disclaimer

In preparing to write this chapter, we talked with a diverse group of advertising practitioners and also conducted extensive secondary research. We tried to be sensitive, unbiased, and ethical regarding the various issues discussed here. Yet, some people may take issue with our content or the tone. Some might say we wrote too much on one issue and not enough on another or that we totally missed the point on others. We did our best to bring these issues out into the open and encourage you to think about them, because "the times they are a-changin'." How you handle them depends on your own perception, sensitivity, and ethical boundaries.

Who's Who?

Marti Barletta—A recognized thought leader on marketing to women, Marti Barletta is CEO of the TrendSight Group, a think tank specializing in marketing to women, and founding member of the Women Gurus Network. Prior to founding TrendSight, Barletta was vice president and director of Frankly Female at Frankel. She is the author of *PrimeTime Women: How to Win the Hearts, Minds, and Business of Boomer Big Spenders* and *Marketing to Women*, and writes a regular column for *Advertising Age*. Her work has inspired marketers to rethink the way they approach marketing to women.

Thomas Burrell—Thomas Burrell started in the mailroom of a Chicago agency and was promoted to copywriter in 1961. During the 1960s, as the race issue gained significance on Madison Avenue, Burrell became a leader in addressing race in advertising. He eventually opened his own agency, Burrell Communications, which was the first African American ad agency. By 1980, Burrell had become the largest African American agency in the United States, stressing the unique experiences of African Americans. Burrell's client list includes Coca-Cola, McDonald's, Procter & Gamble, and Sears, Roebuck & Co. and surpassed $168 million in billing in 1998.[50] Burrell has since retired, and the agency has been bought by Publicis.

Judy John—Judy John wrote her way to the top. In 1993 after only three years in advertising John, of Asian ancestry, was ranked Canada's "Top Copywriter." Her work has won recognition at virtually every major international and national awards competition including two Cannes Gold Lions, a One Show Pencil, and *Communication Arts*. She founded her own agency, Guerrilla TV, and she has worked at Chiat\Day, TAXI, Roche Macaulay & Partners, BBDO, and Ogilvy & Mather. In 1999 she joined Leo Burnett, Toronto, as chief creative officer, and since 2011 she has been CEO and chief creative officer.

Caroline Jones—A copywriter with a long list of firsts, Caroline Jones is often promoted as the first Black woman to have held the position. She helped many clients, including American Express, Anheuser-Busch, McDonald's, and Prudential, make their initial foray into the African American market. Jones began her career in 1963 in New York as a secretary and copywriter trainee at J. Walter Thompson. She rose to creative director in less than five years. In 1968, she helped form Zebra Associates, no small feat in an era with few Black agency principals. She cofounded the Black Creative Group and established Mingo, Jones, Guilmenot, now the Chisholm-Mingo Group. Jones died in 2011.[65]

Exercises

1. Different Voices

Choose a product. Consumer packaged goods can be good. So can home cleaning products or consumer electronics.

- Pick one brand—for example: Swiffer.
- Draw two stick people and imagine they are from two different demographic groups. As a group, create a bulleted list of demographics and psychographics that represent each group.
- Next draw a speech bubble by each stick person. Fill in the speech bubble, considering how they would greet each other.
- Now give each a thought bubble. Consider how the two stick people might think differently about each other. This is the interesting part, because it gets to an exploration of demographic, cultural, and social differences. Now fill in the think bubble. You might even begin to get at some of the deeper ethical issues, which are often hard to discuss.

2. Brands as Global Personalities

How do some brands more successfully move across the globe than other brands? Why do some take a globalized approach and others a standardized approach?

- Begin by thinking of brands as people and be prepared to trace their personalities across cultures.
- Generate a list of 10 of the most influential people on the globe.
- Discuss why each of these people is influential: What about their actions, personality, country of origin/current residence, profession/title, associations, and so on makes them influential?
- From the previously generated list consider the qualities inherent in each person. Now, link a brand to each person.
- Discuss why each of the brands exemplifies that individual.
- Now write a brand personality statement for each brand. Consider how much this statement reflects the person associated with the brand.
- Finally, discuss how these brands move across the globe based on their brand personality and cultural variations. Consider if a standardized or globalized approach is used and why.

3. Is There Really a Difference?

This exercise challenges you to consider stereotypes and how they impact advertising.

- Your instructor will connect with agency colleagues and find a campaign (ads and brief) that involves ads for both the general market and the gay and lesbian market.
- As a class, review the brief and ad for the general market.
- Next, working in teams, brainstorm ad concepts for the gay market.
- Then select your best idea and present it to the class along with a rationale for why it's the best option to reach the gay demographic.
- Finally, your instructor will show you the ad the agency produced for the gay market.
- Open for discussion: What are the differences between the general market ad and the ad for the gay market? What were your assumptions? How did stereotypes play out?

Visit www.sagepub.com/altstiel3e to access these additional learning tools

- Video Links
- Web Resources
- eFlashcards
- Web Quizzes

Chapter

5

International Advertising

It's a Global Marketplace

The globe seems to grow smaller as technology grows more pervasive. In the midst of this, brands seek to leverage their equity across a myriad of cultures, while advertising agencies seek to make sense of shifting global trends. Technology, culture, and global trends—that's a lot to digest. As we're talking a lot about technology in other chapters, we'll focus on culture and trends in this chapter. However, as you'll see, there's crossover everywhere. While the examples we use come from around the globe, you'll notice that headlines and copy are often in English. It's true English is now the global standard for business communication, but in most cases these ads have been translated for international award competitions, and most appeared in their native language in their own countries.

Geographic Context

Let's start simply by thinking in terms of geography. From this vantage point, here are five categories: local, national, regional, international, and global.

Local: Begin in your own backyard where you'll find local brands. These are often retail brands with small local footprints. Alterra Coffee, in the Milwaukee area, is a good example. It's a local coffee roaster with shops only within the metro area, and the advertising represents that local flavor.

National: These brands are wedded to a single country such Russia's Volga automobiles or America's Sonic drive-ins. Both brands advertise exclusively within a single national border, and the tonality tends to echo national cultural norms.

Regional: Here brands advertise within specific regional clusters. The French Orange telecom brand is one such brand with a focus on Europe, Africa and the Middle East, and the Caribbean. Orange is Orange wherever it goes, but the offers reflect the consumers' needs within the individual countries. It's worth noting that the brand had a bit of trouble in Ireland since the color is also associated with protestant militants.

International: These brands have worldwide distribution but employ standardized marketing approaches. They adjust strategies and messages to adapt to local cultures. Unilever has many such brands. For instance, its ice cream brand changes its name and logo as it moves across the globe. In Spain it's Frigo; in Denmark it's Frisko. It's similar, but different. That's a reflection of local culture.

Global: In the global category, you'll find the behemoth multinational brands. They are hyper-consistent in their branding at a global level, with little deviation in messaging regardless of cultural differences. Brands like McDonald's and Coke fit here. While drive-throughs throughout Europe are "McDrives," the McDonald's name and Golden Arches remain the same, no matter where they appear. The same is true for the Coke brand. Advertising images of "happiness" bubbling out of classic red Coca-Cola bottles are ubiquitous across the globe.

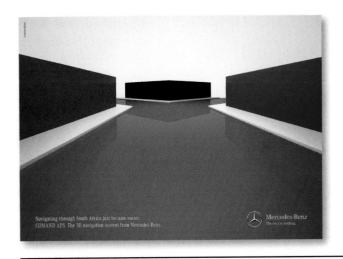

The headline for the Mercedes-Benz 3D navigation system reads, "Navigating through South Africa just became easier." If we saw these graphics from a bird's-eye view, rather than the driver's, we'd recognize the flag of South Africa.

Cultural Dimensions

Having defined geographic frames, let's take a moment to talk about concepts of culture. Understanding the importance of culture will help contextualize the strategies we'll be talking about later in the chapter. An umbrella framework that will help you make sense of culture is the concept of high and low cultural contexts. Under these two concepts are a myriad of cultural nuances that define the overall cultural context—from languages, to social interactions, to food, to courtship and shopping habits. The variations from country to country can go from sublet to extreme. It's an advertiser's job to understand them and strategically decide how important these cultural nuances are, thus leading to how the brand will be positioned within each country.

High-context cultures are what one might consider cultures that value subtlety and privacy. Within these cultures, messages are rarely explicit. In other words, you must understand the local cultural structure to understand the nuances of the cultural messages. Thus, high-context messaging is often inaccessible to an outsider. If you're not part of the culture, you may not understand the message. China and Japan are examples of high-context cultures, where messages are commonly characterized by symbolism or indirect verbal expressions. In these cultures, in particular, having local people on your advertising team is essential. As an advertiser, you will quickly learn that within a high-context culture using familiar cultural codes is essential for advertising success.

Low-context cultures, on the other hand, often use messages that are more transparent. In these countries, interactions between people are generally more open. The codes embedded within messages, be they advertising or personal, are generally more explicit. There is also a strong emphasis on the use of words versus symbolism. The idea of "telling it like it is" is common in these cultures. Thus in low-context cultures words combined with images can quickly be interpreted. In short, these cultures function with more direct forms of communication. In low-context cultures, such as Germany and the United States, even an outsider can relatively quickly pick up on the codes within local messages. Considering that cultural codes in low-context cultures are fairly transparent and direct, it is not surprising that branded messages from these cultures might be understood across the globe with fewer modifications. However, it's important to remember that even if these messages are understood, it does not mean that they

Talk about the intersection of high- and low-context! This Base batteries campaign expresses the power of backup systems with high-context cultural perfection. Wife can replace husband, son can replace mother, or son can replace father—but only if you have a backup, and only if you understand Indian culture and politics. At the same time, the Coca-Cola backdrop expresses the simplicity of messages from low-context cultures. Welcome to India. Welcome to the global marketplace.

will resonate or be accepted. Herein lies the unending debate among those who work in global advertising. We'll get into this debate, which centers squarely on strategy, a bit later. For now, let's take a look at where the growth is.

Global Growth

If you look at the four main geographic regions for global branding—North America, Continental Europe, Asia, and Latin America—you'll see one clear trend in sector growth: digital technology. In North America, seven of the top ten brands are in technology, with Apple way out in front of the others in terms of brand value. The other three brands are Coca-Cola, McDonald's, and Marlboro.[2] No surprises there. In Continental Europe, technology garnered four of the top spots. Luxury brands took four others, with the final two going to the retail sector.[3] The balance of technology and luxury in Europe is also expected. For while Europeans see themselves as players in the Western capitalistic model, they also differentiate themselves from Americans by their passion for art and culture. In the United States, luxury brands are economic status symbols, whereas in Europe they are cultural status symbols. This helps explain the power of luxury brands in Europe. In Asia, half of the top ten brands were in technology,

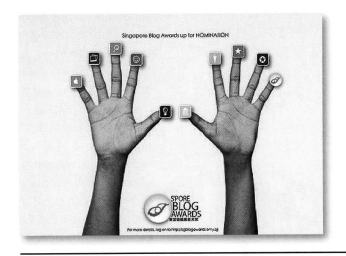

While Singapore is generally regarded as a very conservative, closed society—think high-context culture—it has become a hotbed for creative advertising. At first, that was fueled by a large expatriate community, but now much of the award-winning work is done by Singapore natives.

with three others in banking, one in insurance, and one in the auto sector.[4] Banking and insurance represent growth sectors in Asia. The focus on technology paired with the rise of banking and insurance clearly articulates a region in rapid economic growth. Finally, South America had only seven top brands. Even here nearly half, three, were technology brands. Another three were beer, with cosmetics and oil each garnering one spot.[5] Beer brands taking three top spots might surprise some readers. However, beer in South America is normalized much the way luxury brands are in Europe. It's an embedded part of culture. Knowing that we have only a chapter's worth of space to talk about international advertising, let's focus where the growth is. So, jump on board as we head out to visit the emerging BRIC and MIST nations.

Not long ago the talk was all about the emergence of BRIC nations—Brazil, Russia, India, and China. They are still the economic engines of global growth. However, today the buzz is increasingly about the MIST nations—Mexico, Indonesia, South Korea, and Turkey. While the BRIC nations still represent the powerhouse nations, the MIST nations represent an emerging new breed of consumers. Together these nations represent the bulk of where advertising dollars are flowing. It's predicted that over the next three years the BRIC and MIST countries, along with South Africa and Argentina, will represent half of all global advertising growth.[7] Let's follow the money and take a look at the drivers of change within these nations.

Words of Wisdom

"The other thing is we don't believe in digital marketing. We believe in marketing in a digital world."[6]

Clive Sirkin, senior marketing officer, Kimberly-Clark, Neenah, Wisconsin

BRIC Nations

BRAZIL

When it comes to big spending power, Brazil leads the way, and that's not about to slow down. The middle class now makes up more than half the population. As host to the 2014 World Cup and 2016 Summer Olympics, its economy will only keep booming.[8] Brazilians are known for their passion for life, and that moves across all aspects of culture. It's been said that if "you would like to inspire rapture in Brazil, weave the 'beautiful game' (soccer) into your pitch. Incorporate the spirit of the *joga bonito* (beautiful play) in your ads."[9] Brazilians, long known for their admiration of all forms of beauty, are also huge consumers of cosmetics. Sack's, an online retailer, and Natura, a natural cosmetics line, are leading the way into the global marketplace.[10] Match their admiration of all things beautiful with their love of music, and you get brand-building enterprises like Rock in Rio. This weeklong festival brings more than 350 brands and nearly a million consumers together in a marketing extravaganza.[11] Brazilians are big on technology too, with more cell phones than people and an exploding social media market.[12] While they may love technology and music that embraces their cultural heritage, they also love global brands. That is a call that global brands are heeding. Though Brazil may be a more transparent, low-context culture, Brazilians tend toward searching out people and brands that feel "simpatico"—that they believe understand and respect them.[13] Respect means not being in their face. Thus, it's not a surprise that outdoor advertising has been banned in Rio. This duality is something that advertisers must embrace if they wish to be successful in Brazil.

Leveraging Brazilians' sense of irony and passion for sharing via social media, Volkswagen created a series of 15-second spots: "Son you are adorable/adopted. I love you Bob/your boobs. It's not you. It's me/Melissa." As the sound of texting clicks away, each spot plays off of the perils of texting, driving home the brand message. Accept only an original.

RUSSIA

This enormous country leads the BRIC nations in gross domestic product and has a growing middle class, with a striking number of billionaires. The growth of the Russian economy has been driven by technology and innovation. That has brought brands like Microsoft and Nokia into the Russian market in a big way.[14] The luxury sector with its growing wealth and brands like Louis Vuitton and Gucci are hot. Like Brazil's, Russia's economy will benefit from future international sporting events with the 2014 Winter Olympics and the 2018 World Cup.[15] These events will present huge opportunities for advertising sponsorships. Also like Brazilians, Russians tend to trust global brands over national brands. Thus the biggest challenge Russia faces is persuading Russians to buy Russian. At the same time, Russia brings its big and bold history with it into the present.

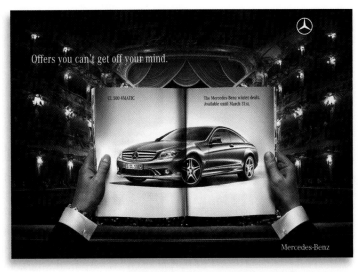

How's this for screaming status? This ad is loaded with symbolic markers of Western status: manicured nails, cuff links, velvet, rich colors, and, of course, Mercedes-Benz. And its location, the theater, has deep and luxurious Russian roots. It's a great example of the mixing of high- and low-context cultural values.

For Russians size matters. They appreciate brand names, big firms, and large-scale promotions.[16] These confounding trends strongly suggest that Russia is a mix of high and low cultural markers. The high-context markers are vestiges of the Soviet era, and the low-context markers signify Russia's growing prominence in the Western marketplace. The key cultural takeaway for Russia? Think like a chess player. Be bold, but thoughtful. Be strategic, but passionate. The messages advertisers send had better reflect these contrasting cultural standards.[17]

INDIA

With a rapidly expanding Indian middle class, which is often employed in technology, India is on the move. Not unlike in China, banking and technology are leading the way. At the same time, India is a country that has historically thrived on mom-and-pop stores. Thus, Western-style retailing, with the rise of hypermarkets, is having a difficult time finding roots in India.[18] Add to that the fact that there are 16 languages in India. Though Hindi and English, a vestige of colonialism, are the official languages, the others have high emotional resonance for those who speak them. Reflecting the trend toward embracing local culture, television advertising is switching from English to Hindi, to better appeal to customers' impulses and emotions.[19] While India's entry into the global marketplace is fraught with economic and cultural dissonance, don't think for a minute that its consumers are not interested in participating in the global consumer economy. For one, India has the largest film entertainment industry on the globe—Bollywood. And it's booming. For instance, the Spanish tourism authority tapped Bollywood to create a movie featuring Indian stars Flamenco dancing across Spain. It was so successful that tourism in Spain jumped 65%.[20]

With consumerism growing in India, Yebhi .com, an online shopping mall, uses visuals to marry traditional shopping with postmodern retailing and technology as the matchmaker. Yebhi could give Amazon a run for its money in India.

The core message of Oreo—twist, dip, and enjoy—took a bit of explaining. But 50 years after its introduction, Oreo is a beloved brand, especially among children. The tagline means "Time for fun, friendship, and closeness. Only with Oreo." Suddenly Chinese characters seem so much simpler.

Indians love more than movies. It's communication generally, with mobile and, surprisingly, newspapers leading the way. Both sectors are thriving.[21] So, it seems that India is a study in contrasts. Yet, at its core, India is a high-context culture. This is reflected by Indians' harsh view of the word "no," which can be said in a multitude of ways, but never simply "no."[22] If you cannot even say "no" and you have 16 languages, imagine the cultural challenges faced by copywriters.

CHINA

Let's put this very high-context culture in perspective. In 2010, China surpassed Germany, a very low-context culture, to become the third-largest ad market.[23] It is also the largest Internet market in the world and has the highest penetration of digital outdoor displays on the planet.[24] Certainly, many Western online media channels are closed within China. To date Google, Facebook, and Twitter are not available in China. If these platforms ever become available, there could easily be over 500 million new users overnight. While media constraints limit advertising accessibility in China, they do not appear to dampen Chinese passion for social media. Big brands like Procter & Gamble, Coca-Cola, and General Motors are flooding into China. To put this in context, in 2011 Procter & Gamble spent 71% of its ad dollars outside the United States, and China garnered the biggest chuck of that money.[25] In this booming marketplace, imported luxury brands from French wines to Gucci bags are flying out of stores, often driven home in Buicks. To support this booming economic growth, the banking, insurance, and telecom sectors are surging. Looking at ad revenues, China's roaring economy, and consumers' pension for global status brands, it's hard to imagine this market is anything but capitalist. Yet, any savvy advertiser knows that the key to advertising messaging in China is a subtle balancing of cultural emotions and political correctness—and we mean that literally.

The BRIC nations are powerful brokers in the global economy. They represent huge global populations with consumers who are eager to spend their growing disposable income on global brands. Over the past 25 years, advertising in the BRIC and MIST nations has steadily grown, while advertising spending in the United States slowed, only doubling over this time. In China, and the overall Asia Pacific region, advertising spending has more than tripled. In Latin America, where Brazil represents the giant

Rising Star

Bonjour de Paris!
I was about to become a typical business graduate, someone with a business degree and marketing internship. In my last semester of college I decided that I wanted to add something to my résumé that would set me apart from my peers sitting next to me with similar internship experiences. I also wanted one last opportunity to travel the world without any responsibilities.

I found an internship program through another university that allowed me to take a few classes and intern part time. It was a great opportunity until I tried to justify spending as much money as I could be making if I graduated and got a job. Regardless, I made an impulse decision, delayed graduation, and headed to London.

My overseas internship offered me much more than any job I could have landed. It proved to future employers that I had the ability to take risks and be adaptable to cultural differences. In addition, I got to see places I only read about in books. At the end of the semester I returned home and found a marketing job to pay off the debt I racked up while traveling.

I hit the ground running and expressed an interest in international opportunities. My internship helped justify why I would be a good candidate. A year and a half after starting my job I was asked to take on an international marketing assignment in New Zealand and Australia. The opportunity forced me out of my comfort zone and helped me to grow. Along the way I got to see one of the most beautiful places on earth.

It's been 18 months since New Zealand, and today I'm working in France as an international product manager. In fact, I'm writing this from my office outside of Paris. So, here's my advice. Set yourself apart. Take risks. Go international. Bonjour de Paris![26]

Erin Regenwether, market analyst, international marketing, Kohler Company, Kohler, WI, kohler.com

---

spender, advertising spending has grown nearly 10-fold. In Central Europe, advertising spending went from almost zero to a 25-fold increase.[27] Multinational brand managers are willing to follow the money and head directly to the BRIC nations and on to the emerging MIST nations. It also tells us that you had better know more than a little about the global marketplace when you enter the job market.

MIST Nations

MEXICO

Mexico leads the way in growth among Spanish-speaking countries in the Americas. As its economy grows, so does its media usage. Mexico is also the production hub for the two biggest Spanish-language television stations, which broadcast across Central and North America. By the end of 2012, it is expected that nearly half of

UN MUNDO TAN COMPLEJO NECESITA UNA BUENA EXPLICACIÓN. MILENIO

Mexican advertising can be dramatic, very emotional, and often playful, as in this ad for the Milenio *newspaper. The tagline is "Such a complex world needs good explanations." A simply brilliant approach, even when the people depicted aren't.*

Mexican households will have access to subscription television.[29] Add to that the fact that Mexicans use cell phones much like Hispanic Americans, with mobile usage outpacing computers as their primary entry point into the digital world. That opens up enormous mobile pathways to connect with Mexican consumers. One thing you can count on is a blatant lack of political correctness among Mexican consumers, who are quick to laugh at stereotypes. Advertisers who leverage this knowledge can reach them with resonance. However, when it comes to big-ticket items, Mexican consumers are collaborative in their decision-making process.[30] As they live in multigenerational homes, brand loyalty tends to trickle down the generational line. However, if you want to build brand loyalty among young Mexican consumers, the so-called "NiNis" (Neither-Nors), you'd better understand their longing for heroes. In fact, "when asked for a famous person they most admired Mexican youth chose Gandhi."[31] In the end, Mexico is a fairly low-context country. It is also a country that is looking toward the future. Thus, aspirational brands like Nike and Gatorade have gained huge traction in Mexico.

INDONESIA

When you talk about advertising potential in Indonesia, you can't help but talk about digital. Indonesia has the second biggest Facebook population in the world. It's probably also the most Twitter-obsessed nation on the planet.[32] BlackBerry is Indonesians' preferred mobile device; iPhone is not even on their radar. China Berry, Apple's Chinese competitor, is nipping at BlackBerry's heels. As in Mexico, computer penetration is low in Indonesia, while mobile penetration is gigantic—six times the penetration of computers. Advertisers are following consumers' lead. Online ad spending grew 200% in 2011. But, that's still a small part of the advertising media pie. Social media, accessed via mobile, lead spending, grabbing a giant slice at 80%.[33] Indonesia is a high-context Muslim culture, and broadcast is highly regulated. If you're going to use traditional media in Indonesia, you'll need to have it well vetted.[34] Thus, advertisers tend to seek nontraditional ways of creating conversation as a way of injecting fresh interest in brands.

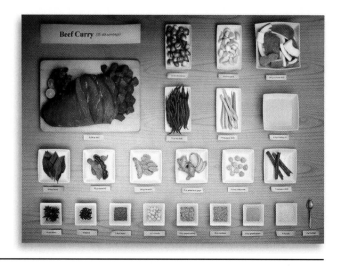

Unilever's Sunlight dishwashing liquid leverages cultural knowledge to send home its message. Beautifully. One tablespoon of Sunlight dishwashing liquid is enough for 40 servings. Period.

SOUTH KOREA

Luxury products have huge appeal in Asia generally, with Japan leading that category and China close behind, after South Korea. However, the luxury market in South Korea has been growing an average of 12% each year since 2006.[35] For South Korean consumers who cannot afford luxury brands, nonluxury retail brands have become a haven for social interaction. International brands like Zara, Uniqlo, and H&M have increased sales two to four times in the past three years.[36] South Korea is a high-context culture, with South Koreans rarely showing emotion in public. However, the younger generation tends to be more demonstrative, still in culturally appropriate ways. This generation is a huge fan of entertainment television, social media, and fashion, hence the growth in nonluxury fashion retail, often driven by consumer-generated social media buzz. Juggling all their passions makes South Koreans avid multitaskers, living a highly e-commerce-driven life. It can be said that "if you want to reach a Korean executive, text him or her."[37] If you want your brand to reach South Koreans where they play, you may consider taking up golf, singing karaoke, and investing hugely in social media, all of which transcend generational boundaries. Both are hugely popular and appear to transcend generational appeal.

TURKEY

Imagine consumer confidence ratings never going below 90%.[38] Welcome to Turkey. In this booming economy, you'll find big shoppers who love their mobile phones. In fact, malls are the number-one hangout spot among Turkish youth.[39] Western-style shopping malls reflect cultural norms embedded in the tradition of open-air markets, but they also represent a connection with the new Western economy. Turks, like the rest of their BRIC and MIST neighbors, are avid users of technology with nearly half expressing the belief that staying up to date with technology is essential to life.[40] However, while technology is one of the top three most important issues for Turks, the other two might surprise you. They are religion and politics, and we dare say their discourse is a bit less raucous than in the United States. This is, in part, because Turkey has a mix of high and low cultural contexts. It is the high-context aspect that most likely keeps things a bit more reserved. But

Throughout Asia electronic bidets, the ultimate private luxury product, are extremely popular. South Korea is no exception. Conway's tagline—"We love your tush"—and visual turn the idea of visual metaphor on its head.

Anadolu Insurance was able to use street vandalism to its advantage. This seven-layer outdoor board in Istanbul drove home the key message and the tagline—"Never lose." It's interesting to note the house looks very Western. Western imagery is not uncommon in product and service categories that tap into the aspirational desires of consumers from emerging markets.

the spirited low-context aspect of Turkish life is driving modern consumption habits. Still, these habits are paired with Turkish cultural values that prioritize authenticity and honesty.[41] Thus, brands like Nokia, Adidas, Nike, and Avon are big in Turkey because their positioning fits well with the cultures that value authenticity. In Turkey, outdoor is alive and well, with television, newspaper, and the Internet also big players.[42] But, as we know, to woo Turkish consumers, the medium is not as important as the message. Here authenticity rules.

Global Survival

Whether BRIC or MIST, African or Arab, American or European, moving brands into new markets takes a considered and culturally driven approach. Every year Millward Brown releases its *BrandZ™ Top 100 Most Valuable Global Brands.* This report helps global marketers understand the trends that are driving global change. It's one of the industry's most valued assessment tools for global branding. We took BrandZ's key takeaways for maintaining a winning global presence and condensed them down to a lucky 13.[43]

Anticipate and understand change: It's a chaotic world. Do your homework and be ready for change. Use consumer insight as the basis for coherent strategy.

- **Stand for something original and consistent:** Your competitors are seeing the same information you are. Make your response original. Then stay the course.

- **Stand for something more:** Corporate social responsibility is good but not enough. Make social action relevant to both consumers and your brand. And be sincere.

- **Innovate and differentiate**: Consumers demand innovation and expect differentiation. Make your brand personality clear and culturally resonant.

- **Converse with customers:** Social media gives consumers a voice. But, the customer is not always right. So, create a dialogue that can persuade.

- **Talk clearly and listen closely:** Invest in content that people will talk about and share, so you will be heard above the clutter. Those who love your brand will talk.

- **Be honest and open:** If you're not, you will be caught. Transparency is key.

- **Build trust:** That won't be easy on the heels of a global recession. But, it's essential for growth.

- **Deliver a great experience and value:** Shiny new objects are fine, but only if they are reliable and do not frustrate consumers. Now, deliver the goods at a fair price.

- **Grow and protect brand value:** Your brand promise must lead and be fulfilled at all times—across all cultures.

- **Be consistent but flexible:** Deliver the same coherent global message across cultures, but express it in a way that resonates locally.

- **Measure and act now:** Track your results and be accountable. Offer something relevant to consumers no matter where they live.

- **Break rules:** When you know why you're doing something, it's easier to break the rules.

Adventure at the Touch of a Button

According to Jeremy Clarkson in *Top Gear,* the BBC motoring television series, ŠKODA's compact SUV, the ŠKODA Yeti, is considered to be possibly the best car in the world.

How can you top such a statement?

Our strategy was to bring a real outdoor feel, which only a truly capable and solid SUV like the ŠKODA Yeti can offer, into the city, because this is where most compact SUVs in Europe are used.

The aim was to differentiate the Yeti from its merely urban lifestyle-oriented main competitor, the Nissan Qashqai.

The campaign idea was to project a real jungle scene onto the city by the "accidental" touch of the ŠKODA Yeti's Off-Road Button—a button that set the car's 4x4 parameters automatically into off-road mode.

As you can imagine, this script needed a lot of imagination to envisage the final results, since the project effect has to be created with computer-generated imagery.

So it was probably no big surprise that when we presented the campaign idea to marketing representatives of ŠKODA's 15 most important international markets, only two markets voted for this idea instantly. The remaining markets wanted to see another campaign idea developed.

However, when the campaign was eventually executed for these two markets anyway, the other markets realized its potential and followed swiftly. The campaign was finally aired in 18 countries, driving the Yeti sales up significantly.

It is said that it is hard to judge a book by its cover, and this seems true even for marketing experts. Nowadays with digital production technologies it requires even more imagination, trust, and confidence to go for great, perfect ideas.[44]

Thorsten Jux, managing partner, Leagas Delaney, Prague, Czech Republic, leagasdelaney.cz

Strategic Approaches

Reaching consumers with resonance is at the heart of what advertisers must do as they attempt to move brands across the globe. So let's take a moment to contextualize this in terms of culture and its impact on branding across the world. In the advertising industry, we often talk about two overarching approaches: globalized and standardized.

Globalized Approaches

These tend to parallel the global geographic category, and take the view that consistent branding supersedes cultural differences. However, that is not to say that culture is not a concern. It is. For brands using a globalized approach the focus is to cultivate the brand and not local culture. Yet, as they do so, they promote a globalized Western cultural point of view. Global strategies offer brands the opportunity to maintain a highly consistent brand image throughout the world. Another appeal is that the global approach is much easier for brand managers when it comes to controlling all aspects of brand life. This approach, as common as it is, is fraught with gaps in cultural connectedness. Yet, it is a favorite among global brand managers.[45]

Brand Perú had problems to solve. It wanted Americans to see it as a good trading partner, a secure place for foreign investment, and a great tourist destination. What better strategy than to come to Peru, Nebraska, to tell your story! Young & Rubicam, Lima created a 15-minute television documentary merging the two cultures. It lives online and as smaller clips. So strategic and smart, sometimes hilarious, and other times touching, it's just about perfect.

Standardized Approaches

On the other hand, these approaches suggest branding consistency, while offering flexibility. These approaches parallel the international geographic category, discussed previously. Brands in this category also have a big footprint. However, while maintaining some consistence, they strategically change their messaging to adapt to local cultural variance. Standardized approaches tend to create advertising messages that are more culturally resonant. When advertising a global brand, you can't afford to ignore the multitude of possible pitfalls. No matter if you choose a globalized or a standardized approach, always be a forward-thinking global corporate citizen.

Strategies for Success

The most important lesson here is not whether to use a globalized or standardized approach, but *how* to use these approaches. And the most valuable work you can do is to understand the cultural imperatives that shape the markets into which your brand will be moving. That's another way of saying pay attention to the cultural nuances related to high and low cultural context. To bring all of this to a more practical conclusion, we suggest six strategies for internationalizing brands based on the work of global brand consultant Marieke de Mooij.[47] These reflect a hybridized way of interpreting the globalized or standardized approaches. Take a read, and then we'll close with a few cases to provide context.

1. **Cultivate established local brands:** Develop national brands into global brands, bringing with your brand its original brand value and strategic orientation, with little variance. Coca-Cola and Dove are brands that have successfully done this.

2. **Global concept, local adaptation:** Develop a single conceptual formula for the entire world. Yet be able to adapt that formula in order to carry local values. McDonald's is a brand that has done this very successfully.

3. **Create new brands:** Recognize a global need and create a product or service to fulfill consumers' wants and needs. Google is the perfect example of such a brand.

4. **Purchase local brands and internationalize:** This is standard practice for most consumer packaged goods companies such as Kraft, Unilever,

and Nestlé. Kraft has done this successfully with a wide range of digestive biscuits from Petit Écolier, to Pim's, to Le Véritable Petit Beurre.

5. **Develop brand extensions:** This is classic marketing. Take the parent brand and create a family of products under that parent brand name. Cartier, originally a watchmaker, has done this elegantly, moving more deeply into the luxury market with leather goods, pens, and perfume, and along the way benefiting from global cross-promotion.

6. **Employ a multilocal strategy:** Develop differing strategies, based on local culture and customs. The equity of the parent brand name remains, while the product adapts to local culture behaviors and norms. Nestlé has done this well, inserting the local country into its overarching branded message, such as "Nestlé, the best of South Africa." You could insert any country into this message with this strategy.

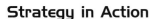

Coffee is, obviously, not a traditional Chinese beverage. Yet, the image employed to pitch it taps into highly traditional Chinese ideals. The ad, which won a Lion at Cannes, clearly implies that coffee will provide the energy to be a better community member. And that's very Chinese. Another cultural note—the worker's parents are first on the pile of dependents followed by the wife who is knitting baby booties.

Strategy in Action

So let's end with a few examples of international advertising that has moved the needle. This time we looked for examples outside the BRIC and MIST nations. As you'll see from the four we chose, none of them feel like advertising as we once knew it. Or maybe it's fair to say none of them use media in traditional ways.

We begin with the work of Swiss agency Jung von Matt/Limmat, which took the little Swiss village of Obermutten with fewer than 80 people and announced it to the world. The promotion set the mayor of the town in the center of the plan, by having him promise to post the photo of anyone who liked the village. With 14,000 Facebook fans from 20 countries and a huge bump in tourism, it's fair to say this was a success. This campaign takes the global concept and local adaptation strategy and turns them on their head, working perfectly.[48]

Argentina's Del Campo Nazca Saatchi & Saatchi helped BHG Electronics move microwaves not by developing a classic advertising campaign, but by developing a brand extension. Rather than the usual microwave that beeps at consumers when it's done, this line of microwaves plays music to announce the food is ready. They sold out immediately. The new line will go into full production this year.[49]

DDB Singapore created a beautiful cross-promotional campaign combining music and fashion. It teamed iTunes with StarHub Music Stores by using RFID tags attached to clothing. When shoppers entered a fitting room, the tag triggered speakers to play a musical track designed to fit the mood of the garment. This was followed by a text sent to the shopper's phone offering a free download. The campaign garnered an 84% click-through rate and boosted paid music downloads by 21%.[50]

Finally, DDB Sweden took a traditional medium, outdoor, and spun it with a very nontraditional direction. They took the global aspect of the Volkswagen brand, its 4Motion four-wheel-drive feature, and adapted the message for a local Swedish audience. The team created a classic car on billboard outdoor board and plunked it in the middle of a frozen Swedish lake. Then they waited for the ice to melt. Progress was live streamed, and the campaign was supported by TV, print, in-store, and banner ads. By the time the outdoor board sank, sales had risen 38%.[51] Ad thieves from Wisconsin and Minnesota, as well as Finland and Siberia, ought to take note.

This Samsung ad from Perú demonstrates the universal nature of technology. The ad could work almost anywhere in the world because it exemplifies our collective understanding about technology and tells the story visually. Samsung is a great example of a brand that used a globalized strategy to cultivate an established local South Korean brand into a global brand.

Lost in Translation

While the previous four campaigns illustrate home runs, you will never be able to completely avoid missteps. Life happens. However, when trying to adapt a global brand or concept to local markets, do your homework. We close with four examples to illustrate the importance of due diligence.

The combination of General Electric and Plessey Telecommunications created the initials GPT. Not a problem in most countries, but in France, pronouncing them sounds like *j'ai pété,* which can be translated as "I farted."

When Coca-Cola introduced their brand to China in the 1920s, over 200 characters could have been used to depict words that sounded like *Coca* and *Cola.* So, without a corporate standard, shop owners created their own signs. Shoppers ordering a Coke could ask to "bite the wax tadpole," sip a "wax flattened mare," or enjoy a refreshing "female horse fastened with wax." Coke finally changed the name to something that sounds like "ko-kou-ko-le," which literally means "to allow the mouth to be able to rejoice." In short, *it tastes good*—at least better than a wax tadpole.

Coke's rival, Pepsi, also had a challenge in Taiwan. Years ago, their international slogan was "Come Alive. It's the Pepsi Generation." Somewhere in translation, the meaning was changed to "Pepsi brings your dead ancestors back to life." Now that's a pretty bold claim.

Finally, Kraft recently named a new snack food, to be launched in Central Europe, "Mondelez." The name was a mashup of terms: *monde* to evoke the idea of "world" and *delez* to convey "delicious." Kraft claimed it had vetted the new name across 28 languages, including Russian. However, to Russian speakers "Mondelez" sounds an awful lot like an oral sex act. The new name lasted two days. Day one, it hit the digital world via *Advertising Age*, went viral, and got trashed. Day two, it got pulled.[52]

Table 5.1 will help organize your creative strategies for global and regional brands.

TABLE 5.1   Global/Regional

Horizontal Strategies	Global	Regional
Positioning	Similar in all markets	Adapted for specific markets
Marketing environment	Similar distribution, price position, product use, legal and cultural conditions	Different types of distribution, varying legal and cultural conditions
Target audience	Similar in each market	Different segments in various markets, localized and highly segmented by income, geography, and social status
Vertical Strategies	**Global**	**Regional**
Creative development	Same slogan, look, and feel in all markets	Variations in themes, appeal, and execution of creative elements tailored to each market
Media selection	Basically the same in all markets with slight variations	Highly localized due to widely variable cultural and technological differences
MarCom tools	Same basic strategies and tactics in most markets	Highly variable based on legal, cultural, and technology conditions

Good-bye, До свидания, and *Adiós*

Whatever your strategy, whatever your brand, as the globe grows smaller with technology bringing us closer together, culture context still matters. Perhaps, more than ever. Be a wise advertiser. Do your homework. Always consider culture. And remember, your brand is a global citizen. If you do the legwork, you just might find the right strategy, hit the right tone, and discover success in the global marketplace.

Who's Who?

Ross Chowles—Ross Chowles is the cofounder and executive creative director of The Jupiter Drawing Room in Cape Town, South Africa. Throughout his stellar career Chowles has mentored generations of young professionals. He's the brain behind "The Ripple Effect," an educational initiative for young people, which he launched in 2004. He has judged shows in New York, France, Canada, and Namibia. He's also won a lot of awards along the way. When not mentoring young creatives or shepherding brands into the marketplace, Chowles finds time to paint portraits of people who have touched his life.[53]

Renata Florio—A Brazilian writer at heart, Renata Florio recently moved to New York as chief creative officer for Wing, Grey Global's Hispanic agency. Florio, from São Paulo, has worked at F/Nazca Saatchi & Saatchi, AlmapBBDO, and DM9DDB, three of Brazil's most creative shops. She has worked extensively with Procter & Gamble over the years and has won eight Cannes Lions for her work in Brazil.[54]

Richard Stainer—A 37-year-old triathlete, Richard Stainer grew up near Belfast. Always one to push himself, he told his mother, at age 5, that he would attend Cambridge. He did, earning a degree in modern and medieval languages. Not long ago he was the managing partner at Bartle Bogle Hegarty, heading up the global Google account, the shop's second largest after Unilever. That led to a move to BBH, New York. Stainer is the perfect example of a truly global advertising executive.

Juan Tan—A native of Malaysia, Juan Tan is creative director at The Brand Union, China. He splits his time between Beijing and Shanghai and takes the lead on a multitude of Unilever brands. Prior to joining The Brand Union, Tan was creative director at TBWA\TEQUILA\China and TBWA\Creativejuice. There his clients included Chivas, Absolut, Adidas, Häagen-Dazs, and Virgin Mobile. In the summer of 2012, he hosted the first-ever Creative Counsel Asia in Shanghai.[55]

Exercises

1. Global Stretching

How far can you take one brand?

- Pick five countries, each from different geographic areas. Then select a brand that does not have a large global footprint.

- Now, generate a list of at least 10 cultural markers for each country.

- Next, find the current tagline and reshape that tagline for each individual country. Explain your rationale for the changes you made or did not make.

2. Cultural Packaging

This exercise will challenge you to think about cultural norms.

- Bring in a consumer packaged good (CPG). As a class, pick one CPG to work with.

- Select a country from one of the BRIC or MIST nations.

- Working in teams, consider the culture of the chosen country, and develop the top three claims that you would highlight on the package. Remember the need for these to be crafted in a way that makes cultural sense (language aside), and be ready to defend why you chose your three claims.

- Next, reconsider the packaging. Beside language, what would you change to make the packaging more culturally resonant?

- If you want to extend this beyond the class, jump online and see if you can find the product, or products within the same category, in the country you were working with. Then discuss how close you came to nailing the cultural nuances.

3. Messaging Across Cultures

This time we are challenging you to see how messaging changes across cultures, or doesn't.

- Using the CPGs from the last exercise, pick another one to work with.

- Make a list of countries and put them in a hat. (Each student draws one.)

- Working in teams, brainstorm thumbnails for a print ad and a social media tactic for the country you drew.

- Finally, pick your best ideas, one ad and one social media tactic, and share it with the class. Try to articulate why, from a cultural point of view, your tactics had resonance and why they worked together.

- Once the whole class has shared, look for cultural commonalities across all tactics. That will say a lot about the strength of the brand. Look for variances that will highlight cultural differences.

Visit www.sagepub.com/altstiel3e to access these additional learning tools

- Video Links
- Web Resources
- eFlashcards
- Web Quizzes

Chapter

6

Concepting

What's the Big Idea?

The word *concepting* usually trips up spell checkers. Usually they try to replace it with *conception.* We suppose in many ways it's similar to creating new life. Another way to say it is "ideation" and "the creative process." In this book, we'll define concepting as the development of the Big Idea. If you have a central thought, that One Thing you can say about the product, how do you say it, and how do you show it? Concepting is the bridge between strategy and tactics, taking you from gathering facts and getting organized to creating words and pictures. At this stage in your career, you don't have to be a great writer or an accomplished art director. But you should start working on becoming a great idea person.

How to Be Creative (Concepting Strategies)

You can find many theories and recommendations on how to be creative. However, it's not a nice, neat, linear process. That killer idea may pop up in the shower. On the drive into work. When you're watching TV. Or in a dream. No one can tell you when and how to think it. Concepting a single ad or a whole campaign is like making sausage. The end result can be delicious, but the outside world doesn't want to see how it's done.

While there is no single process that works for everyone, most people rely on two basic methods:

1. Adapt the strategy to the creative.

2. Make the creative fit the strategy.

Working Backward: There's Got to Be a Strategy in There Somewhere

We've all done it. In a sudden fit of inspiration, you come up with a great headline or find a really cool photo. Now, how can you use it? There's got to be

Words of Wisdom

"Too many young creative teams today . . . look at pedestrian television and print and say, 'Hey, I could do that crap.' Then they get into the business and they do that crap."[1]

Helayne Spivak, CEO, HRS Consulting, and former global creative director for JWT some client this will work for. Maybe it's so great it doesn't matter if it solves the client's problem. Any of that annoying problem-solving stuff can be handled in the body copy. Heck, you can throw in a subhead to explain it. After it's done, you can always go back and rationalize a strategy. Who knows? It might even be on target when you work backwards.

This approach is usually used in the following scenarios:

- Pitching new business: "We don't know much about your product, but we can do wacky stuff."

- Portfolio padding: "The ad looks great, and no one will know if it really didn't sell anything."

- Awards competition: See above.

- Advertising class work: "This was the only decent picture I could find, so I had to build my ad around it."

This ad from China's top refrigerator brand, running in New Zealand, would appeal to most guys anywhere in the world. It's a fresh approach to the old "stylish but affordable" story.

Concepting by the Book

Great concepts begin with great strategy and great research. Garbage in, garbage out. Before you start scribbling, make sure you have the answers to the following questions:

- What is the client's real problem?
- Can I solve the problem creatively with marketing communications?
- Do I know the target audience?
- Do I understand and respect the particular cultural nuances of the target?
- Do I know how they feel about my product?
- Do I know the product features/benefits?
- What is the One Thing I can say or show about this product?
- How much do I need to say or show? Do I even need a headline?
- Where is this product positioned? Where do we want to be positioned?
- Do I know the competition's strengths and weaknesses?
- What should the tone be?

Depending on the product and target audience, some of the answers to the above questions may be "not applicable." For a mature packaged good, such as deodorant, you really don't need an in-depth analysis. But you do need to understand the target audience and find the right tone to reach them.

War Story

In Service of Story

When I went to advertising school, everyone was in search of the brilliant play between words and pictures. The Minneapolis "school" had defined creativity in the annuals with clever headline-visual combinations such as this ad concept for an Alfred Hitchcock film festival: visual—birds on a telephone wire; headline—something about "cast of thousands." Obviously, my recall is spotty, but it was clever, and I distinctly remember thinking: My mind doesn't work like that. How am I going to have a career in this business?

Enter Ron Seichrist, then head of the school I attended, with the following assignment: "Do a bank campaign. But no puns. Base your executions on a personal life experience instead." We came back with a rush of melodramatic, gauzy, tear-jerking stories linked to loans and interest rates. They were bad. But his point—and it was brilliant, even courageous, at the time—was to demonstrate that creative selling could and should be rooted in what I'll call the deepest common denominator: story. Shortly after, John Hancock rocked the advertising world. Wieden + Kennedy wrote "Just do it." The dam had been blessedly smashed to smithereens. And I'd been set free.

Lots of brand work still functions in the old way, muscling toward impact with sheer wit and graphic strength. And art school portfolios are full of this fare, often in threes (the assumption being that three ideas that hang together make a campaign). Wrong. It's not deep and/or wide enough for the needs of brands today to attract and engage audiences over a wide range of media, most notably social media. "Social," after all, means just what it says: having to do with the emotional transactions that take place between human beings at all levels of society and quotidian activity. A pun, or three, isn't going to cut it.

I'm not saying that well-crafted language and visuals don't have a place. I'm saying they're not hefty enough to sit at the core—feeding tens, maybe hundreds, of related executions—of a brand. There's got to be a story. There's got to be shared human experience. There's got to be an observation about existence that—whether witty or serious—gives life and impetus to ongoing, open-ended communication. And "story" doesn't necessarily mean "words." It means narrative in the abstract sense and/or framework for viewing existence. So it can drive both visual and verbal content, both work of duration (film) and the occasional, necessary one-off.

Further, compelling stories have been addicting us since the beginning of the written word. (This is where Shakespeare and the Bible should ring a bell.) Technologies and executional styles will inevitably and relentlessly evolve, but they will never provide, in and of themselves, sustaining ideas any more than the puns of yesterday did. The trick is to learn to use them *in the service of story—the human story*—because that will never fade away.[3]

Charlotte Moore, creative director/ communications consultant, Milan, Italy, @ctwitmo

Concepting Approaches

As we mentioned, developing creative ideas is not a neat, orderly process. Many texts will provide formulas for concepts, which usually work great to describe a completed ad, but don't help to develop a new one. At the risk of falling into the same trap, we offer several simplified approaches to concepting.

1. Show the product: Establish or reinforce brand identity. Period.

2. Show the benefit: What happens when you use it? What does it do for you?

3. Show the alternative: What happens when you don't use it—or use the competition?

4. Comparison: Compare it to other products or present it as a metaphor.

5. Borrowed interest: Introduce something seemingly unrelated.

6. Testimonial/case history: Provide an endorsement or description of what it's done for someone else. It could be a celebrity or an ordinary person.

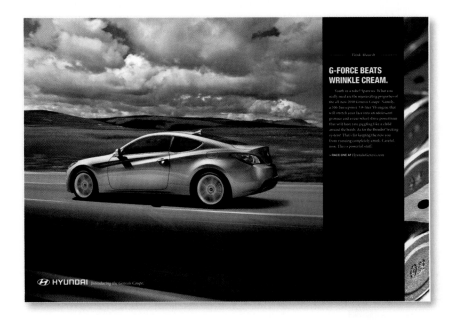

The benefit? Driving fast makes you feel young. Hyundai's improvement in quality and styling is reflected in their more sophisticated advertising efforts. They also do a good job of showing the product.

Show the Product

It sounds boring, but some of the most innovative ads just show the product or logo. The benefit may be buried in the copy, implied in a tagline, or missing entirely. The main purpose is to establish a brand image or reinforce that image. For example, with most packaged goods, it's probably better to show the package or label rather than describe it in a headline. After all, it's what the consumer sees on the grocery store shelf. Sometimes you can set up a concept in a modified question-and-answer format, where the question (or problem) is stated and the product/package/logo is the answer (solution).

Show the Benefit

In many cases this involves a straightforward declarative sentence proclaiming the main benefit. Usually the reader does not have to think too hard to get the concept. Sometimes this is the first thing you think of. From here you move on to more creative approaches. However, it may be exactly what's

Amazon didn't even have to mention the iPad. They just had to match the capabilities and cut the price. Anyone interested in a tablet (except a die-hard Apple fanatic) would have to take a second look at this alternative.

Instead of comparing their soup to the competitor's (remember number one never mentions number two or three), Campbell's compared their hearty 130-calorie soup to a less-than-satisfying 130-calorie slice of ham and cheese wrap.

Showing the alternative: "If you don't have time to get a mammogram, how will you fit six months of chemotherapy into your schedule?" This simple question clearly outlines the choices a woman can make.

required, especially if you can pair your straightforward headline with a compelling, attention-getting graphic. For a soft drink, for example, you may not have any headline, but you show the can or bottle and people having fun. The benefit is implied—your product is connected with good times.

Show the Alternative

This can be a lot of fun. One extreme example is a campaign for Terminix that shows outrageous ways people keep insects out of their homes—turning their living rooms into an ice-covered deep freeze, for one. That's a lot more interesting than showing a clean, bug-free house.

When you go back to basic wants and needs of the target audience, it becomes easier to visualize the alternative concept. In most cases, you think of the opposite of basic wants and needs—hunger, thirst, embarrassment, loneliness, illness, pain, and so on. You can probably think of several extreme images for each of these that are far more interesting than their positive counterparts.

Comparison

You can compare your product to a competitor or, by using a metaphor, compare it to just about anything.

Competitive/comparison concepts: When you go head-to-head against the competition, keep these factors in mind:

> If you are the market leader, don't compare yourself to number two.

> When you compare product claims, make sure you are correct.

A few examples:

Avis claimed they were number two, so they had to try harder than Hertz to win your business. 7Up (the Uncola) was crisp, clear, and citrus-based versus brown cola nut sodas. Both claims were true. Both claims were made by a competitor hoping to gain market share from the leader.

Pepsi has always been runner-up to Coke and from time to time has pursued a very aggressive series of campaigns that involved taste tests, celebrity talent, catchy jingles, cutting-edge concepts, elaborate sales promotions, and take-no-prisoners marketing tactics. While Pepsi has won the hearts and minds of ad critics with their creativity, they are still number two—probably because the consumer still can't perceive a real difference between Pepsi and Coke. Other direct comparisons have pitted Subway sandwiches against their high-calorie rivals from McDonald's and Burger King.

In the above examples, the rival products are basically the same price, except one is presented as superior. Other comparisons involve comparing a lower-priced product to a higher-priced premium brand. For example, the Hyundai Equus has been compared to BMW and Mercedes-Benz in quality, luxury, and performance, even though it costs thousands less. While all that is true, many people buy established luxury brands for the emotional satisfaction the brand provides rather than the actual product features.

Here are some tips for comparison advertising:

1. Try to make sure that your claims are as factually bulletproof as possible.

2. Try to collect hard evidence in advance to support your factual assertions (your lawyer will thank you).

3. Consider the risk–reward ratio—how much incremental benefit will you get from making the specific comparison, versus how much additional risk you court by doing so.

4. Consider including a footnote with additional factual data, perhaps including (a) the applicable version numbers of the products in question and (b) the date of your data.[4]

How do you show the product and position it as a shoe for real or wannabe sailors? This student chose a simple concept that would work well in magazine ads, posters, or billboards.

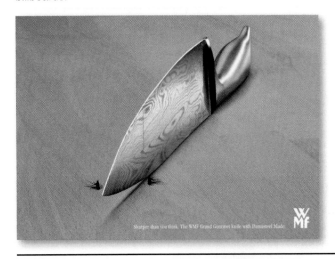

Imagine a knife so sharp that when a fly lands on it . . . you get the picture.

If you're looking for a really hot SUV, how about the Porsche Cayenne? This dealer chose to sell the sizzle rather than showing the car.

Metaphors

Favorites of English teachers and awards judges. Since grade school, you've been instructed to use metaphors to spice up your compositions. Use what you know about metaphors and apply them visually to your ad concepts. Visual

This student-designed visual puzzle says Oxydol gets any smell out of clothes. Look closely and you'll see the "skunk" is actually a pile of dirty clothes.

metaphors can be very direct, such as a grumpy bear morphing into a normal-looking guy after his first cup of coffee in the morning. Or they can be more subtle. Some are very obscure and require a few mental leaps to connect the visual with a product. Sometimes readers appreciate the minor challenge of making that connection themselves. They know the advertiser gives them some credit for having a brain.

Judging by recent awards programs, the greater the distance from visual to benefit or brand value, the higher the ranking, especially if you dispense with headlines or copy to sell anything. Even though you may lose many readers with obscure visual puzzles, sometimes you'll really hook the committed few who take time to study and understand your ads. You need to know if enough members of your target audience can solve your visual puzzle (unless your only goal is to pad your portfolio).

Rather than make excuses, these athletes set records. This bold photo conveys the courage and determination of Canadian paralympians.

Borrowed Interest

Sometimes you can use something seemingly unrelated to make a point. Like the visual puzzle, using borrowed interest relies on the visual for the bulk of the message, but unlike a metaphor, there's no obvious direct connection to the product name or benefit. Usually this approach involves some kind of attention-getting graphic and/or headline that snags the reader. Once they're hooked, the body copy reels 'em in. Sometimes, the only objective is brand recognition, and no copy is needed. Some texts call this the "indirect approach" versus a direct benefit. Whatever you call it, it can work very well as long as the reader gets your intended message and remembers the brand favorably.

Rising Star

Truth or Legend

I don't like talking about myself. Writing this is killing me. It's funny—with advertising it's all about selling. But when it comes to selling myself it's much more complicated.

So, how did I get here? It wasn't planned. I was good at drawing. I thought maybe I could make a living drawing. So, I studied advertising graphic design. That led me to advertising. Thanks to one of my teachers I started as an intern at a local advertising agency. It's pretty hard to get into advertising in Lima. But, once you're in and you're known, everything runs pretty smoothly.

I like my career because I like to think. Advertising makes me more imaginative and, at some levels, more free, less ignorant. A lot of creatives think being creative gives them the right to feel special and different, while I think a true creative does not label himself as such. It certainly doesn't determine who I am.

I'm an introvert by nature. I like my loneliness and to live it. One of the phrases that defines me well is "Why to live in the world when you can live in your mind?" Advertising lets me do that.

But still, nothing should last forever. I believe the Dadaists were right: To grow it is necessary to destroy. Like the founders of Sarah Records, an independent record label, wrote on their goodbye letter, "The first act of the revolution is destruction and the first thing to destroy is the past." It's no surprise that I haven't lasted more than two years at an agency with the exception of Leo Burnett, where the challenges kept me a bit longer. Even so, eventually it was time to move on. Now I'm working at Young & Rubicam, Lima.

I don't know what I'll be doing 10 years from now. I don't have it planned. I just know that now I'm walking. Maybe later I'll start running. Who knows? Whatever you do, don't take my story too seriously. Like John Ford, an English playwright and poet, said, "If you have to choose between the truth and the legend, publish the legend."[6]

Pablo Castillo, copywriter, Young & Rubicam, Lima, Peru, yr.com

How do you show some really jumbo peanuts? Ogilvy & Mather in Indonesia didn't choke on the challenge.

This visual metaphor clearly articulates the product benefit, making a very bold claim.

Testimonials/Case Histories

Years ago celebrities not only allowed products to attach a name to their fame; they actively pitched the product. Today, testimonials, celebrity and otherwise, are still a popular concept. To be effective, they must have credibility—sort of like an editorial feature.

The Concepting Process

Now comes the fun part. Time is running out. Your assignment is due tomorrow morning. You're still sitting in front of a pile of white paper, and your mind is as blank as the first sheet on the stack.

Say It Straight, Then Say It Great

If you're not blessed with a sudden bolt of creativity, how do you get started? One of the best pieces of advice comes from Luke Sullivan. "Say it straight, then say it great."[7] In other words, try a straightforward approach just to get the facts organized and trigger more ideas. You can start with "This ad is about. . . ." Then you can toss that and move on to a more creative way to say it and show it.

This is also a great way to test the strategy internally. Work up a number of straightforward concepts that look like ads. Then review them with the account team. The objective is to get the group to say, "Yeah. That's the main idea. Now how do we make it better?" This not only makes for better concepts; it helps build good relationships with your team. Take their input, and then really go to work to do something great.

You may want to start scribbling down product features or other attributes of a product and keep asking, "So what?" Those questions may lead to something that's interesting.

Brainstorming

Here's the recipe for a great concept: Combine two creative people, preferably a writer and an art director; add stacks of blank paper, Sharpies, pencils, and layout pads; mix in copies of *CA*, stock photo books, and popular magazines; turn up the heat with tight deadlines and client demands; let it simmer or boil over occasionally; if cooking process takes longer, add pizza, junk food, and beer; allow thoughts to cook until a number of rough ideas develop or one of the creative people has killed the other.

From our experience, we've found brainstorming works best with two people. Usually, the dynamic duo is the copywriter–art director team. But it may be two writers or two art directors. Or an art director–illustrator or writer–producer team. Sometimes a third or fourth party gets involved, but it's usually better to bring in those people to validate ideas rather than develop them.

Creating by committee is usually a bad idea, especially if a client is involved in the early process. Sometimes a creative team needs to really rip on the product or brand to get the silliness out of the way and/or really address some marketing problems. That's hard to do with a client in the same room. It's always better to ask a client, "What do you think of this idea?" instead of "What do you think we should do?" The process often isn't pretty. Most times you really don't want to know how it's done as long as the finished product turns out great.

Idea Starters

Sometimes you don't have the luxury of brainstorming with another creative person. Your only companion is a blank sheet of paper, mocking every lame idea that pops into your fevered brain.

In this case, don't wait for the perfect concept to develop. Just start scribbling. Write down anything. Even the stupid stuff. Jot down key words. Doodle different visuals. Write out headlines or taglines. Just keep working and eventually you'll have a stack of ideas. Most of them will be junk. But there just may be a few keepers. Show these to the art director. He or she may be able to work some magic. Or he or she may twist your idea into one that's even better.

This student-created billboard tied two Chicago traditions together in one eye-catching design.

Driving drunk in Canada has the same serious consequences as this Campaign Against Drinking and Driving ad shows.

Words of Wisdom

"Account executives often have big creative ideas, regardless of what some writers think."[9]

Leo Burnett,
founder, Leo Burnett

This student used white space inside and around his main visual to make a dramatic point about memory loss.

In Europe convertibles are called cabriolets. So when you want to take the top down on a VW Beetle, here's a simple way to show it.

Ten Tips for Better Concepts

Through years of trial and error (more of the latter) we've developed a few recommendations for developing creative ideas.

1. **Just do it:** Scribble down everything. Key words. Sketches. Stick people. At this stage, there are no stupid ideas. One key word or visual could trigger an entire award-winning campaign.

2. **Write, don't talk:** Keep scribbling. If something works, then describe it to your partner. If you can't explain it in a few well-chosen words, go back to scribbling.

3. **Throw it all on the wall and see what sticks:** Tack your ideas on a wall and stare at them for a while. If you have the luxury of time, come back the next day and see if they still look good. Invite a couple other people to look at them and ask for feedback.

4. **If you're on a roll, don't stop:** Once the creative juices get flowing, keep tossing out ideas. If you're lucky, you and your partner will get on a streak and not only come up with a killer theme, but enough concepts for a whole campaign.

5. **Does this look funny?** During your concept development you'll come up with a lot of silly ideas. Some may make you fall down laughing, either because they're so funny or because you're totally sleep deprived. Humor is a powerful force, so if your idea still makes you and others chuckle a couple days later, find some way to use it. With that said, don't set out to be funny. Try to be interesting.

6. **Show it, don't tell it:** One picture may be worth a thousand sales. Find an image that grabs a reader. Then develop a tagline or headline that works in synergy with that image, rather than just describing it. Luke Sullivan says, "Try to solve the problems visually if you can. As larger brands become globally marketed, visual solutions will become even more important. Visuals translate better than words."[10]

7. **Don't be different just to be different:** To paraphrase Bill Bernbach, don't show a man standing on his head unless the ad sells something to keep things in his pockets. Sometimes an art director will go crazy with backgrounds, weird typography, and other bells and whistles that satisfy his or her creative muse. But if they don't add anything to the concept, don't do it.

8. **Keep it simple:** Don't lose sight of the main idea. You've got the concept burned in your brain, but does a casual reader get it? If not, adding subheads to explain the idea or cramming in extra inset photos won't help. Simple ideas break through the clutter, they are easier to remember. and sometimes they clarify the strategy.

9. **Don't second-guess the client:** Develop concepts that get attention and sell the product. Then worry about selling them to the client. Don't handcuff your creativity by worrying about what the client will like before you begin. The client hired you to be creative. Otherwise, they'd be doing their own ads.

10. **Build a "maybe" file:** Most of your ideas won't work, but don't throw them all away. File the better ones. They may be the answer for the next assignment. Keep a file of the scrap-stock photos, competitor ads, articles, and other stuff that trigger some great ideas.

Concept Testing

You should test your concepts at three stages, starting with yourself.

Self-evaluation

You've narrowed your stack of rough ideas down to a single concept that you love. But before you start asking the creative director for a raise, make sure you do a little internal evaluation of your ideas.

Level 1: Gut check. The first level of testing begins with you. Ask yourself, does this concept feel right? If you have the luxury of time, put it aside for a few days and ask the same question. This means don't start thinking about it the night before it's due.

Level 2: Two quick tests. The first is the "matchbook test." Can you put your idea on the cover of a matchbook and still convey the One Thing about your product? Another quick test is the "billboard test." If you have written copy and laid out the ad, cover up the body copy so you only see the headline and main graphic. Would it make a good billboard? If so, your creative idea communicates quickly and effectively. If not, maybe you need to come up with some new ideas.

Level 3: Honest evaluation. Your idea looks good and feels good. But it still has to meet some objectives. Remember strategy? So before you fall in love with your idea, ask yourself . . .

- **Is this concept doable?** Can you pull this off within the budget constraints? Can you execute it correctly? Do you have the talent? Props? Locations? All the other things required that make this idea work?

- **Is it on target for this audience?** You love it, but will the intended buyer? You might want to try it out on a few people in the target audience . . . but don't rule it out if all of them don't get it.

Words of Wisdom

"I just see so many wacky creative things that come out of young creatives . . . You can solve these practical issues in very creative ways. BUT there has to be a link back to the product issue. As David Ogilvy said: We sell or else."[11]

Maureen Shirreff,
senior partner, global
executive creative director,
Ogilvy Worldwide

- **Does it have legs?** Will this idea work in an extended campaign? Is it a one-hit wonder, or can you expand this concept for use in other media?

- **Can you sell this to the client?** Is this idea so far out of the box the client will have a heart attack? Can you justify this concept with sound logic?

Level 4: Consumer interplay. OK, you're confident your idea is on strategy. You're not in love with it, though you love it. Now the questions are: Will consumers love it—or not? And, how will they interact with it? You want consumer interaction; you don't want consumer control. This is your baby.

- **Why will they love it?** OK, you've tried it out on a few people, so now probe deeper. Why do they love it? What specially resonates with them? How can you take their reactions and extend them?

- **Once they fall in love—or not—what will they do?** This is the deal killer in today's media world, where consumers exert a lot of control. How will they interact with it? Will your ads become viral? Are they ripe for parody? If so, do you have a plan for how to leverage consumer-generated media? Do you have a plan to address possible negative reactions across social media?

Creative Director/Account Executive Evaluation

The creative director and account executive will also quickly run through the self-evaluation process listed above. They will also apply a higher standard of evaluation that includes the following questions:

- Will the client buy it, and if so, will they love it (and the people who sold it to them)?

- Does the work represent the best of this agency?

- Can we win some awards with this?

- And in some shops, if the idea is really great, how can I get credit for it?

Client Evaluation

Clients are fond of telling their agencies to think outside the box. What is this "box" anyway? Typically, clients confine the box to features and benefits. Some engineering-oriented companies think in terms of specifications. Marketing-driven companies think in terms of solving problems for customers. Your box should be much larger. Once you start working within your bigger box, look for ways to step outside of it. It's always better to have a bunch of crazy ideas you can pull back into the box than having the client tell you to be more creative.

Benetton has always pushed the envelope of good taste to promote their brand. This was part of a series of "Unhate" ads showing some Photoshopped (we hope) affection between some unlikely lovers.

Do the Twist

Not to be confused with a dance from the '60s, a twist is an unexpected element of an ad or a commercial. A TV commercial for Jimmy John's featured a fun twist. In a gritty and very intense bank robbery, all the bank customers were ordered to lay flat on the floor. One heroic hostage secretly pulls out his cell phone and calls, you guessed it, Jimmy John's to deliver lunch. You never saw it coming. Here's another TV twist: A prosperous-looking retired couple relaxes on their sailboat in the Caribbean. It looks like an ad for a mutual fund or insurance company. The twist? It's actually a commercial about paper shredders. It seems that this sweet old couple stole your credit card number, and they're now living the high life because you didn't shred your credit card receipts.

Finding the Edge

It's starting to become a cliché, but people are still looking for an edge—some kind of creative device to separate their advertising from the rest of the pack. "Edgy" ads take risks. They may push the envelope (another overused term) to the breaking point. In summary, creatives who work on the edge:

- Risk offending general audience to appeal to target audience.

- Shock the reader/viewer into noticing.

- Drive a wedge between "our customers" and everyone else (us vs. them).

Going for the edge may seem like the perfect approach. If you are willing to offend or confuse a large share of the total audience to make a stronger connection to a highly defined target audience, it might be OK. However, never forget the risks of pushing the envelope too far. Before you cross that line, you should review Chapters 2 and 5 and reconsider.

Does Sex Sell?

We see sexual content everywhere in advertising. A study in *Advertising & Society Review* found that 20% of all magazine and web ads and about 10% of TV ads involved sexual images.[14] Before you take this route, keep your target audience in mind. If you assume men are the intended audience for images of scantily clad women, don't forget that their wives and girlfriends influence most of the purchases for the home, including beer and cologne. Of course, there are exceptions. In 2005, Go Daddy's Super Bowl commercial showed a "wardrobe malfunction" of a busty model. The network pulled the second ad scheduled for the broadcast. Results: Go Daddy was reimbursed for the cost of the second ad and received an estimated $11 million in free publicity, and their market share jumped from 16% to 25%. Since then, they've continued to create sophomoric sexualized campaigns and now control 53% of the market.[15] If you try to emulate Go Daddy's model, you might not be as lucky. A 2001 study sponsored by

Words of Wisdom

"Advertising needs to have a bit of an edge, whether it's aimed at the neighborhood or the world."[13]

Phil Dusenberry,
copywriter and former
chairman, BBDO

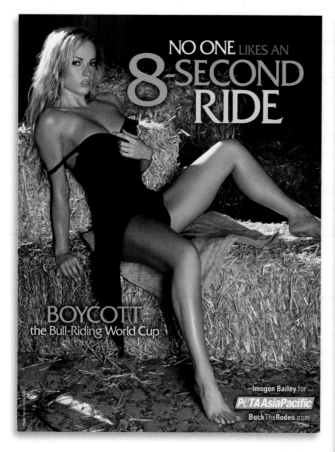

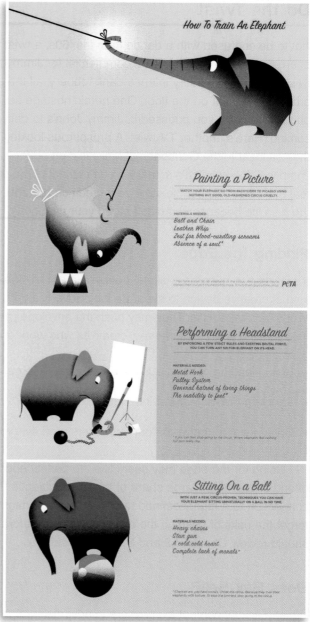

PETA feels they need to get your attention before they can tell their story. Their approach on the right takes a totally different route by mentioning the cruel training practices used for circus elephants. Which concept do you think is more effective in telling the PETA story?

American Demographics found that 61% of respondents who viewed sexualized ads were less likely to buy.[16] Our advice: Develop concepts that focus on the consumer's brain or heart instead of other body parts.

Before You Get Edgy

- Understand the tolerances of the total audience.
- Really understand how far you can push your target audience.
- Consider the risks (legal, ethical, business).
- Check your personal moral compass. Are you proud of the work?

- Be able to defend your idea logically, not just because you think it's cool.
- Have a backup idea.
- Don't try to be different just to be different.
- Get paid before the client goes bankrupt.

Children of parents who smoke, get to heaven earlier.

A number of public service announcements have targeted the effects of secondhand smoking, but few are this compelling. This one states, "Children of parents who smoke get to heaven earlier."

What to Do When You're Stuck

Everybody develops writer's block. Sometimes the slump lasts a few hours; sometimes it lasts a lot longer. Novelists have the option of waiting weeks and months for inspiration. Copywriters don't. So what happens when that blank sheet of paper becomes your worst enemy? We offer the following suggestions:

- **Back up:** Find out where you are, and you might know why you're stuck. Do you understand the product, the market, the target audience, the competition, and the tone? Did you miss something? Do you have enough information to "say it straight"? If so, you are very close to finding ways to "say it great."

- **Go back to the books:** Dig out the old issues of *Communication Arts* and *CMYK*. Check out new websites that feature award winners. Leaf through the stock photo books.

- **Talk about it:** Find a sympathetic ear and state your problem. Don't ask for ideas. Just explain what you know about the assignment and where you're stuck. You might find that by explaining it out loud, you'll find the solution yourself. Sometimes you'll mention an idea that seems kind of lame to you and another person loves it. They might give you just enough encouragement to turn it into a great idea.

Words of Wisdom

"Comfort the afflicted. Afflict the comfortable."[17]

Carl Ally, copywriter and founding partner, Ally & Gargano

So many things are potentially offensive about this ad, we won't state the obvious. The creative team, agency management, and ultimately the client must have decided it was worth the risk. We should add that this was created for a BK franchise and does not reflect the corporate ad standards.

Words of Wisdom

"Rarely have I seen any really good advertising created without a certain amount of confusion, throw-aways, bent noses, irritation and downright cursedness."[18]

Leo Burnett, copywriter and founder, Leo Burnett

- **Take a break:** See a movie. Watch TV. Play basketball. Dig in your garden. Do something totally unrelated to work. This will unclog your mind and may allow some fresh ideas to sneak in. Taking a break is fine, but don't let it extend to an hour before your assignment is due.

Crowdsourcing: Curse or Salvation?

Crowdsourcing, or using social media to solicit creative concepts, is really no more than outsourcing tasks, which clients and agencies have done forever, but the potential list of vendors has grown exponentially thanks to the Internet. Remember the old rule of thumb? Good, fast, cheap—pick two. It still applies to crowdsourcing. While crowdsourcing a client's marketing efforts may be cheap and fast, the goodness is questionable. Unexpected time to manage the project and hidden costs add up.

Crowdsourcing may cost a few hundred dollars per idea, but it can end up costing a company much, much more in the long run. Harley-Davidson, a brand that had been tended with precision by Carmichael Lynch for over 20 years, recently pulled its advertising in-house, ready for a full embrace of crowdsourcing. The thought behind the move was that the advertising had become too familiar, that it spoke only to the devotees. Ironically, the move to crowdsourcing only took the brand deeper into devotee territory. In their rush to embrace crowdsourcing the marketing team walked away from "the ride." Time will tell, but our money's on the ride.

Then there is the issue of copyright violations, something a company does not want to risk. Many creatives reproduce similar designs for different companies, or simply steal existing work of established companies. According to the fine print, they deny liability if there are problems. Many designers are from China, India, Serbia, or developing nations. Sound a bit like an offshore sweatshop? It can be.

Crowdsourcing opens a lot of new opportunities for freelancers. However, the competition may become a lot tougher, which tends to drive down the price and reduce the odds of success. For the client, it can mean a lot more creative ideas from which to choose, assuming someone is qualified to check for copyright infringement and other traps. To an agency that has established a long history with a client as a trusted marketing partner, it's a slap in the face. Crowdsourcing, in its purest form, turns ideas into commodities sold at the lowest price possible.

LIVE CAGE FREE

DISCOVER A NEW KIND OF FREEDOM WITH THOUSANDS OF TEST RIDE OPPORTUNITIES.

*Harley-Davidson's latest campaign touts the crowdsourced tagline "No Cages."
Unfortunately, to understand the tagline you have to be a motorcycle rider. So much for
extending their brand beyond devotees.*

Who's Who?

Carl Ally—Cofounder of Ally & Gargano, Carl Ally is known for cutting-edge and risky advertising that spoke very bold truths. Some of his breakthrough advertising included work for FedEx, Hertz, Dunkin' Donuts, Volvo, Fiat, Saab, MCI Communications, Polaroid, IBM, Pan Am, Piper Aircraft, and several others. He was the man responsible for winning a change in television rules against mentioning the competition in commercials. He was not afraid to take on corporate underdogs, and he changed many unknown companies into household names. He enjoyed taking on accounts that were new or troubled, and he built brands up from almost nothing.[20]

Philip Dusenberry—Philip Dusenberry joined BBDO as a copywriter in 1962 and developed into one of the world's most influential creative forces as he rose to vice chairman at BBDO Worldwide. His impact came chiefly from memorable General Electric and Pepsi-Cola campaigns (including a megamillion-dollar deal with Michael Jackson). Dusenberry also played a major role with advertising's volunteer Tuesday Team, whose "Morning in America" commercials helped reelect Ronald Reagan. As a screenwriter, Dusenberry's credits include *The Natural,* starring Robert Redford.

Charlotte Moore—Born in Chattanooga, Tennessee, and educated in Virginia, Southerner Charlotte Moore found a spiritual and professional home on the West Coast when she began to work for the creative hot shop Wieden + Kennedy (W+K). Over the course of almost eight years, she worked as art director and, eventually, group creative director on accounts including Nike, Microsoft, and Coke. She left the agency in the fall of 1995 but returned as co–creative director of their European headquarters in Amsterdam. Agency ambition was interrupted by love, however, and she followed her heart to Italy where she currently lives with her husband and children. She still works with W+K copywriting partner Janet Champ pursuing creative projects sometimes for money, but more often for personal reasons. Her work has been recognized by *CA,* One Show, and *McCall's* Advertising Women of the Year, and has received four nominations and two back-to-back wins in the MPA's Kelly Awards for best, most effective print advertising.

Millie Olson—Millie Olson is the cofounder and CEO of Amazon Advertising in San Francisco. Olson began her career in Chicago working at N. W. Ayer, DDB Needham, and J. Walter Thompson. She was recruited to Ketchum's San Francisco office, where she spent over a decade, winning numerous awards along the way. Olson cofounded Amazon based on the belief that ideas are sustained by human truths and that strategies should feel like stories waiting to be told. Amazon's client roster includes Kashi, Canon, Philips, and Procter & Gamble's Naturella and Always brands. In March 2009 Olsen was named "Ad Person of the Year" by the San Francisco Ad Club.[21]

Exercises

1. Failing Fast Is Fun

(Contributed by Jeff Ericksen, instructor and founder, Master Ericman's Portfolio School for Mischievous Young Men and Women)

Whether it's an advertising copywriter struggling to nail that one perfect headline or a software developer searching for the next killer app, there can be a method to the madness of creation. We call it Failing Fast Is Fun. Like a jazz musician or an improvisational comic, this technique allows you to build off of ideas or themes and spin them into completely new directions. One thought leads to three. Those new three each lead to another three. And so on and so on. The trick is to not stop too soon. There will be time to edit, rationalize, and flesh out later. Here's what you do:

- Write down the objective at hand.
- Grab a stack of Post-it notes.
- Limit your time. If you're doing this in a class, you might work in small groups and begin with 15 minutes.
- Unlimit your thoughts.
- Jot one idea down per Post-it.
- Review your notes and cluster them by concept. Pick your top ideas, using them as jumping-off points, and repeat.
- Repeat. Repeat. Repeat.
- One you've got three or four killer ideas, see which ones have legs using the same Post-it note technique to extend each idea.
- Repeat. Repeat. Repeat.

2. Spite Can Be Right

(Contributed by: Jeff Ericksen, founder and instructor, Master Ericman's Portfolio School for Mischievous Young Men and Women)

Most kids have the wonderful inclination to do exactly the opposite of what you tell them to do. Then you reach adulthood, and there's a fine line between smart and smart aleck. We're not talking about being a rebel for the sake of being a rebel or not doing what you're told just to be a maverick. We're talking simply about going in the exact opposite direction of where everyone else is headed to find a solution to a problem.

Here are a couple examples. Conventional wisdom would tell you that when starting out and asking investors for their trust, a company should take its name very seriously. Tell that to Google. In the late '90s and early 2000s, bigger was better on American highways. But then came Mini Cooper. So here's how we put not doing what we're expected to do to work. Pretty much do exactly the opposite. Do the twist. Here's what you do:

- Write down the issue at hand in as few words as possible.
- Now, write down the exact opposite next to it.
- Brainstorm around the opposite solution for a few minutes. Maybe use the Failing Fast Is Fun exercise.
- Rephrase your issue in a different way and write it down.
- Repeat the first two steps.

3. Thinking Outside the Box

This exercise is designed to help you immerse yourself in a product. The specific objective is to help bring all of your senses into play. Begin with a partner and then work on your own in this three-step exercise.

Step 1

- Your instructor will stop at the dollar store and buy as many products as there are students, put them all into a covered box, and bring it to class.
- Working in pairs, one person (explorer) will explore a product with the help of their partner (scribe). The scribe will be in charge of taking notes based on the explorer's sensorial responses to the product. The process will then reverse.
- Without looking, the scribe will reach into the box and select a product.
- The explorer must keep their eyes closed through the entire process. Trust your partner!
- The scribe will place the product (still packaged) in the hands of the explorer.
- The explorer will then slowly, and with specific focus on each sense, explore the product—smell it, listen to it, touch it, taste it, and see it (last)—as the scribe writes down their words. They must trust their partner to guide them as necessary.
- Explorers should describe the product's "features" with words and phrases rooted in their sensorial experience. Be as expressive and emotional as possible. Nothing is "wrong."
- Now reverse roles. Select a new product from within the box. Do not return the first product to the box.
- Next begin to generate a list. It could be a list of all the words and images from the product's category. You could also focus on the competitor with a few "suffering points" to show the alternative is you don't use your product. Or you could do the "twist." There's also the possibility of playing with metaphors. Then again you might be so inspired that you'll think of ideas that aren't even ads and go nontraditional. The idea is to brainstorm ideas. Ultimately you will amass a benefits list.

Step 2

- Next consider who the target is and write a consumer profile.
- Spin the features into benefits and prioritize them into the top 10.
- Then write a positioning statement.

Step 3

- Next write 50 headlines, but turn in three. No headline may be more than eight words.
- Then select the most resonant headline and execute it in a font and color that strategically speaks to the positioning of your brand (use at least 36-point type).
- Present your finished headline and discuss your rationale.

Visit www.sagepub.com/altstiel3e to access these additional learning tools

- Video Links
- Web Resources
- eFlashcards
- Web Quizzes

Chapter 7

Design

Worth a Thousand Words

Why me?

I'm not a designer.

Ah! But your eye went right to what you hoped would be the answer. By the end of this chapter, you'll understand and appreciate why your eye traveled as it did and be able to answer the question, "Why me?"

Why Every Creative Needs to Be a Designer

Or at least understand design. Whether your talents lie with the written word or visual expression, if you want to get a job, an internship in the creative department, or even a foot in the door, you'd better learn how to put your concepts into visually interesting layouts. Copy doesn't exist in a vacuum. You need to marry copy with design in an engaging layout. Mind you, we didn't say *perfect*—we said *interesting* and *engaging*.

Just what makes a layout interesting? We'll get to that a bit later. First, let's consider why all creatives need to understand design basics and, for that matter, why everyone on the advertising team should. We begin with a discussion that centers on 2D design or print. However, the same principles generally apply across all media. They have nuances depending upon the medium, but good design is good design.

- Words and visuals do not exist in isolation.

- Design visually expresses the Big Idea and sells the product.

- Good creative should engage the audience visually and verbally.

- Portfolios are important, and presentation matters.

- Multiple skills increase your value.

- Knowledge is power.

This last one deserves a little more discussion, even if you're never going to be a creative. Fine. Now, imagine yourself as an account executive who speaks

Words of Wisdom

"Start your layout knowing that it's a problem to be solved as an integral idea. Treat it as an advantage, not a problem."[1]

Paul Arden, former executive creative director at Saatchi & Saatchi and author

the language of creative and clearly articulates design concepts to the client. Think you'll climb the ladder quicker?

So You Want to Be an Art Director

Art directors don't create in a vacuum. Great ideas, including most great advertising, emerge from collaboration. That's why brainstorming is so important. It gets your creative juices flowing, but it also helps ideas evolve collaboratively. As an art director, you will have to find ways to visually convey the meaning in your copywriter's headline. You'll have to make body copy engaging and readable. Your layout will have to sign strategy. But above all, you must learn how to attract attention, create interest, and stimulate action. In short, art directors share the same responsibility as writers—create artwork that sells an idea or a product.

Of course, as an art director, you need to understand the basic principles of design and execute them with skill and sensitivity. You should also have a mastery of the latest software. Most of all, you'll need the patience to develop multiple concepts *before* you sit down at the computer. Most art directors are conversant with software programs, with a strong focus on the Adobe Suite.

Coming into the industry with software skills is a huge asset, but being an idea person is the key to success. At bigger agencies, art directors are often able to hand their rough concepts off to a production artist, who is adept on software and can quickly interpret the rough sketches of the art directors. Whether your career path takes you to the copy or art side of the creative business, the key is developing and communicating concepts. Advertising is an ideas business.

Don't Throw Away Your Pencil

We know most of you love computers and would rather be playing on your computer than reading this textbook. But creating ads involves ideas, and ideas don't live in computers. You need to start with a pencil. Believe it or not, the pencil is a design tool. Design starts in your head, flows onto paper or napkins or backs of folders or inside book covers via your pencil, and is executed using your computer. Yes, you'll use a computer, but it all begins in your head.

Use technology wisely. If you're seriously thinking about going into art direction, design, or production, you'll need to be competent in the programs that are the current industry standards. For art directors, that means knowing InDesign, Illustrator, and Photoshop very well and being conversant in iMovie and Motion, and maybe a few others. At the very least, learn the basics and keep practicing. But never, never use the

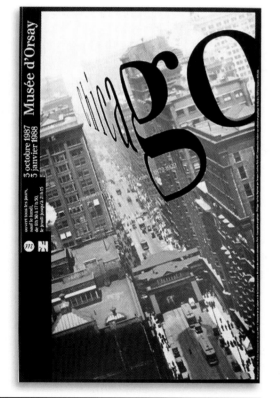

This classic poster leverages hand-rendered type to suggest the expansiveness of both the city of Chicago and the museum exhibition singing its praises. It also demonstrates the power of good design.

computer to go shopping for concepts or visuals before you have nailed down your concept. Perusing the Internet can stimulate creativity, but your ideas—the concepts—should begin as thumbnail sketches. Remember the order: head, paper, computer. You're the genius, not the computer.

Basic Design Principles

Artists define design principles in their own way, and there are many books out there on design. All those opinions might seem confusing, but in reality it's a matter of perception and preference. We think Robin Williams does a great job. Her book, *The Non-Designer's Design Book: Design and Typographic Principles for the Visual Novice,* is terrific. She's clearheaded and succinct. We are taking her lead and focusing on the following four principles of design[3]:

1. Proximity

2. Alignment

3. Repetition

4. Contrast

Before we begin, recognize that the concept of unity underpins these four principles. No matter what you are trying to accomplish and no matter how you execute one, or all, of the design principles, how the layout hangs together—unity—is what matters in the final analysis. For copywriters, a good way to think about unity is to consider thematic qualities in writing. You don't change the subject midsentence, so don't change your design theme midlayout. Use each principle consistently throughout your layout. Carry your visual concept all the way through your ad—from top to bottom, left to right, and page 1 to page 100.

Proximity

The principle of proximity suggests that you group related elements together. You can move them physically closer so the related elements are seen as one cohesive group, or you can move them farther apart, suggesting a less important relationship. And how you align them (the next principles) will help the viewer make sense of your visual story. All the elements have a relationship, and proximity helps viewers understand that relationship. Another way to think about it is this: Think of grouping those elements while considering the target's needs and wants (emotions) and your strategy. See, you really can use the creative brief. If you tap into the target's emotion, if you find viewers' sweet spot, you've hooked them.

The basic purpose of proximity is to help designers and art directors (we'll use these words interchangeably) organize the elements of the layout in a way that brings the strategic concept to life. So what are the elements of a layout? They vary, but the basic ones are headline, subhead, body copy, tagline,

Or buy a Volkswagen.

Simple concept. Simple design. This art director's sketch became one of the most popular in a long line of groundbreaking VW ads.

Do your planning on paper; then build it on the computer.

Proximity is critical to the effectiveness of this ad. Both headlines say the same thing, but their position makes all the difference.

visual(s), and logo. *Visuals* are the images that support the copy. They are almost always either photographs or illustrations. Avoid using the word *picture*. It tends to connote a photograph, which can confuse people or lock you into an unintended concept.

Alignment

Consider alignment as expressing what is rhetorically important. Each element should have a visual connection to another element and flow from a central point. Nothing should be placed arbitrarily. Nothing should hang alone. If your alignment is cohesive, then when you decide to break the alignment (occasionally), it won't look like a mistake. It will scream strategy. Consider alignment as the design principle that makes you a visual storyteller. Think of how a writer connects one sentence to the next, one paragraph to the next, one chapter to the next. Alignment is all about *making the verbal visual.*

Think of the principle of alignment as offering you invisible lines to direct a reader through a layout. Alignment is a system of organization. Organization or unity is central to this principle. How elements are aligned tells the reader that no matter where an element is placed it has a relationship to something else on that page.

The two key points to remember with the principle of alignment are visual flow and lines. Visual flow refers to how readers' eyes follow the layout, how they flow. The art director is in charge of the visual flow based on strategic objectives. Some novice designers start by centering the headline or the visual and everything that follows. That's a center-justified layout. We are not suggesting that you never center-justify anything, because sometimes a centered layout is perfectly on strategy and quite interesting. Rather than following a formula, it's better to let the strategic message, the Big Idea, guide your alignment. A common visual flow pattern and a good standard for beginners to rely on is the *Z* or backward *S* pattern. In Western cultures, our eyes tend to begin reading at the upper left and then naturally flow to the right, just like when we read a

This student-designed OXO ad makes the visual verbal and forms the perfect marriage with the headline. Using visual flow, it tells the readers exactly what the product does.

Lines convey movement, which dovetails perfectly with the directive message—sign the pledge.

This ad from Thailand combines metaphor and directional alignment to demonstrate the natural protection provided by this bug spray.

book (hence justifying the foundation for alignment). Then our eyes travel down, moving from upper right to lower left. Can you imagine the *Z* or backward *S* configuration? This classic pattern is the reason you so often see the logo anchoring the lower right corner of a layout, as we previously suggested. The bottom line is you are in charge of how the viewers interact with your layout.

Lines are the second key element of alignment, and they are central to visual flow. Lines can be the edges of visuals, the ends of lines of copy, the

Repetition, alignment, and color strategically demonstrate the product benefit while reinforcing the headline.

edges of blocks of copy, or actual lines. Robin Williams explains how lines work: "In any well-designed piece, you can draw lines to the aligned objects, even if the overall presentation is a wild collection of odd things with lots of energy."[5] Sometimes those lines are invisible, and sometimes they are literal.

Repetition

The principle of repetition is predicated on, well, repetition. Repeating some design element throughout your layout is essential. It might be shape, color, lines, texture, bullets, or a particular font. It can be anything, but it needs to be visually recognizable and strategically relevant. Think of this principle as the principle of consistency. Repetition does not have to be boring. In fact, it can be downright adventurous. Every ad in your campaign should have a visual repetitious theme. Every page in your brochure should repeat similar visual elements. Every screen on your website should have the same visual familiarity, if for no other reason than to promote ease of navigation. Repetition is what unifies your brand message.

Two main things to avoid when considering repetition are being annoying and overwhelming the viewer. Consider how contrast can work in combination with repetition. We'll cover that shortly. Chances are if your repeated elements are annoying, they are also overwhelming. Once you've overwhelmed or annoyed your target audience, you've lost them.

Contrast

A dramatic use of negative space and contrast.

The two main points to consider when working with the principle of contrast are optical weight and white space (negative space). Optical weight is a huge part of providing contrast. Every element in a layout has optical weight. Thin type seems light to our eyes, and we respond emotionally to that lightness. Conversely, a thick, dark line (rule) looks and feels emotionally heavy. Optical weight can play a significant role in how viewers respond to the contrasting elements in your layout. Make it a strategic role. White space also has optical weight. It is more than just the unused portion of the layout, and it's more than just the background. In fact, white space isn't even always white. White space is the negative space surrounding elements within the layout, and it provides the backdrop for many other elements of contrast. Why use white space? Our eyes sometimes need a rest. White space offers that. It can also frame elements or form a base on which an element can visually rest or float. White space can draw attention to a headline, copy block, or visual. Respect white space. It's an art director's and a copywriter's friend.

Using negative space and repetition within a series, this *Häagen-Dazs campaign whispers purity with the final ad bringing it all together, perfectly.*

As far as we are concerned, there's only one thing to avoid when it comes to the principle of contrast—as Robin Williams says, "Don't Be a Wimp." To test the effectiveness of your contrast, consider *mirroring.* Try to reflect the opposite weight, shape, or size in another part of your layout. Once you've mastered how to contrast visual elements and see how their weight balances the overall layout and works strategically, your design skills will improve.

Some Essentials

Like many of the design choices you'll make, the selection of type and color goes a long way to enhancing awareness and building strategic comprehension.

Typography

SERIF OR SANS SERIF

Serif typefaces, like this have little tails (serifs) at the ends of the strokes. Sans serif fonts, like this do not. Probably the most important thing to remember about serif versus sans serif is that the serifs tend to make the type appear

Here's a great use of repetition in design and a metaphor in concept. This student-designed ad clearly shows the protection levels of various SPF levels of Coppertone.

more flowing and easier to read. Conversely, sans serif type tends to be more stiff or edgy and perhaps a bit more dramatic.

WEIGHT

When we speak of the weight of type we mean optical weight, just like when we discussed contrast. One font may be much heavier than another. That is, the strokes are much more substantive, making each letter visually heavier.

SIZE

In the graphics world, point size refers to the height of type. Interestingly, many styles of type vary slightly in height even if the point size is the same. The main objective is to go beyond legibility and make your copy inviting to read.

Check the visual flow of this ad. Your eye tracks from the benefit headline, through the copy, and to the product and finally lands on the logo.

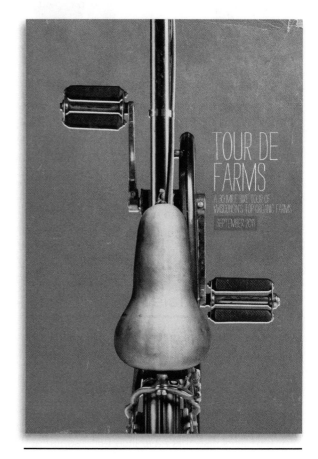

This poster leverages alignment, balance, and color and combines it with an elegant visual metaphor perfectly suited to the event.

This has nothing to do with reading backwards. Reverse type refers to type that is white (actually colorless) because it "reverses" out of a block of color. Beware of using reverse type on low-quality paper. It will tend to bleed, and you may not be able to clearly read your copy. For new designers, we suggest using this technique sparingly.

Over printing is just the opposite. It simply means the type (usually black) is printed over a lightened (ghosted) image, texture, or tone.

MATCH FONT TO TONE

Type plays a big role in creating resonance in the reader. For example, which of the following best matches the image of the brand?

A Diamond Is Forever

A DIAMOND IS FOREVER

A Diamond Is Forever

LEAVE ENOUGH MARGIN

We suggest half-inch margins and that you remember white space. White space will draw your eye in. Don't run your copy edge to edge, and don't cram in so much copy that it becomes intimidating to read. Honor your margins.

Other type considerations: The space between lines of text is called leading. The amount of leading depends on the size of the font, the volume of text, the desired readability, and the designer's personal preference. For example, some European designers like a lot more leading than some American designers. Justification describes how the type is arranged on a line. Most of the time body copy is left justified, which means the text aligns with the left margin with no designated alignment for the end of each sentence. See Tables 7.1 and 7.2 for examples of leading and justification.

The type choices imply savory status while the background color implies purity. The placement of the type balances the layout, drawing the eye to the savory mac and cheese.

Color

Starting with the basics, think of colors as primary or secondary, warm or cool, and complementary or contrasting. From a designer's point of view, here are two key points:

- The human eye is most comfortable looking at warm colors.

- Complementary and contrasting colors should work to visually enhance your strategy.

Some speeches change the world. Some take you to an entirely new one.

The Moon Landing 40th Anniversary.   The JFK Library and Museum wechoosethemoon.org

Type considerations should also include using it as a graphical visual element. This ad uses the body copy to express the inherent meaning in the message.

Whether you're using warm or cool colors or engaging complementary or contrasting colors, you also need to keep in mind the social and cultural connotations attached to each color. Just as with words, colors can have multiple meanings. Think of the social and cultural meanings of each color. Then weigh those meanings against the brand, the colors associated with the brand, and its competitors. Also consider your audience's sensibilities when making color choices. Finally, remember color may be applied to many elements of a layout: type, line, and backgrounds. Visual images too have an expressed color palette.

Make wise strategic choices that you can justify. Some questions to help you select color:

- How will color enhance the Big Idea/that One Thing?

- Are your color choices in keeping with the strategy?

- Does the color support the brand?

- Will the audience relate positively to the colors?

- What are the cultural connotations of your color choice?

- What is your justification for each color choice?

TABLE 7.1   Leading

12/10	12/16
The lines become more compact.	The lines become farther apart.

TABLE 7.2   Justification

Center justified simply means the type is centered with equal distance to each side of the page.
Right justified (as in Arabic and other languages that read right to left) means the type lines up on the right side of the page and is "ragged" on the left side of the page.
Left justified (as in Western literature) means the type lines up on the left side of the page and is "ragged" on the right side of the page.
Justified means that the type is spread evenly across the page, column, or copy block and forms smooth edges both right and left no matter how many characters there are per line (as you would see in most daily newspaper columns.)

Now that we've defined some of the basics, we'll move on to how to apply them across media. We begin with a discussion about the design process. Then we'll explore design for print, move on to digital with a discussion of both web and mobile, and wrap it up with a few comments on social media and nontraditional design. Just remember that content, which is the literal communication, and form, which is the design, are—or should be—indistinguishable.

In a nutshell, the process begins with your creative strategy. Work from your brief all the way through. Once you have a clear idea about what needs to be conveyed and a darned good idea about how many elements might be in your layout, start sketching or collaging. If you're more comfortable with sketching, draw thumbnails until you run out of paper.

Apple used color to support its brand, while giving the iPod campaign legs to beautifully dance across multiple media platforms.

Use your boxes, squiggles, and blocks to mark where various elements will be placed, as well as to indicate the general proportion of each element. Work freely and generate a lot of loose ideas. Move your boxes, squiggles, and blocks around within the confines of your layout. It you're more hands-on, try collaging. The bottom line is good design takes a lot of work. When you brainstorm a headline, you may create 50 or even 100 ideas. Most of which will be schlock. The same process holds true with layout design. Scribble and scratch or cut and paste 50 or even 100 ideas. In the process, you'll come to see what works best for your specific project. One last bit of advice that bears repeating: Don't start shopping for visual images until you've nailed down your Big Idea. We cannot stress enough how much your preliminary work—off the computer—will make or break the quality of the final product. This process holds true whether you are designing for print, web, mobile, or an ambient structure. Only a strong design concept will lead to successful design execution.

Selecting Your Visuals

As you'll see in later chapters, certain words in headlines and copy pull in more readers. The same is true with visual elements—in print, in the digital world, or on television. As with "proven" headline words, don't use cliché visual choices just because they've generated results over the last 50 years. Try to find a new approach that gets noticed. Some of the visual choices that attract readers and viewers include:

PEOPLE, NOT THINGS

Given a choice, people like to see other people. It's all about satisfying those wants and needs. Is that person in the ad benefiting from the product? Is that person suffering because he or she's not using the product? Will I look like that handsome/beautiful person in the ad if I use that product? If asked, any reader would say, "Nah, I don't look at people in ads." But they do. And so do you. The choice of

RISING STAR

Creative Passion

I graduated from the York University/ Sheridan College Joint Program in Design with a bachelor's degree and a professional certificate in digital design. Upon graduation, I quickly joined Karacters Design Group, the branding and design arm of DDB Canada. I began as an intern at Karacters and after only three months was hired on full-time. My projects encompassed brand identity design, environmental design, package design, direct marketing, and retail. At Karacters, I was able to work on large-scale corporate rebrand projects, where I quickly learned to look at brands systematically and holistically. While at Karacters, I worked on brands such as Subaru, Bosch, Milestones Restaurants, and Stratford Shakespeare Festival.

For the past three years, I've been at Zulu Alpha Kilo working on integrated campaigns for Bell, Coca-Cola, Corona, and Workopolis. At Zulu, there is a lot of opportunity for me to work on projects beyond traditional design. Innate in Zulu's culture is its collaborative environment and multidisciplinary creatives. Working at Zulu has given me opportunities that have ranged from creating a 3D animated TV spot to a motion/voice interactive web experience. Because of these diverse projects, my design is constantly influenced by a lot of different resources—from fashion, to architecture, to social media, to experimental art, to fine arts.

My other passion lies in typography, art, and travel. I'm always looking to do my next art project.

Currently, I try to make time for my daily hand typography blog. I started the blog to fill my time during train rides to work. Each word is chosen at random, and most often drawn on ephemera I find on the train, such as newspapers, tickets, and so on. The blog has actually become a great reference tool for work when I need inspiration for a typeface. Another passion of mine is traveling. I try to do at least one big trip a year. Last year I was able to travel around Spain. I fell in love with Barcelona's historic architecture highly contrasted by the graffiti that layers it. You'll most often find me taking photos of signage and graffiti in my travels—I use these as a resource for inspiration. I love type that is formed from asymmetry, nature, and sculptural structures.[6]

Mooren Bofill, senior designer, Zulu Alpha Kilo, Toronto, Ontario, Canada, mobofill. tumblr.com

Words of Wisdom

"Advertising is not a f—ing science! Advertising is an art. No question about it."[7]

George Lois, author of
The Art of Advertising (1976)
and a celebrated Hall of
Fame art director

showing the product or people using the product depends a lot on the product category. For example, showing a medium-long shot of a sexy sports car racing through the night could be the most effective image for that vehicle. But showing a mom with her kids and a lot of stuff to carry may be the best image for a minivan.

MORE VISUAL, LESS COPY

You need to know how to write copy. But you also need to know when to leave it out. While people will read long copy if they're interested, for many consumer ads, you just don't need it. When it comes to print, it's better to use a visual to capture their attention than a mass of intimidating text. Once again, the choice depends on the target audience and type of product. Soft drinks and chewing gum don't need 200 words of copy. A business-to-business (B2B) product might.

ILLUSTRATION VERSUS PHOTOGRAPHY

Years ago illustration was much more common. Now with Photoshop, photo manipulation creates amazing effects that were only available with illustration. However, illustration is a valid option for a lot of reasons:

You can't show it any other way.
Cutaway drawings, blueprints, overlays, ghosted images, and many other graphic treatments are executed as artwork instead of photography and sometimes in a combination of the two.

You want to create mood.
Illustrations create resonance too. Sometimes you need a painting or drawing to elicit an emotion you can't get from a photo.

Your goal is to have dramatic effect.
Illustration can be used to exaggerate a feature, make a problem look bigger than it really is, or enhance a benefit. These visual overstatements are more accepted as artwork than realistic photography.

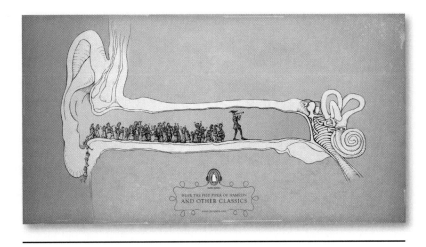

This Malaysian Penguin audiobook ad uses illustration for maximum purpose. The illustration itself conveys, with wit and charm, the action of the product—storytelling—while the pastel color suggests a pleasant audio experience.

Finding Your Visuals

One of the biggest problems faced by students (and most professionals) is where to get the visuals. Searching the web for that perfect image often turns into a shopping trip. You might find something that looks cool but doesn't fit your concept. Try to stay true to your creative strategy, even if you can't find the perfect photo. Fortunately, with stock photo websites, your odds are greatly improved, even if the image is plastered with watermarks.

SHOPPING ONLINE

You can find just about any image you might need using Google. However, the quality is usually not usable for anything other than a rough reference. When searching for images, try to limit your search to Extra Large, if you plan to put them in a layout. Another good source is iStock, which has a great library of still photos, videos, illustrations, and Flash animations. You'll have to pay for them, but the cost is nominal.

MAGAZINES AND OTHER PRINT MATERIAL

If you need an image of a glamorous model in an evening gown, start looking at some fashion magazines. If you're doing B2B work, trade publications can provide a wealth of materials for comping up a layout. Remember you are assembling images for a layout, not a real ad.

CREATE YOUR OWN PHOTOS

Need a picture of a college student eating a pizza? Don't waste your time browsing stock photos. Just shoot your roommate (photographically, that is). With a little planning, you can create all kinds of professional images on your own. This tactic also works very well to create photo storyboards for television commercials.

DRAW IT

If you can't find it and can't photograph it, try drawing it. Don't worry; you don't have to be a great illustrator. The agency will hire one. You just need to express your idea.

Design and Campaign Continuity

The four design elements, along with great copy, tie a campaign together. The use of lines, type, color, and layout style, in particular, provides a certain look that is carried across a campaign. Pay special attention to logo treatment and taglines. They may have to work with a wide variety of executions across multiple media. It takes discipline to maintain graphic continuity in a long-running campaign, especially when new ads are developed halfway through the campaign's run. This is when you really have to understand how the various elements interact to form a unified theme. Without that understanding, a campaign can visually fall.

Better Print Layouts

Robin Williams offers a simple yet effective approach to nurturing the creative process and developing better print layouts: "See it. Say it. Sketch it."[8]

- *See it.* Start keeping a file, scrapbook, or morgue—in other words, a collection of ads that you like. Learn to file anything that strikes you. Your scrapbook will be a great resource for ideas. Use it before you start concepting. Or when you're stuck. It's bound to trigger some fresh ideas.

- *Say it.* Write down why you like the ads you've selected. What makes them sing? Which of the four design principles are strongest? What made each one stand out? What caught your eye? If you can articulate why you like a certain ad, you are well on the way to defending your own ideas.

- *Sketch it.* Sometimes the most dreadful ads inspire great new ads. Cut schlocky ads apart and rearrange them. Or take a piece of tissue paper and draw over it. Make it better. This process may just inspire a great design for your next ad. The point is to put something on paper. You may be tempted to jump on the computer before you have a concept. Don't. Scribble something down first. Try some alternatives. When you're happy with your rough, then turn on your computer. And if you're allergic to paper or you just won't turn off your computer, be sure that you treat each thumbnail document as a sketch. Don't overwork them and don't fall in love with the first one.

Layout Patterns

There are two common organizational layout systems or patterns: grids and chaotic. Each of these layout systems can be experimented with by using that wonderful design tool—the pencil. We will explain each system. But the idea is to quickly rough out four or five thumbnails, sketching in squares or rectangle boxes for copy blocks, squiggles for display copy, and solid block shapes for visuals. Armed with boxes, squiggles, and blocks and using either the grid or the chaotic system as a jumping-off point, you'll be on your way.

Grids (also known as Mondrian layouts) are simply a systematic way of dividing up space using geometric patterns beginning with the basic rectangle, which makes up your page. Grids allow us to see how elements of a layout might be organized. Consider how many elements you have in your layout. That will help you decide how many blocks you'll need to create within your grid.

Don't think of a grid layout as a stack of blocks or a boring "checkerboard" where you have to fill in all the squares. You have a lot more creative latitude. The grid simply provides a system. You use the four principles of design to arrange and rearrange your boxes, squiggles, and blocks. From a practical standpoint, grids are easier to build for print ads, web ads, and websites—which are really a collection of interconnected tables or grids. Columns are much like grids. In fact, sometimes the terms are used interchangeably.

Chaotic layouts (sometimes called circus or field-of-tension layouts) are usually not as crazy as they sound. Generally, the organizing principle that pulls chaotic layouts together is alignment. Thus, the use of lines can bring organization to a chaotic layout. Proximity is another principle that brings order. The seemingly random placement of visuals can be organized, for example, by placing captions nearby or using lines (rules) to connect elements or using repetition to create unity. Use your boxes, squiggles, and blocks to play with the layout. Some chaotic layouts, especially from novice designers, are just that—a visual train wreck. Unless you have a well-defined design strategy and use some organization principles, we suggest you stick with something simpler.

This time a pun works perfectly, while a grid helps organize and showcase the endless possibilities in St. Petersburg and Clearwater, Florida.

Chaotic layouts really do have a purpose. In this case, the parts of the motorcycle flip the headline, building a picture of the consumer. Now that's something every Harley rider can relate to.

Layout Considerations

- Did you consider alternatives? (You can never have too many thumbnails.)

- Did you consider the four principles of design?

War Story

Break the Cycle*

Over 90 years ago, the Kotex® brand invented the feminine care category with marketing and communication that, back then, was progressive and ahead of its time. Yet, skip to the turn of the 21st century, and the Kotex® brand equity and market share were worlds away from where the once number-one and highly trusted heritage brand should be. It was crystal clear. The Kotex® brand needed an overhaul—and quickly.

When we stepped back and really examined the feminine care category, we first noticed the obvious. The products were a sea of sameness: white, boring, and institutional. To top it off, in a category that is so personal and emotional, manufacturers were speaking to women in a purely functional way—talking only about product benefits, and in an often ridiculous way (picture women in white pants riding horses or twirling on the beach—need I say more?!). Finally, society was treating periods and vaginas as taboo, causing a vicious cycle of shame and embarrassment for girls and women. Why was it OK, we wondered, to talk about erectile dysfunction on commercials and on network TV, but to say the "V-word" was completely off-limits? Someone or something needed to Break the Cycle.*

Enter the U by Kotex® brand in North America in early 2010. I was incredibly privileged to be the first U by Kotex® marketing brand manager. Working with teams of talented multifunctional resources at Kimberly-Clark Corporation, and an amazing group of outside agencies (including media, advertising, PR, and digital), we launched an entire line of U by Kotex® feminine care pads, liners, and tampons with bright, bold colors and designs supported by a solid, 360-degree campaign. The campaign spoke to our target consumers in a no-nonsense, straightforward way that has literally changed the face of feminine care, and shaken up the category conversation. We successfully changed the trajectory of the Kotex® brand equity and market share, and got both our consumers' and our competitors' attention.

U by Kotex® started with a few somewhat simple insights that a lot of dedicated and creative people, both inside and outside Kimberly-Clark, rallied around and brought to life. Two years later, U by Kotex® continues to thrive. And, the UbyKotex.com website has challenged nearly 4 million girls to help Break the Cycle* by reading articles, asking questions, watching videos, taking polls, and designing their own, unique, and far-from-boring pads.[9]

Amy Attenberger, global brand manager, Kotex, Kimberly-Clark Corporation, Neenah, WI, kotex.com

- Did you use white space effectively?

- Does your layout have a pleasing and logical visual flow?

- Did you choose a display font that matches the tone of the ad?

- Is the body copy inviting to read—the right size and proportion?

- Did you honor the margins—allow enough space around critical elements?

- Did you keep it simple? (Less is more.)

Basic Web Design

Software makes design and layout faster and cheaper but not necessarily better. If you can't afford to hire out, you might consider open-source web templates. Check out 1&1 or Wix templates that can be customized for every industry. After that, keep in mind the basic design principles previously discussed. And read on for a few more tips (see also Table 7.3). However, if you are serious about learning web design, buy a different book! This book focuses on creative strategy and the creative process. This chapter focuses on design basics. When it comes to design, the basics are rooted in print. And the principles remain the same. Let's take a quick look.

Designing for the Web

Begin by considering a website as a collection of pages. In a brochure or magazine, you turn the pages. On the web, you click links or sweep your fingers across the screen. Regardless, you're turning to a new page. As with any well-designed document, the four design principles—proximity, alignment, repetition, and contrast—work together to create a unified whole. Of course, you need to consider the gestural motion of touch screens, the utility of fast downloads, and the interplay of sound. But really visual consistency is what makes a website great.

Considering the four design principles, when it comes to the web, one stands out: repetition. On the web, nothing is more important. Repetition lets visitors to your website know that they are still on the same site, no matter how deep into your site they travel. Repetition also allows you to create a clean graphic style, and a clean graphic style means smoother and, most likely, faster navigation. Repetition creates rhythm, and rhythm makes websites beautiful. To accomplish a clean graphic style, repeat color schemes and use the same fonts. Repeat the same button styles and use similar graphic elements in similar places on each page. Simplicity ensures fast loading, which is essential if you want to keep viewers on your website.

When it comes to choosing fonts, choose wisely and choose simply. You want fonts that will transfer no matter what platform your viewers are using. We suggest Verdana because it's found on all operating systems. You might also consider Helvetica or Arial. Times and Times New Roman are also pretty safe bets. Whatever you choose, make sure you lay it out in a readable style. Never, ever run your copy across the entire width of the webpage. Online, type is most easily read when it is framed within a textbox or table. In general, shorten the length of your copy within each textbox or table. Yet despite shorter blocks of copy, on the web you can actually provide more information than you can in print. In fact, most people go to the web to find more detailed information. So, when providing more detailed information, simply use shorter blocks of copy but more of them.

TABLE 7.3 Essential Website Design Considerations[10]

- Integrate the design of the website with the brand identity.
- Use hierarchy to create a logical progression through the site.
- Keep the branded experience rich.
- Build easy navigation that is intuitive.
- Respect users' time with fast downloads.
- Make content easy to find, download, and/or print.
- Follow the Americans with Disabilities Act (ADA) Standards for Accessible Design guidelines for web design (www.ada.gov).

The Nike+ site is an example of using rich media to deliver a highly branded experience. Runners are able to engage with the Nike brand in the community, while enhancing their performance with web-based performance apps. On top of that, the clean and energetic design visually expresses speed and performance.

Working with the grids we discussed earlier can really help create structure within a website as well. By using grids you can organize information. Even if you grab a template, grab one that allows you to easily respect and utilize basic design principles. As you build your site, be sure to consider visual hierarchy and rank your visual elements, copy blocks, and graphic elements, in order of importance. After that, be sure that key elements such as the home page button, critical and repeated links and/or tabs, and the title or brand logo remain in the same spot no matter what page a visitor is on.

In the end content, the literal communication, and form, the design, are inseparable. Form should enhance content, while content should dictate form.

Designing Mobile Advertising

The primary thing to keep in mind when you're thinking mobile is that nearly everyone has a mobile phone. Mobile is everywhere, all the time. And for some communities, such as Hispanics, mobile is also often their primary access to the web.

The two key things to consider when you are designing for mobile are utility and entertainment. From mobile games, to mobile programming content, to mobile commerce, mobile is on the move. With utility and entertainment always top of mind, consider first and foremost how you can leverage existing campaign components when designing mobile. Can you help consumers listen to an outdoor poster? Can you offer scannable teaching moments? Or can you deliver the right ad to the right person at the right moment—all with a branded theme? Mobile design is really about concept and strategy (see Table 7.4). And the mobile screen offers you the opportunity to create an intimate relationship with consumers.

TABLE 7.4 Conceptualizing Mobile Ideas[12]

- Relevance matters.
- Make it *utilitarian.*
- Give it legs.
- Make it *entertaining.*

In the end, you'll most likely send apps production outside. Just remember it's the strategic concept that matters more than anything else. As you sketch out your concepts, go back to the grids we discussed earlier. Keep it simple. People who are engaging with your brand via mobile will expect simplicity and ease of use—all framed around entertaining or utilitarian experiences. Keep it fun. Keep it smart. And make your app work *for* the user.

Parting Thoughts on Social Media and Nontraditional Advertising

People use social media for a reason. Sometimes it's social, other times it's practical, and the next time it may be all about entertainment. Whatever the reason, when brands engage in that sphere, they need to be smart and respectful. In social media, it's not unlike mobile—entertain or be utilitarian. If you're a brand in this space, you'd better be offering them something interesting. Robin Landa recommends making the experience relevant, authentic, valuable,

"Don't rely on your art director to save you. A strong idea, simply presented, is far more effective than a weak idea strongly presented."[14]

Jim Durfee, copywriter
and founding partner,
Carl Ally agency

enticing, and shareable.[13] From a design perspective, social media is just like nontraditional because it needs to fit within a strong branded framework.

Nontraditional advertising should surprise consumers. However, from a design perspective, think of nontraditional advertising as a visual extension of the traditional campaign. While it might surprise consumers and live in unexpected spaces and places, its typography, logo treatments, and color palettes should reflect the broader traditional campaign. Use it as a storytelling moment and let the design you choose merge the story into the overall branded campaign.

Putting It All Together

If you really want to become an art director or a designer, it's essential that you take design classes, preferably taught by working professionals who deal with real clients every day. Learn the rules and when you can break them. Above all, there is no substitute for experience, even if most of that experience is trial and error. Practice. Practice. Practice.

Thoughts on Software

You can build an ad in Microsoft Word, Excel, or even PowerPoint. In fact, any program that allows you to import an image and manipulate text can be used to create an ad. But whether you're an aspiring writer or an art director, we *strongly* suggest that you get proper training as early as possible in the following programs: Adobe InDesign for desktop publishing; Adobe Photoshop for photo retouching; Adobe Illustrator for creating vector images such as infographics; iMovie and Motion for developing animated narrations that can be used on the web; Microsoft PowerPoint, Prezi, and Keynote for slide presentations. Try to experiment beyond the standard templates and backgrounds. The only way to become proficient is to practice. So try to execute your pencil layouts as you scribbled them but also experiment with other ideas. How would a headline look in a different font? Should the body copy be in two columns or one? Do you have room for an inset photo of the product? Can you make the margins wider, the logo smaller, and the copy more readable? Once you have the basic elements of your concept in place, you can start playing around with how they should be arranged on the page.

Evaluating Your Work

Writers and art directors may occasionally trade places. Yet even as an account executive or a media director you should still be able to evaluate design and have some good reasons for your opinions—and those opinions should always be tied to strategy.

Table 7.5 is a brief checklist of design tips and techniques. Use this to evaluate your work and the work of others. You may not follow every "rule" listed here. But if you don't, you should have a sound creative reason why you didn't.

TABLE 7.5   Conceptual Considerations

- Does your design convey the big idea?
- Did you design with your audience in mind?
- Did you prioritize elements? (The most important should be the most prominent.)
- Do your visuals and headlines work together?
- Overall, does your design catch the reader's eye?
- Did you keep it simple? (Less is more.)

If you remember nothing else about this chapter, remember this:

Keep it simple. Don't add so many elements, styles, and fonts that no one can figure out what you're trying to say. Less is more. Keeping it simple doesn't mean you can only put one element in an ad. It means you need to unify multiple elements into a cohesive design—so the reader is impressed by your idea, not your technique. Another cardinal rule:

If you emphasize everything, you emphasize nothing. A cluttered, confused, truly chaotic layout repels readers. No one wants to take the time to figure out your message. Once again, less is more.

Who's Who?

Helmut Krone—Helmut Krone developed a clean, uncluttered look in the 1950s that still sets the standards for modern advertising design. Working with copywriter Julian Koenig, Krone created witty, tasteful, intelligent masterpieces for Volkswagen and other Doyle Dane Bernbach clients. Krone sweated print details and advanced professionalism among creatives in his relentless pursuit of perfection. He was elected to the Art Directors Club Hall of Fame in 1976 and has been a perennial award winner as he revolutionized advertising's "look."[15]

George Lois—George Lois gained fame and major awards with bold, clean work for Doyle Dane Bernbach, Papert Koenig Lois, and Lois Holland. In 1976 he penned *The Art of Advertising,* praised as the bible of mass communication. He also became the youngest inductee into the Art Directors Club Hall of Fame. Lois's ads for Wolfschmidt Vodka, Xerox, Allerest, MTV, Maypo, Wheatena, and Edwards & Hanly, and his *Esquire* covers reflected his "loosey-goosey" style and exemplified his idiosyncratic "stun 'em and cause outrage" philosophy. Never an "establishment" model citizen, Lois is defined by his powerful early work.[16]

Woody Pirtle—Woody Pirtle began a successful career in graphic design as an art director at Stan Richards and Associates in Dallas. After his stint at Richards, Pirtle went on to become the creative director at Pentagram in New York, ultimately founding his own shop—Pirtle Design. His work was legendary for its dimensional beauty and creativity, as well as the challenges it posed to the printer. In 2003, he received the prestigious AIGA Medal for his exceptional achievements in the field of design.[17]

Nancy Rice—Nancy Rice was a founding partner in the fabled Fallon McElligott Rice agency, which three years later was named Agency of the Year by *Advertising Age*. Her "Perception/Reality" campaign for *Rolling Stone* was recognized as one of the 10 best campaigns of the decade by *Adweek*. Rice later joined DDB Needham, Chicago, as senior vice president and group creative director, working with numerous high-profile clients from Anheuser-Busch to General Mills. While at DDB, her work garnered an extensive list of awards, including gold and silver at the One Show, Clios, and Athenas. She was the first woman elected to the Advertising Hall of Fame in 2006. Rice, always a passionate mentor, is now program coordinator for the Minneapolis College of Art and Design.

Exercises

1. Endless Possibilities

The goal here is to internalize the idea that there is an enormous range of opportunities when it comes to approaches to creative execution. There are endless possibilities.

- Pick a brand. Not a classic brand, but a new and somewhat hot brand. Something like Netflix.

- As a class, brainstorm—just shout out anything that you think of when you hear the word *Netflix*. Anything. Now you have list of strange and wonderful possibilities.

- Take each item on that list and walk through the variety of possible points of association. Let's say the word is *couch*. Here is a list of options. What colors do you think of when you think of a couch? What sounds do you associate with a couch? What shapes do you think of when you think of a couch? What do couches feel like? Where do you find couches? Who should you share your couch with? And so on. Ask the same questions of each item on the brand association list.

- Now everyone picks one word. With its multiple points of association, create three thumbnails. Use the principles of design to guide your work.

- Everyone shares their thumbnails and provides constructive feedback. Along the way, you'll begin to see the possibilities that brainstorming can unlock.

- You could take this to the next step and write a consumer profile and create a comped layout from each thumbnail. Then spin that into a mini campaign. Imagine the tactical opportunities you've generated!

2. Celebrity Fonts

(Adapted from an exercise contributed by Mike Cissne, group leader, production, Bader Rutter)

This is a good exercise to become familiar with the program's font choices and find personalities that work with font choices.

- As a class, list the top 20 celebrities that you know.

- After creating the list, pick five celebrities and typeset their names, choosing the fonts and colors that work appropriately with that celebrity's present image.

3. Five Lines

(Adapted from an exercise contributed by Mike Cissne, group leader, production, Bader Rutter)

This exercise is teacher driven and designed to help you experience how lines work as a design element.

- Take out a sheet of paper, draw five lines on it, and then sign your name and submit the sheet for review.

- Your teacher will lead a discussion, using the lines you drew, to demonstrate how many details and decisions could be involved to complete any task and that a designer should be aware of all of the choices.

- Now, generate a list all the questions that could be asked before completing a design project that involves lines: Should the lines be thick? Should the lines be thin? Should the lines symbolize something? Should the lines touch each other? Should a ruler be used? Should the lines be short? Should the lines be long? Should the lines be parallel? How much pressure should be used when drawing the lines? Do the lines need to be seen up close or far away? What color paper should be used? What size of paper should be used? What utensil should be used? Where should the name go in relationship to the lines? And many more . . .

- Discuss how we mostly take for granted these decisions, but a good designer runs through all of these thoughts and many more before doing anything.

Visit www.sagepub.com/altstiel3e to access these additional learning tools

- Video Links
- Web Resources

- eFlashcards
- Web Quizzes

Chapter 8

Campaigns

Synergy and Integration

What Is a Campaign?

Before you can create a campaign, you need to define it. From a copywriting standpoint, we prefer Maxine Paetro's simpler description:

> A campaign is a series of ads for a product (or service or company) that work individually and cumulatively to communicate the advertiser's message to the consumer.[1]

In other words, each element of a campaign has to be effective on its own, because that may be the first and only exposure. All the elements also need to work together to build a cumulative image. With a well-executed multi-element campaign, the whole is greater than the sum of its parts. What makes a collection of marketing communication projects a campaign? In some cases, a campaign can include the complete MarCom arsenal, or it can be as simple as a series of three fractional page ads, as long as they meet all of the following criteria:

Common objective: Well-defined target audience, awareness, comprehension, conviction, and action goals within a given time frame. In other words, there should be a campaign strategy.

Unified theme: Whether it's a tagline, graphic design, or copy message, a campaign needs to convey a single message so the consumer can connect that one adjective to the brand. This does not mean every ad has to look the same—but the overall message should.

Coordinated rollout: Depending on the time frame, all elements can appear at once in a blitz, or new elements can be added depending on changing marketing environments, such as seasonality and competitive response. This involves media and promotion planning, but it certainly affects creative strategy.

Overall, if you remember nothing else about campaigns, know this:

The primary purpose of a campaign is to support the brand.

From your clients' point of view, a campaign is a more effective, more profitable, and more stable situation for establishing their brand name.[2]

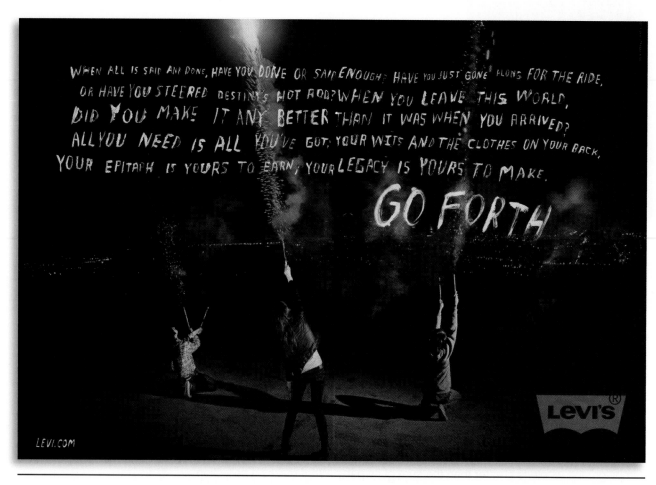

Levi's revitalized their brand with a campaign that celebrated youthful exuberance. Print, television, online advertising, social media, and out-of-home media all worked together to urge young people to "Go Forth."

Campaigns and IMC

In Chapter 1 we outlined a few elements of integrated marketing communications (IMC). In a campaign, the operative word is *integrated*—they have to work together in a planned approach. Campaign strategy can involve the whole marketing communication toolbox, including public relations and media planning; however, we'll limit our thinking to creative elements.

Campaign Components

Think about any recent soda or fast-food restaurant campaign. Where did you first notice it? Probably on television. But you also heard the radio commercials, saw the billboards, checked the coupons in the Sunday paper, got annoyed by the pop-up ads on the web, and probably glanced at a display in a store or restaurant. Each individual component conveyed the message, and collectively they pounded it into your brain. So when you see that soda on the grocer's shelf or in a vending machine, you buy it, probably without realizing how many times you've been bombarded with different messages in the various media. What made you pull into the drive-through to try that new sandwich? Maybe it was the ad on your car radio or the billboard you just passed. Again, you probably don't realize how many campaign components were working together to influence you.

Here are a few of the components that can be part of an integrated campaign:

Advertising: Consumer magazines, trade magazines and professional magazines, broadcast television, cable/satellite television, radio, local newspapers, national and trade newspapers, ambient, out of home, Internet banner ads.

Promotion: Short-term sales contests, special offers, discounts, rebates, incentives, sweepstakes, in-game marketing, product placement, sponsorships, events, cross-promotion with other products, publicity, and, of course, advertising of the promotion—not to mention digital promotion tools like Foursquare and Groupon.

Public Relations: Event planning, publicity of events, print news releases, newsletters, video news releases.

Internet marketing: Websites for computers, tablets, and smartphones; landing pages and microsites; e-mail marketing; search engine marketing; customer relationship marketing.

Social media: More campaigns are using social media as their hub. The focus has shifted so that advertising drives viewers to Facebook, Twitter, and YouTube to continue the conversation.

Direct marketing: Database development, direct mailers (letters, cards, dimensional mailers), fulfillment (mailing information or merchandise). Direct marketing is more than direct mail: It's also telemarketing, direct selling, e-mail marketing, and mobile apps.

If all of the above components are part of a campaign, they all have to work together, yet stand alone as individual selling tools.

How to Enhance Continuity

Continuity Does Not Mean Conformity

The biggest difference between a single-shot ad and a campaign is continuity. Continuity within a campaign means the various components of the campaign have enough commonality that the reader/viewer/listener should perceive a common theme and unified message.

Continuity doesn't require that the TV spot uses the same dialogue as the radio commercial, or the billboards have the exact same graphics as the print ads. While it's nearly impossible to give you one set of guidelines that works for every campaign, remember this:

Don't repeat the same idea in every part of the campaign—repeat the creative strategy with different executions.[4]

Extendability

To create an effective campaign, you need to think in two dimensions—*extending* the creative strategy across the various media and *repeating* that strategy within each medium. The first dimension—extendability—means you use the same theme and common elements in two or more media. For example, can you carry that creative message from print to TV? Will the direct mailers look like they came from the same company as the billboards? Does the advertising support the promotion theme? Does the point-of-purchase material tie in with the campaign?

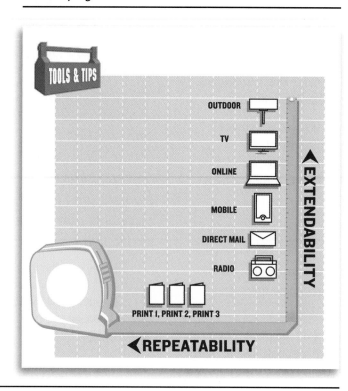

Source: Created by Dan Augustine.

Repeatability

Repeatability is a little different from repetition. It does not mean rerunning the same ad or commercial until everyone is so sick of it they ignore it. That's a media decision. In a creative context, repeatability means using common elements to create a series of ads or commercials. They are not identical, but they are related—being able to stand alone, but also working cumulatively to convey a campaign theme. We can't think of a better illustration of repeatability in a campaign than the "Got Milk?" campaign. This long-running campaign has featured the stars of the day (and days past). If you want to check out its origins, read Jon Steel's *Truth, Lies and Advertising: The Art of Account Planning.*

How to Maximize Extendability and Repeatability

We've already covered some of the creative tools you can use to provide continuity to a campaign. You can use one or all of them to help hold your campaign together.

Repeatability. The design and the Big Idea remain consistent across the board in this Clio-winning outdoor campaign.

MUSIC

When people can't remember the words of a commercial, but can sing the jingle, you know your campaign's music is holding it together. Music is far more

Extendability. To support the launch of the 2012 Focus, Ford created a multimedia campaign aimed at the African American community. The "Inner Child" television commercial celebrated the joyful enthusiasm of driving a new Focus. Radio ads ran on Steve Harvey's and Tom Joyner's radio shows; print ads appeared in Essence and other African American magazines; the Focus was prominently featured in Ford sponsorship of the Hoodie Awards and Essence Music Festival, as well on the Ford Urban site.

This student-designed campaign uses primary colors and a playful tone that matches the target audience perfectly. The body copy also tracks nicely from the headline to hold the whole ad together.

memorable than any other commercial element. For example, you'd have a hard time finding anyone over 40 who doesn't know the Oscar Mayer wiener song. We find it surprising how many students "remember" music from commercials made before they were born. There are as many ways to use music in your campaign as there are songs—probably more, with today's sampling and mixing technology. Thanks to broadcast and online commercials, obscure indie bands become overnight hits as millions are exposed to their music when it goes viral.

VOICE TALENT

Using the same announcer throughout your TV and radio campaigns helps establish a common sound. Here are a few examples:

- **Celebrity on camera:** Just have the celebrity appear in the spots and say something. In this case, the visual of the celebrity is probably more memorable than the sound or his or her voice.

- **Celebrity voice-over:** A lot of very famous people provide voice-overs for commercials without identifying themselves, such as George Clooney (Budweiser), Kevin Spacey (Honda), Morgan Freeman (VISA), Tim Allen (Chevrolet), John Hamm (Mercedes), and Jeff Bridges (Hyundai), to name a few. Using famous actors may be expensive, but they often have a distinctive voice that connects with the viewers or listeners. New research reveals that television commercials featuring celebrity voice-overs are most influential when consumers can't identify which actor it belongs to.[7]

- **Character voices:** People are used to hearing smooth announcers. So a distinctive voice treatment can shock them into listening. The current voice of the Geico Gecko is British actor Jake Wood, although a few others have covered him, including Kelsey Grammer.

- **Announcers:** Using the same announcer, even if he or she is not a celebrity, can provide continuity. Be careful to maintain the tone and delivery style, even though the copy changes from spot to spot.

ANIMATED CHARACTERS/ANIMALS

For years the Leo Burnett agency was known for its "critters"—those memorable animated characters that have been the common thread of many of their long-running campaigns. Before you dismiss these mascots as throwbacks to the 1950s, consider that they've been around for a long, long time. That means the agency has created long-term brand value and, in doing so, has retained clients much longer than most of their competitors. Some characters, such as Tony the Tiger, the Green Giant, and the Keebler Elves, are inseparable from the product.

SPOKESPERSONS: CELEBRITIES

Back in the day when brands were the sole sponsor of radio and television programs, the star of the show was the brand spokesperson. These days, the process is often reversed. Success in show business or sports generates instant recognition, and brands are quick to jump on the bandwagon. The key word is *success*, which transcends any considerations about race, ethnicity, or sexual orientation. Years ago, an African American woman would have limited opportunity to endorse products. Today, Beyoncé has stacked up endorsement deals with American Express, Samsung, Armani Diamonds perfume, Disney, and L'Oréal. And she is by no means the only African American entertainer to command top dollar for an endorsement.

Nowadays, celebrity status trumps prejudice.

In his prime, Michael Jordan was one of the top commercial spokespersons, starting with Coke, then representing Nike, before branching

Animated brand mascots not only contribute to campaign continuity, but they also never grow old, get arrested, or go into rehab.

off to McDonald's, Hanes, and many others. His celebrity transcended his fame on the court. As of this writing, Danica Patrick has not won a major NASCAR race, though she has finished near the top in multiple races. Despite not winning, she is arguably the best-known professional driver in the world. In addition to her racy Go Daddy ads, Patrick also pitches Peak antifreeze, Bell helmets, Marquis jets, Hot Wheels, Tissot Swiss watches, and Nationwide insurance, among others. We can safely assume that her looks might have something to do with her off-track success. With male athletes, that consideration is generally irrelevant. Tiger Woods became the symbol of Nike golf products and Buick, among others. But his commercial empire faded as quickly as his golf game when his scandals dominated the news. Like most male athletes, Woods's sex appeal was not a consideration, but his sordid sex life was. However, if he returns to his prescandal success on the tour, all that nasty stuff will be quickly forgotten. That's the high-reward/high-risk world of using celebrities.

As we discussed in Chapter 6, using a celebrity works best when he or she has some reasonable connection with the product. Whether your celebrity is from the world of sports, show business, politics, or any other public venue, the main considerations should be:

- Can we afford this person?

- Any skeletons in the closet—any future potential for embarrassing the client?

- Will he or she connect with the consumers?

- Will this person enhance the brand image?

Danica Patrick certainly has a connection with the product when she's promoting Peak antifreeze. However, as eye candy for the inane series of Go Daddy commercials, the erotic focus is clear, though we can't help but question what it has to do with search engines or an athlete's personal brand.

Subway has invested a lot of capital in the Jared Fogle story. He has his own page on their corporate website, has his own foundation, and still appears in their TV commercials.

Fiat used Jennifer Lopez to launch their 500 model in the United States. Although they were promoting her "Jenny from the Bronx" persona, social media quickly pointed out a body double drove the car through the old neighborhood and that JLo bought an $18 million mansion in the Hamptons. So much for keeping it real.

SPOKESPERSONS: SYMBOLS

You can create spokespersons, and if things go right, they become celebrities. One of the most successful is Jared Fogle, who lost a ton of weight eating healthy food at Subway. He's been their spokesperson for over a decade, thanks to the brilliant foresight of a local Subway franchise owner who saw Jared's story, "Crazy Diets That Work," in *Men's Health*.

STORY LINE AND SITUATIONS

Story line: Some advertisers use testimonials or case histories, all with a common theme to convey their message. Hospitals, for example, typically feature inspirational stories of survivors who owe their lives to the advanced technology and caring doctors of a given institution. Insurance companies also use this approach with the emphasis on caring for victims of some catastrophic event.

Situations: These are recurring themes or vignettes that involve (1) the same characters or (2) the same premise. Over the years, Budweiser has featured their iconic Clydesdales in Super Bowl commercials. Check out the War Story in this chapter and see how Allstate used a scruffy guy with attitude called "Mayhem" to personify all the bad things that can happen if you don't have the right insurance. For nearly 15 years, William Shatner was the face of Priceline, challenging travelers to negotiate a better price. When the firm switched to a fixed-price model the old "Negotiator" was presumably killed in a fiery bus crash. After seven months, he resurfaced in a new series of commercials, proving it's really hard to knock off a good spokesperson.

DESIGN AND TAGLINE

As we discussed in Chapter 7, design elements can unify a campaign. When it comes to using a symbol and slogan to unite a campaign, no one has done a better job than Nike. As a "hero" brand, Nike campaigns celebrate the fighter in every athlete from top professionals to weekend warriors. As Nike has proved, once a look is established in the consumer's mind, extending it becomes a lot easier, which has made the brand's move to embrace female athletes as simply athletes who happen to be female a welcome and logically branded shift.

Nike sticks with its premier athletes, even when they struggle, proving that "Just Do It" is more than a slogan. Few brands have matched Nike's level of continuity and commitment to maintaining their core message.

Consumer-Generated Campaigns

As social media merged with marketing, advertisers used the Internet to give consumers an unprecedented opportunity to buy into their brands. Technically, anyone with a cell phone camera or a camcorder and a computer (or smartphone) can create consumer-generated media (CGM). Encouraging consumers to create their own commercials involves them in the brand far beyond being a loyal customer. Many national consumer brands have sponsored consumer-generated campaigns. Some, like Old Spice, invited consumers to provide ideas for online videos, while Harley-Davidson fired their agency of record and let consumers determine the new tagline and direction of their current "no cages" campaign. Others, like Mini, ask people to submit scripts for TV spots. And we're pretty sure you haven't forgotten the Doritos spots that ran on the Super Bowl. Despite the current trend, it's important to remember that most of these CGM are short lived, very specific in scope, and limited to a single product or brand extension. Consumer-generated work, well done, should not be used to replace the corporate or brand campaign or the advertising agency. It should be used to generate high consumer engagement. In many cases, CGM could be considered a sales promotion that is supported by other media. Time will tell if CGM will remain a major force in brand support or whether it will be an intriguing bit of marketing fluff.

War Story

Making Mayhem

A poetry teacher once told me that great writing needs objects and opposites. Allstate Insurance had spent years talking about how well their car and home insurance could protect you. But things really got interesting when we decided to show people the opposite of protection . . . mayhem.

Our competitors were dominating the airwaves with messages about low prices. You can't see insurance—it's invisible. And most people don't read their policies and understand what they're covered for until after trouble strikes. So we decided to show people how having the right coverage from Allstate will keep you better protected and save you money in the long run.

Enter Mayhem. He's the personification of all the trouble in the world. He's every reason you need good insurance. And it's all based on hard facts—if you get the minimum property damage liability the law allows and you rear-end a lawyer in a $90,000 BMW 7 Series, you personally are on the hook for about $60,000. And believe me, a lawyer will sue you and garnish your wages.

I think the thing that makes Mayhem really work—in addition to being a strong idea—is craft. Of all advertising, 98.7% isn't well crafted. Mayhem may look easy to come up with, but our team rewrote each script at least 100 times. Every single word was scrutinized. Every piece of action was thoroughly thought out to a fraction of a second.

There are no cutaways to "the product"—Mayhem talks to the camera the whole time. A great example is the "Deer" spot, where Mayhem is a wild deer, "out eating leaves and whatnot," and he runs into the road and freezes in your headlights because "that's what we deer do." He gets hit by a car, and he rolls off the hood and keeps talking to the camera as he's lying there in the road about how stupid you are if you buy the cut-rate insurance, and then he laughs wickedly. It's awesome.

When it came to casting, we looked at about 400 actors, but we kept coming back to Dean Winters. Nobody else had his gleeful sense of malevolence—he really takes pride in his work.

Equally important were the little details our director, Phil Morrison, came up with. Like Mayhem's makeup—he's always bruised, dusty, and cut up, like he just came from blowing up a bridge or something. It was quite a job to convince the client on the set that he should look beat-up, but now it's part of his character and they love it, too. And as we took Mayhem into Facebook, mobile, radio, out of home, ambient, and events, we made sure the details were perfect.

No matter how nice you are—and I'm one of the nicest people you'll ever meet—there's a little part of us that really wants to be bad. Mayhem feeds that dream of our opposite, and I think that's why he's been so successful.[8]

Jeanie Caggiano, executive vice president, executive creative director, Leo Burnett, Chicago, leoburnett.com

If you're planning to use CGM as the main focus or even part of your campaign, keep these tips in mind:

1. Don't separate your CGM from the main objectives for the brand or company—integrate it. Determine how your CGM will support your brand, not detract from the brand message.

2. Be honest about your intentions. You want people to create ads. Don't call it something else. Too many CGM programs have crashed because they weren't transparent.

3. Encourage participation—not just from entrants but also from people who can vote on the best submission. It's like Chicago politics—get them to vote early and often.

4. Facilitate syndication. Use viral seeding to get the videos out to a wider audience. Empower syndication by making it simple to upload and embed in blogs.

5. Consider long-term implications and opportunities. Can your CGM be leveraged into a longer-running campaign? Can it be mainstreamed into your primary branding campaign?

Advertising, in-game marketing, social media, and promotion all blend together seamlessly in this Jeep campaign . . . or is it a campaign to promote Call of Duty: Modern Warfare 3?

Integrated Digital Campaigns

As we'll see in chapters discussing online marketing and sales promotion, the web has become the hub of many advertising campaigns. While consumers may not want to read a 100-word print ad, they might read 500 words on a website. In many ways, the purpose of a multichannel ad campaign is to direct people to a single landing page, which gives them the option to explore multiple methods of interacting with the advertiser.

Even if your gaming experience begins and ends with Angry Birds, you've probably heard about Activision's wildly popular *Call of Duty* series. For 2012, Jeep blurred the lines of reality with the introduction of the Wrangler *Call of Duty: Modern Warfare 3* Special Edition. The tricked-out Jeep is prominently featured in the *Modern Warfare 3* game. But that's only part of the promotion. TV commercials lifted the graphics from the game to launch the new Jeep model, as well as the game. The *Jeep Ops* Experience Sweepstakes gave away the very first production model of the vehicle. To win, you had to "like" the Jeep Facebook page and complete an online entry form. While on the Facebook page, fans were able to play *Jeep Ops*, the brand's online video game. Additional support came from print ads and billboards using the new slogan, "The toughest vehicle in the world. Any world." There was also a lot of buzz created on gaming, automotive, social media, and marketing websites and blogs.

Rising Star

Midwest Ad Cat

I wanted to be Draper decades before the synapse in Matthew Weiner's brain fired and the mega-culture character was born. My father was in advertising, so the idea of being a big-shot, New York ad cat was instilled in me at birth.

Years later? Well, it's not that I gave up on my own dream. I simply realized I had overly romanticized it; the stress and anxiety that comes with Madison Avenue just didn't seem worthwhile. But letting go of having all three—fame, fortune, and fun—wasn't an option either.

So? Nose to the grindstone, I mapped out a route to get everything I wanted.

Unlike many of my peers, I walked across the stage at graduation with a title and business cards: "junior designer." I worked my internship night and day. I engrained myself in the agency culture and made sure I touched every project. I went from a designer to associate creative director in about seven years. I've won more ADDYs than I can recall, collected local accolades, and landed in *Communication Arts,* and I teach copywriting and communication design at local institutions. But what I've accomplished has been at my own pace.

It's not what I wanted when I was a kid. It's better.

You *can* have fame, fortune, *and* fun (g'head, be greedy); the secret is defining these terms for yourself and not abiding by Webster. Here's how I got all three:

Take pride in what you do. Do not be overly concerned with pleasing your superiors. Please yourself first. Be passionate about what you've created, and you will make evangelists of your boss and clients in the process.

Observe. Constantly. Always be seeking new avenues of inspiration. Be an eternal student of culture. Eat things you never have. Listen to music you never would otherwise. Experience all you can. See the beauty in everything and be inspired by it.

Take a break. Your plate will never be clean. Ever. With that in mind, forgive yourself your deadlines and break away. Your brain is a muscle, and it cannot run efficiently without the occasional respite.[9]

Dan Augustine, associate creative director, Noise, Milwaukee, WI, nowhere-somewhere.com

Putting It All Together

Creative strategy for campaigns begins with marketing objectives. As always, you have to ask, "What do you want to accomplish?" The more specific the goals, the better your plan. When the objective is to introduce and reinforce a brand, start thinking campaigns.

Don't limit your thinking to repetition of the concept or even to how it will work in other media. Look at the big picture. The most famous one-shot ad of all time—Apple's "1984"—was actually part of a campaign that involved a huge amount of publicity and public relations. The commercial was shown many times—for free—after its one and only appearance at the Super Bowl, and the buzz put Macintosh on the map. It's interesting to note that the client was so nervous about the approach before the Super Bowl that the agency sold off their time for a scheduled second airing.

Campaign Tips

We've offered a lot of ways to improve the continuity and thus the effectiveness of campaigns. Here's some more good advice from Jim Albright:

- A campaign is a series of planned actions. Think big about a wide, multipronged attack on the marketplace.

- When assigned to write a one-time ad, check to see if the client has an ongoing look and sound and slogan. If so, make the point of the ad under the umbrella of the ongoing look, sound, and slogan.

- If the client has no continuity in its advertising, write the one-time ad so that it could be extended into a campaign, if necessary.

- When writing an advertising campaign, don't repeat the same plot in different media. Repeat the creative strategy with different executions.

- Think extendability from the beginning. Sometimes a strategy is so narrow that only one or two good commercials or ads can be written under that strategy. Think ahead to all the different ways you can execute advertising under your creative strategy. You may have to write a song or have T-shirts printed.[10]

Words of Wisdom

"The greatest advertising isn't great for moving merchandise any more than the greatest literature is great for compelling plots. Somehow—in the service of carmakers and brassiere manufacturers and car rental agencies—these campaigns have discovered our humanity."[11]

Bob Garfield, columnist, *Advertising Age*

Who's Who?

Lauren Connolly—Lauren Connolly has risen to senior vice president and creative director at BBDO, New York, in nine short years. Among her achievements at BBDO was co-creating the 2012 M&M's Super Bowl spot. Connolly also helped launch Cingular's mobile brand with the "Raising the Bar" campaign. She's judged numerous awards shows including the One Club. Most recently, she has begun to oversee work at TotalWork, BBDO's digital shop. In 2012, she make *Adweek's* "20 under 40" influencers list. It's no wonder why.[12]

Marie-Catherine Dupuy—Marie-Catherine Dupuy is a third-generation ad agency exec. Her grandfather founded one of the first French advertising agencies (which later became Saatchi & Saatchi in 1986). Dupuy joined Dupuy-Compton as a copywriter in 1970. In 1984, she became a founding partner and executive creative director at Boulet Dru Dupuy Petit (later to become part of TBWA). As writer and creative director, she has won more than 200 awards in the international competition for clients such as Virgin, BMW, McDonald's, Tag Heuer, Sony, and Bic.

Jeff Goodby—Jeff Goodby was freelancing with partners Andy Berlin and Rich Silverstein while working as a copywriter at Hal Riney. Their freelance client eventually became Electronic Arts and got so big they decided to create their own agency with EA as their first account. It wasn't their last. Their creative risk taking led to breakthrough campaigns for the California Milk Processor Board (Got Milk?), Budweiser (Louie and Frank the lizards and the "Whassup" campaign), Nike, E*TRADE, and the Winter Olympics. That campaign, among others, helped the once tiny agency gain significant recognition, including multiple Clio and Cannes awards. Goodby has been named by *Adweek* as Agency of the Year and grew steadily with the addition of Unilever, Cracker Jack, Intel, and *The Wall Street Journal.*

Tom Monahan—Tom Monahan has helped thousands of people master creative thinking with his popular creative workshops. Through his consulting company, Before & After, he has worked with clients such as Capital One, Frito-Lay, AT&T, and Virgin Atlantic. He is also author of one of the top business-oriented books on creative thinking—*The Do-It-Yourself Lobotomy: Open Your Mind to Greater Creative Thinking.*

Exercises

1. Brand Stories

Here's a chance to learn about how personal stories influence branding.

- Pick a brand and find six people who use it.

- Next interview each person, asking them to tell a story about their experience with the brand. Try to elicit from each person their emotional connection to the brand and record your conversations.

- Review the interviews and transcribe them. Using the stories, generate a positioning statement that personifies the essence of the consumers' experiences with the brand.

- Next write three short branded stories, each with a headline, that embody the essence of the positioning and reflect the stories you heard. Limit your stories to 300 words each.

- As a variation, consider who you would consider to be the perfect spokesperson for a branded campaign and write a rationale explaining why.

2. Next Ones

(Contributed by Kimberly Selber, PhD, associate professor, University of Texas–Pan American)
This exercise works with the concepts of *extendability* and *repeatability*.

- Find several campaigns across various categories.

- Break up into teams, with one campaign per group, and write a creative brief based on what your group sees in the campaign.

- Then, working with the concept of *repeatability,* concept one or two new ads that could seamlessly work with the existing campaign. You can do this with tissue roughs, the existing layouts, or full-blown creative executions.

- Next, working with *extendability,* generate two or three new media placements or touch points for the campaign. Consider the executional opportunities for these new placements.

- Finally, present your group work in class.

3. Endure the Pain and Enjoy the Gain

(Contributed by Jeff Ericksen, instructor and founder, Ms. Coffmansen's Portfolio Finishing School for Good Girls and Boys)

All writers must suffer for their art, right? Now, I'm not talking about pursuing bad relationships, living on the streets, or abusing alcohol. Although some of those things will make for more interesting conversations at dinner parties. I'm talking about soldiering through the painful part of an ad first. Writing the body copy. Here's what you do.

- Start by writing the copy before coming up with the concept or headline. Imagine describing the client's brand, sale, or issue to your grandma in an e-mail. Keep it clear and simple—you know how Grandma gets confused.

- When you've finished this exercise, you've accomplished a few things. You've stated your case in a manner a consumer will understand, and you're no longer staring at a blank page. Perhaps your mind is also opened up to seeing that there could be several ways to solve your problem.

- Finally, consider the subject header of your e-mail. Maybe that's a headline?

- You might consider writing e-mails to the whole family. Who knows? Maybe you'll end up with an entire campaign.

Visit www.sagepub.com/altstiel3e to access these additional learning tools

- Video Links
- Web Resources
- eFlashcards
- Web Quizzes

Headlines and Taglines

First Get Their Attention

We can show you the easy way to get an A in this class.

Got your attention, right?

That's what a headline is supposed to do. It appeals to your self-interest. It can promise a reward. It makes you want to know more. It can draw you into the ad.

Why Have a Headline?

All forms of marketing communications use headlines, even when we don't call them headlines. In television, it's the start of the commercial. In radio, it's the first few words of copy. In a letter, it may be a title or the first paragraph. David Ogilvy stated that the headline is the "ticket on the meat,"[1] which sounds rather simplistic for someone who wrote "At 60 miles an hour the loudest noise in the new Rolls-Royce comes from the electric clock." He found a benefit (exceptionally quiet ride), included specifics (60 miles per hour), and twisted it with an unexpected comparison to an electric clock, probably the last thing you'd think about when buying a Rolls-Royce. At 18 words, it's very long by today's standards, but still memorable.

Not all print ads have headlines, especially visual puzzles. However, it's important to know how to write a good headline first. Then you can decide if you need it.

David Ogilvy wrote one of the all-time great headlines using an obscure fact and a comparison anyone could understand. He didn't have to say "luxury," "quality," or even "quiet" in the headline.

Some texts dissect and analyze headlines in great detail, but we'll boil their functions down to four primary points. A *good* headline does one or more of the following:

- Gain immediate attention (the old fishhook in the brain).

- Select the right prospect (appeal to self-interest).

- Lead readers into the text (they want to know more).

- Complete the creative equation (synergy with visuals).

Types of Headlines

Categorizing headlines is usually more helpful in describing completed work than helping you develop new concepts. Philip Ward Burton developed a list of categories that we like.[3] We modified his list a bit and kept the descriptions brief (see Table 9.1).

TABLE 9.1   *Types of Headlines*

Type of Headline	Use this when . . .
News	. . . you want to introduce a new product, new brand, or new feature.
Direct benefit	. . . you want to promise a reward or highlight the prime benefit in the headline.
Curiosity	. . . you want to intrigue the reader into finding the main idea in the body copy.
Emotional	. . . you want to sell the image and/or invoke resonance in the reader.
Directive (command)	. . . you want the reader to do something.
Horn blowing	. . . you want to impress the reader by being the biggest, the fastest, the first, etc.
Comparison	. . . you want to differentiate your brand from the competitor or use a metaphor to describe your product.
Label	. . . you want to focus on the brand name, product name, or campaign tagline rather than discuss features or benefits.

Source: Adapted from Philip Ward Burton.

Proven Styles of Headlines

Additional research has shown that certain styles of headlines tend to pull better. Once again, it is far more important to write a headline that achieves one or more of its purposes than to have some empty bit of fluff that fits some formula.

It happens every day on America's highways. Police stop drivers based on their skin color rather than for the way they are driving. For example, in Florida 80% of those stopped and searched were black and Hispanic, while they constituted only 5% of all drivers. These humiliating and illegal searches are violations of the Constitution and must be fought. Help us defend your rights. Support the ACLU.

american civil liberties union
125 Broad Street, 18th Floor, NY, NY 10004 www.aclu.org

This comparison headline works because the contrast between the people is shocking. It creates a synergy that draws you in. You want to know more.

These three proven styles are:

- Question
- How to
- Quote

The first two are effective because they involve the reader. If you ask a question (and the reader is interested), you stimulate involvement. The same is true with a "how to" headline, but you have to finish the sentence with something that interests the reader. Quotations can be effective because they are usually connected to a person . . . and people are interested in other people, be they celebrities or ordinary Joes or Janes. A quotation hints at a story, which, if it interests the reader, fosters involvement. There are some examples in Table 9.2.

Know your audience. An ad in Cosmopolitan can get away with this light sexual innuendo. ("Cop at the bar wants to cuff you. He's off duty.") Would you use the same headline in Good Housekeeping?

This directive headline bluntly tells people what to do with their product.

TABLE 9.2   Styles of Headlines

Style	Headline	Visual	Client
Question	Do you really need more proof that drinking impairs your judgment?	Plain girl morphing into a fashion model as it gets later in the evening.	MADD
Question	Ever see a grown man cry?	Broken bottle of whiskey on floor.	Crown Royal
How to	How to convert liters into cups.	Race car and racing trophies.	Acura
How to	How to write an obituary for your teenager.	[All-type ad.]	Partnership for a Drug Free America
Quote	I told my dad I stopped raising hell, and he called me a quitter.	Redneck-looking guy smoking a cigarette.	Winston
Quote	These tables are my voice, and I'm about to holler at the world.	DJ scratching two turntables.	Mountain Dew Red

When you can ask your phone for directions and it can answer, then you've got a smart phone. Apple has done a great job keeping the concept simple and showing the product in use.

Creating Headlines From Product Information

First start with a positioning statement, a description, or that One Thing you can say about the product. This is not a headline, but it will give you some idea starters to build one or several. Figure 9.1 shows how the process starts, using what we call a Creative Tree. You can keep adding more branches as you think of them. As with all creative writing, if you're on a roll, don't quit. Keep writing headlines even if 99% of them are awful. A real stinker may trigger a winner. You may end up with something that has no direct relationship to a specific product feature, but if it attracts readers and pulls them into the ad, you've done your job.

Writing Headlines With Style

If you work on it, you can try to add a little spice to your list of headlines. The following are a few suggestions. Try to work some of them into your long list and see if they lead to anything worth keeping.

Be specific: Let's go back to Ogilvy's classic. Do you think it would have been nearly as good with "This is one really quiet car" or "The clock is louder than the engine"? Without turning it into a laundry list of specs and features,

FIGURE 9.1 *Creative Tree for Headlines*

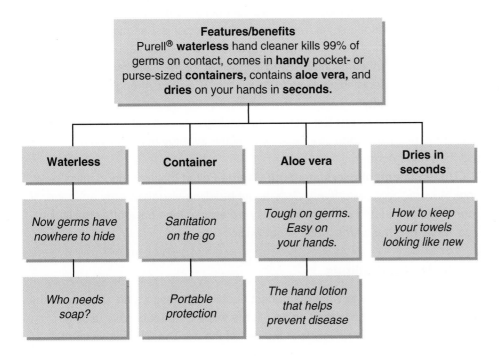

see if you can work some details into your headline. Brooks Brothers, quietly but very specifically, states the value of its brand (reprinting a pitch for a 1942 newspaper ad): "It pays to buy at Brooks Brothers." Consider the economic parallels between 1942 and 2009, and you'll see how timeless simplicity can be.

Rhyme, rhythm, alliteration: As with taglines, using rhyme, rhythm, and alliteration can make a headline more memorable. Some might say a rhyming headline is clever. Others may think the same headline is cheesy. If it's memorable and sells something, who cares? Rhythm usually employs connecting a few well-chosen short words, such as "Coke is it." Alliteration, for those who can't remember English composition, combines two or more words with the same initial sound, such as "The joint is jumping" or "Every kiss begins with Kay."

Judicious use of puns and wordplay: Sometimes puns work. We did an ad for a luxury boat company that showed our product docked at a marina with many other fancy boats. Some of the other owners were checking out our client's product. The headline: "Pier Pressure." Cute? Stupid? You decide. This tip could also include wordplay and double meaning. As with puns, be careful.

Parallel construction: This is just a fancy way to say you're combining phrases or sentences with similar key words to make a point. A few years ago, Florida tourism used the line "When you need it bad, we've got it good." Now, consider the timely rhythm of these words from Crate & Barrel: "Oven-proof. Dishwasher-proof. 401(k)-proof." A student wrote an ad for Purell waterless hand cleaner, making the point that money is full of germs and other nasty stuff. Her headline: "Dirty money. Dirty hands."

Try it with a twist: The headline is part of the concept, so give it a twist now and then. Another example from our luxury boat client: We showed the boat at a pier in front of a very nice house in an even nicer neighborhood. The owners of

our boat were hosting a very fancy outdoor dinner party. The headline: "If your neighbors aren't impressed, move to a better neighborhood."

Be relevant: Hot cultural trends and salient social issues matter greatly, and so does the health of the economy. Always consider what's happening around you. Stuart Elliott, the insightful advertising writer for the *New York Times,* suggests that financial institutions focus on the "S" words: strength, safety, stability, and security.[4]

Involve the product: Sometimes the package or logo can be an integral part of the headline. Then you really have some synergy between visuals and text if it's done right.

Understatement/overstatement: George Felton makes a good point in his book *Advertising: Concept and Copy* about headline-visual synergy and tone. "If your visual is wild and crazy or obviously excessive, then back off verbally. And vice versa. In other words, don't shout twice."[5]

Ineffective Headlines

We can't tell you how to write the perfect headline. Unless it's an all-type ad, the headline usually doesn't stand alone. So the value of a headline is usually related to how well it interacts with the rest of the ad. The ultimate value of a

Single-word headlines are seldom more effective than this one. In an era when advertisers would not risk saying anything perceived as negative, VW gave readers credit for reading deeper to discover the real meaning of this ad.

This single word was the last message a girl saw on her phone before she flipped her car and died. When headline and copy are this strong, sometimes visuals only get in the way.

Ordinary aspirin (Aspirina) may be enough to cope with your boss. But you need extra-strength pain relief (Cafiaspirina) to deal with his or her jokes. The headline draws you in, and the fine print calls out the product and the benefit. Bayer markets the Aspirina brand in Latin America and other regions outside of the United States.

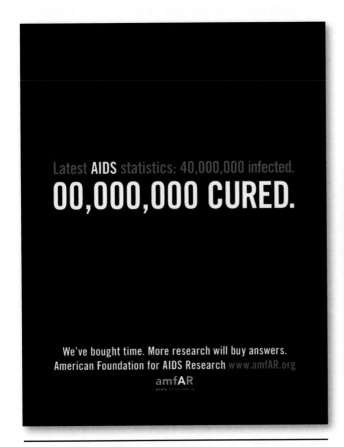

Facts and figures don't always change opinions, but in this case the number of people cured of AIDS makes a strong point.

When you follow the instructions "Fold A to B to see what happens when the house is dirty," you can see how this ad packs a punch. The copy at the bottom asks readers to get involved to prevent family violence.

This split headline promoting Austrian vodka and gin clearly provides a superior use for potatoes.

Cocoa Metro puts a spin on this direct benefit headline, sending the reader away chuckling.

headline depends on the expectations of the client and the results achieved. "Free donuts" may be the most effective headline to attract policemen, if that's your objective. Some headlines just scream, "Think again!" Try harder when you see a headline:

- Asking a question that can't be answered (confusing).

- Asking a question that can be answered with a simple yes or no (no involvement).

- Used as a caption. They describe rather than interact (no synergy with visuals and limit involvement).

- Relying on stupid puns (stupid defined as having absolutely no relation to the product or market).

- Using insulting, condescending, patronizing language that annoys intelligent readers.

- Being clever for the sake of cleverness (trying to impress rather than persuade).

Evaluating Headlines

When writing headlines, you're faced with the same dilemma as with the overall concept. Do you write one that looks good in your portfolio or one that works hard at selling something? Once again, the answer is . . . that depends. Just as most people think they are experts on taglines, even more have an opinion on headlines. Some like straightforward news headlines since there's no mistaking the message. Others like obscure references that hook a select group and leave the rest scratching their heads. Still others think silly puns are the height of creativity, while others just groan.

While there are infinite degrees of cleverness and clarity, our advice is:

If you can't be clever, be clear.

In other words, if you can't come up with a least one different, twisted, unusual, or interesting headline, then say it straight and always keep in mind the visual is there to work with the headline, not to just sit above a caption.

Rising Star

Word Problems

I wrote on everything when I was a kid. Whether it was the bathroom wall with a purple crayon when I was 2, or a notebook filled with stories when I was 12. Writing is just something I did. So it made perfect sense to pick finance as a major in college, right? Ha!

I was miserable. Fortunately, two years in, I figured it out and switched to advertising. When I took my first copywriting class, it just felt like home. I knew this was what I was meant to do.

The economy tanked two months before I graduated. Call it a blessing in disguise. My portfolio was weak. Mediocre at best. There was no way I could compete with the hundreds of post–portfolio school kids for a creative internship. Grad school, here I come!

I spent two years in the copywriting track at the VCU Brandcenter. It was the hardest, best thing I've ever done. But hey, now I'm employed (thanks, portfolio!) and have a master's. There were a lot of late nights (which just means frequenting 7-Eleven and eating out of the vending machine). But I learned discipline. I learned what good work is. And, after getting my work thrown in my face (yeah, literally), I learned to take everything seriously and never personally.

It was never a dream of mine to end up in New York City, but after interning here between my first and second year at the Brandcenter, I couldn't resist. So, here I am, still pinching myself. I work on the Publicis OneTeam where the only account I work on is a financial one. Oh, the irony.[7]

Jennifer Stopka, copywriter, Publicis, New York, jenniferstopka.com

OUR GIRLS ARE A **DIAMOND'S BEST FRIEND**

SOFTBALL PLAYED HARD
NATIONAL PRO FASTPITCH
WWW.PROFASTPITCH.COM

Words of Wisdom

"I've done as many as 19 drafts on a single piece of copy. I wrote 37 headlines for Sears Roebuck last week and I think I got three good enough to submit."[8]

David Ogilvy, copywriter and founding partner, Ogilvy & Mather

Notice the twist on a popular expression in this headline? The tagline has a twist too.

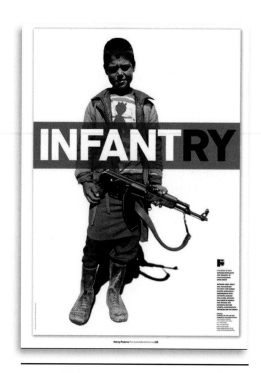

The split headline clarifies the message in one word, while the placement and proximity to the child enhances the chilling message.

Using parallel construction, this B2B headline for the Namibia Procurement Fund states a problem and the solution.

Headline Checklist

Before you settle on one headline, run through the following guidelines. Your headline doesn't have to meet all these criteria, but it should cover some of them.

1. Let your headline sit for a while. Do you still love it the morning after, or do you slap your head and say, "What was I thinking?"

2. Does your headline work with the visual, or is it just a caption or, worse, completely irrelevant?

3. In your vision of the layout, does the headline look important? Is it readable? Does it have the proper proximity to the visual and body copy?

4. Can you do the "billboard test" and still have a concept that makes sense?

5. Does your headline appeal to the reader's self-interest?

6. Does your headline pull readers into the body copy?

7. Be honest. Is this the best you can do? Or can you start round two or three or four to come up with a list of great headlines?

8. Do not use a strong subhead to "explain" a weak headline. Use a strong headline, and you might not need a subhead. (Remember less is more.)

9. Be careful with puns. There's a reason they're called the lowest form of comedy. Don't be cute just for the sake of cuteness. If a pun has a purpose, try it. Otherwise, find a more clever way to say it.

10. Think campaigns. How are you going to follow up that killer headline? Will your next five ads be just as good?

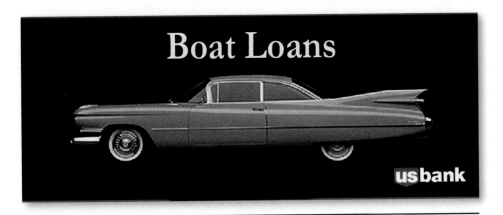

Sort of a pun. Sort of a twist. Sort of a double meaning. Sort of a waste of time, since the client rejected it.

Subheads

As you would expect, the subhead is usually underneath the headline. Sometimes it immediately follows the headline, as if to say, "What we *really* meant to say is. . . ." Other times subheads are used to separate long copy blocks or introduce new thoughts in an ad. In this context, they are sometimes called "breakers."

The four main purposes of a subhead are:

- Clarify the headline.

- Reinforce the main idea stated in the headline.

- Break up large copy blocks.

- Lead readers into the body copy.

Subhead Traps

Too often subheads are used to "explain" the headline. You may feel the headline is too weak or the reader won't get it. So you add a straight line so there's no mistaking the benefit. Many times this is done to convince a skeptical client that your risky ad concept really is a serious selling effort. We don't like subheads

In this ad, the headline alerts the reader that there's a difference between products, and the subhead clarifies that it's a good thing.

used this way for two reasons: First, why write a weak headline and prop it up with a subhead? Write a strong headline in the first place. Second, use as few words as possible to convey your message. Adding a subhead can more than double the copy clutter in an ad.

Another subhead trap: Don't use the subhead to introduce a new, separate idea from the headline. Going back to our Ogilvy headline, you don't want to follow that beautiful headline with a subhead that says, "What's more, the new Rolls-Royce offers the highest horsepower of any luxury car."

Preheads

This is also called the overline. Whatever you call it, it precedes the headline. You can use preheads for a number of reasons, but the four most common are:

- Set up the headline.
- Define the audience.
- Identify the advertiser.
- Identify an ad in a series.

As with subheads, decide if the prehead is needed to explain the headline. If so, rethink the headline, and you may not need the prehead. In many cases, the prehead asks a question that the headline answers or starts a thought completed by the headline. In these cases, you could consider that prehead as an integral part of the headline.

Why Have Taglines?

We call them taglines, but you could also say they're slogans, signature lines, or theme lines. Usually, they are the catchphrases that appear after the logo in a print ad or at the end of the commercial, and, in most cases, they are very forgettable. However, if they're done right, taglines can be the most important element of a campaign. Some clients expect too much from a tagline. They don't want a little blurb to sneak under their logo. They demand a "statement" that (a) defines the company, (b) positions the product, (c) denigrates the competition, (d) reassures the stockholders, and (e) will be approved by the CEO's wife. The more objectives a tagline tries to achieve, the more generic it becomes. When a tagline becomes generic, you can put it under any logo with negligible effect. Too many taglines are written by committees and tested by management panels. They're cobbled together with a few key words that by themselves mean nothing but, when used in a composite slogan, become completely irrelevant. Before you start cranking out slogans you have to ask the client, "What's the One Thing you want to say?" Do you want to convey a general attitude or tone? Do you want something specific about the products? Do you want something relating to your customers? Just what the heck *do* you want? George Felton sums it up pretty well: "Slogans . . . had better do more than just be clever . . . they need to be smart."[10] The smart taglines stick with you years after they first appear. They become part of the popular culture and define their place in time as well as the brand.

According to *Advertising Age,* these are some of the best taglines of all time:

1. "A diamond is forever" (De Beers)

2. "Just do it" (Nike)

3. "The pause that refreshes" (Coca-Cola)

4. "Tastes great, less filling" (Miller Lite)

5. "We try harder" (Avis)

6. "Good to the last drop" (Maxwell House)

7. "Breakfast of champions" (Wheaties)

8. "Does she . . . or doesn't she?" (Clairol)

9. "When it rains it pours" (Morton Salt)

10. "Where's the beef?" (Wendy's)[11]

The primary purpose of a tagline is to establish or reinforce the brand name. To do this, the tagline should do the following:

War Story

Blind Ignorance

I worked on the state lottery account. One assignment I had was to promote an instant scratch game called "Bull's-eye Tripler." The way the game worked was simple: One needed to scratch the card to reveal the image of a dart on a dartboard. If that dart appeared to hit the bull's-eye, a player would win triple the prize shown. Easy-peesy, right?

The policy with the state at that time was to always present three different concepts, but there was one concept in particular that I loved and pushed hard to produce. The premise was simple.

SCENE: Smoky bar. Three friends in a darts league. The last man up is getting a pep talk from his friends. "Come on, Mickey, think bull's-eye, bull's-eye, bull's-eye. . . ." With unwavering concentration, he takes aim and throws the first of three darts. Cut to the dartboard to reveal the dart missed not only the bull's-eye, but the entire board. Looking like a sore thumb, it sheepishly stuck into the wall *next* to the dartboard. Cut back to the friends, who continue to cheer him on. He focuses, throws . . . and again we cut to the medium shot. This time the dart missed the dartboard by a foot! Disappointment for Mickey's team, laughter, and cheers from their competitors. Last dart for Mickey. With his friends pleading, praying, and holding on to hope, he takes aim, tongue peaking out of the corner of his mouth, throws the dart, and. . . . Cut to reveal the worst throw yet. This one missed the dartboard by three feet! The guys lose. The competition cheers, and the game is over. But at this point the camera would suddenly pull back to reveal that Mickey and his friends were actually standing three feet in front of the dartboard the entire time, and still they lost.

VOICE-OVER: "Do you like darts, but find you're not very good? Then play "Bull's-Eye Tripler, where you can win $25,000. . . ."

Fun concept. Nice misdirect. Strategic and not expensive to shoot. The client, however, could not get past one simple problem: Rather than trying to explain his logic here, which I do not think can be done, I will simply quote him:

"We can't show a spot like that on television. It'll offend blind people."

(PAUSE FOR EFFECT, TO TAKE THAT IN.) I assured him that, ahem, *blind people* do not watch television. But he would not budge. I tried everything to assure him there would not be a problem. I even went so far as to tell him that if he got one complaint from a blind TV viewer, I would personally pay for the production of the spot.

No go. He was convinced that those who cannot see would be turned off by what was shown on the screen. Heavy sigh. We had to shoot a different spot.[12]

Dave Hanneken, creative director, Ogilvy & Mather, Chicago, ogilvy.com

Provide continuity for a campaign: A tagline may be the only common component of a multimedia campaign. It can also be the link between campaigns with very different looks. A good tagline transcends changes in campaign strategy. No matter what BMW is doing with their ads, the cars are always "The Ultimate Driving Machines."

Crystallize the One Thing associated with the brand or product: Whether it's staking out a position or implying an abstract attitude, the slogan is an extension of the brand name. When you can mention a brand name and someone else quotes the slogan, you know you've got something. Going back to concepts discussed in earlier chapters, the tagline can help foster *awareness* and *interest* of a brand or product. A few well-chosen words can define the brand, separate it from the competition, and anchor it in the reader or viewer's brain. Think of M&M candies that "melt in your mouth, not in your hand." It's not only a statement of a real product benefit; nobody else can say this. A good tagline increases your creative freedom. When the message ends with "Only in a Jeep," you can have a lot more fun with the content.

How to Write More Effective Taglines

The following are a few tips and techniques for writing better taglines. Of course, not every tagline is going to possess all these traits (unless you find the successor to "Just do it"). These guidelines are offered to help you evaluate your taglines before you submit them to the client.

Keep it short and simple: VW came up with "Drivers wanted" a few years back because it stuck in the mind better than their older slogan, "It's not a car. It's a Volkswagen." After a decade of "Drivers" they came out with "Das Auto" (The Car) which may have taken German simplicity a little too far. The goal is not to keep the word count to two or less or to make something so obscure you need another slogan to define it. However, when you develop a slogan, think of billboards—no more than six words. Three words are even better. As Shakespeare said, "Brevity is the soul of wit." Just make sure your witticism makes sense.

Think jingle: Even if you never put your tagline to music, picture it in a TV commercial. You can use the old tricks of rhythm, rhyme, and alliteration to make it more memorable. For example, no one over 40 can forget "Winston tastes good like a cigarette should," even though cigarette advertising on TV ended in 1971. A modern example: Kay Jewelers says, "Every kiss begins with Kay."

Try to differentiate the brand: Can you come up with a simple way to separate yourself from the competition? Visa used to say they're "Everywhere you want to be," implying that American Express and MasterCard were not. They followed that with "Life takes Visa," which not only gets the product's name in the slogan, but also implies that the card is universally accepted. For nearly 40 years BMW has been "The Ultimate Driving Machine." The ideal slogan can't be used by any other brand. Altoids established themselves as the "Curiously Strong Mint" so well they could extend the tagline to other products such as the "Curiously Strong Sour."

If you have to be generic, go global: Many brands use what could be called generic slogans. They're positive, easy to remember, and can be translated into most languages without changing their meanings. When they stand alone, these slogans could work for just about anyone. The difference is they're supported by millions of dollars of advertising and promotion. So if Joe's Burger Shack says, "I'm lovin' it," no one notices. When McDonald's does it, it becomes major marketing news. If you can remember the innocuous slogans for most mass-marketed packaged goods, it's only because they've been beaten into your brain through relentless advertising.

Play with words: A tagline can be more memorable if you take a common expression and twist it just enough to get attention. Chrysler used to promote their preowned cars as "Brand Spanking Used." Years ago Panasonic

Whether it's used as a headline or a tagline, the alliteration and the jingle in TV commercials make "Every kiss begins with Kay" memorable.

promoted the ergonomics of their home electronics with "So advanced, it's simple." Sometimes you can give your slogan a double meaning. For example, a drug company targeted doctors with "Healthy concern for your practice," indicating that the drug company was successful and cared about their customers.

Don't confuse or mislead: In the effort to be creative, some writers forget that the rest of the world is not as clever as they are. An obscure one-word tagline could be misunderstood or, worse, ignored.

Justify your choices: Everyone is an expert on taglines. So when you submit a list to the client, make sure everyone knows the parameters you were given. Too often the rules change after you've received the initial game plan.

Creating Taglines From Product Information

Writing taglines is a lot like developing whole concepts. Start with the One Thing. Then say it straight. From there you can veer off in several directions, each with a list of possible slogans. Figure 9.2 illustrates a brief template for a business-to-business client, although this technique works for any product or service.

As you've probably noted, the majority of the taglines in Figure 9.2 stink. Most of the time, you'll start with a generic slogan, but as you keep working, you'll branch out. You can have as many branches as you'd like. Don't worry if some of your slogans don't fit a defined category—just keep writing. Don't start

The Ultimate Driving Machine

JOY WINS.
THE NEW BMW 3 SERIES.

BMW EfficientDynamics

The Ultimate Driving Machine

THE BMW 533i.
THE SEDAN ENGINEERED TO TURN FUEL INTO ADRENALIN.

In 1975 BMW staked their claim as the "Ultimate Driving Machine." Nearly 40 years later BMW still holds that position as evidenced in their 2012 London Olympics sponsorship.

editing until you get a huge list. Then weed out the obvious stinkers. Keep refining your list until you have a group of taglines you can live with. So you might come up with something a little better, such as:

- The Power of Innovation

- Solutions in Motion

- We Power Your Ideas

OK, they're still not "Just do it," but don't stop trying. Keep sending out branches.

You'll find one that works as long as it stays true to the values at the base of the tree.

FIGURE 9.2   *Creative Tree for Taglines*

Positioning Statement
SAFCO makes innovative DC fractional horsepower motors for automotive, medical, and appliance appplications and provides complete testing and prototyping services.

Innovation	**Applications**	**Services**
A World of solutions	*We keep you moving*	*Global resources/local support*
The Smart Choice	*Power Solutions Worldwide*	*Technology on your side*

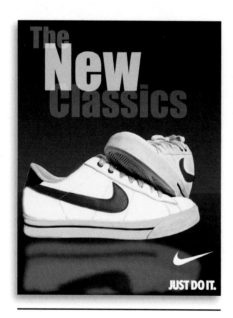

Styles come and go . . . and come back. But through it all, "Just do it" is the perfect slogan for a "hero" brand like Nike.

The classic Rolls-Royce ad at the beginning of this chapter used an indirect subtle approach to make a point. Today Cadillac twists a common expression to make a statement about power and sophistication in a luxury car: "A China Shop in a Bull."

Taglines Need Your Support

Even "Just do it" would not have made much sense if it had been launched in a campaign that highlighted the features and benefits of Nike shoes. It had to be paired with people dedicated to exercise. That synergy made it magic. That's why writing taglines can be so pointless. They're usually evaluated by a committee in a vacuum, without the benefit of massive ad support or even a connection to the campaign. Once a slogan becomes established, you can vary the images and copy in the ads, but they have to be there when that tagline is introduced. Once it's established in the consumer's mind, it becomes part of the brand, transcending the creative execution that may change from year to year.

Who's Who?

Christine Bronstein—Christine Bronstein used one word to launch a brand: *wives*. Her research told her that we all need wives. But, of course, only men have them. She turned the word *wives* on its head. For her, wives are your closest allies and friends. Bronstein founded A Band of Wives as a private social community for women. It provides a safe place for women to ask for and find the support they need, to promote their business and talents and other cool things they do. In her day job, Bronstein is the CEO of one of the few women-run, venture-backed health and fitness companies in the nation.[13]

David Ogilvy—Founder of Ogilvy & Mather, David Ogilvy was, first and foremost, a copywriter. One of the pioneers of image advertising, Ogilvy also wrote two best sellers, *Confessions of an Advertising Man* and *Ogilvy on Advertising*. He was one of the most eloquent and influential voices in advertising and today is still one of the most quotable.

Jane Maas—Jane Maas began her advertising career as a copywriter in 1964. She worked her way up, eventually becoming a creative director and later a top executive at Ogilvy & Mather. Being a woman in advertising in the 1960s was not easy, and Maas, like others, endured what we now call "sexual harassment." With no place to take her complaint, at least back then, she eventually went to the top, speaking directly with David Ogilvy. Ogilvy reassigned her, but made no changes regarding the creative director who had harassed her. She later joined Wells Rich Greene. Her most famous work was the "I Love New York" campaign, which rescued New York City from bankruptcy and still echoes around the world. She has authored three books. Her most recent, *Mad Women: The Other Side of Life on Madison Avenue in the '60s and Beyond*, is a must-read.[14]

Shirley Polykoff —Shirley Polykoff was a pioneer for women in advertising and outstanding creative talent. She started out in advertising as a teenager working for *Harper's Bazaar*. After a career in retail copywriting, she took over the Clairol account at Foote, Cone & Belding, where she penned the classic "Does she . . . or doesn't she?" Polykoff reached the position of executive vice president and creative director at FCB and left to found her own successful agency.

Exercises

1. Chocolate Coke

(Contributed by Roy Winegar, PhD, assistant professor, Grand Valley State University)

Here's a scenario for you: Your team is on the Coca-Cola account at Leo Burnett. You are all gathered in the conference room for a major announcement. The client is ready to introduce a new product and wants to hear some campaign ideas to consider. Typically, this client will consider five ideas before deciding on one to move forward. Your team is given the task to come up with five ideas. As always, it's a very big deal to be the team that comes up with the chosen idea.

- The announcement: Coca-Cola has decided to add chocolate to their line of flavored Cokes, cherry and vanilla. They choke on the name Chocolate Coke, though; and so, to start with, they would like a better name.

- Come up with five ideas for a name for this product and a tagline for each. Knowing what you do about the Coke brand and imagining the possibilities for chocolate Coke, you are encouraged to find the One Thing and then use the Creative Tree to move forward. Good luck.

2. Brainstorming Cubed

(Contributed by Sheri Broyles, PhD, associate professor, University of North Texas)

I have a cube that sits in my office, and sometimes it goes with me to class. It's my brainstorming cube. Like every cube, it has six sides. In addition, this cube has one of the following written on each side: Describe it. Associate it. Compare it. Analyze it. Apply it. Argue for/against it.

I write the topic on the board—say, hot tamales. Then I give the cube a toss into the classroom. The first person who catches it looks at whichever side is facing up, reads it out loud, then instantly responds. "Associate it. Movies." Then the cube gets tossed to another person. "Describe it. Wrapped in corn husks." Another toss. "Compare it. Hotter than Skittles." It flies all over the room, sometimes to a repeat person but eventually to everyone in the class. As the thoughts and ideas are shouted out, I write them on the board. It's very fast, and all ideas count.

When we're done, we have a long list on the board that we can then go back and sort through. Sometimes we'll find new angles. Sometimes we'll find patterns. Sometimes we'll find thoughts that can be combined. We almost always get a broader range of ideas.

It's a quick technique that will allow you to look at your topic from six different perspectives. That may reveal new strategic connections and the One Thing that will lead to the perfect campaign. Along the way, you just might find the right headline or tagline.

3. Energy Drink

(Adapted from an exercise shared by Mike Cissne, group leader, production, Bader Rutter)

- Come up with as many emotions or feelings that you could experience from consuming a brand-new energy drink.

- In class, split into two teams with a captain for each team.

- Discuss what will be more effective in communications: communicating with visuals or with words.

- One team defends words, and one team defends visuals.

- Then in the same teams review separately the list of all the emotions submitted for each team and secretly select the two emotions that feel the most marketable.

- The "words" team writes a headline for each of the two emotions, and the "visuals" team sketches out two simple visuals expressing the emotions.

- Conclude by trying to guess the other team's pair of emotions. See if any of the headlines and visuals match up.

- Finish with a discussion of the power of words and visuals, and the importance of the synergy between headlines and visuals.

Visit www.sagepub.com/altstiel3e to access these additional learning tools

- Video Links
- Web Resources

- eFlashcards
- Web Quizzes

Chapter

10

Body Copy

Writing for Readers

As you've seen in many of the examples in previous chapters, not all ads have body copy or any copy. In fact, many people believe that readers won't read copy in ads, and the best we can do is get them to remember a brand name. That may be true, but a good creative person needs to know how to write body copy for print—magazines, newspapers, direct mail, and collateral. A complete copywriter also needs to know how the rules change for the Internet, mobile, and e-mail, but we'll concentrate on traditional media for this chapter and cover the digital space in other chapters.

Who Needs Body Copy?

You Never Know When You'll Need It

Versatility is one of the keys to survival in the creative field, especially in a tight job market. You might write a cool tagline now and then, but what happens when the client wants a campaign with a series of 200-word spread ads? You should know how to write all varieties of copy well. If you can't write that well, you should at least be able to recognize and respond to good writing from others.

Ads Aren't the Only Place You'll Need Copy

As we'll discuss a little later, there are many reasons to include copy in advertising. But there are so many other varieties of marketing communication where good writing skills are just as important:

Web content: An ad with one line of copy may drive a reader to a website that's chock full of copy. Writing copy for the web has its special rules, but a good portion of it is traditional advertising writing. The objectives are the same as with print ads: grab readers, hold their attention, persuade them to consider your product, and tell them how to get it.

Collateral: Your ad may have only one line that says, "Send for a free brochure." Who's going to write that free brochure? Hundreds of millions of sell

192

sheets, catalogs, brochures, flyers, spec sheets, magazine inserts, and other promotional items are printed every year. Somebody's got to write 'em all.

Direct mail: What makes you open a piece of junk mail? Somebody wrote something that caught your eye. Once you open it, you want to know more. Maybe it's a letter, or a brochure, or some other piece of information. Somebody wrote that too.

Reports, plans books, proposals: Who says creative writing has to be limited to promotional material? Clients appreciate a well-written, crisply edited proposal or plans book. In fact, any manager would rather read something that quickly gets to the point and doesn't waste his or her valuable time. You can take entire courses on business writing, and judging by some documents we've read, not enough people have taken these courses. Using some of the writing skills we'll discuss here will help make all your business writing better, not just ad copy.

What You Need to Know . . . and Use

No matter the length or content of the body copy, you should keep a few basic concepts in mind. These apply to advertising, collateral, business documents, and basically any commercial form of writing:

1. Don't write to impress—write to persuade.

2. What you say is more important than how you say it.

3. Remember the rules of English, but don't feel forced to use them.

4. Write to the individual, not the masses.

Why Do We Need Copy in Ads?

Some ads just work better with copy. Here are a few reasons why:

Considered purchase: Whether it's an industrial flow control valve or a power drill for the homeowner, people want to know more about the product than its brand name. Go back to the foundations of the project and find out how the product features align with the wants and needs of the intended buyer. Prioritize them and string them together with style. That's body copy.

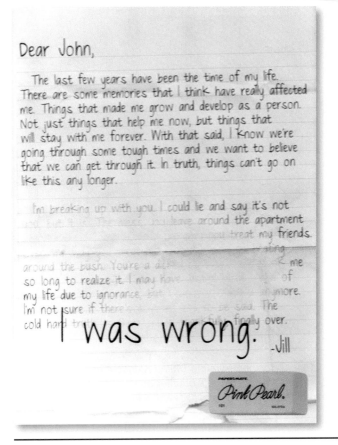

Letter writing is a dying art. But this student used it as great way to promote something as simple as a pencil eraser. The intent of the original copy in the letter is clear, even though some has been erased and replaced with "I was wrong."

ALARM GOES OFF. SNOOZE GOES ON. ALARM GOES OFF. DRESSING GOWN GOES ON. SHOWER GOES ON. SHOWER GOES OFF. TEETH ARE CLEANED. CLOTHES IRONED. HAIR BRUSHED. LUNCH MADE. LUNCH DROPPED. LUNCH IS MADE AGAIN. BAGS ARE PACKED. LOVED ONES ARE KISSED. HOME IS LEFT. THE JOURNEY BEGINS. HEADPHONES IN. EYE CONTACT AVOIDED. OXFORD STREET IS REACHED. DESTINATION IN SIGHT. THE HANDLE IS PULLED. THE HANDLE IS PULLED. THE HANDLE IS PULLED. THE HANDLE IS PUSHED. BARISTAS ARE MUMBLED TO. COFFEE IS POURED. REGULAR SEAT IS FOUND. YOUR CUP IS LIFTED. THE INDELIBLY RICH AND LUXURIOUS FLAT WHITE COFFEE REACHES THE BACK OF YOUR THROAT, WARMING YOU DOWN TO THE FARTHEST REACHES OF YOUR BODY AS THE CAFFEINE SURGES THROUGH YOU LIKE THE SMOOTHEST, MOST VELVETY HOMING MISSILE KNOWN TO MAN.

YOU WAKE.

COSTA OXFORD STREET. WE MAKE IT BETTER EVERY MORNING

This all-copy ad from the United Kingdom describes a day in the life from the morning alarm clock to the first cup of coffee at Costa. The type gets brighter as you get closer to the part where "the caffeine surges through you like the smoothest most velvety homing missile known to man."

Differentiate products: Why should a reader believe a Hyundai Genesis is a better value than a BMW 3 Series? Because the headline says it is, or because the copy details independent testing that shows the Hyundai is faster, corners better, and overall performs better than the more expensive import? Sometimes you have to lay out the facts to make your case.

Multiple features: We hammer that One Thing into your brain. But sometimes there's more than one thing to talk about. You may lead with the main point but then bring in other key benefits to build a more persuasive case for the product. If you don't have the luxury of producing single-feature ads, you may have to find a way to weave several key points into the copy.

Difficult, complicated, or controversial subjects: If you want to change someone's mind or have people do something difficult, a catchy slogan isn't enough. For example, a recent antidrug ad tells parents who smoked pot in their youth not to feel like hypocrites when they talk to their kids about drugs. That's much more effective than "Just say no."

The Case for Long Copy

Writing good long-copy ads (200 words or more) is a fast-dying art. Reason one: It's assumed no one reads ads, so why bother? Reason two: No one knows how to write long copy well enough to hold a reader's interest . . . so see reason one.

Be honest. Even in textbooks that showcase the greatest ads ever written, do you actually read the copy? You probably don't even read the captions if they're more than five lines long. Before television shortened our attention span to 30 seconds, and the Internet cut that to 2 seconds, magazine and newspaper ads had enough copy for a beginning, a middle, and an end. We could feature many wonderful classic ads that read like well-crafted short stories, so damn persuasive that even we want to run out and buy the product. But showing these great ads from another age won't be of much value if your creative solution is a three-word headline plus logo.

When we look at ads from the 1920s through the 1950s, we're amazed at the craftsmanship. The best ads had a rhythm and flow that sucked the readers in, held their attention, and, in the end, left them convinced that the right brand of baked beans or laundry soap could improve their lives. Can you imagine a 400-word ad today for any kind of commodity packaged good like detergent, cereal, coffee, cigarettes, or whisky?

People will read a long-copy ad if they have a reason. John Caples said, "Don't be afraid of long copy. If your ad is interesting, people will be hungry for all the copy you can give them. If the ad is dull, short copy won't save it."[2]

The key to writing copy that's read, long or short, is to involve the reader. If the ad holds no reason to read on, don't expect anyone to get past a headline or visual.

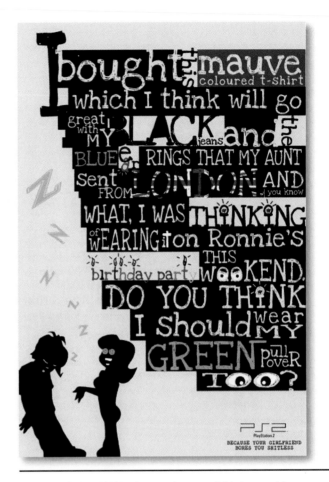

The benefit is buried at the very bottom of this busy ad from India. The inane comments from the girlfriend dominate the copy as well as put the boyfriend to sleep. The reason to buy a PlayStation 2 (and we're paraphrasing): "Because your girlfriend bores you 'senseless.'"

Writing Structure

Types of Copy

Knowing the various types of ad copy will never be as important as knowing how to write a good sentence. However, it can be useful to recognize several copy styles and know when to use them.

The story: This is also called "traditional" copy and features three main components: a beginning, a middle, and an end. Usually the beginning establishes the theme, makes a promise, plays off the headline, and in general sets up the ad. The middle is typically the sales pitch, with reasons why you should consider the product or service. The end is the summary and call to action. It wraps up the selling argument and encourages the reader to do something. A well-crafted story does not have to be a long-copy ad. But it should flow smoothly . . . as if you were telling a story that has a point.

Words of Wisdom

"There is no such thing as long copy. There is only too-long copy. And that can be two words if they are not the right two words."[B]

Jim Durfee, copywriter and founding partner, Carl Ally agency

Every Harley rider has a story. Some are even printable. In this campaign, Harley riders share their personal story in a beautifully designed ad. This is one of the last Harley-Davidson campaigns executed in a long and brilliant relationship with Carmichael Lynch.

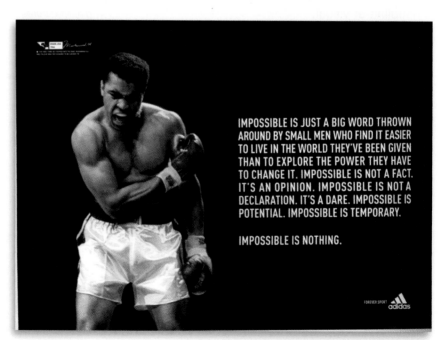

It's not a mistake that this copy is in all caps, nor is the choice of the spokesperson accidental. Who better to personify the idea that "Impossible Is Nothing?" Its powerfully persuasive start and rhythmic end packs a punch.

War Story

What are you gonna start?
sharpie.com

Sharpie ®. Uncap what's inside.
Sharpie® is one of those brands you know you are just going to love working on. It's surely iconic and loved by many, but at the same time, it was a brand that seemed to be struggling to find its place in a world that had changed around it.

When a brand is looking to find a new place in the world, the most critical element you need between you and your client is trust. You can't expect to rely on the same information, the same approaches, and the same tactics. You have to exorcise those demons—early and often. You have to break down the "them" and "us" mentality that permeates so many relationships and create a "we." That is where the power lies.

For our work on Sharpie®, that meant a couple of long, intense, yet well-structured sessions that we brought to bear on the issues facing the business. We worked through what it means to be a dominant, share-leading brand producing incremental growth and talked about creating a new category rather than being prisoners of our own success. We discussed at great length the role of technology and its impact on writing and, in turn, their business. Together, we highlighted the need to be more than a permanent marker in this very real world of the future. And we did the one thing so many brands have a hard time doing on their own—we looked at how consumers behaved *around* the product and *with* the product. We realized that the brand was something not owned by us, but owned by them, and that they had been whispering its real value to us for years.

That value—found in the art, the doodles, the sneakers, and the backpacks—was self-expression. And to be true to that value, we would never own it, but could have a role in promoting and advocating it that could be both powerful and persuasive. We could do something not "to them," but "for them" by celebrating their passion and helping them share it. And that has made all the difference.

Shifting from telling people about us and why they should buy us to showcasing, inspiring, and facilitating their innate passion for the product has changed the brand's fortunes. Yet, without trust and a conscious decision to approach the problem differently as a team, we never would have got there.[4]

Jamie Shuttleworth, executive vice president, chief strategy officer, Draftfcb Chicago draftfcb.com

Seth Godin has written several books about creating more effective marketing communication. In *All Marketers Are Liars,* he outlines some key points that relate to the advertising message, especially ad copy:

- Surprisingly, the less a marketer spells out, the more powerful the story becomes.[5]

- Great stories don't appeal to logic, but they often appeal to our senses.[6]

- The best stories promise to fulfill the wishes of a consumer's worldview: A shortcut. A miracle. Money. Social success. Safety. Ego. Pleasure. Belonging. Or avoiding the opposite of the above.[7]

Bullet points: Many clients will say, "No one has time to read copy. Just list the key points." In many cases, this is just fine, especially if you can't think of One Thing to say and need to list a lot of features. Usually, the points are

PÜR takes care of water by filtering out contaminants. Delivering clean, delicious water right in your kitchen.   www.purwater.com

Body copy doesn't always have be in nice neat blocks. In this ad, Pur outlines the cost savings of filtered tap water vs. bottled water, all within a single drop.

prioritized by the importance of selling features, with the most important always going first. Too many times, the writer and client can't decide what's important, so they list everything and hope the reader will find something he or she likes.

You'll see a lot of bullet point copy in retail newspaper ads, business-to-business magazines, and direct mail. This technique has sort of a "down and dirty" look, so it's usually not appropriate for a high-quality or brand-image promotion. In addition, a long list of short bullet points takes up more real estate than a few well-written sentences in paragraph format. So if saving space is your only justification for using bullet points, measure carefully and reconsider.

One technique that can be very effective is a mix of traditional sentences and bullet points. The bullets highlight key points and, when done correctly, draw the reader's eye to the most important selling messages.

One-liner: Sometimes the headline is the only copy in the ad. Other times the headline and visual work together to convey the main message, and a single copy line adds additional information. If you don't have to explain a lot about the product, need to direct people to a website for more detailed information, or just want to promote a brand image, one-liners (or no copy at all) work just fine.

Body copy doesn't always have to be in nice, neat blocks. In this ad, PÜR outlines the cost savings of filtered tap water versus bottled water, all within a single drop.

Writing Style

Advertising Is Not English (Even in English-Speaking Countries)

In other classes, you were told to write essays and reports with an assigned number of words, paragraphs, or pages. These were graded for spelling, composition, vocabulary, and comprehension. Your teachers were looking not for tight, get-right-to-the-point persuasion, but rather for how you could expand a one-sentence idea into a four-page paper.

In advertising classes and in the real world, your writing will be evaluated on how well you communicate. Period. Using real words. In the way real people talk. Your writing must attract jaded readers and hook them in the brain. You are appealing to a consumer's wants and needs. Not to teachers who get paid to grade papers by the pound. As Shakespeare said, brevity is the soul of wit. Good advertising is both witty and brief. Now this doesn't mean you can completely ignore grammar and spelling. A copywriter can dress like a bum, but you can't write sloppy. Even though you may shatter a few rules of English grammar, the copy should be tight, easy to read, and clearly understood. Your copy style should be tailored to the target audience and the product. Remember tone? That should guide your style of writing. So an ad for a brand of chewing gum can be hip and informal, while a brochure for a million-dollar yacht should be more formal and elegant.

Persuade, Don't Impress

When it comes to ad copy, you don't have to impress readers with how many words you know. Or even by how much you know about the product. Instead, you have to persuade them your product meets their wants and needs. And you don't have a lot of time or space to do it.

A common error many novice writers make is to show the client how much they know about the product, especially for new products or new clients. Or they dredge up every fancy word they can find from a thesaurus to replace the simple language most people use. You should make people believe how good the product is, not how smart you are. Some ads don't say, "Buy me." They say, "Look how I can repackage what the clients told me so I can show them I was listening." That's OK for the first draft. But on the next round, take out the meat-ax and start hacking away.

When you're given a creative brief, or write a copy platform, don't forget to keep looking for the "So Whats." Find out what's really important to the consumer, and then see if the client's priorities mesh.

The "Seven Deadly Sins" of Copywriting

A lot of teachers have told you how to write. Now we're telling you how to write better—by pointing out some common mistakes and how to correct them. We call these the Seven Deadly Sins. When you see them in your writing, make a brief confession and do penance by rewriting. Even experienced writers commit these sins. As with other transgressions, you can't feel guilty until you know it's a sin.

This year, Mum's giving me flowers.

I don't deserve them.

I deserve a good swift kick up the bum.

But Mums aren't like that. No matter how badly you screw up they always say "Never mind love, we all still love you." Doesn't your Mum do that?

Unconditional. That's the word.

All that stuff about your life flashing before your eyes is absolutely true. And I couldn't believe it Mum, you were in practically every scene.

And all those crappy movie scenes about never telling people how much you love them till it's too late? Well they're true too.

Mum, you gave me the gift of life, and what did I do with it? Played with it for a bit, then threw it away.

And now, after all those Mother's Days I forgot because I was too busy with mates or chasing after girls, what does she do? She brings *me* flowers.

I never gave my Mum a thought as I was flying down the road that night.

But I bet a little bit of her was thinking about me as she watched TV in the hours before that knock on the door.

My advice? Treat this Mother's Day like it's your last.

Then spend a year making sure it isn't.

This long-copy ad in an Australian newspaper combines the sentimentality of Mother's Day with a safe driving message.

"Toilet paper should help keep your hands clean, too."

The copy is standard packaged good advertising jargon: "Ready for the straight talk about toilet paper and getting clean?" and "Satisfaction guaranteed. Or your money back." What separates it from old-school ads is the new variety of ways readers can connect with the advertiser—QR code, website URL, and a Facebook page . . . plus all the fine print about claiming a guarantee. Regardless of old school or new school, there's too much going on.

The Seven Deadly Sins are:

1. Advertising-ese
2. Bad taste
3. Deadwood
4. Generic benefits
5. Laundry lists
6. Poor grammar
7. Wimpy words

Let's explore each of these sins in detail and discuss ways to avoid them.

Advertising-ese: Don't confuse using proven selling words with the mindless clichés in some advertising. We've grown up with advertising jargon, so it's natural to write ads that way. Read your copy out loud. If it sounds like it should be on QVC, rewrite it.

The best money can buy. You've seen the rest, now try the best. Isn't that amazing? Don't delay, call today. One call does it all. Nobody else offers this kind of quality at such a low price. Hurry, these deals won't last forever. Unique. New and improved. Exclusive. State-of-the-art. Incredible. More for your money. Often imitated, but never equaled. You deserve the best. Get it now!

But wait, there's more . . . the list goes on and on.

In some cases, advertising-ese includes unsubstantiated claims or boasts of being the best without providing detail to back it up. If you can't prove it, don't say it, because you've just lost all your credibility.

Advertising-ese also includes trite punctuation, especially the dreaded exclamation point. If you have to add ! to a headline or even a line of copy you're shouting that you can't think of anything clever or memorable. You used to see phrases like:

It's just wonderful! The all-new 1965 Oldsmobile Vista Cruiser with the new improved smooth-as-silk Strato-Glide transmission!

Bad taste: Sexist, racist, insensitive, offensive, and vulgar language. In this age of political correctness, people can find hidden meanings in the most innocent messages. When you look at some of the ads from the 1930s and '40s, it's amazing how African Americans were portrayed. In the 1950s and '60s, women were shown as mindless neat freaks, more concerned with whiter shirts than careers. Today, writers who would never use stereotyped racial or sexist language think nothing of using sexual puns, vulgar language, and scatological humor. If you are appealing to a general audience, be careful what you say and how you say it. If you are going for an edgy concept that appeals to a very select group who won't be offended by your bad taste, go for it, and accept the consequences.

Deadwood: This is one of the most common sins committed by beginning writers. They say the same thing several different ways, time after time, in a very redundant fashion that wastes time and space, over and over again, ad infinitum. Say what you mean. Then tighten it up. Look for ways to eliminate unnecessary words and phrases. Don't overstate the obvious. Don't include a description when a visual will work better. This has been stressed by English composition teachers since grade school, but somehow, ad students forget it.

> **Original:** Wamco engineers have developed several new ways to help original equipment manufacturers make products that are accepted better by their customers, which, in turn, makes them more profitable.

> **Better:** Wamco makes your products more profitable.

Generic benefits: Also known as "weasel words," these benefits are so vague they could apply to almost anybody and anything. You may have attached a benefit to a feature, but have you gone far enough? Keep asking "So what?" and you'll eliminate generic benefits. Always lead with the strongest benefit. Readers may not get to it if you bury it at the end of the ad.

Laundry lists: This sin usually involves grouping features with no benefits, and all have equal value. It's hard to find the Big Idea. This is a crutch used by some writers who don't know much about the product, so they throw every feature into the copy and string them together with no relation to each other or connection to a benefit. The temptation is to cram as many copy points into an ad to let the client think you know the product. For example:

> This sleek powerboat features a powerful fuel-injected engine, two-tone gel coat finish, a tandem trailer, removable carpeting, lots of cup holders, an in-dash CD player, and a five-year warranty. Who could ask for more in a family runabout?

Poor grammar: You should make your copy easy to read, and sometimes that means using the proper mechanics of English, such as when to end a sentence, and when to use commas, dashes, colons, and other punctuation. You should understand sentence structure, such as the need for a subject and a verb, and how to use prepositions and conjunctions and phrases. Given that, don't feel compelled to follow every rule of English composition. While you should not try to impress readers with your brilliance, you don't want them to think you are an illiterate slob.

Speaking of punctuation, as we mentioned earlier, don't overuse the exclamation point! Also, don't overuse ellipses . . . they break up the flow and usually indicate you haven't figured out a good transition between sentences. Use commas only when it's necessary to provide a pause or improve the readability. Some writers (David Ogilvy included) don't like to use periods in headlines, even if it's a complete sentence. Others believe a period adds deliberate emphasis. As long as your copy reads well, punctuation is usually a matter of personal choice.

This ad violates most of the rules: reverse copy, small print, and busy design, just to name a few. However, a real Jack Daniel's aficionado would enjoy reading all the short stories that make up this ad. For example, "When it came to music, Mr. Jack was one hell of a whisky maker."

Wimpy words: This category covers a lot of territory. Certain words rob copy of its vitality. Writing in passive voice also weakens copy. Beginning a sentence with a prepositional phrase or subordinate clause also dilutes the power.

Some examples:

- Usually you should never start a sentence with ***There***.

  Bad: There are a lot of reasons why people visit their friendly Toyota dealer. First of all there's the large selection they have.

  Better: People visit their Toyota dealer for a lot of reasons: First, they offer the largest selection . . .

- ***That*** is overused. Try reading it out loud, with and without *that*, and see what sounds better.

- ***Be*** verbs . . . "to be or not to be" is great for Shakespeare but not advertising copy. Derivatives of "to be" include *is, are, was, were,* and *being.*

  Bad: If you *have been* considering purchasing a luxury sport utility, then you *are* in luck.

  Better: Interested in a luxury sport utility? Lucky you.

- **Passive voice:** Your copy should take action rather than being acted upon (even that tip reads awkwardly). Examples:

  Bad: Why do you think Sony computers *were chosen* by design engineers *who have held* senior positions in this industry?

  Better: Why the industry's top design engineers picked Sony.

- **Lead with phrases and clauses:** Get right to the point. Don't put a phrase or clause in its path. Also, don't string a lot of phases together in the same sentence. Short, simple declarative sentences work best. For example:

Bad: After shopping *for your family, on the way* home, stop in *for a cool* refreshing DQ Mister Misty.

Better: DQ Mister Misty: a refreshing treat after a long day of shopping.

Make a copy of Table 10.1, cut it out, and keep it handy when you're writing copy. It's also handy when reviewing other people's work.

TABLE 10.1   *Seven Deadly Sins of Copywriting*

1. Advertising-ese	Write the way people talk, eliminate clichés and useless phrases, and keep it conversational (read it out loud).
2. Bad taste	Watch for sexist, racist, offensive language and symbols. If it feels wrong, it probably is.
3. Deadwood	Weed out weak, redundant, unnecessary words and phrases. Keep the flow of thought moving.
4. Generic benefits	Provide consumer benefits in terms they understand. Appeal to their lives. Lead with strongest benefit. Is one benefit so strong that it is the central truth or One Thing about this product?
5. Laundry lists	Don't list features without reference to what they mean to the consumer. Weave benefits into the ad and prioritize them based on the consumer's point of view.
6. Poor grammar	Watch for errors in spelling, punctuation, and verb tense. Know the rules and when to break the rules. Use fragments if it improves readability.
7. Wimpy words	Use power words, active voice, and short simple sentences. If it doesn't feel strong, it's not.

Good body copy can be persuasive and short. In this ad we are simply asked to save the salmon for its beauty or so we can enjoy eating it at Legal Sea Foods.

Rising Star

Breathing Room

My break into advertising wasn't as easy as it seemed it would be at first. When the creative director of Rethink—a hot Vancouver agency—saw my book at a portfolio show and offered me an internship, I thought I had arrived. Not only was I the first in my class to land an internship, I was going to the shop recently crowned Agency of the Year. I thought I'd waltz in, hit a couple home runs, and be offered a job. But eight weeks later I was back in Toronto.

I accepted an internship at Ogilvy & Mather with the hope that they'd reward my free labor with a job. Yet again, no offer. Four disheartening months later, I got a one-year contract at Grip, an agency full of seasoned creatives to learn from. Now I had some breathing room.

When my contract at Grip was drawing to a close, a senior writer who'd mentored me at school gave me an opportunity at TBWA\Toronto. After 18 months, I had my first full-time job. At TBWA, I developed a work ethic borne out of the realization that nothing in advertising comes easily. Over the next two years, my work improved by leaps and bounds.

Then I learned that Zak Mroueh—a world-renowned creative director I had long admired—was opening his own agency: Zulu Alpha Kilo. Zak was known for having fiercely high standards. And I knew that if I wanted to create world-class work, this was the place to be. After a little badgering I got an interview and eventually a job as the agency's first full-time writer.

The expectations are high and the pace is intense, but the results are worth it. I work with incredibly talented people on some of the best brands in the world. If my future is half as bright as this young agency's, I have a lot to look forward to.[9]

George Ault, copywriter, Zulu Alpha Kilo, Toronto, Ontario, Canada, zulualphakilo.com

Power Writing

We discussed what not to do. Now we'll offer some recommendations that will help make any ad read easier and communicate more effectively.

Mix short and long sentences: Sometimes short sentences work best, but you don't have to make every sentence three words. Mix up short and long sentences. Use the short ones for the sales message, or if you like, use the long sentence for the setup and the short one for the "punch line."

Use simple words if you can: If you're writing a technical brochure for orthopedic surgeons, you're not going to talk about the "shinbone." But in most consumer work, simple language usually communicates best. Remember you are writing to persuade, not to impress readers with your vocabulary. Again, we refer to the venerable John Caples: "Simple words are powerful words. Even the best educated people don't resent simple words. But they're the words many people understand. Write to your barber or mechanic."[10] Caples found a simple word change had an immediate impact on response rates.

Write the way people talk: Most people use contractions and speak in sentence fragments. Try to write copy as if you're talking to a friend. Read your copy out loud. Does it sound like a normal person talking or an announcer from a 1960s game show?

Match the copy style to the product tone: More sophisticated products require more formal approaches (you'll never see "Yo. Check out Rolls-Royce. We got yer luxury right here!"). Copy for technical products should indicate some level of technical competence in the copy. But for the vast majority of consumer products, an informal, conversational style works best.

Active verbs and positive attitude: Don't tiptoe into a benefit. Get right to the point. Use active voice and show excitement for the product. You can't do this with every sentence, but try to make an effort to activate your writing.

Be specific: "A flat-faced, bug-eyed, pig-snorting Boston Terrier" conveys a stronger image than "dog." Rather than using "soon" say "today." Instead of "It's been stated by many physicians," write "Doctors say."

Parallel construction: As with taglines and headlines, you can use parallel construction in ad body copy. But use it judiciously and only to emphasize a point. Otherwise, it can become annoying or something even worse—poetry.

Alliteration, rhythm, and rhyme: These techniques can spice up body copy. But use them carefully. You can emphasize key points, but you don't want your text to look like a string of slogans or a Dr. Seuss book. (So, you do not like rhyming text today, try it and you may I say.)

Tighten it up: The old rule is if you want 100 words, write 200. ~~As opposed to most good things in life, shorter is better. Find a way to say things in fewer words. Don't waste your reader's time. This is very important so~~ if we could say it in two words, "write tight."

Write out loud: Read your print copy out loud. Does it sound as good as it reads? If you need inspiration, read some of the great speeches of all time—fireside chats by Franklin Roosevelt, Winston Churchill's messages during World War II, Kennedy's inaugural, Martin Luther King's "I Have a Dream" speech, and Ronald Reagan's tribute to the *Columbia* astronauts. No matter how you feel about politics, these speeches were powerfully written. They feature simple eloquence, memorable catchphrases, and vivid imagery. Most of all, they resonate in the hearts of listeners long after the speech was delivered.

Checklist for Better Copy

After you've written what you think is your final draft, use this checklist. You might find that you're not done writing.

- **Strong opening line (pull-through):** Is the first line good enough to be a headline? It's got to pull the reader through. Readers take the path of least resistance—make it easy for them.

- **Appeal to consumers' point of view:** Why do I want to buy this product or service? Appeal to the reader's self interest—what's in it for him or her? Remember the "So Whats." Is the style appropriate for the audience? *Tell me about* my *yard, not* your *grass seed.*

- **Clear central idea (the One Thing):** After reading your ad, will the reader be left with the one main idea you want to convey? Does your copy provide mixed messages? Go back to your copy platform to check.

Words of Wisdom

"Fine writing? Do you want masterpieces? Or do you want to see the goddamned sales curves stop moving down and start moving up? What do you want?"[11]

Rosser Reeves, copywriter and former CEO, Ted Bates Worldwide

- **Strongest sales point first:** Lead with your strongest selling point. The reader may not get to it if you bury it.

- **Strong supporting information:** Is the information persuasive, and presented in a logical order? Does it support the main idea?

- **Easy reading:** Is the message clear? Does it say it in as few words as possible and as many words as necessary? Even the most intelligent people appreciate simple language. People will read long copy if they are interested in the subject.

- **Power writing:** Can you use active voice rather than passive? Do you start any sentences with "There are"? Ruthlessly weed out unnecessary words. Get rid of the deadwood. "Avoid clichés like the plague." Strip away the ad jargon and "me too" phrases.

- **Call to action:** What do you want the readers to do? Where can they get more information? Where can they buy the product? For well-known widely distributed consumer products, it may not be necessary. But for retail, it's mandatory. For technical products and other considered purchases, you need to establish a connection that may require several more contacts. The ad is merely a conduit to more meaningful communication.

For a change, we'd like to talk about *your* air bags.

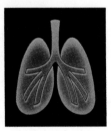

Take a deep breath. Relax. Get comfortable. You are about to read some good news.

Recently, Honda brought its advanced Low-Emission Vehicle (LEV) technology to everyone in America. All fifty states. Voluntarily.

It arrived in the form of the all-new 1998 Accord and the Civic. Both offer engines which meet California's strict Low-Emission Vehicle standard. But now you can buy one not just in California, but in Michigan. Texas. Ohio. Georgia. Wherever you live.

Both cars meet a 70-percent-lower emission standard for smog-contributing non-methane organic gases than is required by the most stringent federal standard. With no performance sacrifice or cost penalty.

Plus, in California and specific states throughout the Northeast, we're now offering our new Accord Ultra-Low Emission Vehicle (ULEV). It's the first auto certified by the California Air Resources Board as a ULEV, making it the cleanest gasoline-powered production car sold in the U.S. Ever.

That means, based on last year's sales figures, more than 60 percent of all new Accords and Civics, some 450,000 cars, will now be more environmentally friendly.

Historically, Honda has continually been a leader in fuel-efficiency and low-emission technology. Because we always think about more than the products we make. We think about the people who use them, and the world in which they live.

Which, in the end, helps us all breathe a little easier.

HONDA
Thinking.

For more about environmentally friendly Honda products, call 1-888-CC-HONDA ext. 109 or visit www.honda.com. ©1997 Honda North America, Inc.

This is what we mean by power writing. Notice the mix of long and short sentences, the use of specific information, the conversational style, and the smooth flow from beginning to end.

You're Not Done Yet

You've just written a modern masterpiece of ad copy. You've avoided all the Deadly Sins. It's passed the checklist with flying colors. So what's next? Honest evaluation.

Give it a rest: The best advice we can give any creative person is "Write hot. Edit cold." In other words, if you're on a roll, keep going. Don't worry about word count, style, or even content. Write what's on your mind. Then put it away. Watch TV. Go jogging. Do anything but think about your ad. After a decent interval, look at your copy. Most people think, "Jeez, that's awful. What was I thinking?" So start the process again, this time with more focus and insight.

Mark Twain offered this advice for editing: "Kill all your darlings." In other words, get rid of words or phrases you think are cute and clever and focus on what really matters. Jim Durfee explains:

> "Kill all your darlings." If a single commandment could be burned into the mind of each beginning writer, it should be this one . . . By shunning that darling of all darlings—the pun headline—I'm left with no-nonsense straight talk . . . By avoiding cutesy-clever copy phrases I eliminate the danger of show-off writing. And when I'm writing long, flowing, beautiful, heart-pounding sentences (like this one) I know I'm in danger of spewing ego-garbage. Which endangers clear thinking. So I start over. Well, usually.[12]

Adjust your work habits: Everyone has a time when they're most creative. Unfortunately, it's usually not during the typical 9-to-5 workday. That's why it's important to write hot and edit cold. When you get an idea, jot it down no matter where you are. If you feel like writing 1,000 words at 2 a.m., that's great. E-mail it to work and edit as long as you can stay awake.

Get help: Most good writers are excellent proofreaders—of someone else's work. They are usually criminally sloppy when it comes to their own writing. For proper editing, you need diligent, objective, and independent proofreaders. Don't rely on a computer spell checker. *You may have the write spelling butt the wrong meaning.*

Mark it up: Whether you're editing another writer or your own work, document the problems or change them. This requires printing a hard copy and scribbling comments just like your great grandparents did. We've included a selection of editing marks in the Appendix. Use these when you're proofing your copy.

Don't stop: We can't think of a single project that we couldn't do better the second or third time (including this book). If you have the luxury of time, keep improving your copy. Replace weak words. Cut out the deadwood. Say it better with fewer words. Keep polishing that copy 'til it shines.

Words of Wisdom

"Advertising is a business of words, but advertising agencies are infested with men and women who cannot write."[13]

David Ogilvy, copywriter
and founding partner,
Ogilvy & Mather

Who's Who?

Janet Champ—Janet Champ started her career in advertising as the 15th employee, the receptionist, at Wieden + Kennedy. But Champ dreamed of being a writer and had the talent to back it up. Over her 15 years at Wieden + Kennedy, she worked on everything from Coca-Cola to Microsoft, but it was her work for Nike Women that made her famous. Champ won gold at Cannes, Best of Show at the One Show, and two consecutive Kelly Print Awards—the only writer in history to do so. She was recognized by the *National Women's Law Review,* the National Women's Health Board, and the Office of the U.S. Surgeon General for the Nike TV spot "If You Let Me Play." In 1999 she was named *Adweek's* Copywriter of the Year. Champ also has the painful distinction of having been sued by the surviving Beatles for the use of their song "Revolution" in the first TV spot she ever worked on. Since 1999, she has been a freelance copywriter "trying to do good, instead of evil."

Jim Durfee—As copywriter and cofounder of the Carl Ally agency, Jim Durfee was one of the leaders of the Creative Revolution. His philosophy was that advertising is a product, not a service. "A product," Durfee said, "is something that is molded, produced, thought out and set out before the person: 'We have made this for you, we think this will help.' A service is hat-in-hand and through the side door. It was a completely different attitude toward what an agency was and what an agency made."[14]

Ed McCabe—Ed McCabe has profoundly influenced the field of advertising. For more than four decades, his ads broke new ground for such clients as Volvo and Perdue chicken. Many of today's most creative advertising professionals follow his innovative teachings and examples. He cofounded Scali, McCabe, Sloves, Inc., and helped build the company into the 10th-largest ad agency network in the world. For 10 years after leaving Scali, McCabe, Sloves, he was CEO of McCabe & Co. At the age of 34, he was inducted into the Copywriters Hall of Fame, the youngest to be so honored.

Helayne Spivak—Helayne Spivak now runs a consulting company (HRS Consulting) and is still considered one of the most accomplished leaders in the ad business. She has run some of the world's top creative departments: At Young & Rubicam, she was chief creative officer; at J. Walter Thompson, she was worldwide creative director. She has won nearly every major honor the industry offers, including numerous Clio Awards and the Gold Award at the Cannes International Advertising Festival.

Exercises

1. Branded Surprise

Do you remember a time when you were surprised by a brand?

- Share a story about a time when you or someone you know was surprised by a brand. The surprise could have come at any point in life. Surprise can be good and bad . . . just look at the element of surprise and the emotions behind it. If the surprise happens with the brand, be ready to spin it into body copy. If it's not, do the *twist* and see if you can make lemons out of lemonade. Remember the old VW ad, "Lemon"? Something not so good sold a lot of cars.

- Focusing on the emotion behind the surprise, write 150 words of copy to express the experience. Think beginning, middle, and end, and tell your story.

- Now trade stories with a partner who will use the Seven Deadly Sins to edit hot.

- Next trade edited copy and rewrite your ad. Add a headline and visual, and you've got a story line ad.

- Shares your ad with the class and be prepared to discuss the strategic strength of your branded story, and consider if it has legs.

2. Consumer Packaged Goods

We've always figured that if you can write copy for a consumer packaged good you can write for anything. After all, shampoo is shampoo is shampoo—until you read the ads.

- *Instructors:* Pick a brand; we like Excedrin Migraine. Provide the students with a brief, so they are all working from the same strategic document.

- *Students:* Develop three taglines each and be ready to share your favorite.

- *Instructors:* Make a list of the tags on the board. Then, across the top, write the tips for effective headlines (see Chapter 9). Use this as a matrix to discuss the merits of each tagline. Get it down to two or three and then have the class vote on the winning tagline.

- *Students:* From here, develop an ad with a headline, a visual, and 75–100 words of copy—using the new tagline. Presents your work to the class and discuss the rationale for your copy choices.

- *Instructors:* Have the class use the *Checklist for Better Copy* to guide their critique. It's very interesting to see how the creative varies and yet how each approach fits with the tagline.

3. Editing the Pros

- *Instructors:* Find a long-copy ad—one with copy that's good, but not great. An ad with multiple components—subhead, captions, and bullets—is preferable.

- *Instructors:* Write up a copy sheet (each section of copy within a Word document) and give it to the students, along with a consumer profile.

- *Students:* Take until the end of class to rewrite the copy. Then rough out a pencil sketch to show copy placement.

- *Students:* Share your copy edits, along with your pencil sketch.

- *Instructors:* Once everyone has shared, show the class the original ad. Imagine the discussion that will lead to.

- *Instructors:* You can spin this in a different direction focusing on design. In this case take an ad that's light on copy, but the copy is very well written. Give students the same two documents (copy sheet and profile). Then let them do a comped layout using the existing copy. They share, and then you show the original ad. Let the discussion unfold.

- *Instructors:* This can also be great on a quiz to test students' comprehension of creative principles.

Visit www.sagepub.com/altstiel3e to access these additional learning tools

- Video Links
- Web Resources

- eFlashcards
- Web Quizzes

Chapter

11

Print

Writing for Reading

We're using print to start our section on writing for each major medium. In this chapter we cover magazines, newspapers, collateral, and out of home. While the trend is toward using less traditional media and more digital, magazines and newspapers still capture a major share of the total advertising dollar. Instead of totally fading away, they are finding ways to integrate themselves with digital marketing tools. We'll begin by looking at creative opportunities with magazines.

Magazines

A magazine ad is an ideal palette for applying all the creative strategies and tactics we've discussed in previous chapters. Magazines also present a lot of creative opportunities based on the variety of sizes, shapes, and multiple-page combinations. Finally, a magazine ad is a perfect size and shape for your portfolio—small enough to fit anywhere, large enough for long copy and to make a design statement.

Why Magazines?

From a creative standpoint, magazines offer many advantages. Specifically:

- *Magazines are selective.* Some magazines are devoted to very narrow interests, such as water gardens or old Porsches. Many general-interest publications print special editions based on region, occupation, or income.

- *In most cases, the printing quality is much better than in any other medium.* Four-color ads really pop. And when you run inserts, the sky's the limit for the number of inks and varnishes.

- *Magazines usually last longer than other media.* Weekly, monthly, and quarterly publications get passed around and reread. Your ads are seen longer and more often by more people.

Words of Wisdom

"We've always been concerned about doing great print advertising . . . just think of all the magazines that have been launched . . . there must be a lot of people reading."[1]

Jay Chiat, copywriter and founding partner, Chiat\Day

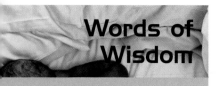
- *Magazines can add prestige.* Publications such as *Architectural Digest* reach an upscale market. So if you're selling expensive cars, jewelry, or real estate, upscale magazines are the perfect choice.

- *Many magazines offer value-added services to advertisers.* For example, many business publications have "bingo cards" in the back where a reader can circle a number to get literature. Others offer advertisers their lists for direct mail or market research databases.

- *Magazines give you a lot of design flexibility.* Whether you use a series of fractional pages, multipage inserts, advertorials, or a series of single-page ads, magazines give creative people and media directors a lot of options.

- *Magazines are integrated with the Internet.* Most major magazines also have websites, which opens all kinds of promotional and cross-promotional opportunities for print and online advertisers.

Magazines and Campaigns

Magazines and campaigns seem made for each other. You can have a campaign within a single issue with multiple insertions. The periodic nature of magazines also fits many campaign strategies. Since readership of various magazines transcends demographics, it's natural to run ads in several magazines to maximize impact. Magazines also fit well as part of an integrated marketing campaign. Here are just a few examples:

- Include a music or interactive CD-ROM as an insert in a magazine.

- Use cross-promotion with a compatible brand to cosponsor a contest, sweepstakes, or special offer.

- Run a series of short-copy ads that direct readers to a website for more detailed information.

- Use tear-out mini-inserts that include coupons.

- If they will fit within a magazine, include product samples in your insert.

Where to Find the Best Magazine Ads

The Association of Magazine Media presents the Kelly Awards for the best magazine advertising each year. Winning a Kelly is a major accomplishment, and all the top creative shops compete. When asked what it takes to win a Kelly Award, Mal MacDougall, chief creative officer of Christy MacDougall Mitchell, gave the following advice:

IT'S EVEN MORE FUN WHEN YOU KNOW WHERE THE FISH ARE.

TAKEMEFISHING.org

Magazines allow unique ways to showcase the printed word. Here the page appears to be pulled up to reveal the selling message and direct the reader to the website for more information.

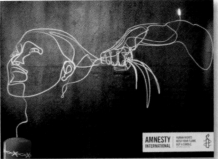

Magazines provide the opportunity for campaign continuity week to week or month to month as well as the ability to dominate the spread in each issue.

QR codes sometimes stick out like sore thumbs in magazine ads. This series of ads made the code from vacation images (and the real code is tucked discretely in the corner). The only purpose of the ad is to send people to the airline's microsite.

Words of Wisdom

"You can entertain people in print. You can make print emotional. And you can sell your product. Print copy can cover all the small differences that add up to a big reason for buying a specific brand."[3]

Hal Riney, copywriter and founding partner, Hal Riney & Partners

Keep it simple. Don't try to be crazy. Don't try to go to your computer and think you can do something off the wall. Do something within a very narrow strategy. The narrower the better. The strategy is a very short sentence; the soul of the brand you're trying to talk about. Simplicity is what's going to work. You cannot win a Kelly award with a complicated message. Get to know who is really reading that magazine. Decide whom you really want to talk to. Narrow it down to a tiny few people. Then you know exactly who is reading this golf magazine, fishing magazine, fashion magazine or gardening magazine. Make your message simple, clear and aim it right at them.[4]

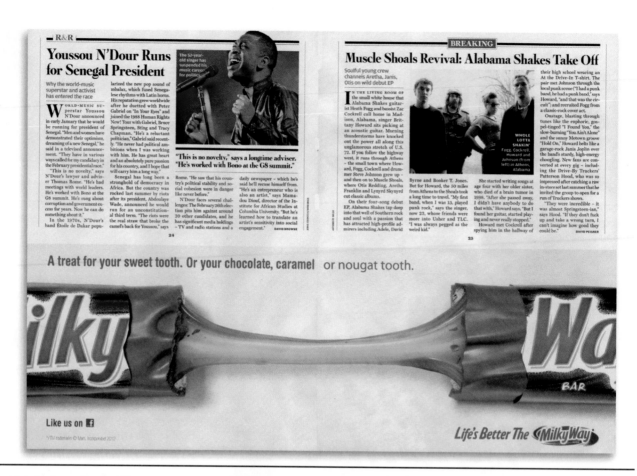

You don't need to buy the whole spread to dominate it.

Another way to dominate a spread is to combine a full-page ad with a facing fractional-page ad. Leveraging editorial content to maximize your product attributes can also be a benefit of fractional-page buys.

UNCOVER YOUR NATURAL BEAUTY

PANTENE PRO-V

Front cover.

PANTENE PRO-V

HEALTHIER HAIR*
HEALTHIER PLANET*

Pantene **NATURE FUSION** Pro-V systems with Cassia make hair up to **10X** stronger.* Plus, new plant-based bottles make a healthy choice for the planet.

PANTENE. HAIR SO HEALTHY IT SHINES*
Check out facebook.com/Pantene

*vs. non-conditioning shampoo
*plant-based plastic has lower carbon footprint per gram vs. petroleum-based plastic
*strength against damage vs. non-conditioning shampoo

Back cover.

NATURE FUSION MOISTURE BALANCE GIVES UP TO 10X STRONGER HAIR*

-Eva Mendes

"WHEN I TREAT MY HAIR WELL, I SEE RESULTS."

"THERE ARE CERTAIN PRODUCTS THAT YOU KEEP COMING BACK TO AND, FOR ME, PANTENE IS ONE OF THEM."

*Strength against damage vs. non-conditioning shampoo

LOOK NATURALLY BEAUTIFUL

PANTENE'S NATURE FUSION COLLECTION COMBINES ADVANCED HAIR CARE TECHNOLOGY WITH NATURALLY DERIVED INGREDIENTS, SUCH AS CASSIA, FOR GORGEOUS RESULTS. HERE'S HOW:

- Pantene Nature Fusion collections blend Pro-V technology with naturally derived ingredients, such as Cassia.

- Moisture Balance shampoo captures the potential of Cassia to strengthen hair against damage, while leaving hair soft, shiny, and feeling moisturized.

- The Moisture Balance conditioner insulates strands to help keep moisture in and protect hair against damage. With ginger, calendula and aloe vera, this conditioner leaves your hair soft and radiant.

- Also available in a Smooth Vitality formula, designed to help seal the outer layer of your hair and lock out unwanted humidity, so you get a smooth, controlled look.

INTRODUCING MORE
ENVIRONMENTALLY
FRIENDLY* PACKAGING THAT'S
100% RECYCLABLE,
EXCLUDING THE CAP.

Each bottle is made with sugarcane-derived plastic, up to 59% excluding the cap—a first in the hair care industry! The new plastic uses **70% less fossil fuels** and results in **170% less greenhouse gases** vs. traditional, petroleum based plastic. Get healthier** hair and take one small step towards a healthier Earth* by using Pantene's Nature Fusion.

**vs. non-conditioning shampoo

ENTER THE FIND YOUR STRENGTH SWEEPSTAKES!

Two lucky winners will get a healthy dose of "look great" prizes from Women's Health:
- One-year membership to a local gym
- Hair services at a local salon
- Gift basket full of Pantene Nature Fusion products

Visit **WomensHealthMag.com/Pantene** and enter for your chance to win!

No purchase necessary to enter or win. A purchase will not improve your chances of winning. Void Where Prohibited. Sweepstakes begins at 12:00 am Eastern Time, Nov. 22nd, 2011 and ends 11:59 pm Eastern Time, Feb. 9th, 2012. Must be over 18 years of age and resident 50 US or DC to enter. For the Official Rules, visit WomensHealthmag.com/Pantene. The Sponsor of the Sweepstakes is Rodale Inc., 400 South 10th Street, Emmaus, PA 18098-0099.

START TAKING SMALL STEPS TOWARDS A HEALTHIER PLANET* WITH PANTENE NATURE FUSION.
FIND OUT MORE AT PANTENE.COM/NATUREFUSION

*plant-based plastic has a lower carbon footprint per gram vs. petroleum based plastic.

Inside spread.

Inserts allow the ultimate in creative flexibility. This one features a double gatefold with die cuts on the right and left panels. The inside spread reveals details of sweepstakes, and the back page features the obligatory beauty shot.

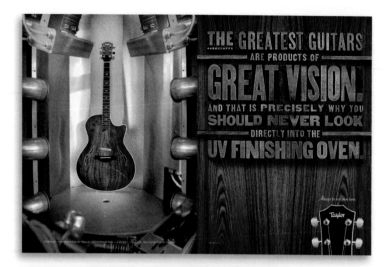

Magazines not only provide a great opportunity to create campaign continuity; they also give you the large palette to pay off big ideas.

Newspapers

What's black and white and read all over? Not necessarily newspapers. Today they use almost as much color as magazines. Read all over? Not anymore. Readership has dropped off drastically, especially in people under 35. Still, in terms of advertising dollars spent, newspapers are a major force, especially when ads are packaged with both the print and online versions of the paper.

Why Newspapers?

From a creative standpoint, newspapers offer many advantages. Specifically, they are:

- *Local:* They fill in small niches so you can pinpoint advertising in a city or suburban area.

- *Timely:* Ads can be changed within hours of appearance; they can promote short-term events.

- *Widespread in their coverage* (although readership is declining).

- *Controlled by the readers:* They can scan, skip, or plod through paper (allowing for long-copy ads).

- *Well suited for co-op opportunities:* National advertisers develop ads and help pay for them.

- *Specialized:* They include supplements and special-interest sections (sports, features, etc.).

- *Believable:* They offer news and sports first; entertainment is secondary.

- *Convenient:* Papers can be taken anywhere—trains, restaurants, bathrooms.

- *Large size:* A newspaper page offers a huge canvas for your ad. A full-page magazine ad is only a fraction of the size of a full-page newspaper ad.

Retail Advertising

About $4 out of every $5 spent in newspapers goes to retail advertising. Retail is also called "local" advertising; however, with national chains running traditional-looking retail ads in national newspapers like *USA Today,* it doesn't seem proper to call them local.

Retail is different from other advertising in the following ways:

- **Urgent:** Consumers act on it quickly ("Buy me today or you miss your chance"). It works quickly or not at all.

- **Price oriented:** Most national magazines do not feature price; most retail newspaper ads do.

- **The cheaper the merchandise, the more elements in the ad:** Tiffany's does not have 24 different items with prices in their ads like Walmart.

- **The store personality is very important:** What is the personality—bargain prices (Walmart), service (Nordstrom), reliability (Target), length established (Jewel-Osco), or class (Lord & Taylor)? Remember, the merchandise can be the same at every store, so making the store image different is the key.

The biggest challenge in designing retail advertising is organizing the various elements. You may have two, four, or a dozen different products featured in an ad. How do you arrange them in an attractive layout that stresses the brand, price, and store personality? When it comes to writing the copy, consider the following guidelines:

1. **Tailor the copy to the customer:** Your tone should be in keeping with the price of the products, the clientele of the store, and the types of products.

2. **Be brief:** Just the facts.

3. **Use direct benefits if you can:** Mention features if you must.

To celebrate Lady Gaga's concert tour in Australia, this fried chicken chain offered some specials on snacks just for "little monsters." Daily newspapers are perfect to tie advertising to current events.

National Newspaper Ads

Most national newspaper ads are like magazine ads. However, if it's a daily paper you can change the message every day if necessary. For large retailers with multiple outlets you obviously can't list every store location, but you can convey a store's personality.

National newspapers are also ideal for corporate image, public service, and open-letter advertising. In fact, national newspapers are great vehicles for any message you want to convey quickly to a large audience.

When you want the best color reproduction or really want to make a spectacular splash, you can produce full-page (or larger) inserts. *USA Today* has included some huge inserts. One for a hotel chain in Florida folded out to 20 × 48 inches.

Sometimes advertisers insert whole sections in newspapers. Many readers pull out these inserts and keep them like brochures.

Newspapers and Campaigns

Newspaper advertising can fit very well into an overall campaign strategy. You can maintain continuity with other creative elements, plus you have the

Newspaper ads provide an ideal space for coupons, discounts, and other limited offers, such as this one for cat litter.

Subway is all about healthy eating, and who is healthier than America's top Olympic athletes? These gold medal winners appeared in TV, online, and magazine ads, plus in-store displays. This unique ad in USA Today *unexpectedly violates the editorial space in the sports section to gain maximum impact.*

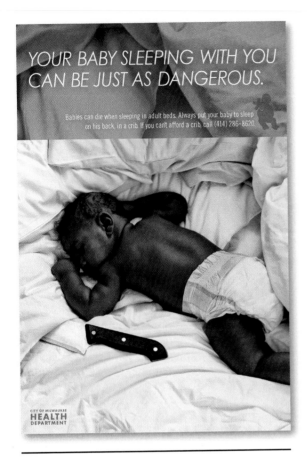

Local newspapers offer a venue to address serious social problems. This is one of a series of ads produced for the city of Milwaukee to point out the alarming rise in co-sleeping deaths of infants.

Newspapers give you a large palette for your creative. This ad for TheLadders, an executive recruitment service, dramatically separates the chair of a six-figure person from all the rest.

flexibility to make rapid adjustments. For example, you may want to use TV and magazines to establish an image for a product but use newspapers to promote its price or guide readers to local retail stores. Many tourism accounts show beautiful images of their destinations in color magazine ads and run price promotions in small black-and-white ads in the Sunday travel sections of local newspapers.

Making Your Newspaper Ads Work Better

The guidelines for writing good newspaper ads are basically the same as for other media. But note a few special rules for retail:

- Establish a store character: A store is also a brand.

- Use a simple layout: Sometimes fine detail is lost in newsprint.

Rising Star

Advertising Found Me

I didn't find advertising. It found me.

I grew up in the middle of Chicago. Not the suburbs. Not DeKalb. Chicago. So I have a certain pride for all things having to do with the Windy City. Except the Cubs. Sorry Cubs fans.

When I was in eighth grade, I interned for a week at Leo Burnett. A Chicago landmark that I grew up walking past on the way to other endeavors, like shopping at Marshall Field's or visiting the Cultural Center. It was a week full of observing focus groups and watching Hallmark commercials starring Fred Savage. All fun. But soon forgotten. High school and college whizzed by, and soon I had graduated from the School of the Art Institute of Chicago with a BFA. Yep. A BFA. So needless to say . . . I was waiting tables. Not walking around a gallery full of my own art with people clamoring to buy it. That doesn't really happen except in movies, which I came to realize only after completing my degree.

If I hadn't been waiting tables, however, I wouldn't have waited on a man who just so happened to be the lawyer for the owner of a small studio in none other than the Burnett Building. He got me an interview, and I got a job in the company mount room. I spent my days and many nights building newly designed cigarette packages and mounting beautifully shot photos of horses and vistas on foam core. From there, I worked my way up and into Burnett where I am now a senior art director on the Allstate and Hallmark accounts.

I didn't have a plan to have a career in advertising. In fact, some will tell you commercial art is the opposite, if not nemesis, of fine art. But I think when advertising is truly great and done right it has the same amount of power to change the world for the better. Plus it pays the ComEd bill. Which is a beautiful thing.[6]

Kate Harding-Jackson, senior art director, Leo Burnett, Chicago, leoburnett.com

Words of Wisdom

"In the good shops, you learn how to write first. And that means print. You don't have thirty seconds; you don't have music; you don't have special effects; it's you and the reader and you have to capture his or her attention, right there and then."[7]

Helayne Spivak, copywriter and CEO, HRS Consulting

- Use a dominant element if you can.
- Let white space work for you (or negative space if your ad is in color).
- State the price or range of prices (especially for retail).
- Specify branded merchandise (especially for retail).
- Urge your readers to buy now (especially for retail).

Collateral

Collateral is a big catchall category that includes printed material used for personal selling, handouts, and sometimes direct mail. The materials can be as elaborate as a coffee table book featuring the illustrated history of a company or as cheesy as a black-and-white single-page flyer stuck under your windshield.

Collateral includes, but is not limited to, the following items:

- Product brochures
- Corporate image brochures

- Catalogs

- Sell sheets

- Capabilities brochures

- Personal selling kits

- Trade show handouts

- Annual and quarterly reports

While virtually every consumer product uses some kind of collateral, much of it is done by a design firm or collateral agency other than the (advertising) agency of record. However, in most cases, business-to-business collateral is integrated into a total communication program developed by one agency or

Collateral includes everything from high-end brochures to inexpensive flyers. A complete creative person should know how to design and/or write multipage brochures.

design firm. When you're writing collateral pieces, especially multipage brochures or a series of pieces, keep the following tips in mind:

- **Have a theme** and carry that theme throughout the brochure, whether it's a graphic or text theme (or both).

- **Think of the brochure as a campaign**—each major element has to work by itself and collectively with other parts of the brochure.

- **Appeal to wants and needs of the readers.** To do this you have to know and understand the intended target audience.

- **Think visually.** Even technical pieces need good, attention-getting graphics.

- **Pay attention to typography,** especially for copy-intensive pieces.

- **Stretch your thinking.** Consider gatefold pages, pockets, inserts, die cuts, windows, and other creative devices to liven up the design.

- **Consider printing limitations when doing your layout.** Don't forget that in most cases you have to *think in terms of four-page units* (unless you have one or more gatefold pages).

There are no other rules for collateral, except following good design and copywriting practices. Other than budget, there are no restrictions on paper stock, number of colors, binding technique, or paper size. Many businesses have drastically cut back on printed literature. Instead, they put their literature on their websites as PDF documents so customers can download them. This not only saves a lot of money in printing costs, but there's no inventory and you can make changes whenever you want. If printing quality is not an issue and you don't need a salesperson to walk a prospect through the literature, it makes a lot of sense.

War Story

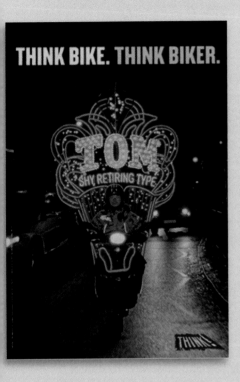

THINK BIKE. THINK BIKER.

Insights Matter

Which ideas have the potential to change behavior and save lives on the road?

In 2009, Flamingo helped develop a creative strategy for the UK Department for Transport, which attempted to answer that question. Our work informed and inspired creation of the *Named Riders* motorcycle safety campaign, by AMV BBDO, their creative agency. The campaign launched in March 2010. *Named Riders* was created to help reduce motorcycle KSIs (accidents in which road users are killed or seriously injured) by promoting better understanding between drivers and motorcyclists. AMV BBDO found a compelling creative device to achieve this, by showing sequences of motorcyclists with their names and personal details lit up by brightly colored flashing signs around them, complemented by voice-overs sharing prosaic yet touching insights into their lives.

Communicating with road users about motorcycle KSIs is a key component of the continuing success of the United Kingdom's road safety strategy. Road accident data over the years provided a series of chilling snapshots of what was happening on UK roads. Long-term trends showed that the roads were becoming safer for most road users: In 2007 KSI casualties were down 36% on the 1994–1998 average, but in 2009 collisions between motorcyclists and drivers continued to account for 21% of deaths on the road. By 2010, motorcyclists represented only 1% of vehicles on the road, but accounted for 20% of all road user deaths. In surveys and questionnaires, drivers demonstrated a low awareness of motorcyclists, yet drivers were involved in 79% of motorcycle-related fatalities.

Through online bulletin boards, one-to-one in-depth interviews, and discussion groups around the United Kingdom, Flamingo worked with both drivers and motorcyclists to build a deep qualitative understanding of their attitudes and behaviors toward each other. This helped identify the most compelling idea for the campaign. More familiar territories we explored with the audiences, around increasing skills, visibility, and even anticipation on the road, were simply not driving reappraisal. We saw a need to humanize the issue and encourage drivers to see the person behind the helmet.

Our recommendations were used to brief the Department for Transport's creative and media partners, AMV BBDO and Carat. The *Named Riders* campaign launched for the first time in 2010, and returned twice with subsequent bursts of activity in 2011 and 2012.

According to figures submitted by AMV BBDO to the Institute of Practitioners in Advertising, the United Kingdom's advertising industry body, over the first campaign period, motorcycle casualties dropped by 8.5% versus the same quarter the previous year. The campaign won an Account Planning Group Creative Strategy Award in October 2011. Sarah Newman, Account Planning Group chair, said it was awarded for "getting to the nub of the relationship between car drivers and bikers, helping to humanize and protect bikers in the process."[8]

David Burrows, group brand director, Flamingo, London, flamingo-international.com

Who's Who?

Maile Carpenter—Maile Carpenter may not be in advertising, but she has a lot to say about it. Carpenter is editor-in-chief of *Food Network Magazine.* Magazines are not exactly guaranteed to be blockbusters these days. But that hasn't slowed Carpenter's work. Since landing at *Food Network Magazine,* after being snared from *Every Day With Rachael Ray,* her magazine's circulation has leaped. In fact it has more than tripled since its debut in 2009. Parent company Hearst has taken note and plans to use her model to advance another network-based magazine, *HGTV Magazine.* Sort of makes you wonder if Carpenter doesn't know something about magazine readership that others wish they did.

Howard Gossage—Howard Gossage influenced a generation of copywriters with innovative and often unconventional approaches to marketing communications. He began his copywriting career at age 36 in San Francisco. Success soon followed with award-winning work for Land Rover, Paul Masson wines, Rainier Ale, Eagle shirts, and Qantas Airways.

Tom McElligott—Tom McElligott and creative partner Pat Fallon started out with a freelance business called Lunch Hour. After winning several awards, the pair launched their own shop in 1981. They quickly recruited art director Nancy Rice and account executive Fred Senn, and the legendary Fallon McElligott Rice was born. Thanks to award-winning creative and rapid acquisition of blue-chip accounts, such as US West, FMR was named Ad Agency of the Year just three years after its founding. A short time later, Rice left and McElligott jumped ship when Fallon sold a majority share to Scali, McCabe, Sloves, an Ogilvy & Mather subsidiary.

Helen Lansdowne Resor—Helen Lansdowne Resor provided the creative spark in the early days of J. Walter Thompson. As the first female copywriter to write and plan national advertising, she opened the door for many women in advertising as she was constantly creating new ways to attract readers. She brought a woman's point of view to advertising, addressing clients' conventions as she managed and supervised two thirds of the business in the JWT New York and Boston offices. She was a revolutionary inventor of a new style in advertising. Among her many achievements is one of the greatest slogans of all time for Woodbury's soap—"The skin you love to touch."

Exercises

1. Branded Shopping

Doing some ethnographic homework to understand consumers can be insightful for every creative. Let's get going.

- *Instructors:* Pick a branded product available at a local retail venue: Toyota Prius, Crest toothpaste, Apple MacBook Pro, Hoover vacuum cleaners, Lancôme cosmetics, or another brand.

- *Instructors:* Provide a consumer profile. Now that students know the product and the target, send them off to observe consumers in the retail environment. But first, have them do some initial secondary research on the brand.

- *Students:* Hit the streets, observing at least 10 shoppers interacting with the product and potentially its competitive set. Then generate a list of questions that will later help you access the retail environment and shoppers' experiences within that environment. What was the retail environment like? How did it feel, look, and sound? What was the sales staff like? How long did consumers spend in the retail environment? How many competing brands did they also interact with? Did they shop alone, and if not, who were they with, and how did they interact? How long did they spend with the brand? What were their physical responses?

- *Students:* Taking your ethnographic knowledge, concept three print ads with the objective of increasing traffic.

- *Students:* Share your ads in class and discuss how your ethnographic research in the retail environment influenced your creative.

2. Retail Roulette

(Adapted from an exercise shared by Sue Northey, Director Research and Measurement, Branigan Communications)

- *Instructors:* Consider a particular retail client, the overall competitive set, and the target audience. Brainstorm a list of 50 adjectives that might apply to the category generally. Put each word on individual note cards (and save them for next semester).

- *Instructors:* In class post the names of your retail brand along with its main competitors. Now hold up each word and let the class shout out which brand it fits. Create a stack of word cards by each brand. Where there is obvious debate toss out the word card. For added depth you can also use images.

- *Students:* Using each stack of adjectives, work in groups to create a profile of each brand.

- *Students:* Now take the adjectives for each brand and use them as a seedbed for generating headlines.

- *Students:* Pick one headline each and write copy for a newspaper ad, dropping it into a comped layout with a visual.

- *Students:* Share your ad among the group and watch the brief come to life.

3. Going Traditional

We sometimes think of print as traditional media and digital as new media. Frankly, today it's more about what works than whether it's old or new. In truth each has a place.

- Come to class ready to share your favorite digital campaign. Your instructor will randomly select one student to present his or her campaign. Be prepared to talk about why you think yours is smart and on brand.

- Next, work in pairs to create a billboard for that brand. The trick is to make the billboard match the digital campaign. You also need to consider geographically where you would place it and why.

- At the end of class, share your concept. Everyone will be surprised what they find out.

Visit www.sagepub.com/altstiel3e to access these additional learning tools

- Video Links
- Web Resources
- eFlashcards
- Web Quizzes

Chapter

12

Radio and Television

Interruptions That Sell

Broadcast media face new challenges from digital media that we couldn't even imagine five years ago. Still commercial radio and television command a huge share of the total advertising dollar. As the lines between broadcast, cable, satellite, and online media blur, many of the tried-and-true principles still apply. We'll cover them here and discuss how to apply them in digital as well as traditional broadcast worlds.

Radio

So how do you get people to listen? More than anything, you break out of the audio wallpaper that radio has become. From a copywriting standpoint, radio presents a perfect opportunity for you to flex creative muscles in totally new ways. You're using words, music, and sound instead of pictures. When you're the writer or producer, the radio commercial is your baby, and the art director can't save your lame idea with a great layout.

Why Radio?

For advertisers and the people who write the ads, radio offers many unique advantages:

- It's everywhere, and it's free. There's nothing to buy (other than a radio) and no effort to find programming.

- You can stimulate immediate action. And, you know if your spots are successful.

- It supports local retailers and national brands. You can combine national campaign themes to support local stores.

- It features segmented markets. You can personalize your messages. Radio has become a very personal medium, so you can tailor specific messages to reach specific demographics.

- Radio personalities sell. Well-known voices have built-in credibility with key listener demographics.

- It offers creative opportunities. It's the ultimate creative challenge to create visuals with music, voice, and sound effects.

- Digital technology, such as podcasts, provides radio programming on demand.

Streaming Music Services Versus Local Broadcast Radio

Commercial broadcast radio's slice of the total advertising pie has been declining for years. Music downloads, legal and illegal, filled up iPods as younger people turned off their radios. Satellite radio, while not living up to its full potential, continues to eat into commercial radio's listener base. Led by Pandora, the Internet radio industry streams free music to its subscribers. Since the music is free, the online music providers live and die by advertising revenue or subscription fees. While the streaming music industry will continue to grow, especially with the rapid expansion of mobile, it still can't match the power of broadcast commercial radio. At the end of 2011, traditional radio advertising generated $15.7 billion versus $800 million for online radio.[1] As an advertising medium, digital's got a long way to go, since 93% of Americans still listen to free local radio.[2] "Broadcast versus digital is a misconception," says Eyal Goldwerger, CEO of digital audio ad platform TargetSpot. In fact, a study from the firm shows that adding digital audio ads to an existing broadcast campaign increases response by 3.5 times![3]

Whether it's traditional broadcast or online, listeners control the content they hear, so advertisers can target audiences based on their musical, entertainment, or informational tastes. Dave Marsey, Digitas' group media director, says, "A genre, station, artist or playlist that's explicitly chosen by the user tells advertisers what mood he or she is in—Nirvana in the afternoon, or Beatles in the morning, for example."[4] As with any advertising, the effectiveness comes from knowing the audience. Listeners of Pandora, Spotify, and MOG skew younger, so digital audio advertising needs to appeal to that skeptical, fickle, short-attention-span, tech-savvy audience. While commercials for commercial broadcast radio have to be produced to reach an older, more traditional listener who's content with blocks of 30- or 60-second commercials interrupting the programming.

This spot written for use on Pandora and ties the brand into the medium.

CLIENT: Cartridge World
TITLE: "Pandora/Colors"
:15

No matter what color you choose—Moody Blues, Red Hot Chili Peppers, Green Day, or even Black Crowes—you'll find it on Pandora. And at Cartridge World—where you can save 30 to 40 percent every day on color ink, black ink, and toner. Thanks for listening.

Podcasting began as a novelty and has become a mainstream advertising medium. Most syndicated radio and many local radio programs are podcast for downloading to computers, MP3 players, smartphones, and tablets. Where popular programs go, advertising follows. However, with podcasting, advertising standards are not as stringent as with the typical broadcast message. For example, Durex, a condom manufacturer, ran ads in podcast programming, which not only reached their key demographic, but also allowed them to be a little more risqué, while skirting Federal Communications Commission decency rules.[5]

This spot uses a straight announcer making some pretty outrageous claims. The right voice and delivery with the right blend of humor and a sales message makes it work.

CLIENT: Seattle's Best Coffee
TITLE: "Overpromising Guy"
:60

ANNCR: I have something . . . shocking to tell you. OK, maybe not shocking. But interesting. We'll go with interesting. (PAUSE) Seattle's Best Coffee now makes three ready-to-drink iced lattes that are so smooth and full-flavored, they can actually bring out your inner morning person at any time of the day . . . and your inner morning person speaks French. Fluently. (PAUSE) That was a lie. I think I am just trying to impress you. But it is true that every time someone discovers their inner morning person, a new star is born in the sky. (PAUSE) That star part isn't true. But the part about the iced lattes being very good is true. And they can be cooled to one thousand degrees below freezing. (PAUSE) Actually that doesn't even sound reasonable. But people do keep them in the fridge. I do know that. So there you go. Iced lattes from Seattle's Best Coffee are cold and delicious, and they help you discover your inner morning person.

Production Considerations

In most cases, the copywriter plays a big role in production. In smaller shops, he or she may be the sole decision maker for production—the person who selects the talent, music, sound effects (SFX), and production studio. As writer/producer, you supervise the recording and editing sessions, making sure everything matches your vision.

It Takes Talent to Cast Talent

As Luke Sullivan says: "Casting is everything. In radio, the voice-over you choose is the star, the wardrobe, the set design, everything all rolled into one. It's the most important decision you make during production."[6]

Where to start: When you're a beginning writer, the list of people who can and will help you is rather limited. Let's see: There's you, your roommate, your significant other, and the crazy guy who works the late shift at the Quickie Mart. Not much of a choice, is it? Just for timing and testing purposes, any voice will do. But before you actually record the spot, think carefully about talent. Perhaps you can work with other beginning writers who are really into broadcast—people who work at the campus radio station or broadcast students. Check out your school's drama department. Those trained actors could be natural voice-over talents. If you're looking for the proverbial man on the street, take your recorder

Words of Wisdom

"Production is where 90 percent of all radio spots fail."[7]

Luke Sullivan, author, *Hey Whipple, Squeeze This!*

down the street and find him. The point is, don't take the easy way out and record your friends the night before a radio assignment is due.

In the real world, when you work for a shop that's able to pay talent, your possibilities open up considerably. If you're not familiar with specific voice talent, you can get demos online from talent agencies. Most voice talents are capable of many different styles, so listen carefully. If you're looking for multiple voices, you don't have to select them from the same agency or even have them work face-to-face, thanks to the beauty of digital editing.

Dos Equis achieved wide recognition as the preferred beer of the "World's Most Interesting Man." The TV campaign established the character, but the radio commercial achieves the same effect with wild claims about his special talents.

CLIENT: Dos Equis
TITLE: "The Most Interesting Man in the World"
:60

MUSIC (IN AND UNDER)

ANNCR: Signs that say this is not an exit don't apply to him. His two cents have overruled Supreme Court decisions. If he rode in your car its resale value would instantly increase.

He likes the word "fog." Were you to pass him on the street and he didn't see you, you would still feel like he said hello and asked you about your day. If you were stuck in an elevator with him you wouldn't want to be saved. Even his tree houses have finished basements. His business card just says I'll call you. He is the most interesting man in the world.

MOST INTERESTING MAN: I don't always drink beer, but when I do, I prefer Dos Equis.

ANNCR: Enjoy Dos Equis responsibly.

MOST INTERESTING MAN: Stay thirsty my friends.

MUSIC: OUT

When you pick your talent, depending on the budget, you may want to hold an audition, especially if you have to sell the client. Many voice talents will do free auditions with your copy. You don't even have to be there. You'll listen to a phone patch, and they'll send you the MP3 via e-mail. It's a great way for a lot of people to listen to a lot of voices. (Beware of selecting talent by committee, though.)

Spend some time considering the voice talent. Even if you just need a straight announcer, there are many styles. Some sound "authoritative"; others are warm and friendly, with "a smile in their voice." The casting of character talent is especially critical. Be very specific about the voice tone, inflection, accent, and timing. You might need to write casting specs to help the talent agent find the perfect voice. Keep a file of voices you'd like to use for future commercials. However, don't lock yourself into the voice du jour—you know, the guy who's suddenly doing every commercial on the air. No matter how great you think your commercial is, it will start to sound like all the others.

Timing Is Everything

Beginning writers (and clients who fancy themselves as broadcast writers) sometimes have a hard time with the immutable time constraints of radio. They write beautiful 45-second spots and can't cut them down to 30s. Or they pack in a lot of useless filler to stretch them to 60s. How to make your creativity fit? One way is count the words. If you have a 60-second straight announcer commercial, you should have between 130 and 160 words. As you approach that 160-word limit, your announcer is likely to talk faster, so the whole spot seems frantic and poorly planned. A 30-second announcer spot should be between 60 and 75 words. The announcer will thank you if your word count runs a little on the short side.

The best way to make your spot fit is to time it! Get a stopwatch (don't try to use your wristwatch) and read the commercial the way you'd like it delivered, leaving room for music and/or sound effects that will take time. If you time out at 60 seconds, it's too long—because nine times out of ten, you'll read it faster than a professional. Try to give the announcer and producer a few precious seconds to play with.

Is This Funny? (Comedy in Commercials)

Few topics are less humorous than a dissertation on comedy. If you are naturally funny, you don't have to be told how to make people laugh. If you're not gifted with a funny bone, chances are no textbook can tell you how to use humor effectively. However, most people can appreciate humor in advertising, even if they can't deliver it. After toiling to write a funny commercial, you may find that drama or music may be a better way to go. Or you may discover that you have a gift. You'll never know until you try. So, what's funny? Comedienne Carol Burnett said, "Comedy is tragedy plus time."[8] Most comedic situations are about pain or the threat of pain—physical or mental. That pain can be as obvious as dropping a piano on a person's head or as subtle as a mildly embarrassing situation.

Rejection is one of our most powerful psychological fears. So being exposed as stupid, uncaring, socially inept, weak, uncool, or just different can be very painful. And even a threat of rejection brings that pain to the forefront. But it's only funny when it happens to someone else, and then you need some distance in time or space to minimize the tragic effect.

The following commercial is for a local sporting goods retailer in Michigan.

Comedy involves pain—to other people. This very simple, low-budget commercial is crafted like the standard public service spot, but the "problem" is easily solved.

CLIENT: Gordo's Snowboard Store
TITLE: "Snow Down the Crack"
:60

MUSIC: GENTLE GUITAR INSTRUMENTAL

IN AND UNDER

MEDIC: As a ski patrol emergency medic I've seen it all. And the thing that I encounter the most, year after year, is snow down the crack. This occurs when a snow boarder is sitting in the snow trying to get in or out of their bindings. In this position, snow easily gets in the back side of their pants, and in a matter of seconds, they get snow down the crack. Oftentimes, a victim, unable to bear the pain, will scream out, "I've got snow down my crack." It's so frustrating because there's nothing you can do. You just have to wait it out and hope for the best. The good news is, it's completely avoidable . . . by simply going to Gordo's Snowboard Store in the Maple Hill Mall in Kalamazoo. You can buy external high back step-in bindings for only a hundred and forty nine dollars. So call Gordo at three-four nine- eighty-three-twenty-eight, and see what he can do for you this winter. And bring an end to the senseless pain of snow down the crack.

MUSIC: OUT

When you're writing radio, first listen to a lot of commercials. Then, think about what makes them funny. We did, and we found some common threads in hundreds of funny radio commercials:

Be outrageous. While radio is theater of the mind, it can also be theater of the absurd. Stan Freberg was a master of using radio to turn the absurd into memorable commercials. To demonstrate the power of radio, one of his spots conjured up images of draining Lake Michigan and filling it with the world's largest ice cream sundae. The helicopter bringing in the giant cherry was the perfect way to top off the commercial.

Do something unexpected. Remember the "twist" in Chapter 6? That's what we're talking about here. You introduce a topic, sound effect, or musical cue, and then take the listener in an unexpected direction. You can also take a seemingly straight commercial out of the ordinary with twisted copy. The deeper you get into it, the more it twists. Avoid the trap of giving away so much that the listener is ahead of the twist. Sometimes the gimmick is too obvious. It's as if you're saying, "Here's the joke . . . get ready . . . here it is . . . the joke is coming . . . and bingo, here's the punch line you already knew."

Use detail. The combination of sound effects, music, and voice can provide a rich visual image. Radio can't provide detailed information about the product itself, but used the right way, details can make a commercial funnier and more memorable.

Combine extreme situations with realistic dialogue. Some of the funniest commercials feature the most outrageous situations but use downplayed dialogue. Some of the most annoying commercials are just the opposite. The casting, timing, unscripted expressions, overlapping of lines, and subtle sound effects combine to make an outstandingly well-produced and funny spot. There is no way to convey this spot in print. You have to hear it to appreciate it.

Again, think about the commercials you find funny. Then analyze them for their structure. Chances are they will fit one of these three formulas. But keep in mind, it's not the formula that makes it funny—it's the content. Don't write a commercial to fit a formula. Instead, consider whether using some of the techniques in the formulas would make your commercial any better. If not, forget the formulas. As Luke Sullivan says, "Being funny isn't enough, you must have an idea."[9] Above all, you have to be honest with yourself. If you're not funny, face it and move on. Most people aren't funny, and those who are funny might be a little screwed up in other parts of their lives. If, after all your introspection, you find that your sense of humor just doesn't come out in your commercials, try a new tactic.

A Word or Two About Dialogue

Some writers forget how real people actually talk. In their effort to cram the client's name and as many features and benefits as they can into 60 seconds, they turn ordinary folks into aliens from Planet Schlock. Here are the three biggest problems with radio dialogue.

Words of Wisdom

"The best advertising comes out of a sense of humor and perspective about life and a realistic perspective on the importance of the product in our lives."[10]

Jeff Goodby, copywriter and founding partner, Goodby, Silverstein & Partners

Radio allows you to paint pictures with words. The more outrageous the mental image, the more memorable the commercial. In this bit of verbal puffery, a handyman is building a life-size replica of the universe, which will take forever. Good thing his Craftsman tools will last that long.

CLIENT: Craftsman Hand Tools
TITLE: "Never Ending Projects"
:60

SFX: BUILDING SOUNDS IN AND UNDER

ANNCR: Tim is building a diorama of the universe . . . to scale. The job is hard, but Tim's will is strong. Because Tim has Craftsman hand tools. With their lifetime warranty, his tools can last forever. So Tim can build something that takes forever. Hence, the universe diorama thing. Which is nowhere near completion, or ever will be. But Tim says it's getting there. Of course it is, Tim. Keep bolting on those sections to the seven rings of Saturn. They're only 74 million miles long . . . each. After that, keep chipping away at the rest of space, which is constantly expanding . . .in every direction . . . forever. Good thing your Craftsman tools will let you keep working forever. Craftsman. Trust in your hands. Available at Sears hometown stores.

Problem: Consumers Become Salespeople

You've heard commercials where neighbors, friends, spouses, or whoever launch into spirited and highly detailed conversations about laundry detergent, motor oil, or feminine protection products. It usually starts with one person stating a problem. The other person comes up with a solution with lots of reasons why it's so great. The first person is instantly convinced and relieved that the problem is finally solved.

Solution: Use the announcer for the sales pitch. Let the characters talk like real people and let the announcer do the heavy lifting. People expect an announcer to deliver a sales message, whether it comes at the end or separates the dialogue.

Solution: Use an "authority" figure. This can be a sales clerk, a doctor, a teacher, or anyone who is expected to know more about the product than the consumer. While the authority may be better suited to pitch the product, you still need to keep the conversation real.

Problem: Stilted Language

Even if characters don't become salespersons, many radio commercial conversations sound awfully fake. In reality, people interrupt, step on each other's lines, slur words, say "uhh" and "umm," and are generally pretty inarticulate.

Solution: Write the way people talk and allow ad-libs. If you listen closely to some of the best dialogue commercials, you'll notice people hesitate, overlap each other's lines, use contractions and sentence fragments, and, in general, talk the way real people talk. To do this right, you need the right talent and the flexibility to let them ad-lib. Give the talent the general premise and have them improvise as they rehearse. The announcer can be as polished and articulate as you like, but keep him or her out of the conversation, especially for dialogue. Read both parts yourself or have someone else read with you. If it sounds phony, keep trying until it sounds natural.

Problem: Gaps in Conversation

Slight pauses between lines ruin many dialogue commercials. In real conversations, most people don't wait a beat before answering a question or responding in a conversation. Sometimes they take a dramatic pause, but more often they start answering while the other person is finishing, so that words overlap. Dialogue should not be a tennis match where everything happens on either one side or the other.

Solution: Compress. Whether you do it in the actual recording or in editing, look for ways to close the gaps. That does not mean you want the spot to be one breathless run-on sentence, but go for good natural flow—in other words, the way real people talk.

The following spot does a good job with natural-sounding dialogue and separates the sales message from the conversation.

Serious topics such as promoting smoking in children require serious dialogue. The realistic dialogue here is far more effective than a standard announcer describing the problem.

CLIENT: *Minnesota Dept. of Public Health*
TITLE: *"Classified Ad"*
:60

SFX: PHONE RINGS

CLERK: Good afternoon, classified ads.

EXEC: Ummm. I wanted to put an ad in the paper.

CLERK: What would you like your ad to say?

EXEC: I want it to read—lost—tobacco executive's soul.

CLERK: (PAUSE) What?

EXEC: Uh. I've lost my soul.

CLERK: What will the rest of the ad say? Just give me the general—

EXEC: The general gist of it is—I'm a corporate tobacco executive and responsible for promotions like giving free cigarettes away to kids during recess in other countries—stuff like that.

CLERK: Oh my goodness.

EXEC: I'm sorry. I missed what you said there.

CLERK: I just—the idea of somebody giving away free cigarettes at recess—it almost knocked me off my chair.

EXEC: Yeah, so I guess you can understand why I feel emptiness inside.

CLERK: Uh-huh. So are you planning on staying with the company?

EXEC: Well, yeah, I mean, it pays really well.

ANNCR: Corporate tobacco knows that if they don't get you hooked before age 18 they probably never will.

Give Me a Jingle

As we discussed in Chapter 8, music can tie a whole campaign together with one catchy jingle. Most original music is not all that memorable, or if it is, it's remembered for being annoying. Maybe that's why you hear so many recycled popular songs in commercials today. As Bruce Bendinger notes, "One of the best ways to connect with a target is by playing the music he or she was listening to at about the age of 14."[11] It's all about resonance.

Here's another example of realistic dialogue. The two actors mention the sponsor, but the announcer does the heavy lifting.

CLIENT: FedEx
TITLE: "Text Message"
:60

WOMAN: Hey, Larry. Do you think you can meet with me and the client later?

LARRY: D-I-Y.

WOMAN: Oh, Do It Yourself? OK.

LARRY: B-T-W, ship C-H-I, A-S-A-P.

WOMAN: Right. We need to get that shipment to Chicago tomorrow. But why are you talking like that?

LARRY: Question mark?

WOMAN: Oh, I forgot. To save time you're encouraging employees to speak in short text message abbreviations.

LARRY: O-M-G, L-O-L.

WOMAN: You're not L-O-L'ing.

LARRY: Oh, Hah-hah-hah.

WOMAN: I have an idea on how we can speed things up around here.

LARRY: OK. 4-1-1.

WOMAN: Well, we can start using FedEx for our overnight shipping needs. They're fast and very reliable.

LARRY: Smiley face. G-2-G.

WOMAN: G-2-G?

LARRY: Good To Go.

WOMAN: Oh, T-T-Y-L.

LARRY: T-T-Y-L? Oh, I got this. Ted Tows Your Licorice.

WOMAN: No . . .

LARRY: They Touch Your Ladle? Lentils! They Touch Your Lentils! That's it, right?

WOMAN: No, that's not right.

LARRY: Tom Tries Yummy Larvae!

WOMAN: It's Talk To You Later.

LARRY: No it's not. Try These Young Leeches!

WOMAN: Really?

LARRY: Taste Three . . . (FADES OUT)

ANNCR: We understand. You need reliable shipping options. FedEx Express.
Go to FedEx-dot-com-slash-we-understand.

LARRY: (FRANTIC) Trek To Yucatan Larry! I got it. You want me to leave!

WOMAN: Larry, you're sweating.

Tips and Techniques

- If you forget every other tip, remember this: **Keep it simple.** One main idea per commercial. Preferably one main idea per campaign.

- **Get to the point early and stick with it.**

- **Identify SFX creatively; don't label them.** For example, if you use a thunderstorm effect, don't have a character say, "Uh-oh. Looks like we're having a thunderstorm." Use something like "Looks like we're stuck inside all day."

- **Use music to evoke a place or mood.** For example, mariachi music in the background says you're in Mexico so the announcer doesn't have to.

- **Repeat the client's name.** Some people say you should do this at least three times, more if it's retail. We don't have a magic formula, but if you do repeat the brand or store name several times, make sure it flows naturally and isn't forced.

- **Capture attention early.** The first five seconds are critical, whether it's drama, comedy, or music.

- **Use voices to create visuals.** For example, an old lady with a soft, kind voice is a loving grandma. The same voice that's harsh is a witch. Remember the importance of casting specs.

- **Make sure your copy is tailored to the market.** A hip-hop music bed is not going to work on a classic hits station.

- **Avoid using numbers,** especially long phone numbers and street addresses. Instead, feature the website where all that information is available.

- **Help your announcer.** Keep the copy a little shorter and watch for hard-to-pronounce words and awkward phrasing. Listen to the announcer if he or she has suggestions for making it sound better.

- **Write the whole spot and read it out loud** before you decide it's not going to work.

Table 12.1 summarizes creative techniques for radio and how they can be applied.

TABLE 12.1   Creative Techniques and Their Applications

Technique	Variations/Applications
Straight announcer	Serious news style
	Humorous read
	Distinctive accent
	Voice modification (fast or slow)
Dialogue/interview	Two or more characters (slice of life)
	Announcer/consumer interaction
	Authority figure/consumer
Dramatization	Mini play
	Reenactment
	News/historical event
	Outrageous situation (comedy)
Testimonial/case history	First-person testimonial
	Story about person's experience
	Celebrity endorsement
Music dominant	Full jingle—original music
	Jingle with "donut" for voice segment
	Popular music
	Adapted popular music—new lyrics
Combinations	Any of the above so that one component is not dominant

Rising Stars

Moving

We graduated in May 2008 from the University of Delaware. Through a connection made while interning the previous winter, the three of us landed full-time jobs with Euro RSCG in New York as advertising creatives. Though we hadn't concentrated on advertising—opting instead for courses in typography, design, creative writing, video editing, and screen printing—we somehow found ourselves living the life of big-city ad guys, not a month out of school.

It wasn't meant to last. Our boss and mentor was soon on to greener pastures, and the three of us, orphaned, with the economy collapsing into Armageddon, decided to quit our stable job, ignore the smart money, and form our own company on April Fools Day, 2009. GrandArmy was born.

We began to build our signature style of expressive typography fused with a modernist sensibility and perfectionist's eye for detail and craft. We created identity systems, typefaces, and video content; wrote campaigns; showed in art galleries; and had no real intention of returning to the agency world.

Soon Wieden + Kennedy came knocking, however, and we three were offered a chance to be founding members of a new experimental team, which in time became Attack. Here we spent the ensuing nearly three years working on a wide range of clients—from ESPN and Brand Jordan, to small pro bono work for public high schools. It was an amazing experience, and yet we wondered what our next move might be.

Then, in late 2011, Draftfcb Chicago offered us the incredible chance to work closely with all Draft clients at the highest levels—and out of our own space in SoHo, to boot. It proved too sweet a deal to ignore. The timing was right, and the opportunity was righter. The SoHo satellite office of Draftfcb Chicago opened officially for business in March 2012. Stop by and say hello.[14]

Eric Collins, vice president, design director; Larry Pipitone, vice president, design director; Joey Ellis, vice president, design director, Draftfcb New York, grand-army.com

Television

Television offers the glamour of show business plus the impact to make or break a brand virtually overnight. Creating a major TV ad campaign not only lets millions of people see your work; it may also shape pop culture for years. As Luke Sullivan says, "Great print can make you famous. Great TV makes you rich."[15] No other medium does a better job of delivering those three motivators—fame, fortune, and fun.

Technological conversion will be most evident in the merging of computer, tablet, mobile, and television set technology. For example, Google TV allows users to fuse their television, web surfing, social media, and streaming music choices into one device. No matter what device is used, we will be able to access live programming, movies on demand, the Internet, social networks, and marketing communication channels we haven't even imagined. If consumers are interested, they will seek commercial messages, rather than the model of commercials interrupting programming.

Changing Standards

Moving into the future the 30-second spot may no longer be the standard. If users seek more information, they may tolerate a two-minute message. Or a

Television advertising has been driving our culture since the late 1940s. But over the decades, one commercial consistently scores the "best of all time" status. The iconic "1984" Super Bowl commercial for Macintosh has become legendary for its incredible design, strong branding, and audacity to "think different" years before that slogan was used.

The premise is simple. A recent grad thinks his neighbor's shiny new Chevy convertible parked in front of his house is a gift from his parents. His joy is so complete they can't bear to tell him the truth . . . until the neighbor drives away in "his" car. The spot combines the best elements of wild exaggeration and humor.

series of 10-second pre-rolls may be all that's needed to reinforce a brand. This convergence allows advertisers to target precise types of traffic and tailor ads based on a user's watching history in a much more accurate way than the old Nielsen reports. However, TV, as we know it, still captures the lion's share of media advertising dollars and will for some time. In the end, copywriters will still need to understand the basics of crafting a television commercial.

Why Television?

In addition to the above considerations, television offers other creative advantages:

- *Impact:* With the exception of the Internet, no other medium does a better job of combining sight and sound.

- *Universal access:* Almost everyone has a TV. Most American homes have three or more sets. TV is the great disseminator of pop culture.

- *Huge audience:* More than 110 million people watch the Super Bowl each year. But even the lowest-rated late-night show attracts millions of viewers.

- *Segmentation (programming, time of day, cable/satellite):* Specialized programming makes it easier to deliver highly targeted commercials.

- *Integrated marketing:* TV is ideal to promote a promotional campaign.

- *It's perfect for cross-promotion:* With advancing technology, TV and the Internet are becoming a seamless entertainment and information medium.

- *More ways to view content:* You can watch your favorite program on DVD, or on your desktop or notebook computer, smartphone, or tablet.

Limitations of Television Advertising

- *Time limits:* Except for some cable channels and infomercials, you are limited to 10-, 15-, 30-, 60-, and 120-second messages. While it's easier to show and tell on TV than on radio, you still have to make every second count.

- *High cost:* Some websites offer cheap TV commercial production for as low as $1,299 a spot, but according to the American Association of Advertising Agencies (AAAA), the average production cost is more than $330,000, with director's fees alone averaging more than $21,000.[16] The cost of airtime is subject to the laws of supply and demand, rising and falling on economic trends.

- **TV commercials are the most intrusive form of advertising:** Everyone says they hate commercial interruptions. It's when people go to the bathroom, get a snack, or just groan about "another stupid commercial."

- **Technology might stifle creativity:** Some people spend a lot of money on TiVo just to avoid commercials. Programs shown online present new challenges to advertisers used to the standard 30-second format.

How to Solve Those Special Problems

Google's "Dear Sophie" commercial shows a young father using Google tools to fill a digital scrapbook with notes and images of his young daughter as she grows. The photos and videos, interspersed with e-mails, resonate with any parent. Adweek says the spot "invariably leaves viewers choked up, and casts Google, often seen as a tyrant, as a facilitator of love. Data never felt so human."[17]

Concepting. Really study commercials. What makes them funny? Why do you remember them? Then analyze them—how do they handle transitions between scenes, camera angles, lighting, sound effects, music, and titles—everything that makes a commercial great? The rest of this chapter offers some ways you can analyze commercials and, we hope, use that information to create your own great commercials.

You may have to limit your concepts to spots you can shoot and produce. You probably can't visit or even simulate some exotic location, indoor shoots present problems without proper lighting, you're not going to have blue-screen or other computer-generated effects, and you're not going to get a movie star for your spot. Be realistic about what you can accomplish if you're planning to actually produce the spot.

Conveying your concept. Computers can help you produce professional-looking print ads. They can also help you put together a good-looking storyboard. Stock photos and scanned images work well in storyboards. If you're showing a progression of scenes using the same characters, you'll probably need to shoot your own still photography. Whether you use photos or marker renderings (hand-drawn art), make sure your storyboard captures the key frames to convey the concept of the commercial.

Postproduction. Since the advent of camcorders, shooting a commercial has not been the problem. The trick has been editing. Now with iMovie, Premiere, and other video editing software, it's easier than ever to make your own commercials. It still takes time, talent, and experience to know how to do it right. Make sure you have the patience to review every frame of your commercial for days until you get it right. The temptation is to say, "It's good enough!" but it usually never is. Also keep in mind that even the slickest production can't save a weak concept.

To launch their new Coupe, Mini asked people to provide the plot for the ultimate test drive in just six words. The winner—stewardess, salt flats, sushi, paratroopers, Falconer—generated a surreal but highly entertaining two-minute commercial that featured not only the car, but also the person who submitted the winning entry. That's him with the "stewardess."

Showing it. If you have a great TV commercial, you can import it into a PowerPoint or Flash program. You can also mix in your print and radio samples to make a multimedia portfolio. If you don't have produced spots, you can put storyboards in your book, but they have to be as good as your print work.

Technology and Trends That Affect the Creative Process

New technology is changing TV as we know it. Some of these technological advances will also change the way you will develop commercials.

Consumer-generated content: Got a camcorder, digital camera, or smartphone that takes video? You can be a commercial producer. In this YouTube generation, the quality of the image takes a back seat to the content. In fact, if your commercial or video looks too slick, you lose your credibility. Consumer-generated content is used by many marketers to generate buy-in from customers, drive traffic to their websites, and, if they're lucky, create a mainstream media buzz on traditional television.

A number of major consumer brands have asked customers to come up with ideas for commercials. Is this a lazy way to avoid paying for creative ideas from their agency or a clever approach to involve customers in the creative process? Doritos has established a tradition of consumer-generated commercials on the Super Bowl. Mini, long known for innovative creative content from several agencies, has entered the consumer-generated commercial world. Mini's agency asked people to imagine their best possible test drive experience for the new Mini Coupe in just six words. They promised to use the winning entry as the plot for a two-minute commercial film. The winning entry: "Stewardess. Salt flats. Sushi. Paratroopers. Falconer." The result was a very surreal film incorporating all six words, the person who provided the winning entry, and, of course, the Mini Coupe. The film was featured as a full-length online video, a shortened pre-roll online, and a full-length commercial in cinemas.

How to Show Your Concept

You have several ways to convey your concept for a commercial. The one you use depends on the stage of development and conceptual ability of the person approving it.

Script

This is the most basic and often the only method you need to show your concept. It's written in the same way as a radio script, except there is a column on the left for VIDEO that lines up with the AUDIO column on the right. As with radio, the directions and effects are in CAPS.

Storyboard

For more detail, you can create a storyboard, with pictures of key scenes from beginning to end. The audio and video directions are under each frame. A storyboard can be sketched by hand or created with photography. Storyboards really help the producer, director of photography, and postproduction crew, as well as the client, understand the spot.

Key Frame

This should be the most memorable scene of a commercial. It may be the "punch line" or "payoff frame" in the spot. Think of the single image that a newspaper or magazine might use to describe a TV commercial, and you'll know what we mean.

Cheerios has repositioned their brand as a tasty way to lower cholesterol. In this spot a kid shopping with his dad keeps asking what kind of prize is in the box. When asked if there is a superhero inside, the dad admits, "Kind of." The spot features believable characters using very realistic dialogue in a subtle, soft sell approach. The announcer handles the sales message so the actors are likeable and more memorable.

Scenario

This is a brief description of the commercial concept. Typically, it starts with an introduction such as "We open on a . . ." The scenario can describe scenes in more detail and can also work in marketing and creative strategies.

Styles of Commercials

Describing different kinds of commercials won't make you creative. However, if you start to analyze the various styles of commercials, you'll see a pattern. You may begin to understand why they are moving, or funny, or hard selling. A lot of the styles blend together, so you may have a celebrity in a problem-solution format or a vignette with a strong musical theme. We offer the following list of styles not as formulas, but rather to help you watch and then create commercials with a critical eye and ear.

Slice of Life (Problem-Solution)

In the so-called Golden Age of Television, many commercials featured a slice of life (which was more often a parallel universe) in which a frustrated housewife couldn't solve some kind of cleaning problem. A helpful neighbor, announcer, or cartoon character told her about the advertised product and, like magic, her problems were over. Today's commercials (except for most infomercials) are not quite that cheesy, but they're still using problem-solution formats.

Demonstration: It didn't take advertisers long to figure out that TV is a natural to show a product being used. Especially one that moves. Demonstrations have also been very effective in showing what a product can do. One of the best demonstrations was a wordless commercial for Cheer that showed a funny little guy putting a dirty napkin into a clear bowl of cold water, adding Cheer, swirling it all around, and pulling out a clean napkin. The following are various types of demonstrations:

- Straight product in use

- Torture test

- Comparison to competitor

- Before and after

- Whimsical demonstration—exaggerated situation

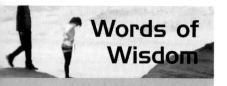
Spokesperson (Testimonial)

You don't have to be famous to pitch a product, although if you do it right, you might become famous, like Subway's Jared. Some brands are associated with a single character, created just to promote that brand, such as the Maytag repairman, played by several different actors over three decades. Whether it's the CEO or an actor, some companies use the same person to represent them on TV. Richard Branson is the personification of Virgin airlines, records, cell phones, and whatever else he's selling today. Vacuum cleaner innovator James Dyson is the perfect spokesperson to hype his own products.

Celebrity

This is perhaps the oldest technique in television advertising, borrowed from decades of use in print and radio. Whether they're sports figures, cartoon characters, or movie stars, celebrities can gain immediate attention and shine some of their limelight on the product. As we discussed previously, make sure the celebrity has some logical connection with the product, even if it's

Honda paid homage to the 1986 film Ferris Bueller's Day Off *with Matthew Broderick as himself, re-creating some key scenes (complete with the iconic music from the original). Honda aired a 10-second teaser, then a two-minute extended version, several days before its Super Bowl debut. It was a top trending topic on Twitter before the big game and earned one of the top ratings for Super Bowl commercials.*

indirect. For example, several years ago, country singer Willie Nelson did commercials for H&R Block because of his well-publicized tax problems. In other cases, TV capitalizes on the flavor of the day, featuring winners of *American Idol* or whatever show is dominating pop culture at the time. The true test of a celebrity presenter is someone who can transcend their fame as an athlete or entertainer and become a credible spokesperson that reflects positively on a brand.

Story Line

This may be a mini-movie, with a beginning, a middle, and an end. Budweiser has produced a series of popular brand-reinforcing commercials featuring their iconic Clydesdales. For example, in one spot a Clydesdale meets a circus horse and chases across the country to find her, and the two run away presumably to be happy every after. Google produced a touching spot that shows the main events in the life of a young girl from her father's point of view, all through the use of various Google products.

The good old storyboard is still the standard for showing a commercial concept in print form. The audio (announcer and music) direction is sometimes indicated below each appropriate video frame.

Vignettes

These are usually made from a series of short clips that are strung together, usually with a strong musical track to hold it all together. Vignettes can be used to show different people using the same product or a variety of products with the same brand. A good example of using vignettes was the global "I'm Lovin' It" campaign for McDonald's. The initial spots showed a wide variety of ages and races. An example of different products for the same brand would include some Honda corporate spots that show cars, lawnmowers, motorcycles, generators, and all the other products that Honda makes.

Apple has perfected the most basic premise of television advertising: Why tell everyone how great your product is when you can show it? Simple product demonstrations were the very first TV commercials, and they are still effective today.

A clueless twentysomething whines that her parents are so lame they only have 19 Facebook friends. As she drones on about her online social life, we see clips of her parents enjoying a real life with their Toyota Venza and their real friends. The spot strikes the perfect tone for active baby boomers who are too busy to worry about adding more fake friends online.

Musical

It's hard to separate music as a category, since it's so integral to commercials today. However, we'll consider this as a unique type when music is the dominant factor of the commercial. For example, Toyota has created some unique commercials for Prius using distinctive music as the hook; San Diego produced a commercial of vignettes of people enjoying local attractions, all tied together by a catchy music track; and Heineken made a wild commercial featuring a hip young couple running through an Asian club with the soundtrack from a Bollywood musical.

Man-eating (and woman-eating) sharks in a focus group are asked to comment on the flavor of their victims. One remarks that "Steve" was especially tasty. The researcher reveals that was because Steve ate a Snickers.

Humor in TV

It's hard to be academic about humor. It's not a science; it just happens. But it touches the most basic human need to laugh at our troubles. Maybe that's why the commercials people remember most seem to be the funny ones. Probably 9 out of the top 10 Super Bowl spots each year are meant to be funny. As with radio, don't start out to create a funny television spot. You may have a good joke, but it's not a commercial unless it sells something. Luke Sullivan offers some excellent advice for writers who want to make their mark with humorous TV spots: "Don't set out to be funny. Set out to be interesting. I find it interesting that the Clios had a category called Best Use of Humor. And curiously, no Best Use of Seriousness."[19]

What Makes It Funny?

Some of the funniest commercials include at least some of the following elements:

- **The unexpected:** Throw in a surprise ending, a twist, a zinger, something they don't see coming. Many times that unexpected ending involves pain—physical or mental.

- **Pain/risk of pain:** The old formula of tragedy plus time works for TV even better than radio because you can show it as well as tell it.

- **Exaggeration:** Making things extremely bigger, smaller, faster, or slower than expected can be humorous. So can giving animals human traits or vice versa. Extreme behavior can be funny too.

When it comes to advertising effectiveness, humor has some limitations:

- Humor may build awareness of a brand, but not much comprehension of what makes that brand better. (Snickers)

- Humor usually doesn't add much credibility to a spokesperson. In fact, an "authoritative" spokesperson is usually a parody. (Alec Baldwin for Capital One)

- Humor works better for radio, TV, and online video, not so much for print. So if your campaign is strongly based on humor, make sure it can be extended to other media. (Chick-fil-A)

- Humor is most effective for younger, upscale, male audiences. (Most beer commercials). Perhaps older, poorer people don't have much to laugh about.

Doritos has earned a lot of great publicity by soliciting independent filmmakers to submit entries for their "Crash the Super Bowl" promotion. Over 110 million people see the winning spot during the game, and millions more catch it online. If it earns the top score in USA Today's Ad Meter, the creator gets a million bucks. Not bad for a spot shot on a shoestring by a guy who works out of his garage.

What Makes It Good?

You need more than a funny situation to make a good commercial. Many humorous ideas fall flat because of poor production. The best humorous commercials need all four of the following:

- **Good direction:** The writer and director need to know when to use a wide shot, when to zoom in, how many scenes to use, and all the other intangibles that make a good spot great.

- **Attention to detail:** Do the sets look real? Are little kids dressed like real children? Are the props accurate for the time frame depicted? Little things mean a lot, and they show.

- **Talent/acting:** This is perhaps the most critical element. The same qualities that make a great comic actor different from a clown apply to commercials. Remember that with TV you can show subtle expressions and nuances in close-ups. You don't need the broad gestures of a stand-up comic or stage actor.

- **Editing:** Well-executed postproduction makes a huge difference. The timing and transition of scenes can turn a "cute" concept into a truly funny commercial.

Tips and Techniques

Aside from the general advice for humorous spots listed above, the following tips apply to nearly all commercials. These are offered as rules of thumb and not as hard-and-fast guidelines you must follow. However, experience shows that you can have a lot better results if you heed most of them when you are critiquing commercials.

- **Get immediate attention.** The first 3 to 10 seconds are critical. Make the first couple of seconds visually interesting.

- **Stick with one main idea.** Keep it simple. Don't try cramming more than 2–3 scenes per 10 seconds or more than 10 scenes per 30. If you're using vignettes, you might need a lot more.

- **Think about brand awareness.** Show the product and involve characters with it.

- **Use titles to reinforce key points.** But not so many that viewers feel like they are reading the commercial.

- **Think visually.** Consider how you want to move within a scene, transition between scenes, and change scenes.

- **Don't forget synergy.** Don't show what you're saying or say what you're showing.

- **Audio is still important.** Use music/SFX to describe place or mood.

- *Make every word count—count every word.* Rule of thumb is about words per second and about 60 words for a 30-second spot. That's less than radio.

- *Give the viewers some credit.* Let them complete the creative equation.

- *Don't overexplain.* They'll remember it better, too.

- *Keep conversation real.* Dialogue should be natural, not forced. Let the announcer be the salesperson, if you have to have one.

- *Don't save it all for the ending.* A commercial should be entertaining through the whole spot. Don't have a sloppy buildup to a punch line.

- *Think in campaigns.* Make your commercial compatible with, but not identical to, the other elements. It should not be a video version of the print ad. Think in terms of extending a concept without repeating the same idea in subsequent spots.

- *Study great commercials.* Look for style, camera angles, editing techniques, and so on. Understand what makes them great.

Chrysler produced a two-minute Super Bowl commercial that featured Clint Eastwood giving a "halftime" pep talk to America. Very few cars and trucks were shown, and Chrysler was only identified at the end.

Power Writing for TV and Video

Power writing isn't limited to print or the Internet. Television and video are perfect places to tell a brand's story, and using power writing techniques helps make that story more memorable. One of the best examples of power writing was used in the 1998 Apple "Think Different" launch. Actor Richard Dreyfuss delivered the 60-second "tone poem" but the sentiment is pure Steve Jobs.

Here's to the crazy ones. The misfits. The rebels. The troublemakers. The round pegs in the square holes. The ones who see things differently. They're not fond of rules. And they have no respect for the status quo. You can quote them, disagree with them, glorify them, or vilify them. About the only thing you can't do is ignore them. Because they change things. They push the human race forward. And while some may see them as the crazy ones, we see genius. Because the people who are crazy enough to think they can change the world are the ones who do.

Checklist for Your TV Commercial

When you've finished your script or storyboard, let it rest, if you can. Then come back to it and check the following:

- Does the video tell the story without audio, and how well?

- Did you specify all the necessary directions? Could a director take your script and produce the spot?

- Do the audio and video complement each other, and are they correctly timed for each other?
- Are there too many scenes (can some be omitted)? Do you need more scenes?
- Have you identified the product well?
- Does your script win attention quickly and promise an honest benefit?
- Have you provided a strong visualization of the One Thing that will linger in the viewer's memory?
- Could a competitive brand be substituted easily and fit well?
- Is it believable?
- Are you proud to say you wrote it?[21]

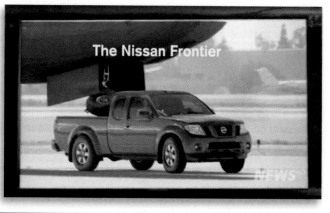

This commercial for the Nissan Frontier depicts a fake a news story about a 727 dropping its broken nose gear neatly in the bed of a speeding pickup truck. Would a reasonable person believe the Nissan can defy the laws of physics in a torture test demonstration, or would they see it as only a clever piece of puffery?

Presenting Your TV Commercial

OK, your spot meets all the requirements in the checklist. Now you're ready to show it to the boss. It's not a print ad that you can just hand in. You have to sell it. The following is a pretty good procedure for presenting a TV commercial, especially to a small group.

- If it's a stand-alone concept, review the creative strategy and state the One Thing you want to convey.
- State your main creative theme for the commercial.
- Describe main elements—music, effects, actors.
- Walk through the video portion; describe what's happening.
- Hit the key visual points, with emphasis on the key frame.
- Once the visual path is established, go back and read the copy.
- Summarize the action in a brief scenario.

Any airline.
No blackout dates.

thankyou
PREMIER
citi

0000 1234 5678 9010

L WALKER

This commercial features a voice-over of a young woman shopping with her boyfriend. Her fancy new shoes are for rock climbing, her "nylons" are ropes, and as far as someday getting a diamond, the rock she really wants is at the peak of a mountain. The Citi card slides in as we are treated to a breathtaking view of her on the very top.

⭐
TRADE MARK
Heineken®
open your world

facebook.com/heineken

Some commercials take some bizarre twists and turns to covey a brand message. In "The Date," an energetic couple runs through the kitchen, behind the stage, and through the dining room of a rowdy Asian club. The action is underscored by the driving beat of a song called "Jaan Pehechan Ho," which came from an Indian movie. The spot was produced in Amsterdam and received heavy play in the United States. See what we mean by twists and turns?

War Story

When Marketing Becomes Entertainment

Most marketing sucks. It's annoying, it interrupts content, and people will go to great lengths to avoid it, but every so often you'll find an exception to this rule.

While at Modernista! I had the opportunity to create one of these rare exceptions with the *Dexter* Alternate Reality Game—a transmedia experience, with a bold narrative, that got thousands of *Dexter* fans to invest two months of their lives into the hunt for a make-believe serial killer.

We launched the game at the 2010 San Diego Comic-Con convention. Here *Dexter* fans discovered a blood-smeared crime scene and were invited to join a crowdsourced investigation team led by the "Serial Huntress." Inside the kill room players found clues intentionally left by the "Infinity Killer."

At one point in the game players discovered a real eBay account with a clue for sale. This sparked a bidding war among players, driving the price from just $8 to $300. At another point, players discovered a fake recipes website with encrypted geographic coordinates. These led to a real abandoned hospital in Los Angeles. When one player actually went and checked in via Foursquare, she found a phone number. Calling it activated a pager hidden in the bushes nearby, and revealed the location of more clues. And perhaps the most impressive moment of the entire game was when players stayed up 22 hours observing a live-streaming video, looking for out-of-the-ordinary clues—a three-legged dog, a ballerina with seven balloons, and so on. They eventually discovered that each of these strange sightings denoted one numeric digit of a phone number.

All along the way the fans played an integral role in the game's narrative, and in the end, they even determined the game's outcome by voting for which of the main characters to kill—they ultimately chose the killer.

As with any story the *Dexter* ARG came to an end, but that didn't keep the players from demanding more, so we hosted a Q&A session for them. It was our first direct communication, and yet we felt a strange connection as we'd shared this unique and somewhat bizarre experience with them. They asked a lot of questions, and some even begged us to produce a sequel, but there was one important issue that never came up: the fact that the entire experience was a clever marketing tactic. Maybe that's because, at least for the players, it wasn't. Maybe for them it was something more. Maybe it was, dare I say it, entertainment.[22]

Adrian Alexander, associate creative director and creative consultant, Third Culture Kidz, Los Angeles, thirdculturekidz.com

Beyond Television

Computers, mobile devices, and tablets provide a much wider audience for commercial messages. They can be 10-second pre-rolls before longer video content, repurposed 30- or 60-second spots, or longer versions of broadcast commercials. Advertisers also have the ability to add content such as behind-the-scenes action or include information about the stars of the commercial or the product itself. Commercials and other video content on the web are covered in Chapter 13 and in the War Story above that describes extending the marketing connections for the popular *Dexter* television program.

Who's Who?

Mary Alderete—Mary Alderete joined the Levi's brand in 2009. As vice president of global brand marketing, she is responsible for leading marketing strategy that integrates brand experience. Alderete was one of the driving forces behind the development of Levi's first ever global marketing "Go Forth" campaign. She has more than 20 years of advertising and brand management experience. Before joining Levi's, Alderete led strategy teams for Old Navy and Banana Republic. She has also worked on the agencies side for Foote, Cone & Belding, BBDO, and J. Walter Thompson.[23]

Lee Clow—Lee Clow was the art director and creative force behind some of the most influential advertising of his generation. His work for Chiat\Day and later TBWA\Chiat\Day includes the famous Apple "1984" spot as well as the Taco Bell Chihuahua, Nike's "Air Jordan," and the Energizer Bunny. Dan Wieden of Wieden + Kennedy, another creative giant of the modern era, described Clow this way: "Lee Clow's heart has been pumping this sorry industry full of inspiration for longer than most its practitioners have been alive. He is the real thing. He is indefatigable. I hate him."[24]

Jennifer Siebel Newsom—Jennifer Siebel Newsom is a filmmaker, actress, and women's advocate. She is the writer, director, and producer of the 2011 Sundance documentary film *Miss Representation*, which explores how the media's misrepresentations of women have led to the underrepresentation of women in positions of power and influence—including advertising. She is also the founder and CEO of MissRepresentation. org. As an actress, Newsom appeared in numerous films and television shows including *Mad Men*. Newsom is a passionate advocate having spoken at corporations, universities, nonprofits, and conferences including TEDxWomen. In 2011, Newsom was named a "Power Woman" by *New York Moves* magazine. She has also been featured in *O, The Oprah Magazine*; *The Huffington Post*; *Forbes*; *Vogue*; and *SELF* and on Fox News and NPR. In 2012 *Newsweek* and *The Daily Beast* named Newsom among their "150 Fearless Women" in the world.[25]

Hal Riney—Hal Riney achieved creative excellence by getting people to like his clients. His work for Saturn cars, Bartles & Jaymes, President Reagan, and others celebrated a unique American spirit that was confident yet at times self-effacing. While working at the San Francisco office of Ogilvy & Mather, he was part of the First Tuesday team, which created ads for Ronald Reagan's reelection effort. In 1986, he took over the office, renaming it Hal Riney & Partners, and went on to mastermind General Motors' Saturn introduction with dazzling success.

Exercises

1. Sketching in Words

(Adapted from an exercise shared by Kimberly Selber, PhD, associate professor, University of Texas–Pan American)

This exercise will help you get outside the demographic cube and into the psychographic menagerie and get you closer to radio, TV, and video production. Create a character sketch of someone you know—as if you were describing a character in a movie or novel.

- Write a short one-paragraph introduction of who this person is, and what your relationship to this person is.

- Next describe the following in great, juicy detail:

  - Physical appearance: gender, age, body type, hair, eyes, facial features, dress, posture, movements, mannerisms, speech . . .

  - Background: education, religion, family, childhood experiences, financial situation, profession, marital status, other relationships, habits, surroundings/environment, health . . .

  - Personality: distinctive traits, self-image, yearnings/dreams, fears/apprehensions, sense of humor, code of ethics, attitude (optimistic? overly sensitive?) . . .

  - Other details: hobbies, skills, favorite foods, colors, books, music, art . . .

- Evaluate as a class, focusing on the following: Did you bring the person to life for the reader? If an actor was going to play the role of this person, would he or she have enough insight to justly portray the person?

2. Audio Hunting Expedition

Let's see how sound can inspire you.

- Think of one brand—a brand that is a big part of your everyday life.

- Go out on an audio hunting expedition to collect audio recordings of sounds connected with this brand. Then record 10 people expressing their affection for the brand—anything goes.

- Now do some secondary research on the brand. Consider if anything you found out about the brand matches the audio images you've collected.

- Inspired by your audio hunting expedition and grounded in secondary research, sketch out a quick 30-second radio spot.

- If you're really adventurous, record it using some of the footage you've collected. You could do your own voice-over or find a brave and willing friend (preferably from the drama department!).

3. Telling Your Story

This exercise is designed to help you craft a story line that feels real—a story line that identifies your brand.

- Craft a 60-second commercial that tells the story of your brand: "brand you."

- Here's the rub. The story has to begin with your first day of college and end with you landing your advertising dream job. The point is not about the job you land but about telling the viewer who you are in a resonant way.

- Your instructor will collect your scripts at the beginning of the next class, without your name, which will be added later, and randomly hand out scripts.

- Take a few minutes to review the script you received (it could even be your own).

- Now, present the script you received. One by one try to identify which script belongs to which person.

- The idea here is to see which scriptwriters were able to create a story that resonates with who they are—resonates enough that the class could identify "brand you."

Visit www.sagepub.com/altstiel3e to access these additional learning tools

- Video Links
- Web Resources

- eFlashcards
- Web Quizzes

Chapter

13

Digital

Second Screen, Third Screen, and Beyond

Our Predictions Came True: We Didn't Know Anything!

Almost every prediction about the long-term future of marketing technology has been wrong. That's why we left a blank page on our last book when we had to predict the future of digital media.

When we began writing the second edition of this book, Facebook boasted an astonishing 100 million users. As of this writing it's close to a billion. Back then 3 million people had Twitter accounts; today more than 300 million people are tweeting. LinkedIn, the social media leader for business, is now worth 10 times what it was in 2008. Apps were introduced in that year, and we have now downloaded over 16 billion apps and counting. YouTube is now the second most popular search engine. Google continues to evolve, grow, and dominate nearly every corner of the digital space. Smartphones were expensive toys a few years ago but now account for more than half of new phone sales and outnumber new PC sales. Gaming consoles are integrating the web with TV to create a single access point to integrate the analog and digital worlds. The cloud-based mobile age has already passed the desktop computer era, and we're still in the early adopter stage.

Keep in mind the advertising world fell off the cliff with the rest of the economy in 2008 and hasn't been all that rosy ever since, which makes the exponential growth in digital advertising even more significant. In the early days, advertisers created mass media to carry their messages. Today, brands are scrambling to keep up with consumers using new methods of entertainment and information. They're shifting to the digital space not only to get consumers' attention, but to interact with them.

Procter & Gamble announced in 2012 that they planned to cut $10 billion from their marketing budget over the next five years. Part of the cost-cutting strategy meant shifting to digital because it is always on, is more engaged with consumers, allows faster midcourse corrections, and integrates so well in a complete campaign. Oh, and it's also cheaper when it's done right. Paula Bernstein reports, "Advertisers have been spreading their digital spending over a dizzying array of options: digital display, video, rich media, search engines, mobile, social, tablets, apps, content sponsorship, to name just a few. With so much to choose from, the challenge becomes finding the optimal mix to create a truly integrated marketing campaign."[1]

Advances in digital technology will dictate how we develop marketing communication tactics. For example, the 2012 Google I/O developer's conference unveiled a new version of the Android phone; Google Play, which offers TV shows and movies; the Nexus 7 tablet; Nexus Q, "the first ever social streaming device"; and Google Glass, which builds mobile access into a pair of sunglasses. There's no telling what Apple and the others have planned for the future, but we can be sure the digital world will be defined by new ways to access technology, not by traditional advertising models.

Our challenge with this chapter is to not get too bogged down in *how* things work or even where this business is headed. Instead, we will gloss over the technical jargon and try to deal with how to make all that left-brain stuff merge with right-brain creativity. So we will focus on two main areas of discussion:

1. Digital advertising: banners and beyond.

2. Web content and search engine optimization (SEO): strategy, concept, design, and copy.

Social media is woven so tightly into so many advertising programs that we find it hard to isolate it as a separate topic. However, there is so much to cover in the social space that we have pulled most of it out of this chapter and address it in more detail in the next one. Writing blogs also is a specialized skill best covered in Chapter 14. While e-mail is certainly a digital marketing communication tool, we'll discuss it in the context of direct marketing in Chapter 15. Mobile marketing also fits in the digital realm, but we will discuss it more as a technology best suited for direct marketing in Chapter 15.

Words of Wisdom

"The irony is that while there have never been more ways to reach consumers, it's never been harder to connect with consumers."[2]

Brad Jakeman, chief creative officer, Activision

The Three Things

Despite all the changes in devices, the basics of online marketing are pretty simple. When you are creating a website, microsite, landing page, or mobile site, there are only three main things you need to do:

1. Get them to come.

2. Get them to stay.

3. Get them to come back.

Do all three, and you will be successful. They have to find you. They have to find something interesting when they find you . . . and you hope you can persuade them to form a favorable opinion, request more information, give up their e-mail address, "like" you, and ultimately buy something, whether it's direct from your site or through some other channel. Finally, they have to keep coming back to extend the relationship. The following sections will discuss how all of this can happen.

As one of the top manufacturers in the business, Burton realized that not only are snowboards different for men and women; so are their attitudes. Burton has a section on their site called "Burton Girls" featuring blogs from 12 "Burtonistas" as well as articles on clothing, heath and beauty, and travel.

Digital Advertising

It finally happened. In 2012, online ad spending surpassed the total spending for newspapers and magazines.[3] Advertisers are also moving ad dollars from TV toward video advertising on the web, thanks in part to standardization of formats and technologies that allow advertisers to reach larger audiences across multiple sites. As social network platforms such as YouTube and Facebook mature into credible advertising vehicles, we'll see more opportunities to personalize both video and display ads. With much more refined segmentation, video ads have become more than repurposed 30-second TV commercials. At the same time, new online media firms can place ads on thousands of sites, so advertisers can not only personalize but also achieve incredible reach. The fact that digital advertisers are considering Facebook as a "publisher" and are using well-known metrics such as gross rating points, demonstrates that digital advertising will continue to grow as a credible and measurable marketing tool.

Digital technology makes it easy to test and measure web advertising and website readership. Because changes can be made in minutes with a few keystrokes, it's easy to test multiple concepts. This is called A/B testing (Version

A vs. Version B). Website analytics measure traffic, page popularity, and visitor behavior to help make informed decisions about optimizing your site.

Banner ads have been the staple of Internet advertising. The most common size is 468 × 60 pixels, and they usually appear at the top of a commercial webpage. They are priced on a cost-per-thousand-page basis. Prices vary based on targeted sites and whether the banners are static or pop-up. Traditionally, banners have not been all that effective for generating traffic but can still have a powerful branding effect. The trick is matching content to the brand and getting people to respond. Banners have to be creative to stand out in all the clutter of a typical webpage. Better targeting methods and more accurate analytics have made banner ads less of a hit-or-miss proposition. Highly targeted advertising networks can place your ads on specific sites frequented by key target segments based on browsing history, past purchases, demographics, or hundreds of other variables. Online advertising networks also offer the convenience of reaching many sites with a single buy, helping you save time and make the most effective use of your budget.

Banner ads can rotate between advertisements or be locked into a specific space. The rates vary with the position, size, and longevity on the site. As in newspapers, premiums are paid for "top of the fold" locations.

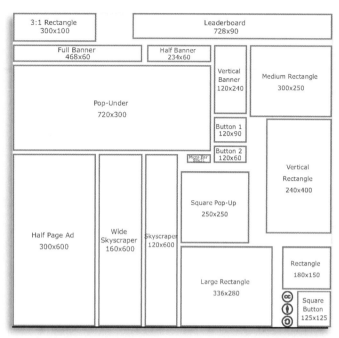

Popular sizes for banner ads

Rich media banners go beyond the ordinary banner ad to add dropdown boxes, sound-on mouse-overs, animated bits, and even interactive games. Rich media banners and badges provide advertisers with ways to present additional content and interaction within traditional ad sizes. According to studies, they can also lead to significant increases in response, brand perception, and recall.

Here are some tips and techniques for creating effective banner ads:

- **Think billboards:** Your little banner ad has to compete with the space around it just like a billboard.

- **Keep it simple:** Just like a billboard, the fewer the words, the better. You have to get attention first. Then they can click for more detail.

- **Offer an incentive:** Everyone probably knows your brand. So convince them they'll get a special deal, a discount, free stuff, or whatever if they click on your ad.

- **Change the offer:** People check their browsers several times a day. Keep your message fresh with new looks and new incentives. This not only increases involvement; it also functions as a good test to measure which appeal pulled the most click-throughs.

- **Engage the viewer:** Use a contest, quiz, and ask provocative questions.

- **Don't forget the brand:** Don't get so caught up in cute gimmicks that you forget what you're really selling—brand recognition.

Web Content

We won't delve very deeply into website design. There are millions of new examples added daily. You can design a site from scratch, but more and more companies are relying on the rapidly growing selection of open-source web templates. Companies like 1&1 and Wix advertise templates that can be customized for every industry.

Content Management Systems

A content management system makes it possible for just about anyone with opposable thumbs to populate a website. Some are easier to use than others, but basically the idea is that if you can use Microsoft Word or drag a photo from a file, you can build a site. While we love the idea of making the web accessible to the masses, here are some caveats regarding content management systems:

- *Have a plan:* It's empowering to select from hundreds of cool templates, but first figure out what you want to say, how you want to look, and what you want people to do when they visit your site.

- *Set the rules and enforce them:* A professional needs to select fonts, image sizes, colors, and all the other elements. It's tempting to experiment and introduce new elements or create a new look just because you can. Don't forget about the principles of branding, campaign continuity, and good design.

- *Limit access:* A committee can approve websites, but never let a committee design one. Nor should you give too many people admin privileges.

- *Don't walk away:* Someone needs to be in charge of updating content and reviewing the overall look and feel of the site. Don't think the job is over when the site goes live.

As a copywriter, you may be involved in website design in several ways, ranging from developing a total site to writing a headline for a banner ad. As an art director, you may have to develop a design for whole sites down to fourth- or fifth-level pages or landing pages that instantly capture the user's attention. No matter your role, you need to have a Big Idea for the site. What's the One Thing that people will take away from looking at your landing page or website? Beyond that, you need to know if your ideas are practical and affordable. Your role in website development begins with understanding the client's wants and needs as well as those of the customers. What does the client want to accomplish? Do they want an e-commerce component? Is this site only for information? Do they have opportunities to include consumer-generated videos, blogs, or interactive games?

If your website is the hub of your marketing communication program, the goal is to have a lot of spokes and make sure they're well connected. Your traditional print, out of home, direct mail, and broadcast should all point to your site. Here are some tips for using online tactics to increase traffic.

1. Always feature the URL in your traditional advertising. If you don't have an easy-to-remember URL, get one.

2. Create one or several landing pages with unique URLs rather than forcing the user to wade through all the information in a complicated or hard-to-navigate corporate site.

3. Get serious about SEO.

4. Avoid doing the whole site in Flash. It's not searchable.

5. Sometimes you have to invest in a sponsored search, buy keywords, and bid up your rankings on search engines.

6. Develop an e-mail program that gets read and stimulates action. Give recipients the means to respond immediately or a way to opt out.

7. Make sure your banner ads and text links go exactly where they should. Too many hot leads end up getting lost.

8. Consider QR codes, but keep in mind the limitations of mobile sites and a "cheesiness" factor of clunky QR codes junking up a nice design.

Separate from the corporate site, this microsite combines social media and traditional branding to enhance the Porsche ownership experience. Users can add their own experiences as part of an ever-growing mosaic of Porsche brand stories.

If your website is not well designed and easy to read, it doesn't matter how clever you are. People will not stay. Here are some considerations for making the content of your websites more engaging.

- **Think campaigns.** Your pages have to work individually and cumulatively. Make sure your design has the same look and feel throughout the website, even though many pages will have different functions. Most designers start with the most complicated page. If you can make that work, the simpler pages will be easier to lay out.

- **Design at different levels.** Your site map is usually headed by the home page, which should set the tone for the whole site. Then the next level, or first-level, pages are used to hold content for the main sections. Each of these first-level pages has buttons or links to second-level pages, which in turn may have links to third-level pages, and on it goes. Your first-level and subsequent pages should have the same look and feel as the home page, even though they have different functions. This does not mean they have to look exactly the same, but consider font size, colors, graphic style, and all the other design elements that hold together a campaign.

- *Prioritize.* To paraphrase Howard Gossage, people read what interests them, and sometimes it's a website. But there is a limit to what they are willing to read, and website visitors have short attention spans. There's just too much to see on any given site, so it's natural to jump around. It's critical to put the most important information up front and display it prominently. For example, if e-commerce is an important marketing activity, make sure the casual visitor is directed to that section of the site.

- *Don't forget the navigation.* Think about how visitors find their way around your website. *Primary navigation* on a home page directs visitors to the major sections or first-level pages. *Secondary navigation* directs visitors to content inside a specific section. *Universal navigation* is on all pages—for example, links to the home page, "search," or "contact us."

- *Keep it simple.* Besides overdesigning a website from a graphic standpoint, you can also overdo the technology. Too much movement is annoying and pulls readers away from the text. Don't use technology for its own sake. Instead, concentrate on strategy: what you want to accomplish, not how cool you can make it. A webpage template is basically a table—a grid. The navigation sections can go anywhere on the page, and the main content can be anything that fits in the window.

Microsites

Most corporate sites have become so dense, it's hard to introduce a new product, showcase a promotion, or provide specialized content on the home page. Like a small-space ad in the newspaper, anything new gets lost in the clutter. Even worse, many corporate sites are so rigidly designed and controlled that you're handcuffed by their template, fonts, and color palette. So how do you stand out from the corporate site? Create a microsite—a new landing page or collection of pages meant to function as a discrete entity within or in addition to the corporate site. The microsite's main landing page most likely has its own domain name. Microsites may be created just to include keyword-rich content so search engines rank them higher. This not only moves you higher up the Google page, but it can also lower the cost per click.

Widgets and Apps

Many sites have little added features that help keep people on the site longer and, more importantly, get them to come back more frequently. Apps (short for applications) are opened by a dedicated shortcut on the page. They're there, but you have to click on them. Widgets are special apps that are always running, such as a weather report, calendar, or clock. But apps or widgets don't have to be

The corporate site on the left has to provide a lot of information about the company, products, history, distribution, and a million other facts. So when this company wanted to announce all of its plumbing products were lead-free, they launched the Zero Lead microsite with its own URL. This not only provided more emphasis for that topic; it also aided SEO.

utilitarian. When Harley-Davidson wanted to promote the annual Sturgis Bike Week motorcycle rally, they developed a Google gadget offering a live feed from the streets of Sturgis, South Dakota, and interviews with bike designers. The widgets were promoted on biking blogs and websites. In a week's time over 25,000 users downloaded the widget to keep tabs on the daily happenings in Sturgis.[4]

Writing Web Content

While most of the basic writing guidelines we've presented in previous chapters apply, writing copy for websites also has its own set of rules. First of all, people do not like to read online—mainly because it's harder to read a screen than the printed page. Instead, they scan copy, much the same way they look at full-size newspapers. Bold headlines and pictures catch their eye and may draw them into the copy for more detail. In many cases, visitors print pages to read later rather than wade through a lot of text on-screen. Here are a few tips for writing website content that people will want to read:

- ***Call out important words.*** Use boldface and/or color to highlight important words. But don't overdo it. You still want to make it easy to read.

- ***Use subheads to break up major copy blocks.*** Since people scan rather than read, make sure your subheads have some meaning related to the body copy. Don't be so cute with your subheads that visitors miss the point of your content.

- ***Keep it simple.*** Stick with one main idea per copy block or paragraph. Don't introduce too many new ideas per section. In some ways a text-heavy website is like a bad PowerPoint presentation—too much copy on too few slides.

- **Convert paragraphs to bullet points.** This is especially critical if you have several key features and/or benefits. Make it easy to see the key copy points.

- **Limit your text links.** The beauty of the web is the ability to navigate within and to other sites. However, too many links interrupt your message. You don't want to hook readers and then lose them to another topic or even another website, which may take them to yet another destination.

- **Lead with the main message, then drill down.** This is the inverted pyramid style of journalistic writing. You state your main message up front and gradually add more detail to support that message. Many times, the opening paragraph will be enough to hook the readers or at least get them to download the whole message.

- **Keep it short.** The rule of thumb is to use half as many words as you would for a comparable print piece. As we mentioned, people read text on-screen much more slowly than they read print.

- **Avoid scrolling.** If at all possible, try to keep a short block of text within the window, so readers don't have to scroll down. Since people don't like to read online, they really hate to take any special effort to read even more text.

Writing for a Worldwide Web

Except in countries where local governments crack down on Internet access, you have a global audience. So writing for global brands presents some challenges. For example, a simple literal translation into Spanish or French may mean your word count could be off by 30%. More importantly, people in other countries think differently, buy differently, and see things differently. Translating your text may not be enough. You have to think like your intended audience. That's why truly global brands tailor their sites to local tastes. For example, in the United States, Budweiser can show their rich heritage as a leading brewer. But in other countries, such as Mexico, Bud's just another American brand in a country loaded with local brews. So the website focuses on promotions and special features, rather than history.

Major consumer brands have to reach a diverse consumer base in their home country and wherever their products are sold. The corporate site for Budweiser in the United States can be easily converted to Spanish, but when they are promoting their brand south of the border, the site takes on a totally different look with more promotions and less corporate history.

Web Copy and SEO

Even if you follow all of the above tips, your brilliant web copy will just lie there unread if no one visits. That's why you need to consider optimization to dive traffic to the site. One of the secrets to SEO is to make sure your body copy is rich in keywords. These are the words or phrases that represent the content of your text and, ideally, the words people will use to search for information. For example, a site for Excedrin PM may include keywords such as *migraine relief, migraine symptoms, migraine facts,* and *migraine remedies*, as well as *Excedrin* and *Excedrin Migraine*. Search engines look for words and phrases to grab. If used correctly, the more they find, the higher your site will rank on a search list. Constantly monitor the guidelines for the major search engines and tailor your copy to maximize organic search potential.

Here are some other ideas for optimizing your web copy:

- Place keywords strategically in the article as part of a sentence or phrase. Don't just repeat them. Search engines consider that cheating and will move you down the list. A good rule of thumb is a keyword density of less than 10% of the total word count.

- Don't forget headlines and subheads. That's the first place search engines look for keyword relevance.

- Pay special attention to the first and last paragraphs. Search engines tend to put more emphasis on these areas.

- Don't forget to use keywords for images. For example, instead of "iStock1234567.jpg" rename the photo "Patient relieving migraine symptoms with Excedrin Migraine."

- Keep your copy short and to the point. It not only reads better, but there's less clutter for search engines to sift through.

- Try to include words that have the same meaning as your keywords, especially in the middle part of your copy. For example, for Excedrin Migraine, you might use *headache, light sensitivity,* or *stress triggers*. This not only attracts users who type in these words; it also gives you more tags without appearing to "spam" the search engine with too many keywords.

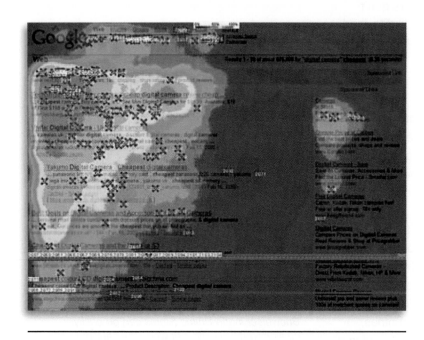

Where do people look first on Google? Researchers have devised the Golden Triangle, with the red area indicating the first and most noticed areas and other colors indicating lower readership. Any doubt why being at the top of the Google page is important?

Bounce Rates

Once you get people to your site, how do you get them to stay? One key metric is the bounce rate, which measures how long people stay with the site. Keep in mind some of the things that people like so much about websites are also factors that have a negative impact on bounce rates. The main thing is to keep measuring and see what works and what doesn't.

- Do whatever you can to minimize page load time. People hate to wait.

- Get rid of pop-up ads. People hate them too.

- Limit the number of external links or have them open in a new window. Don't give people too many opportunities to leave your site.

- Make sure the navigation is easy to use.

- Make sure the content is relevant to the intended target audience (duh!).

- Be careful with music. Give people the option to mute it. Same with videos and slide shows. Let the viewer control what's going on.

Branded Entertainment

We discussed some of the key topics related to online video in Chapter 12. One of fastest-growing areas of online video is branded entertainment—basically telling your brand message in a format and style people will actually enjoy watching. There are many forms of branded entertainment from consumer-generated fake commercials to repurposing TV commercials on the web and even sponsoring a series of slickly produced webisodes starring well-known celebrities. For example, Pampers' "A Parent Is Born" campaign was a popular web series that showed a real-life couple getting ready to have their baby. Because the characters faced real challenges, the series resonated with other expectant couples. It was less about the product and more about people.

Sometimes a company gets lucky with a one-hit wonder. Toyota's "Swagger Wagon" rap hit online gold with more than 10 million views. Why did this video work? (a) It was really funny; (b) one video like this is much easier to share via e-mail, Facebook, and Twitter than several videos rolled out over a long flight date; and (c) taste-making social bookmarking sites like Digg, Reddit, and BuzzFeed focus on one-offs and not series. Sometimes you don't need to do a series of 10 videos when you can create one very special video that can potentially live on the Internet forever.[5]

Branded entertainment isn't as much about selling the brand as it is about selling the "coolness" factor of the brand. First and foremost you need to entertain. Once you're sure you've accomplished that, you can address integrating your brand message in a way that's subtle, even tongue

Rising Star

Fantastic Voyage to a Career in Online Advertising

Marketing was preceded by my desire to pursue an interest in journalism. Although I thought I could write on and on about topics I actually cared about, there was a regimented element of professional journalism that drove me to the dark side—guhh—advertising.

I thought of advertising as an opportunity to create ideas off paper and see them as living, breathing brands. As I switched majors from journalism to advertising my sophomore year, the transformational element of marketing embraced me with open arms.

But with plenty of media channels to explore, I wondered if I should keep copywriting as my focus and continue hoping something (i.e., an internship) would "pop up."

Meanwhile, in South Africa, the experience of a lifetime was in the making.

On a whim, in my junior year, I enrolled in my university's service learning program based in Cape Town and began interning at a community development nonprofit known as Sibanye Economic Empowerment. I was given the challenging task of spearheading the redesign of Sibanye's wholesale catalog website, crucial for organization exposure. This was my entrance into digital advertising.

Utilizing the experience in South Africa as a springboard, I landed my first job as a project manager/SEO manager for a digital shop in Connecticut. Wait . . What's SEO?

I obviously had no idea at the time, so like any other well-learned, resourceful Marquette graduate would do, I learned on the go. Organic search marketing or "increasing Google rankings" was the course. After tons of trials and errors in SEO copywriting and "rinse, watch, repeats" in formulating my process, I began to understand. And understanding led to more opportunity.

Fast forward a couple of agencies later: I'm sitting in a Manhattan boardroom concepting strategies for increasing traffic to the Volkswagen U.S. product site leading up to the Super Bowl, living the brand.[6]

Matthew Hill, organic search manager, Catalyst Online, New York, @matthill728

in cheek. That is part of the brilliance of Old Spice's "Man Your Man Could Smell Like" campaign. It is so over-the-top, so blatantly commercial, that audiences embraced it in huge numbers. Old Spice is in on the joke, winking along with everyone.[7]

Advertisers, entertainment networks, studios, and talent will continue to invest in digital platforms beyond the web. Branded entertainment will also become more interactive, more selective, and more accessible through mobile devices and tablets.

Consumers will lead and brands will try to catch up, mainly because no other marketing channel generates a powerful buzz as quickly as the Internet. For example, "A video of a buff, but sensitive fireman and a fluffy grey kitten helped to create online buzz for Sauza Blue tequila as part of the women-focused Make It With a Fireman campaign, its first all-digital initiative. The video, which attracted 2.3 million views in less than three weeks, was supported by a

FIGURE 13.1

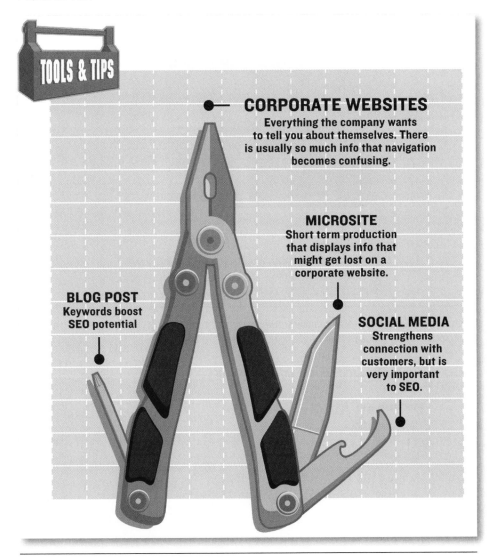

TOOLS & TIPS

CORPORATE WEBSITES
Everything the company wants
to tell you about themselves. There
is usually so much info that navigation
becomes confusing.

MICROSITE
Short term production
that displays info that
might get lost on a
corporate website.

BLOG POST
Keywords boost
SEO potential

SOCIAL MEDIA
Strengthens
connection with
customers, but is
very important
to SEO.

Source: Created by Dan Augustine.

broader campaign, including banner ads on targeted sites, a newly designed
website, blogger outreach, downloadable coupons and sweepstakes promotion
on the Sauza Facebook page."[8]

Web 3.0 and the Future

So where is all this leading us? Web 2.0 has been more or less defined by social
media, user-generated content, and phasing out passive browsing. It's about
customizing content and focusing on well-defined target markets. In the days of
Web 1.0, content was king. In Web 2.0, content is still king, but curating (the
compilation and integration of content) is God.

Pampers' "A Parent Is Born" branded entertainment campaign was a successful web series that documented the joys and challenges of a real-life couple going through pregnancy.

FIGURE 13.2   Branded Digital Entertainment

Source: Created by Dan Augustine.

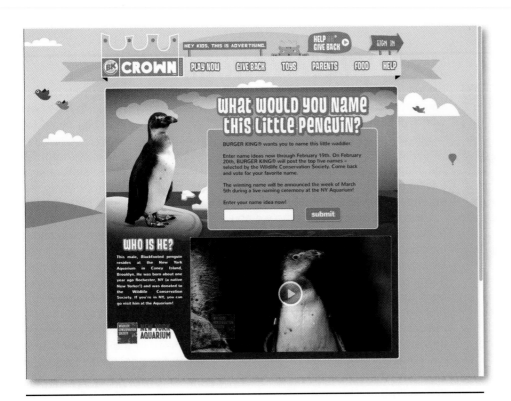

Chances are children would not notice the "Hey Kids, This Is Advertising" disclaimer at the top of this website. They'd rather watch the video. Or check out the toys or play online games. Responsible consumer brands that target kids on the Internet have to walk that fine line between positive engagement and exploitation. Naming a penguin is one thing. Promoting unhealthy food is totally different.

We're well into the next phase—Web 3.0. One of the best ways to describe this new era is the virtual blending of online and offline worlds. Web 3.0 is the seamless integration of your digital and analog lives (or even Second Life, if you're into that). Let's say your computer or smartphone remembers that you like sushi. Your browser becomes like a personal assistant when you look for the best Japanese restaurants in a new town. Web 3.0 requires a giant leap in computer intelligence. In other words, the Internet does all the work for you. All you have to do is tap into it.

So how can you as a creative professional use this technology to create something that sells? Consider the all the possibilities of putting your product in a virtual shopping mall. Or using artificial intelligence to create truly helpful customer service. Or creating an avatar that anticipates the next move, instead of being directed. If having too much information defined Web 2.0, Web 3.0 will be about organizing and filtering that information in a format that comes closer to our "real life" experiences.

No one can predict the exact shape or dimensions of Web 3.0. We expect the merging of desktop and mobile to accelerate. As Apple continues to dominate tablets and mobile devices, Flash will struggle for relevance. HTML5 may take its place to help designers build digital ads. Consolidation of advertising and technology will make it easier to create cross-channel

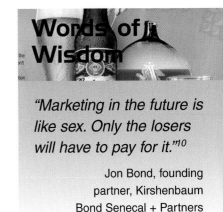

Words of Wisdom

"Marketing in the future is like sex. Only the losers will have to pay for it."[10]

Jon Bond, founding partner, Kirshenbaum Bond Senecal + Partners

War Story

The Perfect Door Opener

The Fernet Stock Z Generation was being introduced as a new variant of the classic Czech bitter spirit to a younger target group. The new Fernet was supposed to be more about enjoying the taste with less alcohol inside. But how do you sell something with less alcohol to a target group that wants one thing from a spirit—the alcohol?

We tried to communicate the new brand as a smarter, more social way of having fun. The TV campaign succeeded in that by showing sketches where people talked at a bar using only words starting with "Z." But our goal was one step further. We had to make the young people experience this feeling of doing something differently and having fun in the process.

We looked for people who we could activate in this way, and at the end we chose university students. Here is why. Lots of the students live in university dormitories, and dorms have always been the source of many new friendships. But today this is often not the case. Students often use their dorm only as a place to sleep and surf on the net. Getting to know their neighbors is not very high on their list. We wanted to give them a reason to knock on the neighbors' doors.

We made an offer for the students: Get together as many neighbors as possible and spell out the letter "Z" on your building using the lights in your rooms. The building with the most votes wins a party paid for by the Fernet Z. We invited eight major campuses around the country by choosing a well-known student at each dorm. This student then had to start connecting the neighbors. With our help, each of them succeeded in getting all the students on board. Students spent a lot of time rehearsing and getting to know each other in the process. The light show at the end functioned both as social glue and as a medium for promoting the new Fernet Z.

One in every four students at the participating campuses took part in the execution of the light show or came to watch the final show. That is almost 5,000 people, and another 10,000 watched the lighting on the web, in real time.[11]

Michal Charvát, general manager, OgilvyAction, Prague, Czech Republic, mather.cz

campaigns. Specialized content will make digital advertising even more valuable. Of course, none of these things may happen. Or the Mayan calendar may actually predict the end of the world in December 2012, which means you probably won't need this book.

Fasten your seat belts. It's going to be a wild ride.

Who's Who?

Peter Vesterbacka—Peter Vesterbacka is one of the culprits responsible for the addiction of more than 400 million people around the world. His crime: being chief management officer for Rovio, the creator of Angry Birds. As of November 2011, more than 30 million people play it every day. The genius of Angry Birds goes far beyond the quirky game itself. Rovio, the tiny Finnish company that markets Angry Birds, also licensed T-shirts, plush toys, Silly Bandz, puzzles, party kits, Halloween costumes, card games, flip-flops, key chains, lunch boxes, board games, and even a TV show. As of this writing, the popularity of Angry Birds in the analog world is surpassing its digital success.[12]

Simon Fleming-Wood—Simon Fleming-Wood was named the first chief management officer for Pandora, the online music service. After 10 years of solid growth (125 million registered users as of February 2012), Pandora needed someone to be the shepherd of the brand and build more disciplined approaches to add new customers. Prior to Pandora, Fleming-Wood was on the founding team of Pure Digital Technologies, the creator of Flip Video. Fleming-Wood stated, Pandora's Music Genome Project is a hand-built database "of musicological DNA that allows people on the fly wherever they are to find music that they love."[13]

Tara Lamberson—Tara Lamberson leveraged her experience with Walt Disney Co., Fox Television, and EarthLink to become vice president of marketing at MindComet, a digital solution agency. The range of services include social networks, podcasting, blogs, viral seeding, e-mail marketing, iPhone development, and brand monitoring for blue-chip clients such as General Motors, Disney, AOL, and Tyco. She received a bachelor's degree in media arts and design from James Madison University and coauthored the book *Understanding Y: Inside the Mind of Millennials.*

Rebecca Rivera—Rebecca Rivera is a digital writer and occasional creative director who recently gave up agency life to go freelance. Rivera revels in her new freedom. She believes marketers get shortchanged when the people most likely to buy their products, usually women, aren't in decision-making roles at ad agencies. She should know. For more than 20 years, Rivers was a player at agencies Team One, DDB Los Angeles, McCann Erickson, Publicis & Hal Riney, Digitas Boston, and Digital Influence Group. Today she leverages her experience to bring her insights to clients, without the agency structure hemming her in.[14]

Exercises

1. It's a Quirky World Out There

- Think of something quirky about yourself, something that sets you apart. Do you collect comic books? Are you the only unicyclist on campus? Have you been a closet juggler since middle school? Are you the only one you know who has lived through five surgeries before age 18? Do you have four toes? We guarantee there will be some quirky people in your class!

- List all the benefits of having your quirk. Have some fun with this. After all, this is advertising.

- Now write a 200- to 250-word story, along with a headline, expressing your quirkiness in vivid detail.

- Now it's time to reveal your alter ego or remain anonymous. Hop on blogger.com and create a blog that tells the world about your own unique quirk. That's right, create a blog dedicated to your very own quirkiness. You might even want to follow some of the tips in this chapter.

- Once you're done, track it for three weeks and keep blogging. Track how many posts you have each day. Are there patterns? Who is posting? What kinds of things do they have to say? At the end of the three weeks make a list of all the branded opportunities that could be leveraged by people who share your particular quirkiness. You might be surprised by how many others share your eccentricities.

- Share your findings with the class. Yes, your have to reveal your quirkiness, at least to the class. If you like your blog, keep it and expand it. If not, game over.

2. Digital Transference

- Find a long-copy ad for a B2B brand.

- Dissect the copy into a series of benefits. Prioritize them based on the key message within the ad.

- Now go online and search for your brand. See if the benefits in the ad match up to the brand's web presence. If not, choose one of two options: (1) Rewrite the ad to fit the digital brand presence, or (2) rewrite the web content to fit the ad. The goal is to create seamless branded transference and make suggestions for visual consistence.

- Now that you have created a consistent print and Internet presence for the brand, suggest two other tactical opportunities that would be consistent with the revised brand voice.

3. Virtual Artifact Room

Pick a product. Any product. It's time to find the articles that are associated with that product.

- Do enough secondary research so you are familiar with the target, and then draft a consumer profile.

- Now, take your ethnographic feet on the road to find objects—toys, food, music, products, photos, clothing—anything and everything that their consumer might have in his or her world. Gather it together into one place. Create an artifact room. Do this individually or as a class. We recommend doing it as a class.

- Spend time in the artifact room and get to know what objects the consumer holds near and dear. See what you can learn about the consumer's lifestyle from these objects. Compare how you "see" the consumer with how your classmates "see" the consumer.

- Now get out your pencil or pen or laptop and start writing. Begin by revising your consumer profile. Next write a story about your consumer, then another, and another, and another. These are the foundation for the branded story.

- Now cluster the objects in the artifact room and consider how you can make the artifact room come to life digitally! How can you make all the objects, and what they symbolize, available to your target virtually? Is it a website, a blog, wallpaper, an app, or perhaps an alter ego? Do they arrive via a podcast, a text, or a gadget? Maybe your brand is the next to be "Simpsonized"!

- Mock up your concept and share it with the class. If you are really tech savvy, go live.

Visit www.sagepub.com/altstiel3e to access these additional learning tools

- Video Links
- Web Resources
- eFlashcards
- Web Quizzes

Chapter 14

Social Marketing

Creating Communities That Buy

A few years ago, agencies and companies were scrambling to find social media experts. In many cases, they said, "We need to get into this social media thing. We don't understand it, so let's hire some kid out of college. They do that Facebook thing, so they must know something." A lot of college grads who didn't or couldn't fit into a traditional agency role found careers in social media. Today, the stakes are higher. And the "let's hire some kid" mentality has matured to "let's see if we can find someone who can work social media into an integrated marketing communication plan with measurable results." Having 700 Facebook friends does not qualify you for this increasingly competitive marketplace. The challenge is defining and then maximizing return on investment for social marketing. When we all agree on some standards for measurement and set some benchmarks to define success, social media will achieve its potential as the driving force of modern marketing. In many ways, that day has arrived. Hash tags now show up on TV commercials, and "like" buttons are slapped on virtually every ad you can find. Jeffrey Zeldman, a designer, writer, and publisher, sums it up pretty well: "Social media will be baked into everything we use, from desktop software, to mobile, to the web, to the thermostat and phone in our hotel room."[1]

Use of social media is a global phenomenon. For example, most Facebook users are outside of the United States, and that does not include China, which does not allow Western social networks. Social media is also cross-cultural. An OMD Latino study found that 90% of online Hispanics use social media at least once a month and that 9% voice opinions about brands, compared to only 4% of general market shoppers.[2]

In some ways, social marketing is similar to the early days of the Internet. Remember how marketers first felt about the web? Interesting and potentially useful at the beginning, eventually it became an integral part of everyday life. Many think that *social media* as a term is already becoming irrelevant. Jeffrey Zeldman comments, "The phrase 'social media,' already used only by a small subsection of the public (tech journalists, consultants, investors, unemployed designers) will fall into complete disuse as social media becomes smarter, monolithic, and ubiquitous—the background noise of all our lives, as little noticed as the electrical hum in our homes."[3] Perhaps in the next edition, we'll talk about engagement through all forms of online communication and not isolate social media.

Social Media Versus Social Networking

We tend to lump all the various aspects of social marketing into a big basket called social media. However, if we are going to be accurate, we need to define *social media* as a communication channel and *social networking* as active engagement between a consumer and an advertiser. The following guide from *Social Media Today* outlines the key differences:

1. By Any Definition

Social media is a way to transmit, or share information with a broad audience. Everyone has the opportunity to create and distribute. All you really need is an Internet connection and you're off to the races.

On the other hand, social networking is an act of engagement. Groups of people with common interests, or like-minds, associate together on social networking sites and build relationships through community.

2. Communication Style

Social media is more akin to a communication channel. It's a format that delivers a message. Like television, radio or newspaper, social media isn't a location that you visit. Social media is simply a system that disseminates information "to" others.

With social networking, communication is two-way. Depending on the topic, subject matter or atmosphere, people congregate to join others with similar experiences and backgrounds. Conversations are at the core of social networking and through them relationships are developed.

3. Return on Investment

It can be difficult to obtain precise numbers for determining the ROI from social media. How do you put a numeric value on the buzz and excitement of online conversations about your brand, product or service? This doesn't mean that ROI is null, it just means that the tactics used to measure are different. For instance, influence, or the depth of conversation and what the conversations are about, can be used to gauge ROI.

Social networking's ROI is a bit more obvious. If the overall traffic to your website is on the rise and you're diligently increasing your social networking base, you probably could attribute the rise in online visitors to your social efforts.

4. Timely Responses

Social media is hard work and it takes time. You can't automate individual conversations and unless you're a well-known and established brand, building a following doesn't happen overnight. Social media is definitely a marathon and not a sprint.

Because social networking is direct communication between you and the people that you choose [to] connect with, your conversations are richer, more purposeful and more personal. Your network exponentially grows as you meet and get introduced to others.

5. Asking or Telling

A big no-no . . . with social media is skewing or manipulating comments, likes, diggs, stumbles or other data, for your own benefit (personal or business). Asking friends, family, coworkers or anyone else to cast a vote just to cast it, doesn't do anyone much good . . . and it can quickly become a PR nightmare if word leaks out about dishonest practices.

With social networking, you can tell your peers about your new business or blog and discuss how to make it a success. The conversations that you create can convert many people into loyal fans, so it's worth investing the time.

Social media and social networking do have some overlap, but they really aren't the same thing. Knowing that they're two separate marketing concepts can make a difference in how you position your business going forward.[4]

Source: Mind Sprout Marketing. "5 Differences Between Social Media and Social Networking." Accessed March 21, 2012, from http://mindsproutmarketing.com/blog/2010/05/5-differences-between-social-media-and-social-networking. Copyright Mind Sprout Marketing.

Social networks have consolidated into a few major players with start-ups launched every day. So we won't spend a lot of time discussing the flavor of the day that will probably be out of business by the time this book is printed. Nor will we concentrate too much on new offerings from the social networking giants because they are constantly expanding their technology and marketing grasp. Instead, we'll cover some basics of how social media and social networking can be used for marketing. We'll focus on a few established social networking channels and outline how they are used to change attitudes, build brands, or spur short-term sales. Remember, for the sake of this book, it's not about how many followers you can add; it's about selling something. We'll limit our discussion to the following topics: word-of-mouth marketing, viral marketing, blogging, and companies and organizations who have achieved results using Facebook, Twitter, and other social networks. Case in point: the Ford Fiesta Project. When they introduced the Fiesta for the North American market, Ford let 100 people use the cars for six months. In return the test drivers had to post blogs and give their comments on Facebook and Twitter. There were no restrictions, but most comments were positive. The second phase of the Fiesta Project resulted in a set of eight nontraditional videos, which brought in a million viewers on YouTube and Fordvehicles.com, as well as 5,000 conversations on Facebook, Twitter, and YouTube. To maximize exposure, Ford used a viral seeding agency. Through the automaker's microtargeting approach, the Fiesta Project was able to reach niche online communities with a custom message. "We know we have to get creative if we want to reach and engage our target audience online," said Jonathan Beebe, Ford's digital communications manager. "The response to the Fiesta indicates that we're making a real connection between the product features and their real-world lives."[5]

We know it's impossible to highlight all the successful integrated social campaigns or to even segment them all into nice neat categories, so forgive us if the lines blur between sections in this chapter.

Word-of-Mouth Marketing

How many times have you heard "the best advertising is word of mouth"? Today's it's more than a tired cliché, because new technology is creating a whole

Words of Wisdom

"Social media is about sociology and psychology more than technology."[6]

Brian Solis, principal and digital analyst, Altimeter Group

Kindergartens are learning on iPads

NOT chalkboards

No doubt you've seen a version of "Social Media Revolution" by Erik Qualman. It's based on his best-selling book Socialnomics. *This program is continually updated to add more statistics, all of which confirm that social media is becoming even more powerful as a global marketing force. Check out socialnomics.net for the latest version.*

new word-of-mouth (WOM) category. WOM is simply the act of consumers providing information to other consumers. Sometimes it's an honest appraisal. Sometimes the buzz is manipulated. When WOM can be manipulated, accelerated, and multiplied exponentially, you can make the case that it's a legitimate form of advertising. In fact, when it's managed to deliver a defined result, it's called word-of-mouth marketing (WOMM).

Why is WOMM so important? Research shows that when people are happy with a product or service, they each tell three people. When they're unhappy, they tell 11.[7] When you consider the impact of social media, you may be talking about 11 million. Marketers are taking note. WOM spending in the United States should double from 2011 to 2015.[8]

Don't you want as many people as possible telling three (or 3 million) friends about your wonderful product? When people naturally become advocates of a product because they are satisfied customers, it's called *organic word of mouth*. When marketers launch campaigns to accelerate WOM—that is, when it becomes WOMM—"influencers" spread the message. The key to successful WOMM is not about how many consumers you please, but rather about how many influencers you reach to spread the message for you. Viral seeding agencies will place your cool product-oriented video on hundreds, if not thousands, of websites, blogs, and social sites. The advantage of online WOMM is that your message does not fade after a one-on-one conversation. It keeps multiplying, even if it's a decelerating rate. Your guerrilla marketing efforts may be picked up by mainstream news media and online news sources where millions will see your message, comment on it, download it, and send it to their friends. Your provocative ambient advertising will be photographed by cell phones and posted on Facebook, where hundreds within minutes and millions within days will see it. As long as we're tossing out old clichés, with properly managed WOMM, one picture is worth a thousand downloads . . . more likely, a thousand times a thousand. Another thing to remember about WOMM is that traditional media also influences the influencers, those people you recruit to spread your message. They'll see a story on CNN, watch the video on YouTube, or get an e-mail, which will accelerate their dissemination of your WOM message. When WOMM is discussed, other terms get thrown around like *buzz marketing*. It's simply another way to get people talking, hopefully in a positive tone. As we discuss in other chapters, be very careful about trying to manage buzz. If it's perceived as too heavy-handed, dishonest, or manipulative, it will definitely generate a buzz, but not the kind you want. Remember those 11 people (or 11 million) who hear negative news?

Vail Resorts built WOM three ways: RFID technology embedded into season passes and lift tickets allowed passive check-ins so riders could learn where they rode, when they rode, and how many vertical feet they traveled. Second, riders could earn pins for a variety of achievements, and it became a game to motivate and challenge riders to push themselves. Third, riders could log into a free web and mobile app to see their stats, add friends from Facebook, send messages, and see where their friends were on the mountain. Shortly after the program went live, over 100,000 people activated their account and generated more than 36 million social impressions.[9]

Whether you call it WOMM or buzz or whatever, one of its real powers is to create and sustain a brand. Where would Harley-Davidson be without a small, but rabid, gang of brand evangelists in black leather jackets? Ben & Jerry's would be just another ice cream if people didn't talk about their support for worthy causes. Macintosh might just have been another futile experiment in operating system development if dedicated art directors, designers, and other right-brainers didn't spread the word within and between agencies and studios.

No matter how many success stories you dig out, the value of WOM as a marketing tool will remain anecdotal until more accurate metrics are developed. BzzAgent, a Boston-based WOMM agency, fixed the value of one conversation at about 50 cents.[10] David Bank, an analyst for RBC Capital Markets, commented, "I might think I'm paying X amount for a CPM [cost per thousand]. But if virality is 30 times that, I'm paying so much less."[11]

Social Media and Word of Mouth

Social media has altered the landscape of WOM, helping spread buzz faster and more efficiently than face-to-face communications. It's done more than simply turbocharge WOM. It has also brought this "alternative" form of marketing to the mainstream. WOMM is based on the simple premise that a recommendation from a friend carries more weight than an ad message. But social media has blurred what that means. Social networking has given WOM marketers a clearer way to measure the impact of their campaigns. Marketers can see how far an influencer's opinion spreads by analyzing retweets or shares. It also becomes easier to see if an influencer's discussions are relevant and in line with positioning. Plus it all occurs in real time. When combined, WOM and social become a dynamic duo. Conversations begun online continue in person, and recommendations spread more quickly, allowing communities built around brands to gain traction. "You start conversations in one channel, continue them in a second and finish them in a third," says Karin Kane, vice president of client services for evolve24, a Maritz Research company that uses business analytics and research to measure brand perceptions, reputation, and risk. "When communication is happening in so many channels, it becomes almost impossible to separate online and offline."[13]

While we can't ignore the impact of social networking on WOM, it's important to note that 90% of brand-oriented conversations are still held face-to-face or over the phone.[14] Is a "like" as influential as an unsolicited recommendation shared in person? Are fans and followers as trustworthy as friends? With more than 2 billion brand impressions created by WOM every day, you can see the 50 million Facebook "likes" are just a small percentage of that total. It's also wise to remember that influencers are not always advocates. The number of active brand evangelists is far lower than the number that simply "like" a product. Regardless of the impact of social media, WOM will continue to grow in importance. Ann Jurman of MagicBuz, a firm that specializes in online conversations, says, "The precision of search engines, coupled with the willingness of consumers to become review publishers in their own right, means that participating in word of mouth is now essential for all marketers."[15]

Viral Marketing

How many times a day do you receive an e-mail, a tweet, or a Facebook message asking you to look at something really cool? Sometimes it's a photo, but more often it's a video. Through WOM and direct marketing, advertisers are also sharing pictures or videos, or telling others about them. When they can foster product or brand awareness via unsolicited testimonials, they not only multiply their media dollars; they also benefit from more effective communication. Then the message takes on a life of its own, and marketers can pronounce the magic words: "It's gone viral."

The factors that make viral marketing so effective are also the things many marketers hate—randomness and lack of measurement. That's why some early adopters started using *viral seeding agencies* to ensure placement of brand-promoting videos on a wide variety of blogs and websites. However, the resistance to being manipulated by marketers has led to widely unpredictable results as marketers try to control the viral buzz. For example, "Dove Evolution" was uploaded to YouTube, and it took off like wildfire, drawing over 2.5 million viewers. It was an instant viral hit. Several parodies made the rounds, which further enhanced the buzz for the original. On the flip side, carefully planned rollouts of slickly produced videos often bomb, especially when skeptical consumers feel they're being manipulated. Brian Morrissey writes, "There is still some debate over what constitutes a true viral campaign. As some feel it's one that happens organically, not planned out like a regular ad push." Christian Dietrich, head of the gaming unit at Tribal DDB, said smart creative that speaks to an audience will win out, and a low-key approach is often better to achieve grassroots appeal. "There's too much risk of it coming across as false or commercial."[17]

Writing Company Blogs

Access to the blogosphere means anyone can become a journalist. Unfortunately not everyone is a good one. The cost of traditional publishing prevents most hacks from inflicting their drivel on the public. Unfortunately there are no such restraints online. As a result, fact checking, grammar, and basic civility sometimes take a back seat to self-expression. Because blogging is such a personal activity, we'll focus on using the blogosphere to sell something. Company-sponsored blogs sometimes try to emulate personal blogs. For example, Bill Marriott of Marriott International hosts a blog for customers and employees. His personal replies to positive and negative comments give the impression that he cares about his customers. Or they can tell stories about a company as Southwest Airlines did to show what a happy, fun-loving airline they are. You can use a blog to inform stakeholders, as the Obama campaign did to keep supporters and donors up to date on recent developments.

Blogs can be used for public relations purposes, such as Starbucks' blog to discount rumors that it did not support American military personnel. Kryptonite Corporation was caught off guard when a blogger reported that a simple Bic pen could pick the company's bike locks. Videos soon appeared to show how to do it. The mainstream media eventually picked up the story, and within days the company blogged about their $10 million product exchange to provide Bic-proof locks. Blogs are sometimes useful when a company is mired in an ongoing controversy such as BP and their oil spill disaster in 2010. While not many consumers expected the whole truth, at least BP made the effort to tell their side of the story and to respond to people's concerns.

If you're writing your own blog or one to promote a company's point of view, here are a few tips:

1. **Be transparent:** If your blog is about your brand, don't try to hide it. Eventually, the truth comes out, and people will resent trying to be tricked. Brands that try to hide behind some thinly disguised fake consumer-generated effort suffer the consequences.

2. **Be original:** It's more difficult to come up with something truly creative. Once again, if you're writing a commercial blog, don't try to mimic a personal narrative.

3. **Be relevant:** Do you have a good reason for doing it? If not, forget it. No one wants recycled news, old information, the standard corporate line, or unfocused personal journalism.

4. **Be responsive:** When someone comments on your blog—positive or negative— reply as soon as you can. Thank the positives and try to persuade the negatives that you are at least sincere in your opinions. Direct e-mail replies as well as public acknowledgement on social networks help establish positive engagement.

A blog was just one of several social media tools used during the Obama reelection campaign. No other presidential candidate has used new media more effectively.

Social Network Platforms

As we mentioned earlier, we can't keep up to date on all the latest upgrades to Google, Facebook, Twitter, and all the rest. So we will cover the very basics and describe how these powerful platforms have been used in integrated marketing campaigns. Besides creating online communities that interact with your brand, social media also provide the means to measure that interaction. Facebook servers handle upward of 50 million "likes" each day. Google indexes some 200 million tweets every 24 hours. Tweets and "likes" are being used as measures of marketing efficacy because of their promise to go beyond mere followers. They are proof positive that the brand's message is getting across.[19]

Until recently, monetizing social media has been one of the biggest challenges facing marketers. Facebook and Twitter have both concentrated on turning regular content into ads. Facebook's Sponsored Stories and Twitter's Sponsored Tweets have added a new twist to their advertising efforts. With Sponsored Stories, when a user interacts with your brand on Facebook (whether through a "like," check-in, wall post, or custom app), your brand will appear twice: in the user's news feed, and in a sponsored ad that features that user's name. The blend of a user's activity with a relevant message from an advertiser adds another dimension to the marketing effort.

War Story

Can Advertising Make People Happier?

Despite our reputation internationally for being amongst the nicest people in the world, we noticed that on a day-to-day basis, Canadians aren't really all that nice to each other. Clearly, there was something wrong here, and we felt it was time to do something about it. We use our creative talent to sell products and services every day for our clients. Why not use it to make Canadians happier?

We set out with the lofty intention of putting our collective talent toward making Canada a better place. The trick was figuring out where to start. Research indicates that a positive attitude improves health, so from there we determined that being nice could actually make Canadians happier and healthier.

We formed a coalition and called it *People for Good*. Our first mission was to run a campaign that would capture the nation's attention by igniting the world of social media and attracting national media coverage. We had over $15 million in donated media to work with, thanks to our media partner and cofounder in the movement, Mark Sherman and his team at Media Experts.

When we began observing how Canadians interact with each other to gain insights, what we saw wasn't pretty. We witnessed people letting elevator doors close in spite of people running toward them, and seniors standing on the subway as nobody gave up a seat. People were caught up in their own little worlds, oblivious to those around them.

We had to jolt people out of their self-absorbed mind-set. We deployed brightly colored billboard executions with large, attention-grabbing headlines that couldn't be ignored, urging Canadians to start doing good deeds. Billboards around the country touted positive sentiments such as "Don't carry grudges. They weigh a ton" and "Give your fellow driver five fingers. Wave."

We kicked off the campaign with a manifesto that ran in newspapers prompting readers to join our People for Good movement. Each piece drove traffic to peopleforgood.ca to pledge support, contribute to the ongoing list of good deeds, and watch the inspiring video diaries from those who took a 7-Day Good Deed Challenge. The campaign also featured radio spots with celebrities Lisa Loeb and Jason Priestley imploring Canadians to join People for Good, along with a mobile app that generated location-specific good deed suggestions.

So did it work? The campaign made an undeniable impact right out of the gate. It instantly garnered national media attention, including headlines in all our national and local papers, plus praise on numerous national television programs.

It quickly became clear that People for Good was resonating with Canadians as support poured in from all corners of the country. Thousands of people joined our online community, and within the first week of launching, the mobile app was featured on iTunes as "New and Noteworthy."

Most importantly, the campaign achieved its goal of jolting Canadians out of their own little worlds and, as a result, is helping to make Canada an even nicer place, one good deed at a time.[20]

Zak Mroueh, president and executive creative director, Zulu Alpha Kilo, Toronto, Canada, zulualphakilo.com

Just before Facebook went public in May 2012, General Motors announced they were suspending Facebook advertising. They explained that Facebook was still an important platform for interacting with consumers, but that it was not an effective vehicle for advertising. After the stock prices started to slide shortly after the IPO, it was disclosed that Facebook's mobile app does not support advertising very well, severely limiting future revenue streams. On top of that, despite having 900 million users, about half the people surveyed thought Facebook was a passing fad and that the initial stock price was set too high.[21] Ouch! It's important to consider ROI before you decide if social media advertising is the new savior of marketing communication.

Google has evolved into an advertising powerhouse with AdWords, AdSense, Google+ for business, support programs like Google Analytics, and we're sure a half-dozen more that have been launched since we wrote this. Whether it's paid search, display ads, embedded content, or whatever, Google can provide the eyeballs for your marketing communication efforts. We're not promoting Google, just reporting the facts, and God knows they don't need our help.

YouTube, owned by Google, is usually regarded as the third most popular Internet site after Facebook and Google. In 2005, YouTube launched the site with one video. Seven years later, they stated over 4 billion videos are viewed per day.[22] Video is probably the most powerful tool on the web, so YouTube's dominance, with the power of Google behind it, will continue to be a potent force. In 2012, YouTube introduced a new ad model—selling sponsorships rather than TV-style demographics. Suites of channels have themes such as Moms, Young Hollywood, and Automotive. Keyword targeting is used rather than demo statistics. YouTube gives the advertiser a grant for video production, then splits the profits from ad sales with the advertiser after the initial investment is covered.

Here are a few other social sites that have grown in popularity. Not all are well suited for large-scale marketing communication programs, and none of them yet match the power of Facebook, Twitter, and Google. While many of the following are great for personal communication or entertainment, we'll concentrate on their potential for marketing brands or retail outlets.

- **LinkedIn** is the social network for business professionals and students who want to be professionals. It's great for personal branding, but no so much for promoting products or services, although you can put promotional messages and ads in user group sections. LinkedIn is also useful for cross-messaging with Twitter and Facebook.

- **Foursquare** is a location-based web and mobile social networking platform where users can choose to have their check-ins integrated with other social platforms, such as Twitter and Facebook. The Foursquare Brand Platform allows companies to create pages of tips and allows users to "follow" the company and receive special, expert tips from them when they check in at certain locations. Users can unlock special badges with enough check-ins, playing into the growing trend of gamification.

- **Instagram,** a photo-sharing platform launched in 2010, grew to over 35 million users by May 2012. Any medium that attracts that many users also attracts advertisers. For example, Delta Air Lines, a fashion eyewear company, and Volvo employed Instagrammers to post photos connected to their brands. *Adweek* reported, "The tactic is a smart one for visually driven brands in industries like fashion and travel—especially those already dabbling in influencer marketing."[23] Instagram was purchased by Facebook shortly before that company went public.

- **Pinterest** provides an alternative to word-driven social sites by allowing users to create and share theme-based image collections. As a start-up, Pinterest was the fastest website to reach 10 million unique visitors a month—the vast majority of them female.[24] The challenge is to connect relevant marketing messages to content created just for fun.

- **Second Life** is an online virtual world where "residents" interact with each other through avatars. Some companies have found success with an ongoing presence in Second Life—for example, Intel technical discussions or online concerts. Others, like the Weather Channel, have created places with activities to engage residents. Brands can get involved in Second Life, such as when the Nesquik Bunny attended several events. As with other role-playing sites, you can pay to have your ad displayed in Second Life, by either location, time, or pay-per-click.

The above list barely scratches the surface. We could talk about the rise and fall of Myspace and its relevance in the market today. We could mention the many music and movie sites, sales promotion sites like Groupon or LivingSocial, or user review and local search sites such as Yelp. We could probably devote a whole chapter, and maybe a whole book, to the status of social networks at the time of this writing, and it would only be a snapshot that will fade as established players evolve and startups emerge.

Facebook: The Rise of "Likenomics"

Although it started later, Facebook passed Myspace in total number of users and hasn't looked back. At the beginning of 2012, Facebook had more than 800 million members and was on its way to having over a billion. Advertising revenue has more than doubled, and Facebook now controls nearly 20% of all U.S. display ad income.[26] New advertising tools and improvements in accountability have helped make Facebook the leading social networking platform for marketing. Brands want your loyalty, so Facebook makes it easy to say you "like" them. Turning those "likes" into measurable assets has been called "likenomics." Posting an opinion online is the easy part. But winning and keeping loyal advocates for your brand is something else. When someone "likes" your brand, they let the world know they have moved from a passive consumer to a brand advocate. Their friends trust their judgment, so they may be more inclined to also "like" that brand, or at least have a more favorable opinion of it. All that improves ad recall, awareness, comprehension, conviction, and action. David Rowan says in *GQ*'s "Digital Life" column, "The social graph generates transactions. Those 'Like' buttons influence your friends to buy what you're buying—which is why brands like Levi's are building 'social stores' on Facebook to reveal which jeans your peers consider cool."[27]

Since Facebook is the dominant player in the social graph, it makes sense to use that platform to increase engagement not easily achieved through traditional media. For example, Frito-Lay teamed with Zynga to promote its new healthier product formulations. They developed an online game tied with heavy emphasis on social media to reintroduce the brand to the new generation of health-conscious moms. Facebook fans were offered a sweepstakes for a new kitchen, webisodes to watch, and testimonials from farmers discussing healthy ingredients. The *Guinness World Records* book named the promotion the fastest-growing Facebook brand page within 24 hours: 1.8 million "likes" a day.[28] This is another example of gamification used for promoting a brand.

Another snack food company learned that just being on Facebook was not enough. When Little Debbie brand set up their first Facebook effort, they posted updates, TV ads, and other self-promoting marketing material. The results were not very sweet. However, when they ran a sweepstakes with a Smart Car as a prize, their fan base grew from 5,000 to 125,000 in just 12 hours. The company received over 6,000 comments from fans saying they just loved Little Debbie snack cakes—a sweet deal for everyone involved.[29]

Facebook's Impact on Retail

Of the consumers who follow a brand on Facebook, over one third cited special deals as the main reason they became fans.[30] Using social media is an ideal way to share information about short-term sales promotions. It's no surprise so many retailers and credit card companies have used Facebook to get the word out quickly before major events like Black Friday, the biggest shopping day of the year. Department stores like Macy's and big-box retailers such as Walmart and Best Buy shared their Black Friday deals early with their Facebook fans. Amazon and Target offered special deals, contests, and other incentives to persuade consumers to "like" their brands. Best Buy created an event page for Black Friday. Facebook offers the advantage of trusted information from a chosen source, rather than impersonal intrusions from traditional media. What's more, an e-mailed or snail-mailed coupon is seen by only one recipient at a time. A special promotion or discount on Facebook can be seen by millions at the same time, and they can share it with millions more if they choose.

Frito-Lay's Facebook fans were offered a sweepstakes to win a new kitchen, webisodes, and testimonials from farmers discussing healthier ingredients.

Facebook was also used as a means to spread the word about Small Business Saturday. In an integrated campaign using television and other media, American Express encouraged shoppers to buy from local merchants. Two days later, Facebook was a major platform to share information about deals on Cyber Monday, the traditional peak of online buying. The rest of the year, Facebook has proven valuable to many retailers, big and small, as a means to provide information about sales, new products, contests, and other promotions. T.G.I. Friday's partnered with an incentive company to create the "Buy Your Friend a Beer" Facebook page, separate from the corporate page. Within a month, 13,000 users paid $5 to send their friend a coupon for a beer. Users provided their credit card and billing information, and the recipient got a blast on his or her Facebook wall and news feed. While the campaign is a good example of translating social gifting into a real-world experience, many critics wonder if entering credit card information into a Facebook application is a great idea.[31]

This Facebook page was part of a campaign for American Express Small Business Saturday, an effort to encourage shoppers to support local independent retailers (between Black Friday and Cyber Monday). Participating small business owners also received access to marketing tools, advice, and free geo-targeted advertising.

"Who Killed Deon?" created for the London Metropolitan Police, won the most awards for an ad campaign in the United Kingdom for 2011.

Beyond the Brand: Social Networking for Social Good

Facebook advertising goes beyond selling products to trying to solve social issues. The "Who Killed Deon?" campaign, created for the London Metropolitan Police, was the most award-winning ad campaign in the United Kingdom for 2011—and arguably the world.[32] The interactive campaign was designed to educate young people (ages 13–15) that playing any role in a serious crime can lead to conviction. In this case, only one person stabbed "Deon," but five others had some connection to the murder. The one who cooperated with the police was not charged. The others, even though some of their involvement was relatively minor, were convicted of murder. The fast-action, split-screen video featured realistic actors and graphic violence, sometimes telling the story from all six points of view at once. Ads on youth-oriented TV channels and radio were used to drive young people to view the film and comment on Facebook. Street teams distributed DVDs to the target audience in tough South London neighborhoods. Some Facebook comments showed a change in attitudes. Others resented the authorities invading their social space.

Twitter: Tweeting Its Way Into the Mainstream

Twitter is a *microblog* with each tweet limited to 140 characters. Unlike texting, Twitter is web based, so posts are indexed by Google and readily available to anyone with Internet access. Although it started slowly, we've gone far beyond the perception that Twitter is primarily used to tell the world what you had for breakfast. Companies and organizations are learning that Twitter can be an effective marketing tool when used correctly. Some monitor tweets as a measure of customer satisfaction. JetBlue, Comcast, H&R Block, and Southwest Airlines, among others, monitor tweets from customers and respond to let the customer and everyone else know they made the effort. Sometimes they can even turn around a negative opinion. A travel writer from Boston tweeted a very negative experience at the Milwaukee airport, which colored his view of the whole city. The airport authority saw his tweet, was sympathetic to the writer's bad experience, and offered to treat him to the best Milwaukee had to offer. The response impressed the critic, who wrote a glowing article in the *Boston Globe* about the friendly, helpful, and caring people of Milwaukee (although he still considered the airport and the rest of the city as pretty crummy). By using monitoring sites' services such as HootSuite, marketers can monitor influencers, set schedules, and manage reach.

Increasingly, organizations and companies use Twitter proactively. For example, Barack Obama's campaign used Twitter to keep volunteers up to date with late-breaking developments. Twitter has proven very effective in some retail promotions. As they do with Facebook, most big-box retailers use Twitter to promote their holiday sales. Walgreens used Twitter to promote their mobile app, which will send coupons to the smartphones of people who download it. Disney Store rolled out an interactive Twitter campaign that included a Twitter "concierge." When KFC introduced a grilled chicken item, they placed a link for a free meal coupon on Twitter. The link was quickly forwarded to millions of people. In fact there were so many tweets, it crashed the site, and KFC franchises were overwhelmed with coupons.[33]

American Express launched a program on Twitter that allows card members to "tweet their way to savings" by synching their AmEx card with Twitter and tweeting a number of merchant-specific *hash tags* to load credits to their account. Participating merchants included 1-800-FLOWERS.com, Dell, Seamless.com, Zappos.com, Best Buy, Century 21 Department Store, The Cheesecake Factory, FedEx Office, FTD, Gulf, H&M, McDonald's, Sports Authority, Ticketmaster, Virgin America, and Whole Foods. American Express Vice Chairman Ed Gilligan said, "American Express is turning Twitter content into commerce by connecting card members to merchants and delivering real world value to both." American Express promoted their Twitter partnership during a live-streamed concert from South by Southwest (SXSW) on the "AmEx Sync Show Presenting Jay-Z" on YouTube.[34] American Express is also taking the lead in integrating social media platforms with their card. Card members can sync their cards with Foursquare, Twitter, and Facebook. When American Express card holders sync their cards with Foursquare, they receive location-based deals and offers directly to their AmEx cards. Those who sync their cards with Facebook, as part of the "Link, Like, Love" program, see deals in their newsfeed on Facebook, based on the companies they talk about and like. Consumers who sync their cards with Twitter get savings loaded directly to their cards when they tweet using special-offer hash tags. The "Link, Like, Love" program lets brands and retailers tie sales back to efforts on platforms such as Facebook, Twitter, and Foursquare, using the AmEx application programming interface.[35]

Words of Wisdom

"You are what you tweet."[36]

Alex Tew, creator of the Million Dollar Home Page

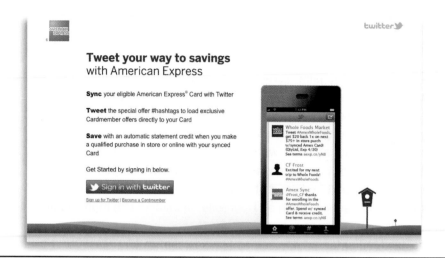

By tweeting special-offer hash tags for selected merchants, Twitter users could receive automatic credits to their AmEx card.

Social media by its nature is unpredictable, as McDonald's discovered with their #McDStories campaign on Twitter. Their #MeetTheFarmers campaign, designed to promote the wholesomeness of their food, drew some nice comments. When they changed to #McDStories, so customers could share their positive McDonald's moments, people began to tweet about getting sick from the food, dirty restaurants, animal abuse, childhood obesity, and virtually every other social ill they could attribute to the Golden Arches. The company pulled the plug on the promotion, but an enterprising Twitter fan created #McFail, which continued the anti-McDonald's tweets.[37]

Despite all the potential for using Facebook and Twitter marketing tools, not many companies are ready to abandon all traditional marketing efforts for the social space. Besides the randomness and risk of negative conversations, the numbers are just not big enough—at least for now. Keller Fay Group, a company that measures brand conversations, said this about Coca-Cola's Facebook marketing program: "There are 860 million offline conversations about Coca-Cola each month and about half are active recommendations to buy or try products; there are 36 million Facebook 'likes' but only 56,000 are active."[38] A survey reported in eMarketer found that 54% of Facebook users who "liked" a company were "somewhat more likely" or "much more likely" to purchase that brand. But the survey went on to report that only 1% of fans of the biggest brands on Facebook actually engage with the brands in the social space. The study examined Facebook-based activities such as "likes," comments, posts, and shares and found nothing substantial to link a brand's Facebook presence with loyalty.[39] What's more, in terms of media efficiency, Facebook ad performance is much weaker than traditional media. Advertisers may use Facebook to drive traffic or sell products, but most traditional brands use the site for its social value alone. A study by Webtrends reported, "Out of the ads we measured, we found that interest-targeted ads began to burn out after three to five days. Eventually the rotting CTR [click-through rate] leads to Facebook deactivating the ad, and it's back to the drawing board."[40]

Words of Wisdom

"Social marketing eliminates the middlemen, providing brands the unique opportunity to have a direct relationship with their customers."[41]

Bryan Wiener, CEO,
digital agency 360i

Keeping Up With Social Trends

Where is social marketing headed? We're sure to see better metrics for accurate evaluation of advertising messages. We can also expect to see more blending of content and advertising. What's more, we expect to see trends toward more consolidation by the major platforms, but also more startups taking hold. But if you really want to stay ahead of the game—guess what? You can't. Even the experts miss trends and have to relearn new tricks as marketing and technology evolve. As graphic designer, web developer, and social media marketer Larissa Harris states, "The urgency to stay on top of what is going on with Facebook, Twitter, and YouTube, and the relentless need for content to fuel blogs, is the most difficult part of social media marketing. Change is constant and the social media marketer must know as much as they can to get the greatest exposure for their clients. So how much do we need to study? I would advise: as much as you can read in an hour a day."[42] She also offers this advice to those who want keep up:

1. Follow the Right People

Perhaps it's cheating, but I rely on others to stay up-to-date with social media. I follow Mashable.com and TechCrunch, create Google Alerts, and follow the experts on Twitter and YouTube. Set aside time each day to read the posts or watch the videos so you don't feel guilty about it. It really is important research for your business. Some people are even helpful enough to answer questions and provide advice.

2. Learn the Tools

It's hard to tell what you need to invest your time in learning. My takeaway from the Facebook changes is to let someone else learn the technology when you can. Then use the products they develop to do what you need to do. Facebook apps are wonderful, and allow you to create great custom pages without knowing any code.

3. Have a Plan

Determine your purpose in creating the social media campaign. My social media clients usually want to:

- Increase their website's traffic

- Establish credibility and build their brand

- Provide support to their overall SEO efforts

- Find potential customers

- Promote their products or services

4. Be Active

Once you've established momentum (your members, followers, etc., are increasing and are active), take advantage of it and be consistent in actively promoting and updating.

5. Use the Feedback

Monitor what people say about your clients on Facebook, Twitter, and other social media communities. Track your progress and change the marketing plan (or even the product) if necessary. To be successful, you need the right resources, tools, and training, as well as technical support. Test out emerging trends, but don't invest too much of your time—it will all change tomorrow.[43]

Rising Star

Rock On

I really wanted to be a rock star, but I chose advertising. Or should I say advertising chose me? No, that will be a cliché like the thousands we see every day in advertising campaigns. I've been in the business for a while now, and, I must say, the most difficult part is to get good work produced. The majority of the ads we see every day are just there for people to ignore them. That's why if you're not passionate about advertising, you shouldn't be part of it.

I've worked a lot of places on my way to get where I am. My career began in Colombia, my native country. Flash websites were a hit in the early 2000s, so with a couple of classes I started making some money while still in college. When the opportunity came to work at Lowe/SSP3, I thought, if I know how to design a website, I can be an art director. Later I realized I had a better future as a writer. After that I worked at Sancho BBDO and Leo Burnett. Then I tried to get transferred from the Colombia office to Chicago, but things didn't work out in that moment. Fortunately I had a backup plan. I packed my bags and headed to Chicago to improve my English writing skills at a portfolio school. A couple of months later, things worked out with my work visa, and I started working at Lápiz, the Hispanic agency of Leo Burnett in Chicago.

It's good to always have a backup plan. It's also good to try to be the best in what you do and give everything in every single project. It's a tough business, but it has something that others don't have: the power of an idea. All you need is a good one to shine brighter than any star. As the title of Paul Arden's book says, "It's not how good you are, but how good you want to be." That, for me, is the key to success.[45]

Nicolas Mejia, senior copywriter, Lápiz, Chicago, @nicolasmm

It's Not About Technology—It's About Engagement

We won't take a snapshot and use it to predict a trend. We can report the facts as they stand when we write this, but they may change before this book is published and will certainly be old news by the time you read it. So it's foolish for us to say how the social graph will evolve in the next three or four years. However, we can say with some confidence, when platforms do a better job to engage their users, they will be able to attract more advertising revenue than their rivals. As marketers look for better metrics and more accountability, engagement will be an important component of ROI—far more important than a cute name, cool graphics, and impressing your friends as "mayor" of the coffee shop. If people spend more time on a site, share it more often, and respond to the content, advertisers will find their way into that site, whether it's embedded in a story or a plain old banner ad. Site developers who want to become the next dot-com billionaire understand that, even though many say they reject advertising based on principle.

FIGURE 14.1   *Time spent on a site is a good measure of engagement. Facebook is the clear winner based on minutes per visitor per month. However, this is a snapshot, not a forecast. Our only prediction is these numbers will change.*

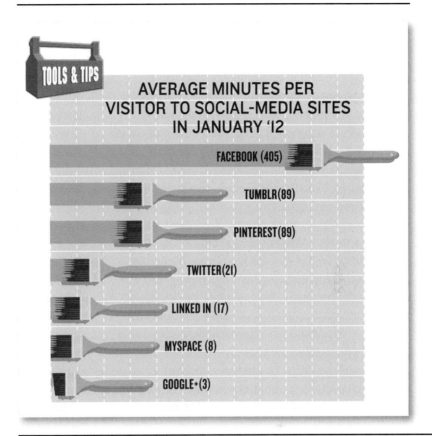

Source: Created by Dan Augustine.

Figure 14.1 shows comScore data for January 2012. Facebook was the dominant player with the average user spending nearly *seven hours a month* on the site. Pinterest and Tumblr are tied for a distant second place, with Twitter coming in fourth. Despite its early promise, Google+ ranked at the bottom and was even clobbered by the increasingly irrelevant Myspace. Google reported different numbers from their internal audit, claiming 90 million users, 60% of which actively use the site daily. While that may be true for the total Google universe, those numbers probably reflect use of their other products, such as Google search, YouTube, or Gmail.[46] As we mentioned earlier, these numbers will change, and ultimately the market will sort out the winners and losers.

Who's Who?

Steven Chen—Steven Chen is the cofounder and former chief technology officer of YouTube. Born in Taiwan, Chen attended high school in the Chicago area and graduated from the University of Illinois at Urbana-Champaign. He was one of PayPal's early employees, where he met Chad Hurley and Jawed Karim. In 2005, the three founded YouTube. On October 16, 2006, Chen sold his share of YouTube to Google and is now an employee of Google.

Jack Dorsey—Jack Dorsey is best known as the creator of Twitter and the founder of Square, a mobile payments company. Dorsey was a computer prodigy at age 14 when he developed web-based dispatch routing software for taxis. Dorsey, Biz Stone, and Evan Williams cofounded Twitter after taking all of two weeks to develop the prototype. As CEO, Dorsey saw the startup through two rounds of funding by the venture capitalists. In 2008, he was named to the MIT *Technology Review* TR35 as one of the top 35 innovators in the world under the age of 35.[47]

Clara Shih—Clara Shih, as cofounder and CEO of Hearsay Social, has been called the most influential thought leader in social marketing on the vendor side. After being named to the Starbucks board last December, the Stanford grad—whose résumé also includes stints at Google, Microsoft, and Salesforce—stands to play a major role in the coffee chain's future. Expect Shih, the author of the bestseller *The Facebook Era*, to keep the company tuned in to all the latest trends—and what its customers want.[48]

Ian Tait—Ian Tait was one of the driving forces behind the "Man Your Man Could Smell Like" campaign for Old Spice. As executive interactive creative director for Wieden + Kennedy, Tait developed the web sensation called "Response," which resulted in 185 personalized videos in reply to tweets. It created considerable buzz for the Procter & Gamble brand and was a vivid example of how social media can be paired with on-the-fly production.[49]

Wall   Frito-Lay · Everyone (Top Posts)   To interact with Frito-Lay you need to sign up for Facebook first.

Share: Post Photo Video   Sign Up

Wall   Frito-Lay · Everyone (Top Posts)

Want to like or comment on this page?

To interact with Frito-Lay you need to sign up for Facebook first.

Exercises

1. Social Media Monitoring

(Contributed by Daradirek Ekachai, PhD, associate professor, Marquette University)

Social media only works if it is well monitored. Here's one way to approach that process.

- Pick a company or brand. Generate a specific set of keywords, which might include the company name, an acronym for the company or brand, topics, issues, the tagline, and leadership (CEO names).

- Review and select a monitoring tool. Tools could include Addictomatic, IceRocket, Technorati, Google Blog Search, Social Mention, Google Alerts, and Google Insights.

- Now, identify what elements you wish to monitor.

- Having chosen a monitoring tool and elements you which to monitor, record what you find from the online conversations and/or videos about the chosen organization or brand over the course of two weeks.

- Write a one-page report including a purpose, methodology, results, and a conclusion— and share your findings with the class.

2. Twitter School Ambassador

(Contributed by Daradirek Ekachai, PhD, associate professor, Marquette University)

This assignment has two objectives. First, to familiarize yourself with Twitter, its writing style, its lingo, and how to tweet professionally. Second, to get you to move above and beyond tweeting what you had for breakfast or sharing what you think is cool.

- For this exercise, you will act as both strategist and writer—and you'll be a brand ambassador for your university.

- The goal is to tout the best your college has to offer via Twitter.

- Pick a topic or focus related to your school and promote it. You must begin early in the semester and tweet regularly for 10 weeks.

- Your tweets can be in the form of an original text tweet, a retweet, a reply to other Twitter users, or pictures (use photo services such as Twitpic or Instagram, or Yfrog). You could also pose questions you'd like others to answer. (Tip: Use hash tags so nonfollowers can find your tweets.) Remember that your tweets are your public "digital footprints," so be sure to mix professionalism with your own personality.

- Your instructor will create a hash tag for the class and share it with the students. You are encouraged to use the class hash tag so that tweets can be easily followed. (If you like, you can have your tweets automatically update your Facebook status by placing #fb at the end of your tweet.)

- Additionally, you must follow at least five people/accounts from within the university or related advertising or public relations media. You can also refer to Chapter 18 for ideas on whom to follow.

- After 10 weeks, turn in a summary of your tweets, including an analysis of how well you were engaged with this assignment. In other words, you will be asked to access how successful your Twitter-based promotion was.

3. Conversations With Mom

This exercise is crafted to help you explore and analyze the power of social media through the eyes of mom bloggers, one of the most influential groups of bloggers. This assignment could be easily reshaped to target other groups as well.

- Do a quick search of the most influential mom bloggers. We like this resource: http://www.babble.com/mom/work-family/top-mom-bloggers/

- Pick a blog and track conversations on the blog over the course of a two-week period. Be sure to note topics, images, responses, and branded sponsors.

- At the end of the two weeks, write a short summary noting topical trends as well as how copy, images, and outside links were used to support stories. Finally, note the kinds of branded sponsors the blog hosted and how the content dovetailed (or did not) with those sponsors.

- Share the finds in class and, again, look for trends.

Visit www.sagepub.com/altstiel3e to access these additional learning tools

- Video Links
- Web Resources
- eFlashcards
- Web Quizzes

Chapter 15

Direct Response Marketing

Hitting the Bull's-eye

Direct Marketing Defined

Even seasoned marketing professionals sometimes confuse all the terms relating to direct marketing. Some call it direct response. Some only think of direct mail. Others think door-to-door selling is its main component. Obnoxious telemarketing is a direct response method. But so is an opt-in e-mail campaign that people really want to read. For this text we'll use a definition created by Bob Stone and Ron Jacobs that covers all direct transactions.

Direct marketing is the interactive use of advertising media, to stimulate an (immediate) behavior modification in such a way that this behavior can be tracked, recorded, analyzed, and stored on a database for future retrieval and use.[1]

In short, direct marketing is *interactive*, stimulates an *immediate response,* and is *measurable*.

According to the Direct Marketing Association (DMA), the three purposes of direct marketing are to:

- Solicit a direct order.
- Generate a lead.
- Drive store traffic.[2]

In addition, we would add that direct marketing should also:

- Generate a measurable response.
- Grow the long-term value of a relationship between the marketer and the customer.

Why Direct Response Marketing?

From a creative standpoint, direct marketing, whether it's direct mail, e-mail, mobile advertising, telemarketing, or personal selling, offers many benefits.

- *It's specific.* With good data, an advertiser can zero in on specific demographics and lifestyles to create a more powerful message.

- *It talks to the individual.* It's as close as you can get to one-on-one marketing.

- *It can be high impact.* If you correctly tap those wants and needs, you provide something of real value to the recipient.

- *It can be localized.* A mailer for a nationally advertised brand can include the names and addresses of local retailers.

- *It can generate sales where there are no stores.* In other words, it generates a direct response, whether it's mail order or online.

- *It can help gather information.* Given the right incentives, many people send back snail-mail or online surveys.

- *It can be used to encourage trials of new products.* Samples and discount coupons help launch many new products.

- *It delivers instant results.* You know almost immediately if your mailing is successful, based on direct sales, phone orders, visits to a location, return-of-reply cards, or other measurement methods.

- *It can be used as part of an integrated marketing program.* For example, sending direct mail fulfills requests for information in a magazine ad; you can direct people to a website for more detailed and interactive messages.

As we've discussed in other chapters, digital technology has changed the face of marketing communications, and that certainly includes direct marketing. Traditionally we thought of direct marketing as direct mail. However, there are many more methods of direct response marketing communication. So in this chapter we will explore direct mail, but also e-mail and mobile communication.

Components of Direct Response Marketing

No matter if you're developing mail, e-mail, mobile, telemarketing, interactive TV, or door-to-door, every direct marketing effort contains these three elements:

1. **The List (or Media):** Simply put, this is who you are talking to. As we'll say repeatedly, the value of the direct response marketing effort is only as good as the list.

2. **The Offer:** The offer is a promise of a reward. Is it a limited-time discount? A bonus product? Something they can't buy in a store? A new product with an incredible competitive advantage? Why should the recipient be interested?

3. **The Creative:** How do you show it/how do you tell the story? What will get their attention, generate their interest, flame their desire, and, most of all, get them to act, and act now? The bulk of this chapter will focus on these tactics.

Database Marketing: Using the List

We can't stress this enough: The most creative concept ever devised is no good if it goes to the wrong person. The better the list, the more on-target your creative message will be. The more you know, the more personal the message. Some of the information you might need to develop your message is listed below. The importance of these categories will vary depending on the type of product, the marketing situation, price points, the buying cycle, and other variables.

Where to Get Information to Build Your Database

You may wonder when you pick up a stack of junk mail or when your inbox fills up with urgent requests about Nigerian bank accounts, "How did they get *my* name?" If you're a direct marketer, you will *never* have an accurate, up-to-date mailing list. Ever. But you can try to make it as accurate as possible so the names on your list better match the profile of the people you want to reach. Rather than go through the intricacies of database management, we will assume you will employ the tips and techniques we offer below *after* you have secured information about your intended direct response marketing recipients.

Customer Relationship Management

Customer relationship management (CRM) tracks and organizes the interaction between the advertiser and current and potential customers. CRM usually refers to the software used to manage customer relationships, but it's just as important for the marketer to really understand the customer's wants and needs, as well as knowing who they are and when they buy. CRM is a key component of campaign management. It coordinates operational and analytical functions to target groups from a database, send e-mails or snail mail, and track the results, as well as store and analyze the data. Successful CRM is a convergence of traditional direct response marketing, database marketing, and online marketing. So what does all this have to do with the creative component? The key is to know the wants and needs of the target audience, because without that, there's not much of a relationship to measure.

Direct Mail

Direct mail (often derisively referred to as junk mail) may not have the speed and immediacy of e-mail, but it can often be the best way to put an advertising message in the hands of a potential customer. Unlike other forms of print media, it has no competing messages (advertisers or editorial) attached to it. Direct response marketing not only invites; it also provides recipients with the means to take real, measurable, physical action. Carol Krol in *Direct Marketing News* comments, "The workhorse benefits of mail remain: it is highly customizable, it

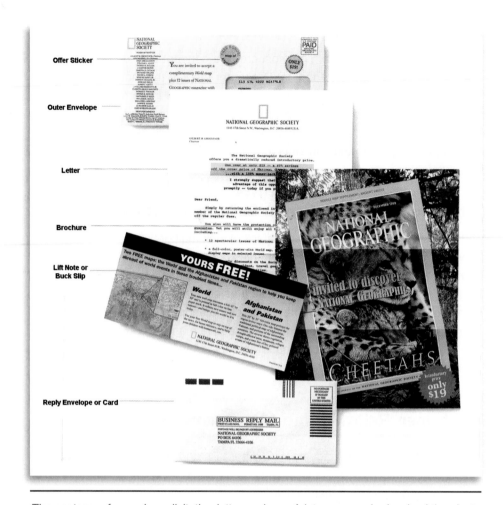

Offer Sticker

Outer Envelope

Letter

Brochure

Lift Note or
Buck Slip

Reply Envelope or Card

The anatomy of an order-solicitation letter package. A lot more can be involved than just a letter and an envelope. Each component plays a key role in getting the recipient to return the reply card, pick up the phone, or log onto the website. It's like having a mini campaign in every envelope.

enables marketers to communicate more information in a single package, it's trackable and it can be particularly effective when integrated with other media channels."[3] She continues, "I'd also argue the mystique of the so-called 'mail moment' has been tough to replicate in any other marketing channel to date."[4]

Several categories of direct mail formats are available. The choice depends on the budget (production and postage), content, type of product, purchase cycle, and response mechanism.

Envelope Mailers (Letter Package)

Anything you put into an envelope applies. It may be as simple as a letter or as elaborate as a 10-piece multicomponent mailer. Keep in mind that every component has a purpose, even the envelope itself. The basic components can include a letter, a brochure, and a reply device, such as a prepaid reply card. You want the outer envelope to say, "Open me." You can do this several ways:

- **Teaser copy:** It could be a special offer or some twist on the message. For example, one envelope for a Florida resort said, "Open carefully: contains white sand, dolphins, seashells and coconut palms."

- **Blind envelopes:** These are usually standard-sized envelopes that suggest normal business or personal correspondence rather than direct mail advertising. Sometimes a stamp is used rather than a meter stamp to make it look more like personal mail.

- **Official envelopes:** These look like government correspondence, a check, or a telegram. While you might get some immediate attention with these, you're more likely to annoy people by deceiving them.

- **Personalized copy:** Sometimes this is effective; other times it may offend people who wonder, "How do they know so much about me?"

This letter package really did contain an X-ray, which turned out to be an invitation to see the hospital's expanded facilities.

Flat Self-Mailers

A self-mailer contains the mailing address on some part of the piece itself rather than on an envelope. Some traditionalists don't like self-mailers. They claim letter

Direct response marketing involves the list, the offer, and the message. In this postcard for a Botox spa, the offer is an open house, the message is "Face to Face," and we assume the list includes women who don't mind frozen faces.

Jumbo postcards are an economical way to get your message out. Treat them like billboards on the front and provide more detail on the back. They're great for integrated campaigns or a series of mailers.

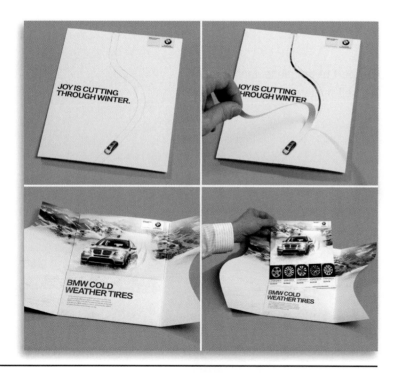

Direct mail allows the inclusion of many pieces that work individually and collectively to encourage an immediate response.

package will always out-pull a self-mailer. A letter is more personal, while a self-mailer shouts, "I'm an ad!" However, a well-designed self-mailer can be cost efficient and effective from a creative standpoint. Types of self-mailers include:

- Postcards.

- Folded mailers—one fold, two folds, and multifolds.

- Brochures and pamphlets.

- Newsletters.

Dimensional Mailers

Some of the most innovative (and expensive) direct mailers are three-dimensional. Basically, they can be anything that can be mailed or shipped. Many times the box will include a separate item, sometimes called a *gadget.* This may be a sample, a premium item that might have some use, or something totally off-the-wall that makes a selling point. The limits to 3D mailers are governed only by your imagination and your budget.

The Fine Art of Writing a Cover Letter

When is the last time you wrote a letter? We mean a real letter, not an e-mail, a text, or a thank-you note to your grandma. Chances are you have never had to write a letter that was intended to persuade someone to buy something or change their opinion. So we will attempt to explain that *well-written* letters can be effective marketing tools. Usually they take the form of a cover letter—that is, a letter that accompanies other marketing messages in a mailing. A cover letter is an introduction, a sales pitch, and a proposal for further action all in one. Cover letters are typically one-page documents and, in most cases, have a beginning, a middle, and an end—usually an introduction saying who you are and why you're writing, followed by a sales pitch for what you have to offer, and then a closing in which you propose steps for further action. These three components often amount to three or four paragraphs, but there are no ironclad rules about how to break up the information. Philip Ward-Burton offers some good advice for cover letter writers in *Advertising Copywriting*.[5] We've paraphrased a few of his suggestions:

Cover Letter *Outline*: 7 Steps

1. Promise a benefit in the headline or first paragraph—lead with your strongest sales point.

2. Enlarge on your most important benefit.

3. Tell the reader what he or she is going to get.

4. Back your statements with proof and endorsements (testimonials).

5. Tell the reader what's lost if he or she doesn't act.

6. Rephrase the benefits in your closing offer.

7. Incite action—set a time limit ("Buy now").

Cover Letter *Style*: 7 Steps

1. Start with a short opening paragraph—four lines or shorter.

2. No paragraph should be longer than eight lines.

3. Vary the length of paragraphs.

4. Use deep indents and center bullet points.

5. Close with a two- to three-line summary.

6. Don't forget the envelope (teaser).

7. Don't forget a follow-up letter—reinforce the message/refine your data mining.

The letter in Table 15.1 contains a persuasive sales message in a format that's easy to digest. Keep in mind, no matter how well it's written, it has to reach the right target audience.

This student-designed 3D mailer was sent to members of Congress, urging them to vote for anti–land mine legislation. The box contained a single small shoe that was formerly worn by a child whose leg had been blown off by a land mine.

Words of Wisdom

"There are few things as certain as the effects of lumpy mail. If there's a mysterious bulge in a letter, it will get opened . . . when it comes to mail, 'lumpy lives.'"[6]

Connie O'Kane, former senior editor, Advertising Specialty Institute

Customization and Variable Printing

We've been saying that you must know the wants and needs of the consumer, and technology today allows you to know more and more every year. Sophisticated database software not only provides spot-on identification but

TABLE 15.1   Cover Letter Example

Dear Jack:	**Personalize with name and other information.**
Here's how you can keep your Sea Ray 230 looking showroom fresh—above and below the waterline.	**Promise a benefit up front.**
During the boating season, you work hard to keep your Sea Ray 230 looking shipshape. But when you haul it out in the fall, you know you're facing many long hours of scrubbing that green slime off the bottom. It won't come off with a pressure washer. And don't think about using harsh acid cleaners on your fiberglass hull.	**Enlarge on that benefit.**
Here's a better way.	**Vary the length of sentences and paragraphs.**
New BoteBrite hull cleaner cuts through that grungy bottom grime to restore your boat's original color and shine. Without hard scrubbing. Without abrasives. Without dangerous acids.	**Tell the reader what's lost if he or she doesn't act.**
Just spray BoteBrite on the bottom of the boat—wait 15 minutes—and rinse with a garden hose.	
That's all there is to it!	
• BoteBrite is a unique detergent that dissolves organic stains from algae and dirty water. • BoteBrite will not damage fiberglass, plastic, metal, or your driveway when used as directed. • BoteBrite is easy to apply and even easier to clean up.	**Use deep indents and bullet points to call out key features and benefits.**
BoteBrite has been approved by the industry's leading manufacturers, including Sea Ray. It's safe, easy to use, and effective against tough bottom stains.	**Back your statement with proof or testimonials.**
After you pull out for the season, will you spend a weekend scrubbing and breathing chemical fumes? Or spraying on BoteBrite and rinsing off a whole season of crud in just minutes?	**Tell the reader what he or she is going to get.**
For a limited time, we're offering a Buy 2–Get 1 Free deal on BoteBrite. Just bring the attached coupon to any BoteBrite retailer before September 30 and get a free 16-oz. bottle of BoteBrite when you buy two 16-oz. or larger sizes.	**Incite action.**
When it's time to clean your boat this fall, take it easy. Use new BoteBrite for fast, safe, and effective boat cleaning.	**Close with a benefit summary.**

also matches it to very specific information for that recipient. So the message can be personalized using variable printing techniques to deliver unique messages. However, just because you can personalize a mailing doesn't mean you have to.

It can be annoying for consumers to receive mailings from a company that pretends to know them, especially if they make the appeal too personal. Grant Johnson of Johnson Direct LLC offers this advice: "Let the target audience define how it wants to be marketed to and via what channels, then test various offers and messaging platforms based on that date to gauge results."[8]

He offers examples of marketers who excel and are exploiting the personal relevance of their brands and why they are successful:

- Starbucks. How I want *my* coffee is different from the way *you* want yours.

- Harley-Davidson. How I customize *my* bike is different from the way *you* do it.

- Apple. The music on *my* iPod is different from the music on *yours*.

Is personalization a bad thing? No. But we need to let our customers and prospects tell us how to proceed.[9]

PURLs: Where Direct Mail Interfaces With the Internet

A PURL (personalized URL) is a landing page created for one person. Actually it could be one of hundreds of webpage templates that allow placement of an individual's name and information derived from a database that is relevant to that person. An example of a PURL would be JohnR.Smith.TravelAdventures.com. When John Smith clicks on the link, he goes to a customized TravelAdventures landing page that may have a headline reading, "Hey, John Smith. Looking for a new adventure?" Copy on the page would use his name and weave in some information such as hiking, photography, and whitewater rafting, based on data compiled for him. John is given the opportunity to request a brochure, chat with a travel consultant, look at a blog of like-minded adventurers, and, of course, book travel online. All the time he is providing information to TravelAdventures, who is recording the information, analyzing it, and preparing future contact with John, including more mailers, e-mail blasts, and possibly telemarketing.

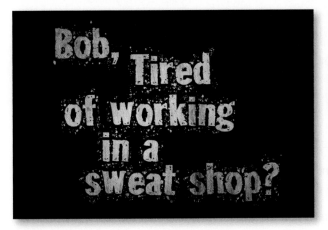

This B2B campaign used variable printing and personalized URLs (PURLs) to connect plumbing contractors with a new way to join copper pipe. In this case, Bob Johnson was told how he could change from "sweating" the fittings to using the ProPress system. When he logged on to a customized site, he could also register to win a prize.

WE KEEP WAITING FOR SOMEONE TO DEFEAT CANCER. WE'RE NOT WAITING ANYMORE.

Every sixty seconds, one more person in America dies from cancer. Every single day, 1500 people are taken away. One out of every two men, and one out of every three women, are diagnosed with cancer in their lifetimes. And we can't wait anymore.

So we're joining together to fight cancer for once, and for all.

Stand Up to Cancer is an organization unlike any other. Along with the American Association for Cancer Research, we will create and fund scientific "dream teams" of the most visionary minds around. All work will be absolutely collaborative. Completely transparent. From the most established to the extraordinarily innovative. Fast-tracking treatments and therapies to those who need them most. And need them desperately.

Today the SU2C movement begins, with the launch of StandUp2Cancer.org and a groundbreaking nationally televised event September 5 on ABC, CBS, and NBC. We have the brilliance. The technology. The desire. All we need now, is you.

THIS IS WHERE THE END OF CANCER BEGINS.

Stand Up to Cancer, Friday, September 5, on ABC, CBS and NBC

ST2C STANDUP TO CANCER
STANDUP2CANCER.ORG

Stand Up to Cancer
Pro bono can soothe your soul, but it can take part of it at the same time.

When the chance to do something moral and noble raises its head in this business you think ah, yes, pro bono. Respect, good deeds, doing what's right for people who will be grateful for everything you put before them . . . what could go wrong? And the answer is: hang on for the ride.

Like fashion or car accounts, charitable organizations tend to look the same when it comes to advertising. They want to make waves, yet want those waves to be containable, un-tsunami-like in nature. And charitable organizations are run by community, a nasty euphemism for "we will pick apart everything until there is nothing left." A community made of well-intentioned, sure. But a community where all decisions aren't left to one person, but to dozens who want to leave a mark upon this earth—this "earth" being your layout, your script, ad nauseam.

Yet they believe in their cause, and so do you. So you jump in and swim. And hope somewhere there will be a life raft.

Now stellar pro bono has been around forever: look at the United Kingdom and Asia alone. But great creative work needs champions on both sides. It takes someone to refuse that ugly word *settle*. And more: currying favors. Then begging for them. Refusing to think of pro bono as "less" or "lucky to have you" or "something you do in your spare time." It takes believing you're saving the world, even if you're not.

For Stand Up to Cancer we were lucky from the start. We had Laura Ziskin, one of the most powerful women in Hollywood, leading the cause. She hired Rick McQuiston and I at inception to create a manifesto, and she understood what the hell a brand actually means. Money was tight. But a launch needs bigness. We came back with a huge spot and one director: David Fincher. He was a friend; he believed in the cause; he respected Laura. Fincher came on board, donated everything. I won't say it was easy. We still had committees to placate. It was tireless, difficult, endless. Screaming ensued. But the work, worked. The creative fed the cause and the money raised was phenomenal. Since then we've had Jesse Dylan and Mark Webb and the work continues. We believe we've helped save lives. And if you're going to burn a candle at both ends as creatives anyway, why not burn it for something that makes a difference in this world?

Pro bono needs great work by people who believe in it. That little word *belief* is everything.[10]

Janet Champ, freelance writer and creative director, Portland, OR, moderncopywriter.com

STEP 1: Print PURLs on each direct mail piece. Include personalized copy.

STEP 2: The recipient clicks on the PURL, which leads him or her to a personalized landing page built specifically to support the direct mail piece.

STEP 3: The personalized landing page provides information and captures the viewer's activity for additional follow-up and lead generation in real time. Reports can be generated later to display response rates, visitor patterns, and more detailed lead information.

E-mail

E-mail represents the best and worst of what direct marketing is all about. On the plus side, e-mail is great for customer retention and relationship management, especially if the recipient has opted in to the campaign. E-mail also has been effective in viral seeding to gain attention and interest among new customers. The downside—one word: spam. Spamming and its evil cousin phishing (using legitimate-looking e-mails to scam people) have poisoned the perception of e-mail. As a result, sophisticated mail filters screen out many legitimate e-mails and even quite a few that people might actually want to read. Because spam has the potential to harm your computer and potentially suck money out of your bank account, many people fear it more than ordinary junk snail mail. However, there are ways to take advantage of e-mails' benefits and reach recipients who actually want to see your message.

Permission marketing allows e-mail recipients to opt in, so messages are sent only to people willing to receive them. Permission marketing programs are offered on websites and by telephone, direct mail, and e-mail. Results are improved even more when permission marketing programs segment customers by demographics or buying history. Over time, recipients may get bored with a constant stream of messages, so enhancements can be introduced to renew interest. These can include sweepstakes, free information, quizzes, or other methods to keep the recipient engaged. The following list describes the steps in a permission marketing program:

1. Provide the means to allow customers to easily opt in. Empower them by giving them the choice.

2. Promise the kind of information the customer wants . . . and deliver it each time.

3. Reinforce this information with incentives when necessary to strengthen the relationship.

4. Try to ramp up the level of participation by offering more incentives to gather more information about the customer. Make their higher level of participation worth their time.

5. Continue to stay in contact and encourage feedback through social media.

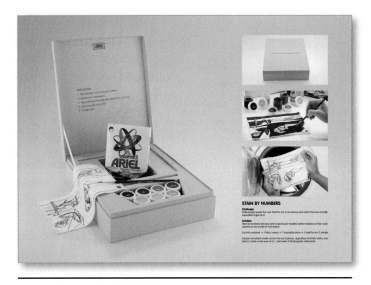

Direct mail can be as elaborate as your budget will allow. This mailer for a laundry detergent was created by a Dubai agency. The recipient is encouraged to color in the designs with the paints that are supplied, then wash them out with a sample of the detergent.

Subscription services: Using RSS (Really Simple Syndication) you can reverse the flow from your computer to check for updates on blogs and news sources and instead have updates from your favorite sites sent to you. To make it work you need to subscribe to a reader such as Google Reader or My Yahoo. Then you visit your favorite sites and click on the RSS logo to make the connection to your reader. Updates will be sent to you as they happen so you won't have to search for new stuff.

Rich mail allows graphics, video, and audio to be included in the e-mail message. When you open up a rich e-mail, your e-mail client automatically calls up your Internet connection and launches an HTML page in your browser. E-mail clients who are offline will invite you to click on the link when you have your Internet connection open again. If your e-mail client does not support graphics, you will receive the e-mail in text only. Most HTML pages instantly appear as complete with the visuals and don't require the added, and often annoying, step of downloading the graphics. As with the most successful e-mail marketers, give recipients the opportunity to opt out by having a "please remove me from your list" reply.

Writing More Effective E-mails

Like a snail-mail letter, an e-mail has several components that are intended to spur the recipient into action. The first is the subject line, which is so important we'll discuss it in much more detail later. The next most important element is the opening line. Like the opening line of a print ad, it should hook the reader and offer a promise—why it would be worth the reader's time to keep reading. The rest of the copy should concentrate on three principles: (1) Stay on topic—provide just one message; (2) provide value—tell the readers how they will benefit from taking action; and (3) ask for action—what do you want the person to do?

Subject Line

The subject line is even more powerful than the headline of a print ad. It has to do all the heavy lifting without the benefit of slick graphics to attract a reader. So here are a few tips for crafting a better subject line.

- **Not too long. Not too short:** Try to stay in range of 50 to 90 characters (if you're tweeting, this should be easy).

- **Keep it real:** People would rather get a message from a person than a company. Try to make it as personable as possible but not unrealistically cheesy. No one likes phony friends.

- **Provide a benefit:** Don't make unrealistic claims or use advertising jargon. Try to be specific with a benefit rather than saying something generic like "Free advice on how to save big money."

- **Get their attention:** Sometimes you have to shock a reader into reading. We recently got an e-mail from a stock photo house that said, "Fake people suck." Made us look, if for no other reason than to see if they were talking about us.

- **Ask, don't shout:** As with print, sometimes asking a question hooks a reader.

Your first paragraph or two should contain a mini-version of your whole e-mail. So instead of carefully spreading out your AIDA (attention, interest, desire, and action), you should try to get all these elements in early. Online users have little patience in general, and they need to understand your whole offer fast. Avoid using hard-sell techniques. These tend to produce poor results. Readers on the Internet expect to see information on the benefits and how to order, but the tone must remain helpful. If it's too slick, your e-mail will be trashed. Shorter is better. If some of your prospects require more information before they make purchasing decisions, include a click-through to an expanded version of your e-mail. Consider viral marketing techniques. Prospects can pass your messages on to others they think would be interested. *Always* include an opt-out statement. The only thing more powerful than goodwill toward your company is ill will.

Years ago direct response marketing pioneer John Caples developed a list of words that were proven to increase readership and response in direct mail pieces. Today, some of those same words have just the opposite effect. When skeptical and spam-weary readers spot these words, they hit the delete button. More than likely, their e-mail program has already routed them to the junk folder. We suggest *not* using the following words if you want anyone to open your e-mail:

Buy	Money
Discount	New
Free	Profit
Help	Sale
Hey (recipient's name)	Save
Investment	Special

And don't use ALL CAPS or exclamation points! Really good copy invites the reader in. Desperate screaming usually has the opposite effect.

E-mail and Integrated Marketing Communications

E-mail by itself can be a powerful tool, but if massive e-mail blasts are the only means of communication, success is merely a numbers game . . . sort of like buying lottery tickets. Most people recognize spam, and response rates are appallingly low. Response rates increase significantly when e-mail messages are coordinated with the look and feel of a company's website and other marketing communication materials. For example, e-mail that's integrated with direct mail,

Words of Wisdom

"Historically, clients came to us . . . to work on their direct marketing. Now we get involved in their work from a strategic standpoint and we see what makes sense—direct, promotion, experiential—providing them the broad range of services."[12]

Howard Draft, CEO, Draftfcb

While some recipients can't receive or don't want to receive more advertising in their inbox, HTML e-mails allow marketers to create more impact than regular messages. If the recipient has opted into a permission-based marketing program, they will welcome the added content.

social media, telemarketing, and online tools, such as a webinar, have a much better chance of being read and generating a response. In addition, diligent use of web analytics can trigger an e-mail response that helps close a sale. Let's say an online shopper bails out at the shopping cart. Sending an e-mail to these shoppers may get them to conclude the transaction. Targeted e-mails have a conversion rate 5 to 10 times higher than the rate for mass e-mails, and revenues from these follow-up e-mails are 3 to 9 times higher.[13]

"Mocial"—Integrating With Social Media and Mobile

As we've seen in other chapters, we can't isolate each marketing communication channel into discrete silos. The highly targeted one-on-one nature of e-mail makes it a natural partner for mobile and social media. Some marketers are staring to call this integration "mocial." Loren McDonald of Silverpop describes three key trends to consider:

- Social media is emerging as an effective broadcast messaging channel.

- The process of checking and reading email is changing with the emergence of mobile.

- People are moving in and out of different *mocial* channels throughout the day.[14]

E-mail spurs readers into action, helps build databases, and connects readers to a brand. So does social media. They don't compete, but are really the perfect partners. Shar VanBoskirk of Forrester Research comments, "Email programs are made stronger with social content, and the awareness of social programs comes from email. Smart marketers have some understanding of how these two channels work together."[15]

Future of E-mail

Despite its many advantages, e-mail can be a terrible way to communicate. Nuance, satire, humor, and sincerity are hard to express in print . . . and unintentional gaffes are impossible to unsend. Many companies are phasing out e-mail in favor of internal social networks and text-based programs, such as Yammer, Google Talk, and Google Voice, among others. As alternatives to internal e-mail grow, we might see a reduction of external e-mail for direct response marketing purposes.

Rising Star

My Coffee Addiction

When I was a little girl I would wait, very excited, for commercial breaks. Once I had to stay with my uncle for a couple of weeks. He would always fast-forward through them, and I always got really mad.

Time flew by. I had a hard time figuring out that I wanted to be in advertising. I knew I wanted to be creative, do stuff that mattered, create something that people would talk about. As a kid I experimented a lot with writing. Then in high school I tried journalism, photography, psychology. In college I finally decided to go for marketing. After graduation I landed my first job as an account manager in a small agency in Moldova. I was soooo envious of the creatives in the agency. All I could think about was how could I become one of them. I soon realized that in Eastern Europe there was not much good creative going on. It seems like we mostly translate the commercials that are produced by big agencies in the United Kingdom, the United States, France, or other big fancy places.

That was it! If I wanted to be part of something big, that's where I needed to start—a big fancy place. That's exactly how I landed in an ad school in San Francisco, 11,000 miles away from home.

Then, I realized that I actually knew nothing about advertising, especially after a teacher almost failed me in my first quarter. I almost quit. As time goes by, though, we all catch on to what's going on—including me.

After I graduated I headed to New York. I started freelancing in a couple of places, including Mother, whose work I always admired. Getting into Mother wasn't easy, but it was fun, and remains rewarding.

What absolutely blew my mind was something that happened last summer, right before graduating. One of the school projects I was working on with my partner (a book swap) got selected for Alex Bogusky's *Common Pitch*. Presenting it on stage with Alex Bogusky, in front of 500 people, and many others watching online—now that made up for all the commercials I watched (or that I missed while staying with my uncle), the total of 33,000 miles I traveled, and the two years of double-shot espressos.[16]

Teodorina Bazgu, freelance creative, Mother, New York, @teobazgu

Mobile: The Third Screen Has Come of Age

Mobile marketing is different from most other kinds of direct marketing communication because the consumer typically controls the flow of information— the user often initiates contact with the advertiser and must give the advertiser permission to contact him or her. Now that smartphones account for more than half of all new phone sales, m-commerce has gained critical mass. LocalResponse, a mobile marketing agency, delivers location-based ads via social media. They collect check-in data from direct sources such as Foursquare and Yelp, but also from indirect check-ins such as mentions, photos, and geotags on various social platforms.[17] This helps make mobile ads more relevant and personalized, based on their geographic location and proximity to retail selling specific brands. Mobile commerce is expected to reach $31 billion in revenue by 2016, and mobile ad spending is already well over $1 billion.[18] Having said that, mobile sites and ads still have a long way to go to catch up with their second-screen cousins. The problems are threefold: (1) size of the screen, (2) lack of

bandwidth for rich media, and (3) mobile dead zones. Sites designed to look good on a 15- or 17-inch laptop look terrible on an iPhone unless they are optimized for mobile, and even then they usually don't look that great. The technology is still catching up with the potential for effective mobile advertising.

At least most developers now see the need for customized mobile content rather than trying to fit a desktop solution into a smartphone screen. Most smartphone users are annoyed with mobile ads even as ad spending increases by double digits. Some people don't like ads intruding on a device they consider much more personal than the TV or desktop. Others just don't like the creative content crammed into a 3-inch screen. Of course, the growth of tablets opens up more space for creativity. But even that larger palette minimizes the impact compared to desktop and laptop screens. Right now, a new generation of creatives is working hard to bring impactful, rich media sites and advertising to smartphones and tablets. For example, a rich media campaign for Discovery Channel's *Storm Chasers* gave viewers a bird's-eye view of a tornado, and viewers' phones even vibrated. They delivered more than 5 million impressions across multiple apps. Another mobile ad involved a promotional game for Buick that generated four times the click-through rate for static creative. And an award-winning campaign for Mini made the smartphone the center of a location-based game to track virtual cars, with the winner receiving an actual Mini.[20]

Named as one of the world's "happiest brands," Campbell's Soup spread the joy with an iPhone mobile campaign—banner ads on news and other mobile sites that were linked to a mobile-optimized site about the wonders of Campbell's soups.

So if we assume that more people will rely on their phones and tablets for information and entertainment, how do we use them for efficient direct response marketing? The Mobile Marketing Association (mmaglobal.com) provides a set of guidelines and standards for the recommended format of ads, presentation, and metrics. They continually update the guidelines, so it's always a good idea to check them out before embarking on a new mobile campaign.

QR Codes and Tagging

Two-dimensional bar codes have been around for over 40 years, but since smartphones have taken over, brands and consumers can connect in much more meaningful ways. A whopping 72% of smartphone users said they'd be likely to recall an ad using a QR code.[21] We've seen those ugly little pixelated black-and-white codes crop up on billboards, posters, point-of-purchase displays, and print ads—just about anything, including textbooks.

The Microsoft Tag is a high-capacity four-color bar code. But those are not the only ways to connect mobile devices with brands. Old Navy partnered with Shazam Entertainment to develop a multichannel campaign that let consumers tag campaign-specific songs and receive product information, contest, and giveaway details and digital coupons.[22] Consumers with the Shazam app could

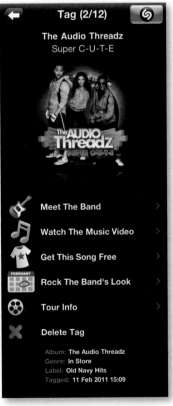

Old Navy launched their "Super Cute" campaign with a fake Kim Kardashian (is that being redundant?) and a partnership with Shazam. Just tag the TV commercial and get all the super cute details.

tag Old Navy's TV commercials to connect to their site and ultimately buy something online. This makes measuring the effectiveness of a "Shazam-able" commercial very accurate.

Home Depot shoppers who aimed their smartphones at the QR code embedded in a flyer for Martha Stewart–branded merchandise got more than a price check. They could receive more detailed information about the products—colors, dimensions, materials, and even a product video starring Martha herself. Fortunately, there was an opt-out feature for that.

Take One Tablet and You're Hooked

Users interact with their tablets at a different level than with other mobile devices. Tablets are called "lean-back" devices, meaning consumers use them in a more relaxed mode, compared to laptops and smartphones. As a result, tablet users are more engaged with the content, whether it's a magazine, a book, a movie, or an ad campaign.[23] For example, Google's catalogue app for the iPad has encouraged many direct retailers to consider swapping paper for pixels, but most see the emerging technology as another exciting channel, not a full replacement. A digital catalogue on a tablet allows the inclusion of music, video, and interactivity on a screen people can actually use.

Tablet users also tend to be more affluent than the typical mobile user. Tablet users spend over 50% more per purchase than visitors who use smartphones and over 20% more than computer users.[24]

When is ketchup green? Heinz wanted everyone to know they were using environmentally friendly packaging. So they put QR codes on the backs of their bottles in restaurants. Diners were invited to click on the code not only to learn about the green initiative, but also to enter a sweepstakes to win a hybrid car. The microsite was avaialble for computers but also optimized for mobile.

The Changing Face of Direct Response Marketing

As long as the postal service pretends to deliver mail efficiently, direct mail will be a powerful marketing tool. Some people still need to hold and feel a real letter or brochure, if just for the satisfaction of throwing it away. The trick has always been to produce something that people want to open. While direct mail has always been integrated with other marketing communication channels, the potential for e-mail, social media, and mobile marketing opens up new possibilities direct mail marketers couldn't even imagine years ago. Two reasons direct response integration works so well: connection with an individual consumer and measurability. New technology not only makes direct response marketing tools such as e-mail and mobile more accountable; it also links traditional media such as television and out of home into a customized and highly measurable effort that enhances the connection between a consumer and a brand. So in addition to having our list, offer, and creative, we'll also have a lot more engagement.

Who's Who?

Drayton Bird—As worldwide creative director of Ogilvy & Mather Direct, Drayton Bird was a key to the success of the world's largest direct marketing agency. He went on to found what became the United Kingdom's largest direct marketing agency. With more than 40 years of experience in direct marketing and advertising, Bird wrote and published *Commonsense Direct Marketing, How to Write Sales Letters That Sell,* and *Marketing Insights and Outrages*—all best sellers. He also writes regular columns for marketing and advertising publications in the United Kingdom, the United States, Malaysia, India, and Europe. David Ogilvy said of him, "Drayton Bird knows more about direct marketing than anyone else in the world."[26]

John Caples—Often called the father of direct response advertising, John Caples was one of the most influential copywriters of all time. He spent a lifetime researching the most effective methods of advertising. His direct approach for writing headlines cut through the clutter and grabbed the readers, pulling them into the ad. Caples penned one of the most famous headlines ever written: "They laughed when I sat down at the piano, but when I started to play!"

Howard Draft—Howard Draft was CEO of the 10th largest agency in the United States, Draftfcb. His rise to the top began at a 13-person Chicago shop that specialized in direct response advertising. When that agency partnered with the much larger Ted Bates Worldwide, Draft moved to New York and set up a direct marketing branch that was soon billing more than his old shop. By the mid-1990s, Draft owned the agency, now called Draft Direct, which grew to $600 million in billings. In 2003, he merged with FCB, one of the best known agencies in the world to form Draftfcb, now billing over $3 billion.[27]

Cindy Gallop—Cindy Gallop is founder and CEO of IfWeRanTheWorld. Gallop's web-meets-world platform turns good intentions into action—one microaction at a time. She launched it as a beta demo at TED 2010. She is also the founder of www.makelovenotporn.com, which she launched at TED 2009. Gallop's background is brand building, marketing, and advertising. She started her career in advertising at Bartle Bogle Hegarty in New York in 1998 and in 2003 was named Advertising Woman of the Year. Gallop acts as adviser to a number of tech start-ups and consults for companies around the world. She has a reputation as a highly compelling and inspirational speaker at conferences and events around the world on a variety of topics: Her talk on "The Future of Advertising" has been described on Twitter as "the most brilliant speech on the future of advertising ever—not the usual buzzword-laden bullshit."[28]

Exercises

1. Right Cause-Right Brand

(Contributed by Kwangmi Ko Kim, PhD, associate professor, Towson University)

The focus of this exercise is to help you understand the importance of using the "right" cause to appeal to the "right" target market in cause-related marketing. In short, how to link the right cause to the right brand.

- Find one or two brands popular among certain demographic groups (maybe through brief interviews with groups ages 18–24, 25–34, 35–44, 45–54, and 55+).

- While interviewing them, you need to also ask each demographic group what causes are important to them. Narrow down their responses into two major causes.

- Study the cause-related marketing practices used by the brands identified in the first step.

- Now compare whether there is any congruence between the causes identified by each demographic group and the causes affiliated with their favorite brands or if there are any perfect partnerships waiting to happen.

2. Visual Word Associations

This exercise is designed to demonstrate the visual power of word associations.

- Think of a brand. Let's say: FedEx. Generate a benefits list.

- Pick the top three benefits and find the keywords for each.

- Now go to visualthesaurus.com and type in each keyword. (It's free the first time, and then it will cost you, but not much. We think it's worth it.) You will see a graphic clustering of associated words. Talk about proximity! For example, with *dependable* the clusters are (1) *good, safe,* and *secure*; (2) *honest, reliable,* and *true*; and (3) *steady-going* and *rock-steady.* (You can also click on each word and go deeper.)

- Now you have three concepting approaches. Generate three layouts that visually express each of the three clusters. Have each layout focus on a different direct tactic.

- We think visualthesaurus.com is a very cool site. It's great for headline generation too.

3. Passionate for a Cause

Letting your passion show is a great way to engage the target audience, and with direct marketing engagement is paramount.

- Choose a nonprofit or social cause that you are passionate about such as the American Red Cross, Greenpeace, Big Brothers Big Sisters, breast cancer awareness, or a host of other great causes.

- Then create a print ad with headline, body copy, visual, and tagline. As this is part of a direct campaign, be sure to pay special attention to your call to action.

- Now, consider the strategically ideal direct medium in order to reach your target audience. Then execute your direct tactic.

- Present your direct tactic and your print ad and sell the class on why your two-part campaign has the potential to be extended—why it has legs. But, also give a rationale for why, even with just these two tactics, your call to action will be heard and responded to. Sell the class on strategy. After all, this is a cause you are passionate about.

Visit www.sagepub.com/altstiel3e to access these additional learning tools

- Video Links
- Web Resources

- eFlashcards
- Web Quizzes

Chapter

16

Beyond Media

Everybody Out of the Box

So far just about everything described in the book has been applied to measured media. However, a big part of the marketing communication spectrum includes tools that are difficult to measure. They're even harder to define. Some call this support media. Others say it's alternative. Or below-the-line. So many of them blend together that you can't put them in nice, neat categories. We've also included the most traditional form of advertising ever known, one that was developed eons before the printing press—out-of-home.

Out-of-Home Advertising

We used to call this outdoor advertising. But what do you call signs inside an airport terminal, posters in a subway station, or three-dimensional displays in a shopping mall? Some people call this ambient advertising, which we'll describe in much more detail later in the chapter. So we're using the term *out-of-home* to cover all advertising that's seen outside the home but is not in the point-of-sale category. That's not a nice, neat definition, but bear with us. We think this will make sense by the end of the chapter.

Why Out-of-Home?

From a creative standpoint, out-of-home offers many advantages. Specifically, out-of-home is:

- Flexible: The location, timing, structure, and dimension of the concept give you a lot of options.

- A high-impact medium: Nothing gives you a bigger canvas.

- Exclusive: You can select a specific location.

- Economical: Low cost per impression.

- Ideal for establishing brand image and building rapid awareness.

Running out of TP is a really big problem. This memorable billboard provides the solution.

- Ideal for promoting packaged goods.

- Effective for reinforcing existing brands.

- A medium that combines selling with entertainment.

Out-of-home is a great medium for copywriters and designers because it quickly conveys a concept. You have to make the point in 10 words or less and often without any words. If you can create a great billboard or transit shelter, you demonstrate solid skills that carry over to other forms of print advertising.

Posters and Bulletins (aka Billboards)

People in the outdoor advertising business don't talk about "billboards." The two main types of outdoor displays are the *painted bulletin* and the *outdoor poster*. The difference is the way they are displayed—posters use sheets of preprinted paper glued to backboards, and bulletins traditionally have used hand-painted images. Today, painted bulletins have given way to Superflex vinyl-coated fabric that gives them almost magazine-like quality. For simplicity's sake, we'll use the layperson's term *billboards*.

Posting companies offer a variety of sizes, usually described in poster terms, such as 36-sheet, 30-sheet, 24-sheet, and 8-sheet. A typical 36-sheet poster is 48 feet wide by 14 feet high—about a 3.5-to-1 ratio. Painted bulletins typically have a 2.5-to-1 ratio.

For layout purposes, all you have to know is that billboards are very wide and not very tall. So if you're using an 8.5 × 11–inch sheet of paper and your design is 10 inches wide, it should be about 4.5 inches high to have a 2.5-to-1 ratio. The reason we mention this here is that too many students treat billboards like magazine ads. When you start thinking about how they are different, it opens up a lot more creative opportunities. Which means they are much better suited to show a hot dog than a wedding cake.

Beyond the dimensions, billboards are available in several different formats or combinations of formats:

Smart people read The Economist, *but anyone walking under this interactive billboard can see the light.*

- **Standard static boards:** Your basic poster or bulletin that fits within the limits of the sign's borders.

- **Extensions:** Part of your image violates the boundaries of the board.

- **Motion boards:** These can be motorized images on a static board with sliding panels that reveal a totally different message, usually another advertiser.

- **Illuminated boards:** The board can be lighted for night viewing or, more dramatically, to include neon, moving lights, and selective spot lighting.

- **Digital boards:** These high-definition boards project a very bright, crisp image. However, these are tremendously more expensive than traditional boards, so time on the board is usually sold by the second. Some cities regulate the time of the display, requiring longer display times so there is less distraction to drivers.

- **Three-dimensional boards:** You can add dimensional objects to and around the board, such as a car crashing through the middle, people sitting on the top edge, or parts of the poster removed to reveal the backing framework.

Billboards aren't the only ways to extend an outdoor campaign. This campaign won Best of Show at the Obie Awards for outdoor advertising.

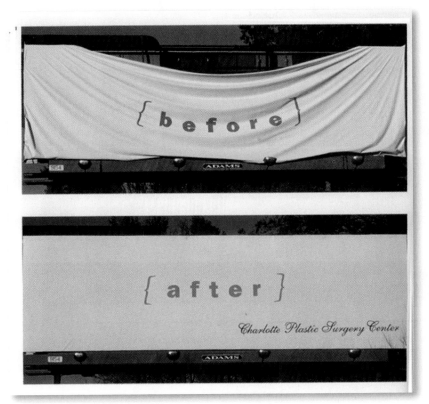

A fixed location offers creative opportunities. The first board with the saggy "before" captures attention. When it's replaced by a taut "after" and the advertiser's name, it all makes sense . . . and gets people talking.

Extensions give your outdoor advertising a lot more visibility. This student wanted to demonstrate just how light Kraft Mac & Cheese could be. She suggested a 3D extension for this digital board. While almost nothing is impossible for out-of-home, sometimes some really great ideas aren't practical.

Look closely in the left corner. Audi playfully challenges BMW to make the "next move." It didn't take long for BMW to answer with a bigger, bolder statement. It was their way of saying "game over."

Global brands like Pepsi sometimes have to adapt to the language and culture of various countries. In this Russian billboard, the brand takes on a totally different look and feel than in the United States.

War Story

India

France

Brazil

"Let's Colour"

Our mission for the Dulux paint brand was to create a unified global brand message around color—and turn Dulux into the first brand in consumers' minds when they think about color.

As part of a big worldwide integrated campaign, we created events where, together with the local communities, we painted urban spaces that were in need of a bit of color. The objective of the events was to show consumers how any environment can be improved using just a bit of color—establishing Dulux as the first brand that comes to mind when they think about color.

We developed an ongoing project helping to organize local communities to change their own environments. First we set up a blog to follow each step of the events. The events were also shot and edited into brand film. A documentary director traveled with us, creating films about the relationship each country had with color. We seeded content through a variety of social channels. Our launch campaign began in Brazil, France, England, and India.

The "Let's Colour" campaign demonstrated that a bit of color could transform any environment. The events created were the best way of putting our words into practice: how a bit of color could change any environment. They also were the best way of creating a direct relationship between the consumer and the brand.

After the first four countries, the project started to get thousands of spontaneous requests to host events all around the world. Because of this response, 14 other markets decided to promote the project in their countries, and there are many more happening today. The "Let's Colour" line became the open invitation to an ongoing project, and the campaign helped position Dulux as the color authority in the global paint market.[2]

Russ Lidstone, CEO, Euro RSGC, London, eurorscglondon.co.uk

Digital and Interactive Out-of-Home Media

As technology evolves, out-of-home is increasingly integrated with mobile devices. For example, in Stockholm, McDonald's gave pedestrians in a busy intersection an opportunity to interact with a digital billboard using their mobile phones. Users who lasted 30 seconds in the "Pick n' Play" game received a coupon and directions to the nearest McDonald's. The two-day engagement used digital out-of-home and mobile technology to drive foot traffic to the restaurants. Rather than downloading an app, users visited picknplay.se and had their locations verified by geolocation technology.[3]

Motion-activated displays, such as those patented by MonsterVision, can be displayed in store windows, at airport and train terminals, at trade shows, and basically anywhere people congregate. These displays can be quite expensive, so many advertisers use them to promote special events, launch a new brand, or introduce a new ad campaign.

Tips and Techniques

The following recommendations are based on the collective wisdom of outdoor advertising professionals and our personal experience. They're not hard-and-fast rules, but factors you should consider when you're creating out-of-home advertising:

- **Be telegraphic.** The rule of thumb for billboards is nine words or fewer, with the emphasis on fewer. Some say six words is the limit. Keep in mind that someone driving by has about five seconds to get it.

- **Think big.** You've got an ad that can be seen from 600 feet away. The images and the type should be huge. Text should be at least 1 foot high to be legible—3 to 4 feet high is preferable.

- **Use bold, sans serif fonts.** Stay away from thin lines and remember that heavy fonts blur together.

- **Go for a strong visual-verbal connection.** Think metaphors and visual puzzles. Many times you don't even need copy.

- **Stick with one main idea.** Above all, keep it simple!

- **Take advantage of location.** A sign on the side or back of a bus can be different from a static billboard because it's constantly in motion. The message on a billboard can be very local. Be aware of the season—in winter avoid whites and grays that blend in with the snow and overcast skies. In summer avoid greens that blend with foliage.

- **Use all caps for short headlines and uppercase/lowercase for longer heads.** Using all caps makes long copy harder to read.

- **Use short words when possible.** They're easier to read and you can get more on a billboard.

- **Use bold colors, not pastels.** You're trying to attract attention. That's why you see so many yellows and reds in billboards. Even white space draws attention, as long as it surrounds a bold color. High contrast is the key. Avoid colors that vibrate like red type on a blue background.

- **Use few elements.** Remember, keep it simple!

- **Use product packaging instead of words.** Show the Coke bottle or can, not the word *Coca-Cola*. Some outdoor media companies suggest making the logo take up half the board.

Transit

Transit advertising also has its own special terminology. To make it simple, think of transit as advertising that goes on the outside or inside of things that move and at the places where you wait for things that move.

Examples of transit advertising include:

- Inside- and outside-bus cards.

- Outside-bus murals.

- Bus shelters and benches.

- Kiosks.

- Train, bus, and subway stations.

- Airports.

- Mobile billboards: car, truck, and trailer ads.

Posters

Posters can be a creative person's best bet to pad a portfolio and win awards. Technically all you have to do is print one, post it somewhere, and, *voilà,* you've produced a real-world advertisement, seen by someone other than your roommate.

Ambient Advertising

The standard billboard is fairly easy to buy from a media standpoint—you figure out how many people drive by in a given time frame and figure out a payment for a number of showings. But what if you want to make an impact where people walk, shop, recreate, commute to work, travel, or go to school? In other words, how do you make your message part of their ambient world? For the sake of this discussion, we'll consider ambient advertising as a freestanding display that attracts attention of passers by. The ultimate goal is not only to catch people's eye, but also to get them to talk about it to their friends, snap a picture to put on Facebook, or shoot a video for YouTube. As with so many other forms of marketing communication, the impact of ambient is enhanced by word of mouth and social media.

Guerrilla Marketing

In the 1980s, the term *guerrilla marketing* came to represent a number of nontraditional marketing communications tactics used to gain awareness without spending a lot of money (at least not as much as for traditional TV advertising). Some ambient advertising has been called a guerrilla tactic—because it's relatively low cost, but it gets people talking and the media to cover it to get even more people talking.

Other guerrilla tactics involve a number of weapons to multiply the coverage. The campaign for Aflac is a prime example. Their duck icon was

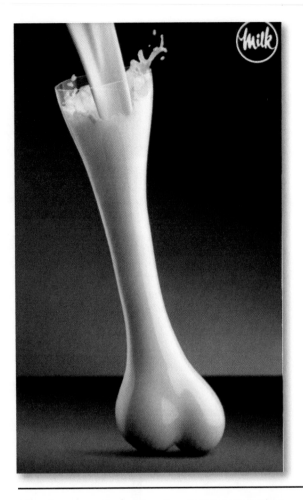

How do you say the calcium in milk helps strengthen bones? You don't say it; you show it.

Words of Wisdom

"Billboards are most effective if you can say these two magic words: 'Next Exit.' If you can't, they work best as a reminder of your other marketing."[4]

Jay Conrad Levinson, author,
Guerrilla Marketing Attack

The big idea here is to demonstrate how much water a lawn really needs as compared to how much most citizens actually give it. A series of two big outdoor ambient media placements tell the story, with copy to be sure you don't miss the point.

HIP (Having Involved Parents) developed several interactive displays to make learning fun for both parents and their kids.

supported with a relatively modest $45 million ad budget. But the behind-the-scenes effort multiplied the impact. In four years, awareness of the company grew from 12% to more than 90%. The following blurb from the *Wall Street Journal* describes how it works: "Creating a breakout ad character is in some measure a matter of luck and circumstances, but Aflac lowered its odds considerably by supplementing its TV ads with a well-orchestrated, behind-the-scenes guerrilla public relations campaign. Instead of simply buying lots of TV ads, a team of four ad and marketing executives are focused on getting the duck on TV at no cost to Aflac."[5] Some of their actions have included handing out plush duck toys to people on the outdoor set of the *Today* show, sponsoring a water tank for synchronized swimmers on David Letterman's show, getting coverage on CNBC (which ran the commercials for free as part of a news story), and lobbying consumers to vote for the duck in a Yahoo/*USA Today* poll on favorite ad icons.

When it comes to out-of-home, using guerrilla tactics can be very effective. Keep in mind that by its nature, guerrilla marketing is meant to provide big results for less money than traditional media. The goal is to generate a buzz—word of mouth (either in person or through viral channels) and earned media coverage that generates far more coverage than you can afford with traditional advertising.

Once again, the point of using these tactics is not to saturate a mass market. It's to get people talking about your brand. So it's important to make sure the creativity does not overshadow the brand message. You don't want people to remember the gimmick but not the advertiser. Now, Coca-Cola is not exactly strapped for advertising dollars. However, they created a very effective guerrilla/ambient effort to promote their "Share the Happiness" theme. A Coca-Cola "Happiness Machine" was placed on several college campuses. The first purchase from the machine produced a bottle of Coke as expected. Then another. Then another. So the happy recipient began sharing her Cokes with fellow students. Then the machine started handing out flowers. Pizzas. Sub sandwiches. And more Cokes. All the time drawing a bigger crowd of happy students, who love to get free stuff, even it's from a multinational corporate monster they are taught to hate. This happy branding effort combined guerrilla marketing and online video on social media networks and won Best of Show in the 2011 Web Marketing Association awards.

In Belgium, Carlsberg beer conducted a social experiment and made a great statement for their brand. They packed a movie theater with some tough-looking biker dudes. Only two seats were open. So when an unsuspecting couple walked into the theater they had to make a choice—sit with

Coca-Cola's "Happiness Machines" handed out more than Cokes. By giving out free stuff, they attracted a crowd, which in turn helped generate some great video clips for a viral campaign.

An unsuspecting couple finds that the only two seats available in a movie theater are surrounded by some tough-looking guys. The couples that took their seats were rewarded with Carlsberg beer and warm congratulations from the boys.

We're sure some people can be as annoying as fleas and ticks. But in this case the humans only represent the pests. The oversize floor vinyl was placed in an Indonesian shopping mall.

To raise awareness of human rights abuses in Burma (Myanmar), a small "prison" was built in the middle of Grand Central Station. Each cell held a picture of a political prisoner with ballpoint pens forming the bars. People passing by were encouraged to take one of the pens to sign a petition, so they not only indicated their support, but also symbolically removed the bars of the prison. The petition books were sent to the United Nations and Burma. Over 150 political prisoners were freed, proving that sometimes, the pen is mightier than prison bars.

the bikers or leave. Whenever a couple took the seats, the bikers broke out the Carlsberg, and everyone celebrated. The promotion demonstrated that you can't always judge people by appearances and that movie theaters are great places to drink beer with a bunch of friendly tough guys. Of course, the whole thing was a viral hit.

Out-of-Home and Campaigns

Out-of-home advertising is usually used as a secondary medium. Billboards and posters are great reminders of a slogan, logo, package, or other aspect of a total campaign. Keep the two key aspects of campaign continuity in mind when using out-of-home. Can you extend the message by using out-of-home, and can you repeat the theme created for out-of-home?

When you are developing concepts for a campaign, you might want to go with out-of-home first. Nothing crystallizes a concept like a billboard. If you can communicate that One Thing with one billboard, you've got something you can build on.

Rising Star

Meritocracy

At my first advertising job, I met two creative guys who shared an office. One went to Harvard, and the other had spent some time in prison. The ex-con generally had better ideas and wore sweaters. The Harvard guy was covered in tattoos and wore leather. No one really knew which guy was which, and it didn't matter.

Advertising is a meritocracy: The best idea wins. If you're the one who comes up with a great idea and you're the lowest rung on the totem pole, no one cares. If you know the inside of a penitentiary better than a library, fine. Everyone just wants an original, unexpected thought. That drove me when I started out, and it keeps me on my toes now.

I didn't go to advertising school. I started out as an account guy. About four months into the job, I was bored to tears. I hated my job. So, in the inebriated state that is the advertising company Christmas party, I begged the woman who ran our creative department to let me have a job on her floor. "You'll do expense reports and never be a copywriter," she said. "You cool with that?" Totally cool with that.

I dutifully did everyone's expense reports and at night, when everyone went home, I worked on my portfolio. Eventually, it paid off. Six months into my role as an assistant, I had convinced enough creative directors to give me a shot on a few small writing assignments. Six months after that, they made me a copywriter.

Obviously it doesn't work this way every time. My path isn't the way you're supposed to do it, and it's a far cry from a guaranteed gig in a creative department.

That said, it reinforces that tenet of advertising I love: The best idea wins. Whether you went to ad school or no school, college or prison, this business is about coming up with a big, great idea. Which, I'm sure you've been told, generally comes to the person who works the hardest.

I'll also say, because the people reading this are probably thinking of joining the industry, be nice to people. Everyone, not just your superiors. Every asshole I know in this business eventually gets what's coming to them.[8]

Pete Harvey, associate creative director, copywriter, Goodby, Silverstein & Partners, San Francisco, goodbysilverstein.com

Sales Promotion

Promotion is one of the four Ps of marketing. In its strictest definition, all marketing communication is a form of promotion. However, in this text we'll call it *sales promotion* and define it as an activity that stimulates purchases by adding a *short-term additional value* to a product or service. In other words, the advertiser is bribing you to buy something quickly. That bribe may be as basic as a discount or as lofty as a donation to a worthy charity. Too many students think of promotion as nothing more than a boring discount coupon, two-for-one sales, and free merchandise when you buy something. But when you explore all the facets of promotion, you'll understand why it's one of the hottest fields in marketing, and when marketers cut traditional advertising in tough times, their dollars often shift to sales promotions.

Most (but not all) sales promotions have specific short-term goals. They are designed to produce results quickly. Once the promotion is over, sales can slip, sometimes prompting an unending chain of new sales promotions.

In some professions, sales promotions are still rare—you probably won't see a plastic surgeon advertising a free tummy tuck with every nose job. However, the use of sales promotion is increasing, even in the service sector. Many marketers have seen diminishing returns from their traditional advertising efforts. Sales promotions, for both trade and consumer, give their sales that extra boost. This is especially common in the cutthroat world of packaged goods, where the only perceived differences between products are in their promotions. Traditionally, three fourths of the total marketing communication budget for packaged goods goes to trade and consumer promotion, while the rest goes to traditional advertising.[9]

Sales promotion is actually more of a product than an advertising medium. To be successful, promotions must be promoted. Mobile technology and social media are making sales promotion a much more powerful marketing tool to boost short-term sales.

Why Sales Promotion?

For a copywriter, sales promotion offers many advantages, especially when it's integrated into a total campaign. Some of these advantages are as follows:

- **It's fast.** Sales promotion accelerates the selling process and maximizes sales volume.

- **It can cover the whole distribution channel.** Targeted promotions reach wholesalers, retailers, and consumers.

- **It can help retain customer loyalty.** Promotions provide a way to stay in touch with current customers and to give them incentives for continuing their relationship with a brand or business.

- **It can increase early adoption.** You provide an incentive for a customer to try a product for the first time. With the proliferation of new brands, incentives shorten the path from awareness to action.

- **It's measurable.** In most cases sales promotion is designed for short-term sales increases, not long-term brand image. You get results (or lack of results) almost immediately.

- **It supports retailers.** The growth of *account-specific marketing*, or *co-marketing*, requires customized sales promotion programs for retail chains. For example, Sony might offer a promotional program just for Best Buy stores.

- **It fits the consumer's expectations.** On the plus side, consumers are receptive to promotions. On the minus side . . . that's coming later.

- **It fits into an integrated marketing campaign.** To be successful, most promotion needs to be promoted by traditional media.

Why Not?

For each of the major advantages, there is a flip side:

- Because of their short-term, price-oriented nature, most sales promotions do not help build long-term brand equity.

- Although incentives can help retain customer loyalty, they can also encourage brand switching. If a brand has no perceived advantage, the consumer will base the purchase on price (or added value).

- Retailers are demanding more, and they are getting it. So in addition to slotting allowances, retailers are demanding more generous account-specific marketing programs that often include expensive sales promotion programs.

- Customers not only respond to promotions; they expect them. Automakers would love to get out of the endless chain of rebates, discounts, and other incentives. But when one offers them, the others follow suit until the whole industry suffers.

- Most promotions can't stand alone. So the advertiser has to weigh the short-term increase in sales against the cost of the incentive and the cost to advertise it. Sometimes an advertiser will settle for breaking even, or even a small loss if it means retaining a retail account or gaining market share. For example, an automaker may offer very generous year-end deals just to say they're the number-one seller in the rest of their advertising.

Types of Sales Promotions

CONSUMER SALES PROMOTIONS

With the exception of long-term PR tactics such as sponsorships, most consumer sales promotion is considered to be *non–franchise building.* Promotions are intended to jump-start sales and do almost nothing to build brand image. Another purpose is to gather information (give us the data, and we'll give you a prize). Either way, the ultimate goal is to stimulate action. Examples of sales promotions include the following:

- *Contests/games:* The consumer actively participates in some way by writing an essay, taking a quiz, or engaging in some other mental activity that would not challenge a first grader's intellect. In return for providing some marketing data, you have a one-in-a-gazillion chance to win something.

- *Sweepstakes:* These involve chance more than contests do. Just enter and you may already be a winner. Sometimes you don't have to do anything except wait for your prize. The laws governing contests and sweepstakes vary from state to state. A few years ago, Pepsi announced a chance to win a billion dollars. Although no purchase was necessary, you can bet the winner probably bought some Pepsi along the way.

- *Product giveaways:* Buy the product, and you might get the next one free. Fast-food restaurants and soft drinks use this quite a bit. You have to buy something first, but you have a better chance of winning.

- *Samples:* You can get them in the mail, in magazine inserts, or from little old ladies in the supermarket. You can give away more than pills, perfumes, and fabric softener sheets. Years ago AOL gave away millions and millions of CD-ROMs in every imaginable way.

- *Paper coupons:* Essentially these are little slips of paper that ensure a discount. They are distributed in a number of ways: traditionally, in magazine and newspaper ads; in freestanding inserts (FSI) in newspapers; in direct mail packs (such as Valpak); and online, in a form that consumers print at home.

- **Digital coupons:** Anyone who's bought anything online probably knows about discount codes that can significantly reduce the price. Downloadable online coupons have been around for a while too, and act basically the same way as traditional paper coupons. Location-based technology allows delivery of coupons to mobile phones when a shopper enters a specific section of a store or when the user scans a QR code. Social coupon services such as Groupon and LivingSocial have had mixed success in attracting one-time buyers, but offer opportunities to promote savings to millions of potential consumers every day.

- **Discounts:** These are temporary price reductions. *Temporary* is the key word, because a permanent price reduction creates no urgency to buy.

- **Bonus packs:** The consumer gets more of a product at the regular price. For example, detergent boxes may be bundled in a buy-one-get-one-free promotion. Bonus packs provide more value to the consumer. However, if the consumer is already a loyal customer, there is no incremental value to the manufacturer.

- **Rebates:** Consumers are offered money back if they mail receipts and packaging to the producer. This requires more effort, and the seller bets that a large percentage of people will not bother. If they do, they have to provide information for the seller's database. Many times, prices listed contain "after rebate" in the fine print.

- **Premiums (merchandise):** Instead of money back, the consumer gets stuff. It can be as simple as the toy in a Happy Meal (marginally harder to digest than the food) or as elaborate as thousands of dollars in water toys with the purchase of a new boat. Premiums can also be intangible items, such as frequent-flier points.

- **Loyalty programs:** These reward customers for continuing to purchase the same brand of a product or service. Airline frequent-flier plans are the most obvious form of loyalty programs. But retailers such as grocers, discount stores, and electronics stores, where customers shop frequently, also use loyalty programs. Many consumer packaged goods companies have frequency programs that award points for purchases. The points can be redeemed for gifts, such as merchandise, or for discounts.

- **Cross-promotion:** Some products just seem to complement each other. If so, they can work together to multiply their promotional dollars. For example, a cookie company may offer coupons for milk. Other times the lead brand in a promotional campaign will bring in partners. For example, BMW's test-drive program to raise money for breast cancer also included Harman Kardon and Michelin, which are used in BMW cars. Pepsi has teamed with Apple to promote free iTunes with purchase of Pepsi.

TRADE SALES PROMOTIONS

If you're a manufacturer, how do you motivate your sales staff, move product through distributors, and encourage retailers to stock your brands? Trade sales promotion is used for business-to-business products and for wholesale transactions for consumer goods. Some trade sales promotions include the following:

- **Financial incentives:** Lower interest rates, reduced freight costs, price discounts, and extended payments can encourage retailers to stock up on products. Some of these include *slotting allowances* to provide shelf space, *buying allowances* to reduce the introductory price, and *promotional allowances* for short-term promotions. These allowances are usually meant to be passed on to the consumer, but some retailers pocket the savings and charge full retail prices, which does not help to move the product. To counter this, some packaged goods companies have dropped their everyday prices and cut back on trade allowances. *Push money*—also known as "spiffs"—can be an extra commission paid to sales force, wholesaler, or retailer.

- **Trade contests:** Salespeople, wholesalers, and retailers receive rewards for increasing their sales. The more you sell, the more you get. These often involve travel incentives, such as a trip for two to Hawaii or tickets to a major sporting event.

- **Sales support:** The manufacturer provides displays, posters, counter cards, signage, and other point-of-sale items. Products sell better with attractive displays, which are often accompanied by price deals. The manufacturer may also provide special promotional literature for the dealer to hand out.

- **Training programs:** The manufacturer trains the distributor or dealer employees in selling the product.

- **Trade shows:** Manufacturers display their products, salespeople meet and greet potential customers, distributors and wholesalers check out new lines, and everybody sees what the competition is up to. Trade shows can be small regional events with nothing more than a few 10- by 10-foot booths or major extravaganzas such as the Consumer Electronics Show, which generates worldwide coverage. Some manufacturers spend millions every year on trade shows—for elaborate booths, celebrity talent, high-profile events, extravagant banquets, contests, and handouts. Trade shows provide a lot of opportunity for creative people. Dozens of details require creative planning: the booth design itself; displays, posters, and handout literature; event planning, preshow promotion, and premium selection; audio and video displays; and more. In a way, a trade show booth is a campaign in itself, with components that work individually and cumulatively to convey a single message.

- **Cooperative advertising:** Basically, the manufacturer helps the retailer pay for advertising its products. Sometimes the ads are provided, and all the retailer has to do is slap a logo and address on the bottom. In many cases, the co-op ad is similar to the national brand advertising done by the manufacturer. Other times, the manufacturer provides images and copy that the retailers use to build their own ads. If you ever have to produce co-op ads, always keep the intended media in mind. For example, don't try to convert an elaborate four-color magazine ad into a black-and-white co-op ad for a local newspaper.

Like consumer sales promotions, trade promotions usually have to be supported with some form of marketing communications, usually print advertising, direct mail, and the Internet.

Promotional Strategy and Tactics

Promotional strategy stems from marketing objectives. For example:

- Get 20% of Brand X users to try Brand Y within three months.

- Get 40% of current Brand Z users to increase purchases from 5 to 10 packages per month within six months.

- Expand distribution for Brand A from 40% to 80% in all X-Mart chain stores within one year.

You need to first have a clear idea of what the client wants to accomplish before you create a promotional program.

Components of the Promotion

Assuming you know the client's objectives, you need to follow these steps:

1. **Think campaigns.** If the promotion is part of a total campaign, make sure your sales promotion will fit the way the product is positioned in the market, the brand image, the target audience, and how it is sold.

2. **Develop a promotional theme.** It's like a tagline. Use some of the guidelines for taglines in Chapter 9.

3. **Consider the incentive.** What will you offer that adds value to the product or service and encourages quick sales? As with the theme, you have to consider the target audience and brand image. For example, a free trunkful of frozen pizzas may get a prospect into a Hyundai dealer, but it probably won't motivate a potential Audi customer.

4. **Promote the promotion.** Once you have determined the theme and the incentive, how do you let people know? Your marketing of the promotion also depends on the target audience and brand image. Using multiple media, such as the Internet and print, provides for more interaction and greater involvement with the product.

Daimler AG doctored a picture of communist rebel Ernesto "Che" Guevara to introduce its "revolutionary" automotive technology at the International Consumer Electronics Show in Las Vegas. Note the Mercedes logo on the beret. A firestorm of protest forced the company to issue an apology. Daimler said they did not condone Guevara's terrorism, and we're sure the communists were not too thrilled about their icon selling luxury cars.

Tips and Techniques for Promotion

- Use a memorable theme.

- Relate to the product attributes (brand image).

- Keep it simple.

- Make the benefit (reward) clear.

Promotional Public Relations

The term *public relations* covers any nonpaid information from a third party that mentions an identified product or service. It's also called *earned media*, since the placement of a story depends on convincing an editor to run it rather than just sending in an insertion order. There are many kinds of PR, and we're not going to address them here. Instead, we'll focus on the publicity aspect of PR and how it applies to promotion and integrated marketing communications. Examples include event sponsorship, donations to causes, charitable foundations, and other good things companies do that deserve positive mention. PR can also be used to announce a sales promotion activity.

A dedicated public relations practitioner would probably be outraged to see PR relegated to a subhead in a discussion of promotions. We do not mean to dismiss the value of public relations. In fact, we believe PR should be the foundation of most marketing communications plans. In this context, however, we will discuss public relations in terms of creative strategy, with special emphasis on how public relations can fit into a promotional campaign.

One function of public relations is getting credit for the good things your company does. So many promotional PR efforts concentrate on charitable acts. For example, your promotion could be about donating money to research against diseases such as breast cancer, supporting national parks, building local playgrounds, and cleaning up river walks. In addition to doing the good deed, you need to promote it through publicity releases and editorial contacts as well as traditional and nontraditional media. Marketers can't always be assured they will earn space in a publication or TV news story. So they produce ads and commercials touting their good deeds.

Public relations advertising uses traditional advertising messages to promote the good deeds of a company. For example, a company may run TV ads stating that they'll donate a percentage of the purchase price to a charity. Or, as was the case with a pharmaceutical manufacturer, they may announce available support plans if patients can't afford the drugs.

Even before they could shut down their leaking oil well in the Gulf, BP used the whole MarCom tool kit for damage control. After disastrous footage of oil-soaked birds and polluted beaches (and their inept CEO whining about

BP invested millions to rebuild badly damaged goodwill in the Gulf region as well as the rest of the nation. National television spots promoted tourism for the four Gulf states; they set up a recovery webpage and their own YouTube channel about Gulf restoration efforts, as well as Facebook and Twitter pages. Print advertising and other media supported the effort to restore the Gulf and BP's reputation.

getting *his* life back), the company settled in for a long-term campaign. As the public outrage faded, BP continued to provide updates on their cleanup and restoration efforts. They used every medium possible, with heavy emphasis on the digital space. To their credit, they shifted the discussion from themselves to promoting tourism for the affected Gulf Coast states. This became a win-win situation where the people of the Gulf benefit from tourist dollars and BP gets credit for doing something positive. Litigation will continue for years, but as long as tourists aren't ankle deep in sludge, they'll keep coming back to the Gulf.

South by Southwest has become a major cultural movement, which naturally attracts big-name sponsors, which naturally attracts more attention.

As America's second most popular spectator sport, NASCAR provides a wealth of sponsorship and cross-promotional opportunities. The drivers and cars are covered with logos from advertisers who pay as much as $20 million to be a primary sponsor.

Event Marketing and Sponsorships

Event marketing and sponsorships are specialized forms of promotion that link a company or brand to a specific event or themed activity. Event marketing and sponsorship are sort of like public relations because they can be long-term goodwill efforts that can enhance brand image. Marketers often participate in event marketing by attaching their brand to a sporting event, concert, fair, or festival. In event sponsorship, a brand or company name usually precedes the name of the particular event. Examples include the following:

- Corona beer presents Kenny Chesney in concert.

- The Sprint Cup NASCAR series.

- The FedEx Orange Bowl.

Event marketing has become very popular because it creates the perfect opportunity for engagement with a brand—sight, sound, sampling, positive association with a cause or performer, and a warm fuzzy feeling of being there in person.

The live event is only one part of the promotion. Websites, e-mail, text messages, and social media all work before, during, and after an event to keep the engagement going strong. For example, South by Southwest (SXSW) has grown into a major organizer of conferences, trade shows, and festivals, with events that include music, film, interactive, and education activities. In the last few years, social media has accelerated that growth, supported by a host of major sponsors. The 10-day extravaganza in Austin started small but now ranks as one of the top music festivals in the country as well as a showcase for emerging technology.

Cross-media event promotion can be very effective cross-culturally too. Tecate beer launched a promotion centered on Mexican Independence Day that touted three major boxing matches in Houston, Las Vegas, and Los Angeles. Special events and promos surrounding the event included key restaurant and bar accounts, ticket giveaways via local radio partners, thematic point-of-purchase displays, mail-in rebates for HBO pay-per-view events, and autograph sessions with local boxers.

Product Placement

Some companies specialize in placing their clients' products on game shows as prizes. Others concentrate on getting their clients into movies and TV shows. For example, in *ET: The Extra Terrestrial* the hero was lured with Reese's Pieces because M&M's would not pay for product placement. Short-term sales of Reese's Pieces skyrocketed. So when you see a character reach for a box of Cheerios, drink a Coors, or drive a new Honda, it's no coincidence. Product placement, also called *embedded marketing*, is negotiated with the producers and, as we noted above, can run into tens of millions of dollars for a single film or television program. James Bond films have become notorious for product placement. The latest, *Skyfall*, set a new record with $45 million for product placement—one third of the production costs.[10]

Product placement isn't limited to television programing and movies. Lady Gaga featured nine different products in her "Telephone" video—including such mundane brands as Wonder Bread, Diet Coke, and Miracle Whip. *Advertainment* is another form of product placement. These sponsored video programs are meant to entertain but weave the product into the story. The classic example is the award-winning series from BMW called "The Hire," featuring Clive Owen.

Even though product placement enhances brand awareness, it still can't match traditional ads for effectiveness.

Mission: Impossible—Ghost Protocol *was a very popular film that showcased the talents of its two leading stars, BMW and Apple. We heard Tom Cruise was in it too. BMW also ran TV commercials promoting the "Mission to Drive Sales Event."*

According to MediaPost, 52% of viewers would buy a product after watching the commercial for it versus only 23% after product placement. Consumers are more likely to recall brands in traditional ads than through product placement.[11]

In-Game Advertising

In-game advertising (IGA) uses computer and video games as a medium to deliver brand messages, logos, and products in use within games as a way to offset development costs for increasingly sophisticated graphics. Advertisers see in-game advertising as a direct path to the coveted 18–34 demographic, which is becoming increasingly hard to reach with traditional media. Early games featured static displays such as billboards in the background, or logos on stadium scoreboards. With ad revenues increasing rapidly, IGA has become big business—big enough to merit the attention of Nielsen Media Research (GamePlay Metrics) to measure ratings of ad messages inside games. As online gaming grew, advertisers could develop dynamic ads that change the messages depending on who is playing the game, where it's played, and when, since ad messages do not have to be hard coded into the game. IGA ads went beyond simple background graphics to increased engagement with the gamers. Here are some examples. In 2008, Barack Obama was the first presidential candidate to run ads in a video game—*Burnout Paradise* (no comment on whether that turned out to be an appropriate title). Earlier in the book we showed how Jeep created an integrated campaign of television commercials, online ads, and in-game promotion of the special-edition *Call of Duty: Modern Warfare 3* Wrangler. In a free demo of *Madden NFL 12,* players who completed a specific play were given a code on the game's Facebook page, which would enter them in a contest to win a Chevy Cruze. Axe created a mini game targeted to Sony PlayStation gamers. The *Even Angels Will Fall* game asked players to spray an in-game avatar with Axe Body Spray to win a T-shirt. In less than a month, 500,000 consumers had played the game. Brands such as Lipton and Degree Women have created interactive hubs with Xbox Live and PlayStation Network that operate outside of specific game play.[12] While game marketers and advertisers like the potential of IGA, what about gamers? Some gamers may see in-game ads as another way for the corporate world to invade their world. However, a study by Nielsen and IGA Worldwide showed that 82% of consumers did not object to in-game ads, and 61% expressed a more favorable view of the advertiser after they played.[13] In-game advertising works best when the brand has a connection to the action. When it's forced or misdirected, the backlash can be devastating, such as when *Fight Night Round 3* inserted Burger King's mascot into the ring with disastrous results.[14]

Social Gaming and Marketing

Electronic Arts (EA), one of the recognized leaders in gaming, took their in-game ad business in-house, rather than using an agency to place ads. *The Sims Social*, their most popular game on Facebook, is a natural for ad placement because avatars can interact with the products. Brands such as Dunkin' Donuts, Dove, and Toyota are thoroughly integrated into the game, and because the advertisements offer virtual goods for free, players don't mind interacting with the product placements. *The Sims Social* offers a fairly large global audience, attracting roughly 3 million daily users and 17.2 million monthly active users to make it one of the top 15 games on Facebook, according to AppData.[15]

Dave Madden, EA's senior vice president of global media solutions, explains the four ways advertising works in *The Sims Social*:

1. **Traffic drivers** encourage players in the game to visit a brand's Facebook page, where they can download a free in-game virtual good.

2. **Quests** force players to take a number of steps inside the game to earn a valuable item at the end. For instance, Toyota launched a quest where players earned a Prius.

3. **Store tabs** appear in a virtual goods store where users will see one or several items offered by a particular brand.

4. **Media integrations** involve a short video advertisement or other type of media, to unlock a virtual good.[16]

Hybrid Marketing

Hybrid marketing takes product placement one step further and integrates it into commercials before, during, and after the program as well as the programming itself. Hybrid ads include customized ads, branded promotions, vignettes, interstitial, and micro-series where sponsor messaging is combined with program or entertainment content.[17] Some examples include a customized 40-second hybrid ad sponsored by CoverGirl cosmetics on *America's Next Top Model* to announce the Meet the Model Sweepstakes, and a T-Mobile-sponsored 35-second custom ad on the American Music Awards telecast to encourage viewers to text message their votes with a T-Mobile phone or go to abc.com to vote.

Hybrid ads are often placed before episodes of programs telling the viewers to visit the sponsors' websites and buy products that will appear throughout the episode. Media critic David Hauslaib comments, "Hybrid commercials work regardless of what field you're in. So Toyota, Keebler Cookies, and Travelocity can enjoy the same bump from their symbiotic show relationship as any other product, as long as they can somehow make their item correlate with the show in people's minds."[18]

Who's Who?

Jay Conrad Levinson—Jay Conrad Levinson is the author of a wildly successful series of books about "guerrilla marketing" tactics. He cites many examples of unconventional marketing and communications programs that generated spectacular results. Typically, these guerrilla tactics use existing marketing communication tools, such as direct mail or outdoor, but in highly targeted, very creative ways.

Dennis Crowley—Dennis Crowley was named one of *Fortune* magazine's "40 under 40" list of rising business stars. In 2003 he cofounded Dodgeball, which was bought by Google two years later. In 2009, along with Naveen Selvadurai, he developed another version of Dodgeball called Foursquare. By mid-2011, the location-based social networking service had over 10 million users.[20]

Cliff Marks—Cliff Marks is the creator of "pre-movie" showings in theaters. His CineMedia company pioneered the introduction of high-quality advertising content on the big screen. Marks and his company introduced The 2wenty, a digital pre-feature program that included traditional 30-second spots and longer-format ads. While some moviegoers don't appreciate the intrusion of commercials, most accept the advertising, especially the slick longer-format spots that are different from typical TV advertising.

Juliana Stock—Juliana Stock thinks like an entrepreneur and has been quietly changing the way people at Condé Nast, the consummate purveyor of print, think. She's heads up Condé Nast's new-business incubator that develops digital enterprises. Her work has brought consumers Idea Flight, an app that allows people to share presentations on the iPad. She's also developed Santa's Hideout, a digital and shareable version of a children's wish list. As of this writing she is spearheading the gaming app Gourmet Live. No wonder she made *Adweek's* "Young Influentials" list.[21]

Exercises

1. Brand Sensing

- Make a grid. In the first column make a list of brands such as Aflac, Apple, Birkenstock, BMW, Chevrolet, Coke, Dell, ESPN, FedEx, *GQ*, Kashi, Marlboro, Motorola, NBC, Nicorette, Nokia, Starbucks, State Farm, UPS, Wii, and so on.

- Make six more columns. In each of the next five columns note how you might experience each brand based on the five senses. How does Brand X look, feel, taste, sound, and smell? Leave the final column blank.

- Now, in class, discuss each brand and list how consumers might experience the brand with each of their senses.

- After completing the entire brand list, return to the first brand, review the sensory aspects, and in the last column list nontraditional options inspired by the sensory list.

- Continue down the list and see how the senses can lead you to see options you might never have thought of before.

2. Unusual Matches

- As a class, generate a long list of highly unexpected touch points—places you might never have thought of finding advertising messages. *Unexpected* is the key word. You are encouraged to push the envelope.

- Your instructor will come to class with a predetermined list of brands, the same number of brands as students, and toss the brand names into a hat.

- Select a brand. Quickly, and relying only on your personal knowledge and/or experience with the brand, write a positioning statement.

- Now, present the positioning for your brand. Follow this with a discussion of who the target audience is.

- As a class, decide which touch point would best fit with the brand. Keep a running list of brands next to each touch point.

- Switch it up to the next student.

- At the end see which touch points have the most brands associated with them and discuss why that might be.

3. Talking Products

(Contributed by Dorothy Pisarski, PhD, assistant professor, Drake University)

Think of times when someone might select a Hershey's chocolate bar from all the other snacks available at a point-of-purchase display.

Begin the list as a class and then continue on your own, writing five more.

- Examples: (a) on a long road trip when paying for gas inside the convenience store; (b) before a camping trip, in anticipation of making s'mores; and (c) when someone needs a not-too-serious Valentine's gift.

Then take on the role of the chocolate bar. For each purchase occasion, complete the sentence "You won't regret buying me because _____."

- Examples: (a) I'll sweeten up your trip and make the miles go by more happily; (b) authentic Hershey's quality is needed for the best-tasting s'mores; and (c) no Valentine can resist the aroma and flavor of a Hershey's chocolate bar.

One product may have several benefits that are the result of different target groups and different behavioral situations.

Visit www.sagepub.com/altstiel3e to access these additional learning tools

- Video Links
- Web Resources
- eFlashcards
- Web Quizzes

Chapter 17

Business-to-Business

Selling Along the Supply Chain

B2B: Challenges and Opportunities

Some beginning copywriters dread business-to-business (B2B) assignments. The products aren't fun. The target audience is deadly serious. You're mostly stuck with trade magazines and collateral pieces. Many creative directors tell their team, "There are no boring products, only boring advertising." But many times, you don't know enough about a product to make it interesting. Too often even the clients don't know why anyone should buy their products. So they settle for a sterile recitation of facts and figures. While it doesn't take a rocket scientist to figure out beer, soap, or toilet paper, you have to know something about your subject as well as the customer when you're creating business advertising.

While creating good B2B concepts can be a challenge, it also presents a great opportunity, especially for entry-level creatives. Rather than being stuck with a small piece of the account, you're more likely to work on a whole campaign. You might be able to work out a whole integrated plan that uses a lot of fun promotional and web components in addition to print ads and collateral. You can probably work in some cool guerrilla marketing ideas. Some clients love that, since they think they're getting more for their money. In *Hey Whipple, Squeeze This,* Luke Sullivan praises B2B: "Trade ads are just as important to your client's economy as its consumer work, and they're usually a better gig than a consumer campaign."[1]

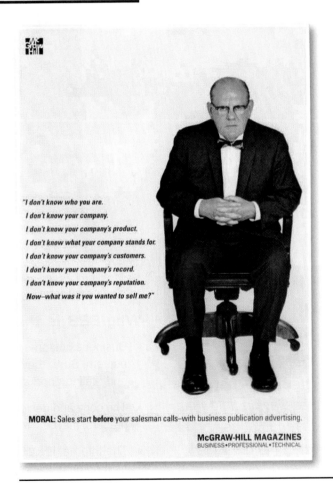

"I don't know who you are.
I don't know your company.
I don't know your company's product.
I don't know what your company stands for.
I don't know your company's customers.
I don't know your company's record.
I don't know your company's reputation.
Now—what was it you wanted to sell me?"

MORAL: Sales start **before** your salesman calls–with business publication advertising.

McGRAW-HILL MAGAZINES
BUSINESS•PROFESSIONAL•TECHNICAL

Many years ago, magazine publisher McGraw-Hill made the case for B2B advertising. The grumpy little man in the chair may not represent typical buyers today, but they still want answers to the questions in the headline.

Why B2B Is Different

- The customer is buying products with his or her company's money.

- Traditionally, the copy has been more factual and less emotional than what's usually found in consumer advertising.

- In general, the emphasis is on generating immediate response rather than on long-term brand building.

- Ad budgets are usually much smaller than with mass-appeal consumer products, restricting many creative options.

- Most business products are not sold retail, which means they are either sold direct to buyers or through dealers or distributors.

Visual metaphors work for business ads too, especially when you're discussing rather complicated subjects like improving data processing speed.

Why B2B Is the Same

- Business customers still have wants and needs—saving money, success, self-esteem. Sure, they want facts, but ultimately it's about making more money and feeling good about it.

- The copy and design principles discussed in previous chapters apply to business readers, maybe even more than they do with some consumer products.

- The Internet is just as important, and in some cases even more important, as a communication source and as part of an integrated marketing communications campaign.

- Branding for business products and services is becoming hugely important, especially as companies merge and change affiliations. Sometimes the brand name is the only constant.

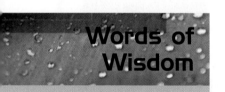

- Even though the numbers of business customers may be smaller, using traditional mass media such as television, radio, outdoor, and newspapers may be an effective way to reach them.

- Companies do not buy products and services. People do.

Don't Forget Those Wants and Needs

A salesperson who just got rejected by a heartless purchasing agent may disagree, but business buyers are human. They may use economic rationales, but they still have wants and needs similar to those of other consumers. For example:

- An office manager responds to a direct mailer from an office supply store that offers free delivery. This saves her time, so she can get more work done; she can save her company money, which makes her look good to the boss, which might mean she gets a raise. All of which satisfies her needs.

- A factory manager sees an ad for a robot that stacks boxes on pallets in minutes, saving valuable time and labor. This will save his company a lot of money, making him look good, which may mean a promotion and more money. (Starting to see a pattern?)

- A doctor reads a brochure, sees a medical journal ad, and checks a website for a new blood-thinning drug. She gets more information from a sales rep, including research reports. She prescribes the drug, not because she'll make more money, but because her need is to help her patients. Sometimes business is about more than making money.

Most of this chapter will deal with trade advertising generally aimed at businesspeople who buy products or services sold direct or through dealers, wholesalers, or retailers. For example, sump pumps sold to plumbers; bathroom fixtures for schools; lumber for housing contractors; engines for jet planes; and a million other products we all take for granted. Besides trade, there are several other B2B specialties:

Agricultural Advertising: It's Another Animal

Agricultural advertising requires a special approach. Farmers are consumers who buy industrial products—tractors, buildings, seed, chemicals, and the like. They ride boom-and-bust cycles that would make the most daring stockbrokers nauseous. When you talk to a typical farmer, he will always complain about the weather, the government, the markets, and whatever else is bugging him today. But for the most part he wouldn't trade his career choice for any city

WinField Solutions promoted their InterLock product through highly impactful 3D mailers, customized websites, video, collateral, and sales promotion.

job. Some of the hottest creative shops have taken on ag clients and won a ton of awards. Someday you just might work on an ag account, so here are a few tips:

- Many successful farmers are college-educated businesspeople and should be treated as such, not as bib-overall-wearing hicks. Appeal to their business sense, not to the nostalgia of a small family farm that disappeared years ago.

- Farmers are extremely sensitive to detail and very concerned about being up-to-date. Show a 10-year-old tractor, a CRT computer monitor, or an out-of-date satellite dish in your ad, and you've killed your sales message.

- You can have fun with the product, but never mock the farmer's country, family, profession, or lifestyle.

- Be careful with claims. If anyone recognizes BS, it's a farmer.

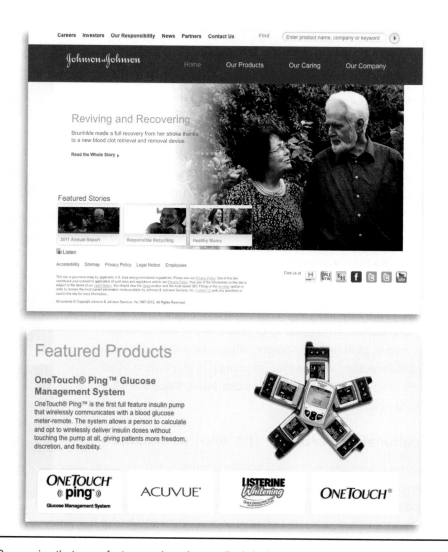

Companies that manufacture and market medical devices use the Internet to provide facts about their company in addition to highly detailed information about their products and services. The tone is professional and fact-based rather than promotional.

Here's how one company used an integrated approach to reach farmers, who are notoriously tough to impress. WinField Solutions developed an integrated campaign to convince growers to use a product to improve the effectiveness of the chemicals they spray on crops. A lockbox was sent to farmers along with a PURL (personalized URL) that would provide the code to unlock it. The box contained product information and a free sample of the product. The personalized website had a video as well as other product information. The site also promoted a contest to win a John Deere Gator vehicle if the visitor provided an e-mail. Results: Colle + McVoy, the agency who created the campaign, reports a 50% open rate versus the usual 6%.[3]

Professional Advertising

Not that we don't think other businesspeople are pros at what they do, but in this context *professional* applies to teachers, engineers, lawyers, accountants, doctors, dentists, architects, and other people who have specialized careers that usually require advanced education and training. Professionals read journals that are often the official publications of their profession, such as the *Journal of the American Medical Association*. Professionals operate under a code of ethics, so journals that allow advertising frown on wild, unsubstantiated ad claims; unauthorized use of a product; or any image that would denigrate their field. That's why so many professional journal ads play it safe and don't risk offending their readers. Other publications that appeal to professionals may be given a little more creative latitude, but remember, these professionals worked hard to get where they are, and it's not something to trivialize with silly advertising.

B2G: A Specialized Target Audience

Business-to-government (B2G) marketing is a specialized kind of B2B that's sometimes called public sector marketing. It involves marketing goods and services to all levels of government—local, state, and federal. B2G can include all the marketing communication tools used for traditional B2B, but government buyers have much stricter guidelines and usually have prenegotiated standing contracts and set prices. Nevertheless, through traditional and social networks, B2G marketers can influence a sale. For example, Xerox helps the federal government streamline their print service management, electronic collection, and Medicaid claims processing. With the new social media tools available, Xerox can provide much more information to their federal government customers. Edward

Insitu, a subsidiary of Boeing, makes unmanned aircraft used by a number of military branches and government agencies. While the sale is strictly controlled by government policies, the manufacturer still promotes the products to reinforce the buying decision, perhaps influence future sales, impress nongovernment buyers, and keep investors happy.

Gala, vice president of marketing, explains, "When you get a message from Xerox, it comes with links to videos on YouTube. It comes with links to whitepapers and analyst reports that are accessible online. It comes with invitations to webinars where you can learn from thought leaders on a particular topic, whether it be security or sustainability or cost reduction."[4]

The 2011 Federal Media and Marketing Study researched the social networking use among federal employees:

- 46% can access social networking sites.

- 51% use Facebook at work.

- 34% use YouTube.

- 19% use LinkedIn.

- 9% use Twitter.[5]

(We assume all this time online is our tax dollars at work.)

B2B and Campaigns

Many B2B marketers have discovered that magazines may not be the primary method to reach their customers. Using integrated marketing communications (IMC) for B2B makes sense because customers are easier to define and locate. All the IMC components listed in previous chapters apply to B2B. Because the number of key customers is sometimes very small, you may be able to create expensive high-impact communication tools that generate higher response rates.

When InfoPro changed their name to Roundhouse, they didn't show computers in their new launch campaign. They talked about information technology for the fashion and retail industry as a "beautiful thing."

As with consumer advertising, you need to think of how many different ways you can reach a customer. Do you go for a few high-impact "rifle shots" or use a lot of different marketing tools?

Here are some examples:

• A Japanese engine manufacturer wanted potential customers to recognize their commitment to the U.S. market. So they sent a large box to the nation's top industrial engine buyers. On the box lid was the slogan, "Take Power Trip." Inside was a high-quality garment bag embroidered with the company logo. In the pocket of the bag were vouchers for two plane tickets to the company's North American headquarters in California. Also enclosed were a cover letter from the U.S. general manager, product literature, and a corporate brochure. Each mailing cost about $200, but when compared to millions of dollars in engine sales, it was very economical. Just as important, salespeople from the engine company called potential customers after the big boxes arrived. You can be sure the prospects remembered the mailer, which made it much easier for the sales force.

• A manufacturer of construction equipment launched a new line of telescopic material handlers. They used print ads but also produced a series of sell sheets, full-line brochures,

When you're talking about personal responsibility for a company's profit, it's a lot more serious than MasterCard's "priceless" approach used for consumers.

You could talk about all the technology that makes an Epson cash register the best choice. Or like this approach, you can show how it makes the retailer's job a little more pleasant. While it makes a good point about serving customers better, does it unfairly portray older people as "slow, ornery and frightening"?

It's been several years since Andersen Consulting split from Arthur Andersen and changed their name to Accenture (to reflect their accent on the future). This ad was part of a campaign in print and television to demonstrate that the world's biggest consulting firm still can move quickly to help their customers.

Every meeting room looks pretty much the same, no matter where it's located. The Vancouver Convention Centre stresses this sad fact, but hints that a meeting in their facility will be inspirational. The ad's sole purpose is to lead readers to the website, which provides details on the facility and the city of Vancouver.

head-to-head comparisons with other brands, a walk-around guide to help salespeople sell the machine, a feature/benefit video, an operational video showing applications and attachments, an interactive multimedia program to show potential customers, a co-op advertising kit, a dealer sales kit, a point-of-sale display for dealers, a complete trade PR program on CD-ROM, and oversized posters and motorized displays for trade shows. The company's dealers had the tools they needed to sell to their contractor customers, who were also very familiar with the new products after seeing the ads and direct mailers.

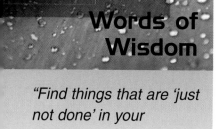
- A marketer of veterinary products launched a line of products to help vets treat ear problems in dogs. They produced a magazine insert that folded out to form a poster for the vet's exam rooms. They ran spread and single-page ads in professional journals. The company offered audiocassettes about building a clinic's business by using these new products. A direct mail kit included a 100-page technical guide. They provided handouts for clinic customers and even ran ads in consumer publications to encourage dog owners to visit their vets.

Here's one way to sum up the use of IMC for B2B campaigns: Imagine that in order to sell something, you have to open a big iron door. Run a few magazine ads, and you're throwing pebbles at that door. Use all the integrated marketing tools at your disposal, and you've got a big boulder that'll knock that door wide open.

Online Marketing Tools for B2B

Many B2B clients adopted the Internet long before consumer brands did. Whether it's used strictly for information or for direct selling, the Internet provides B2B marketers with tremendous advantages over "traditional" media, including the following:

- Provides more detailed information that you can't fit into an ad.

- Shows streaming video, animation, and interactive media.

- When used as part of an integrated personalized direct mail program using PURLs, it can build customer relationships faster than with traditional methods.

- Includes links to co-op partners and/or affiliated companies.

- Provides updated product information such as spec sheets, catalogs, parts forms, and troubleshooting guides that can be downloaded.

- Delivers company news; announces new promotions and special offers.

- Sets up merchant accounts for direct sales.

- Identifies dealers, shows their locations, and provides links to their sites. Widgets such as Google Maps can be integrated into the site for more impact.

- Tracks inquiries, builds databases, and establishes customer relationship management (CRM) programs.

When building a B2B site, don't forget the three things you need to accomplish—get them to come, get them to stay, and get them to come back. When you want to drive customers to your site, trade ads, direct mail, articles in trade publications, banner ads on other sites, and all the other tactics used in business-to-consumer (B2C) marketing apply. As far as keeping them there, the focus should be on education, motivation, and generating action, not entertainment. Even if viewers feel like playing games, watching videos, and reading blogs, chances are their bosses would rather see them downloading specs, comparing prices, and saving time on the web. When you want to get them to come back, it's the same as with consumer sites—keep the content fresh and let them know you have a new product or service worth checking out. Businesspeople are looking for updated sites that offer a wide range of web-based tools for sales leads, direct mail marketing, telemarketing, and CRM. RSS technology is a proactive way to send news to subscribing businesspeople.

Online Events

According to a recent GlobalSpec Industrial Marketing Trends survey, 47% of industrial companies are increasing their spending on online events. Online events, sometimes called virtual events or online trade shows, are a trend made possible by high-bandwidth availability and emerging technologies that allow media companies to produce and host highly interactive experiences.[7] Online events targeted to a specific audience provide an excellent opportunity to showcase a product line, build

Rising Star

Creative Pants

Working in some sort of creative outlet was an eventuality for me. It's one of those things you just know about yourself. Usually you feel out of place most everywhere until you meet a copywriter or an art director or spend some time hanging out at an agency and you realize there are a lot of people like you out there and you can too get away with putting goofy stuff on a résumé and not having to wear a suit ever.

If you like being creative, it's something you do all the time. You're addicted to making things, telling stories, and solving problems, and your mind really doesn't want to stop. And you really want to wear jeans at work, so that motivates you too.

In my situation, that meant using most of my free time in college to work on building a portfolio of spec advertising, with a few short stories and cool logo designs thrown in for good measure.

There's also the built-in desire to want to share your work, but only if people will like it. Opening yourself up to criticism is tough, because in your mind people not liking your work is the same as people not liking you, and if there's one thing you learned in high school it's the pain of people not liking you. But that's the only way to make the work better. Plus there's the potential upside of winning awards and getting hired. I showed my work to a lot of people in a lot of different cities, and I don't think I cried once.

The good news is that dedicating yourself to doing what you love can pay the bills. Don't ever let anyone tell you otherwise. Creativity and a unique perspective and the ability to make things aesthetically pleasing will always be in demand somewhere and is probably the only skill set that can never be acquired by robots. Especially robots in suits.[8]

Jeff Wolf, Copywriter, Tom, Dick & Harry, Chicago, @jmwolf847

---

brand reputation, provide content, and connect with prospects and customers.[9] For example, a company that provides continuing medical education can provide online courses and testing programs. A manufacturer with a new plant in Mexico can't bring customers to their facility, but they can provide a virtual plant tour online. Another company can do a podcast of speeches at their annual shareholder meeting. The possibilities are limited only by bandwidth and imagination.

B2B and Social Media

Many B2B clients were slow to embrace social media, and many still consider it a sideline activity. As with B2C marketers, the biggest challenges are (1) understanding the potential of social media for business and (2) committing the personnel and time to make it work.

Many companies use social media as a means of handling customer complaints. As long as unhappy customers are willing to vent on Facebook or Twitter, the companies feel they need to address the problem, calm down the complainer, and let the rest of the world know they are concerned. To do that effectively, a company needs to react quickly and take the right tone. That kind of instant, online customer service is certainly important, but it barely scratches the surface of social media's potential for B2B marketers. The following case study shows how social media, when integrated into a complete campaign, can really improve the bottom line.

Cisco was ready to launch their new Aggregation Services Router (ASR). In the past, the traditional tech product launch would include:

- Fly in more than 100 executives and press members to company headquarters.

- Rehearse and prepare CEO and other executives' presentations.

- Create and distribute detailed press releases to the key media.

- E-mail customers.

- Run print ads in business newspapers and magazines.[10]

For its ASR launch, Cisco aimed to execute entirely online, leveraging social media, and in doing so engage network engineers in a more interactive, fun way.

Cisco met its audience where they were—in online venues and the gaming world. Here's how:

- *Second Life:* The company built a virtual stage to mimic an actual product launch event. Customers (network engineers) or the press could board their own "personal transport device" to surf through a virtual router. To generate pre-launch buzz, the team held a concert in Second Life featuring eight bands over seven hours.

- *3D game:* More than 20,000 network engineers played a 3D game, where they "defended the network" using the ASR. (Research shows that 17%–18% of IT professionals play games online every day.) Top scorers went on to a championship round with the winner bagging $10,000 plus a router.

- *YouTube:* Video gets eyeballs. Cisco's "Future of Shopping" is up to 3.3 million views.

- *Pass along links via social sharing:* The company used video to educate consumers and the media about ASR.

- *Video conferencing:* The company's next-generation video conferencing technology, Cisco TelePresence, brought customers together at local offices around the globe. Executives back in San Jose could see the audience's facial expressions and vice versa.

- *Mobile:* A video datasheet engaged engineers on their mobile devices.

- *Facebook:* Hard-core network engineers could connect on the Cisco Support Group for Uber User Internet Addicts.

- *Social media widget:* Cisco assembled videos, collateral, and images in a widget format and embedded it into "social media" news releases and launch pages. Bloggers and others could spread the information easily with the embedded code.

- *Cisco blogs:* Videos and other content engaged bloggers and customers, encouraging viral pickups.

- *Online forum:* Cisco seeded its Networking Professionals Technology Community Forum with launch-related discussion topics and gave customers an "Ask the Expert" function.

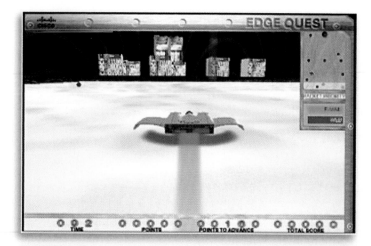

Cisco scrapped traditional live presentations and print media to launch a new product using a combination of Second Life, videoconferencing, customized games, Facebook, Twitter, YouTube, blogs, forums, widgets, and mobile. This resulted in a $100,000 savings and exposure to 90 times more people.

The whole campaign spanned three months with the launch in the middle. During pre-launch, launch, and post-launch, Cisco kept the audience engaged by encouraging discussion with and among its audience. Results: More than 9,000 people from 128 countries attended virtual launch events. That's 90 times more than past launches. Top execs only had to spend about an hour recording their presentations versus weeks of preparation. Without travel they saved about 42,000 miles of gas. Print advertising costs were replaced with nearly 3 times as many press articles and more than 1,000 blog posts and 40 million online impressions. Best of all, the whole launch costs one sixth of a similar launch using traditional methods. Cisco saved over $100,000 using this approach.[11]

War Story

Business Technologists Shall Inherit the Earth

I always wanted to play soccer for Scotland. However, I was rubbish so instead I became a copywriter. My ambition consequently changed from scoring the winning goal in the World Cup final to penning a fundamental creative idea for a blue-chip brand, which would not only be the advertising platform, but also be the brand's strategic linchpin.

Unfortunately I wasn't up to that either.

However I am mighty pleased that last year the IAS creative team, led by Director Reuben Webb, had the distinction of achieving that very feat for the world's premier B2B brand, Siemens. This is how it happened.

Siemens IT Solutions and Services' original raison d'être was to service the needs of its master brand, Siemens AG; however, the innovative and industrious nature of Siemens' people turned it into one of the world's foremost IT outsourcing organizations. But this was evolution, and Siemens was looking for revolution, desirous to develop a stand-alone brand for IT Solutions and Services with a positioning reflecting both market and thought leadership. Everyone dreams of revolutionizing their market, but the conditions are rarely right. This time, though, IAS discovered an opportunity to do just that.

We found during the insight-gathering phase a hard core of industry leaders, advanced observers, and mega-geeks forecasting the demise of IT. In its place, a new category was being discussed—business technology (BT). It stemmed from increasing demand in corporate boardrooms for senior executives to align business strategy and technology. More and more, the chief information officer was changing from the biggest IT guy to a master operational strategist. The more the market and competition were analyzed, the more we realized BT was not just a category in the making, but a category for the taking. The strategy, therefore, was to take ownership of this.

We carved up the challenge in two parts. For the first part, like all the best ideas, the answer was simple: to reposition the Siemens brand as *the* Business Technologists. The second part was to use this as a platform to command a big share of voice normally dominated by the likes of IBM, HP, and Capgemini by using IAS's highly sophisticated TECS (Technology Enabled Contact Strategy) model to develop a global launch comprising a mix of traditional and the latest digital channels. Highlights included internal activation, outdoor advertising, trade press advertising (off-/online and advertorials), direct mail and e-mail, mobile advertising and sponsorship, social media penetration and ads on LinkedIn, search engine optimization, and pay-per-click.

To exploit the fact that Business Technologists is a people-centric positioning and Siemens corporate guidelines stipulate all ads must show people, a creative platform of *Business Technologists of the world unite* was developed. To represent this visually, a photo shoot was commissioned of Siemens people and other members of their ecosystem literally posing as Business Technologists. But the real creative breakthrough was found in the realms of proclamations. In the context of the Business Technologists' story, phrases, quotes, and proverbs were explored that exist in the cultural consciousness of the target audience. Thus, in addition to *Business Technologists of the world unite,* other complementary copy lines were penned: *Business Technologists will inherit the earth,* and *Business Technologists enter where IT fears to tread.* With a spend of less than a million Euros, over 8 million Euros of new revenue was generated, but the true value of the investment is immeasurable.

The repositioning of Siemens IT and Services as Business Technologists helped parent company Siemens AG sell Siemens IT and Services in a deal worth over 700 million Euros plus a major shareholding to Atos, the French IT specialist. And yes, you've guessed it—the Atos people have adopted the positioning and are now the Business Technologists.[12]

Rob Morrice, managing director, IAS B2B Marketing, London, iasb2b.com

Who's Who?

Kathy Button Bell—Vice President and Chief Marketing Officer Kathy Button Bell is responsible for global marketing and corporate branding for Emerson, a $24.2 billion diversified global technology and engineering leader. She led the development and launch of Emerson's corporate branding program in 2000, which put in place an entirely new brand architecture and brand strategy across the company's more than 60 businesses, as well as the first corporate logo change in more than 30 years. Soon after, she initiated the company's first-ever global advertising campaign, which she expanded in 2006 to include the company's first television commercials. In 2009, the global, *integrated* "It's Never Been Done Before" campaign was launched to include translation into multiple languages and expanded social marketing strategies.

Reid Hoffman—Reid Hoffman is best known as the founder of LinkedIn, a social network used primarily for business connections and job searching. Hoffman was instrumental in the creation of PayPal before he went on to found LinkedIn. He has cowritten *The Start-Up of You: Adapt to the Future, Invest in Yourself, and Transform Your Career.* He serves on the boards of Do Something (organization for young people taking action), Mozilla (creator of Firefox), and Endeavor Global (an international nonprofit development organization that finds

and supports high-impact entrepreneurs in emerging markets).

Sheila Kloefkorn—Sheila Kloefkorn is president of KEO Marketing, a Phoenix-based online marketing agency. As president, Sheila is responsible for developing comprehensive online solutions for businesses of all sizes across the United States, and more than 100 countries around the world. Some of the companies for which Sheila has provided online strategy include General Motors, FedEx, and many more. Sheila has also held senior positions with iCrossing, a leading search and digital marketing agency.[13]

Harry Jacobs—Harry Jacobs exploded the myth that great advertising could only be done in New York. Under Jacobs's leadership, the Martin Agency in Charlotte, Virginia, became a creative powerhouse for consumer as well as agricultural and other B2B products. Today, the agency works on national and international accounts such as Coke, Hanes, Mercedes-Benz, Seiko, UPS, and Wrangler, to name a few. The Martin Agency has also been an incubator for the nation's top creative talent, developing creative directors who achieved acclaim at Wieden + Kennedy, Wells Rich Greene, Fallon, DDB, and Chiat\Day. Upon retirement from the Martin Agency, Jacobs was a founding board member of one of the top creative schools in the country, the Adcenter at Virginia Commonwealth University.

Exercises

1. Spinning B2C to B2B

This exercise is all about finding the One Thing and linking it to strategy.

- Find several campaigns for major consumer packaged good or service brands with at least three ads. Online options, such as adsoftheworld.com, are great because you can download the ads.

- As a class, select one campaign for which the brand would have strong B2B opportunities.

- Write a copy platform or creative brief, based on the concept in the B2C ads. The trick is to make the strategy, evolving out of the B2C ads, equally relevant to B2B consumers. End with one sentence describing the overarching concept in the campaign—the One Thing.

- Now concept an ad that is consistent with the brand, but solves the problem of moving the brand through the B2B marketplace.

- Present your ad, sharing your rationale. It's great way to see a wide range of strategic interpretations.

2. Who's Your Target?

This is a great exercise to show how brand messaging shifts depending upon the audience.

- *Instructors:* Pick a classic service brand such as FedEx. Before class, write a positioning statement and provide a short list of features and services.

- *Instructors:* Before class, go to the library and pick up as many B2B publications as you have students. Get obscure pubs like *Pulp & Paper* or *Curator: The Museum Journal.* Pull from the broadest range possible. Slip each publication into its own envelope.

- *Instructors:* Introduce the brand and the strategic information. Tell the students they will each be writing a print ad, with 150–200 words, to run in a B2B publication.

- *Students:* Randomly select an envelope. The publication inside represents the target audience you are to reach, pitching FedEx's services. The ad will run in the same magazine.

- *Students:* Once the ads are complete, execute one other strategically conceived tactic based on what you learned about that industry.

- *Students:* Once both pieces are complete, present your work. You will be amazed at how different each approach will be, thus demonstrating the importance of understanding your B2B audience—any audience for that matter.

3. Let's Talk Business

Everyday students are surrounded by B2C ads. But what do you know about reaching the B2B target? Sometimes not enough. It's time to find out more about this demographic.

- Pick a national brand that is commonly carried at Walgreens, CVS, or another similar retailer.

- Do a SWOT (Strengths, Weaknesses, Opportunities, Threats) analysis of that brand. Then, as a class, and using your SWOTs, craft four questions that could help you understand the strengths, weaknesses, opportunities, and threats from the retailer's point of view.

- Next, go to the retail site and ask the manager the four questions.

- Bring the answers back to class and share them. As a class, look for patterns and insights.

- Taking what you have learned, create a promotion that will reignite retail engagement with the brand, while addressing the strengths, weaknesses, opportunities, and threats that you explored.

Visit www.sagepub.com/altstiel3e to access these additional learning tools

- Video Links
- Web Resources
- eFlashcards
- Web Quizzes

Chapter 18

Survival Guide

Landing Your First Job and Thriving

We designed this book as a "how to" guide to help you develop better creative work. Now we'd like to share some of our personal insights about how to break into the business, as we feature inspiring work by students and rising stars. We've also gathered some gems from some of the top names in our business, our fellow teachers, and creative recruiters to help you survive and thrive in the creative jungle. Gary Goldsmith, a former chief creative officer at Lowe New York, sums it up nicely: "They [students] are entering a business where the staffing is leaner and deadlines shorter than ever before. A business that has less and less time for the necessary teaching and mentoring that is required more than ever before. . . . The more those of us in teaching and in the business can do to increase their chances, the better."[1]

Three ingredients are crucial to making it in advertising creative. Talent. Persistence. Luck. Talent is essential. Persistence is crucial. Luck is the bonus you earn. So start laying the groundwork to get lucky and come out ahead of all the persistent people who are just as talented as you are. Janet Kestin and Nancy Vonk, former co–creative directors at Ogilvy in Toronto, left in late 2011 to form Swim, a training consultancy dedicated to training and nurturing creative staffers. Kestin and Vonk have been committed to mentoring junior creatives for a long time. Before Swim they launched a website dedicated to mentoring creatives—ihaveanidea.org. Kestin and Vonk have a column called "Ask Jancy" and have helped to build it into a powerhouse of information. Eleven years later it's the hub of who's who and what's what in advertising creative—and a site you need to bookmark.

How to Build Your Portfolio

This is a tough business. But as Ellen Steinberg, vice president and group creative director at McKinney in Durham, North Carolina, said, quoting Tom Hanks in *A League of Their Own,* "There's no crying in baseball!" There's no crying in advertising. It's business.[3] The time to start preparing for this business is now. Take the advice of Joyce King Thomas, chief creative officer

Words of Wisdom

"Go for face time with senior creative people at any shop that's of interest. Offer to buy a coffee or just pop in for 15 minutes to hear their perspective on what they look for in a young creative."[2]

Jancy (aka Janet Kestin and Nancy Vonk), cofounders of Swim; former co–creative directors, Ogilvy Toronto

at McCann New York: "Show your book every 6 months and never stop working on it."[4] How many items should be in your portfolio? Every creative director may have a different answer. The following is a compilation from dozens of creative professionals who have suffered through reviews of thousands of bad portfolios:

Inside a Junior Copywriter's Portfolio

- **Hard assignments** like consumer packaged goods where the only real difference is the quality of the advertising. As one creative director said, "Show me something I never would have thought of."

- **Complete campaigns** from multiple product categories with a combination of print, outdoor, nontraditional, web, TV, and radio. Make sure it all looks like a campaign. Show your unique creative perspective and in the process make yourself an asset that their agency can't live without.

- **Print ads** that clearly show concepting ability and always show a series. Demonstrate that you can extend your ideas.

- **Billboards** or **posters** that demonstrate exceptional creative and strategic thinking.

- **Long-copy ads** or **brochures** that show you actually can write copy.

- **Website** or **blogs** of substance. Show them you can write and maintain consistency across time and space.

- **Mobile** application ideas would be good too. Demonstrate that you can think about how to reach consumers anytime and anyplace.

- *Overall*, demonstrate that you are **great** at **concepts** and trainable as a writer and be ready to explain the strategy behind every piece in your book.

Inside a Junior Art Director or Designer's Portfolio

- **Logos** and **brand identity projects** including several examples across different product categories.

- **Complete campaigns** from multiple product categories with a combination of print, out-of-home, nontraditional, mobile, and web executions. Make sure it all looks like a campaign. Show your unique creative perspective and in the process make yourself an asset that their agency can't live without. Pay special attention to the layout, typography, and color.

- **Print ads** that clearly show concepting ability and always show a series. Demonstrate that you can extend your ideas.

- **Billboards** or **posters** that demonstrate exceptional creative and strategic thinking.

- **Nontraditional** to show that you can think conceptually and maximize every dollar.

- **Brochures** or other collateral pieces that show you actually can lay out different kinds of marketing tools.

- Overall, demonstrate that you have **good design sense** and superior concepting ability, you know design software, and you can be trained to create great-looking stuff. In short: Ideas. Ideas. Ideas.

What *Not* to Put in Your Book

- Anything that is predictable such as ads for hot sauce, condoms, and animal shelters. If the product calls for an obvious approach, don't bother putting it in your book.

- Brands with well-known advertising. Do you really think you have a better TV commercial than Bud Light or Apple?

- Too much television. Put your TV on your website. If nothing else it's an opportunity to drive them to your site. The truth is most entry-level people won't touch TV for a few years.

- Radio scripts. Your book should be a fast-moving visual delight. Scripts slow it down or interrupt the flow; besides, you've got them posted on your website.

- Creative briefs, creative strategy statements, and consumer profiles. It's assumed you know this. But be ready to verbally demonstrate your strategic brilliance.

- Sentimental favorites. Don't include a sample just because your ad ran in the school paper or your poster design was used by your Ad Club. A good concept that never saw the light of day is a much better option.

- Too much stuff. Half a dozen great samples are better than 20 or 30 mediocre ones. Interviewers don't have a lot of time. They can spot great ideas instantly. Always think "campaigns."

Breathe the fragrances of Catalonia

Pares Balta, a Spanish vineyard trying to break into the Italian market, was the perfect challenge for students in a cross-cultural summer creative program at Universitat Autònoma de Barcelona. Spanish creatives and a lone American teamed up to energize a group of Italian students. The result: great sensory-based advertising.

Maxine Paetro has written the ultimate book on portfolios—*How to Put Your Book Together and Get a Job in Advertising.* It's chock full of great advice from the author and some of the top names in the creative field. One of her portfolio strategies is to build a "killer sandwich." We have taken that basic idea and offer our own recipe:

- First entry in your book—the very best thing you've ever done. If you could put one thing in the book, this would be it.

- The last thing in your book—the second best thing you've ever done. Something so good it took a coin toss to move it to the back.

- Everything in between—first, think "campaigns" and be sure most of them have a nontraditional execution. Second, have examples across multiple product categories. You don't need a lot, but all of it needs to kick butt.

The student who created this billboard tweeted about it. That night she got a re-tweet from Rishi Tea. The next day Rishi asked to run it and offered her an internship. Liquid Zen, indeed.

Why put the best at the beginning and end? Psychologists say people remember the first and last thing they see (the theory of primacy and recency).

Pregnant or not pregnant? Rather than providing the obvious answer, this student-designed ad uses parallel construction to show the implications of both conditions.

How Should You Format Your Book?

If you can actually show your work in a one-on-one meeting, nothing beats a hands-on portfolio. However, it's expensive, and you will want to leave something behind. So it makes sense to prepare a few mini books. You can do more than one at a time, or you can customize them for each interview. The latter is best, but it's also the most time consuming. Mini books can be created at an office supply store or through an online service like Shutterfly. Don't forget the "killer sandwich" approach, and only put the best stuff in your mini book. Most recruiters prefer electronic. Just remember the book always comes first. You can also e-mail samples of your work by attaching JPEGs or building an instant-loading HTML e-mail page. But we don't recommend this unless the recruiter or HR people request it. Chances are it will end up in the junk mail folder. Your best bet is putting your work on your own website or posting it on sites dedicated to showing student work. If you can segment your work into categories, you have the opportunity to show more variety—your best six print ads, your best 10 photographs, your best three videos, and your best five logo designs. Whatever categories you decide on, keep the site alive by changing things up with new work. For a copywriter a well-concepted blog with great writing can also go a long way. And when it comes to promoting yourself use social media wisely. Twitter and Facebook will follow you forever. Every word that flies off your fingertips matters.

How to Write Your Cover Letter

Your résumé tells the basic facts of your academic and work career and, as we mentioned, probably should not be the place for wild flights of fancy. However, your cover letter can be the one place to demonstrate your writing ability and creativity. As with a cover letter for a product or service, you can follow the basic structure we described in Chapter 15. Except *you* are the product. What can you say about yourself that will get attention, stimulate interest, create a desire to know more about you, and ultimately generate action—an interview? One letter for an applicant started with "I knew I'd be the right person for this job when the toilet fell on my head." That got our attention! The letter went on to describe how an accident at Home Depot convinced the applicant that he should pursue a career in advertising instead of in a big-box store. You can find hundreds of websites that will help you craft a cover letter. Your college career office will also help you with this. Most of them give you a formula for a pure vanilla letter. So before you take the easy way out, think about the wants and needs of the customer—your potential employer. How do you meet those wants and needs? What do you bring to the table? Then figure out a creative yet professional way to present the features and benefits of the world's most unique product—you.

How to Write Your Résumé

Most creative directors or others who hire creative people demand a résumé from applicants. Too many aspiring creatives assume that this is the time to demonstrate all the creativity they can muster. So they put their names on bowling balls, bananas, toilet paper rolls, and a million other objects, in the hope that their unique résumé package will pull them out of the pack. The truth is no one wants to file a bowling ball, keep a banana in a drawer, or forward toilet paper to human resources. As cute as these gimmicks are, they usually won't help and, in most cases, will put you at the bottom of the pile.

War Story

Google TV: Ivan Cobenk

Logitech is a major manufacturer of computer peripherals like mice, keyboards, and other devices. While extremely successful in creating products that are omnipresent and essential to consumers' digital experiences, Logitech, the brand, was largely invisible.

Our task was to bring Logitech out of anonymity and establish them as an entertainment brand through the launch of a new product—the Logitech Revue With Google TV—a platform that integrates Chrome browser technology to bring shows, movies, web videos, and all the wealth of information Google provides right to your television.

Now imagine for a minute that you're the creative team on the other side of this brief. At first blush, it's not all that sexy: Create a 60-second product demonstration to explain this new technology. So we started thinking about what it means to infuse TV, a one-way medium, with the connective, informative, and interactive power of the Internet.

To illustrate that the Revue would delight even the geekiest fanboy, we chose Ivan Cobenk—a Kevin Bacon–obsessed superfan—and created an amusing demo of the Revue and its ability to instantly access all the Kevin Bacon–related information that Ivan could ever want.

In the spot, Ivan shows the viewer all of his favorite Kevin Bacon memorabilia including an oil painting that he's had commissioned of him and Kevin even though they've never actually met. We see him maneuver the Revue, sharing his favorite Kevin Bacon movies, shows, and YouTube clips. He fondly reminds us that this wife has warned him, "If I watch any more Kevin Bacon, I might actually turn into Kevin Bacon." At this point, Ivan innocently looks around and crosses his fingers in hopes that someday this actually happens.

It's at this point in the ad, during the final close-up, that it becomes clear that Ivan Cobenk is actually none other than Kevin Bacon himself.

The commercial was applauded widely on tech blogs and entertainment sites and got over 1.7 million views on YouTube within six weeks. It won awards in shows like Cannes, D&AD, Art Directors Club, Clio Awards, and the One Show. And, most importantly, Logitech began to emerge from obscurity.[8]

Margaret Johnson, executive creative director, associate partner, Goodby, Silverstein & Partners, goodbysilverstein .com

Here's what the vast majority of creative executives who hire entry-level writers and art directors are looking for:

- Keep it clean, easy to read, and simply designed. Designers may be able to show off a little, but applicants for writing jobs should stick to a basic design. Remember, the résumé is for identifying you. The portfolio and cover letter are where you can leap to the head of the line.

- Your name, address, phone number(s), and e-mail address are always at the top.

- Include your education, where you went to school, your major, relevant courses, or special programs such as study abroad. GPA doesn't matter—really.

- Sorry to tell you, but fraternity or sorority membership and athletic achievements aren't likely to wow them. So only add them if you have room on one page.

- What will wow them, beyond internships, is community service that leveraged your talents.

- The most crucial part of your résumé is your professional accomplishments or achievements and how they relate to the job for which you are applying. The key here is insight. Don't give a laundry list of tasks. Show them what you've learned. We think this is so important, we want to show you a couple of examples from one of our students who turned tasks into *insights* and landed jobs.

This aspiring art director used great creative thinkers from across the globe as the link between Pentel and consumers. She's now at Miami Ad School building a killer portfolio.

TOUR GUIDE, MARQUETTE UNIVERSITY

- Brand ambassador for Marquette University (task).

- *Learned how to read people* (insight).

ART CLUB EXECUTIVE, MARQUETTE UNIVERSITY

- Organized and promoted Student Fine Art Night at the Haggerty Art Museum (task).

- *Recognized that creativity takes courage* (insight).

What *Not* to Include

- A picture of yourself. The truth is some places will automatically toss your résumé due to nondiscrimination in hiring practices. Besides, they can always access your LinkedIn profile and Facebook page if they really want to see what you look like.

- Typos. One misspelled word or faulty punctuation will automatically send you to the bottom of the pile or to the circular file.

- References. You can put those with the cover letter. Hardly anyone checks references until you're much further along in the interview process. Besides, for entry-level positions, very few employers care if your professors or summer job boss liked you.

How to Get That Entry-Level Job

What Agencies Are Looking for in Entry-Level Creatives

CORE COMPETENCIES

- Digital. Digital. Digital. Understand the content of the digital world and the software that supports it.

- For art directors, mastery of the Adobe Suite is imperative.

- For copywriters, a working knowledge of the Adobe Suite is helpful. However, mastery of Word, WordPerfect, or other word-processing software and Excel gives you an advantage.

- For anyone in creative, PowerPoint, Prezi, and Keynote are important to be conversant with.

- Find, assemble, and organize background research.

- Understanding of agency structure, agency-client relationships, and the traditions of the advertising business.

- Understanding of basic marketing principles and key advertising terms.

- Mastery of the English language, including correct grammar and spelling.

- People skills. You cannot afford to hide behind your computer or text your way up the ladder. You need to be confident and comfortable when it comes to social interactions.

CREATIVE SKILLS

- Ideas. Ideas. Ideas. And having the ability to explain them.

- Combine headlines and graphics into a single idea.

- Connect reader/viewer/listener with advertiser.

- Create campaigns with elements that work independently and collectively.

- Ability to create ideas that live across multiple media platforms and within multiple touch points.

- Skills to execute ideas for multiple media platforms.
- Present ideas with confidence and enthusiasm.
- Ability to accept criticism and use it to improve.

PROFESSIONAL SKILLS

- Present. Present. Present. Be able to sell your ideas, as well as those of your teammates.
- Clear ethical boundaries that you are comfortable expressing.
- Leadership ability, including being a team player.
- Willingness to learn about clients' businesses.
- Strong work ethic and the willingness to check a bad attitude at the door.
- Confidence without arrogance.

How to Survive as an Entry-Level Creative

OK, you're in. Now the hard part starts. If you're lucky, you've had a few internships. If you're really lucky, you were a sponge, picking up survival tips along the way. In this age of entitlement, keep in mind that very few advertising students get their dream job.

And fewer still keep it for very long. Jean Grow and Sheri Broyles, of the University of North Texas, talked to some of the top creatives across the United States and Canada. Here's some of what they learned:[9]

SURVIVAL TIPS FOR EVERYONE

- Be a sponge.
- Don't have an attitude unless it's a good one.
- Have guts and balls.
- Don't be arrogant.
- Nothing matters but the quality of your work.
- Do more than you're asked to do.
- Know the digital landscape.
- Challenge the status quo.
- Be nice to everyone. Advertising's a small industry.

The copy tells a story that deserves an exclamation point, and that's exactly what Nano provides. This student ad won silver at the Milwaukee 99. Just a few years out of portfolio school the art director launched a web start-up.

- Be a squeaky wheel. Speak up.

- Have a sense of humor.

- Be brave.

- Be yourself. Don't try to sound like everyone else.

- Ask questions and observe your environment.

- Don't say no to any assignment.

- Keep your head down and get the work done.

- Understand brands and consumers, and never ignore the client.

- Hang around with account planners and others at the agency, not just creatives.

- Be aggressive about your career. Always be looking for your next move.

- Keep your eyes on the prize and you'll always be in demand.

- Let your work be the great equalizer.

- Learn to present your work.

- Find a mentor.

What Every Junior Woman Creative Needs to Know

There are a lot more men than women in creative departments—a lot. Women make up only about 15%–20% of all creatives.[11] Sites like adwomen.org and weareshesays.com are proactively seeking to engage in discussions about this issue, while looking for ways to solve the problem. On Twitter the World's Most Influential Female Creative Directors (WFCD) keeps the dialogue on this topic lively. But the reality is there simply aren't a lot of women out there. At the top it's even worse. To proactively address this, the first female creative directors conference—"The 3% Conference"—was hosted in San Francisco in September 2012.

While the number of women in creative may be small on the industry side, in the last 10 years we have noticed a shift in the enrollment of women in the courses we teach. Even without detailed research, we could safely say at least 60% of our advertising students are female, maybe more. Again, it raises the question: Why do men outnumber women by such wide margins in creative departments? While we can't give you a definitive answer on why men outnumber women, we can look to today's top creative women for some tips on how to survive and thrive. Our "Junior Women's Survival Guide" is a compilation of insights from women at the top of their game, from CEOs to creative directors.[12] They include Jeanie Caggiano, Leo Burnett; Nina DiSesa, McCann; Kara Goodrich, BBDO New York; Susan Hoffman, Wieden

+ Kennedy; Karen Howe, Due North; Margaret Johnson, Goodby, Silverstein & Partners; Janet Kestin, Swim; Maureen Shirreff, Ogilvy & Mather; Ellen Steinberg, McKinney & Silver; Linda Kaplan Thaler, Kaplan Thaler Group; Nancy Vonk, Swim; and Christina Yu, Lowe Roche. Here's to "making yourself known."

JUNIOR WOMEN'S SURVIVAL GUIDE

- Take risks.

- Hang in there.

- Don't limit yourself.

- When a man gets a compliment, he says, "Thank you." Learn those two words.

- Don't be a girly girl.

- Use your instincts about women as consumers.

- Don't allow yourself to be pigeonholed in the Pink Ghetto ("women's" products).

- Don't ignore sexism if it exists. Confront it. It won't go away on its own.

- Use your emotional buttons to persuade.

- Learn from men—don't resent them.

- Don't let yourself be intimidated.

- Look for mentors and network—especially with other women.

- Work really hard while you don't have kids.

- Enjoy the guys, and if you can't stand the heat, get out of the kitchen.

- Make your book so good no one notices you're a woman.[14]

Words of Wisdom

"Write for yourself. Never write for your creative director. Neither of you will be happy with the result."[13]

Jim Durfee, copywriter and founding partner, Carl Ally agency

How to Talk the Talk

Here are a few basic acronyms you can throw around and that'll make you look like a genius. While you may get people to nod knowingly when you sprinkle these into your conversations, we suggest that you understand what they mean before you have to explain them in a client meeting.

AAAA (known as the "4As")—American Association of Advertising Agencies

ABC—Audit Bureau of Circulations

AIDA—Attention, Interest, Desire, and Action

ANA—Association of National Advertisers

AQH—Average Quarter Hour audience

Rising Star

Breaking Family Traditions

I was going to keep family traditions and become a doctor, but unfortunately chemistry and physics was never my strong side and I didn't get into medical school. I had one year off and no idea what to do with myself. By accident I found an announcement for a one-year school: Organisation of Advertising. It wasn't exactly advertising school and I didn't find out much about advertising, but I did discover I'm creative and I could be a copywriter. In the meantime I changed my college major to psychology. After one year of studying psychology I knew it is not what I want to do and I applied for internship at BTL, a local ad agency.

As every lucky intern I started packing direct mail. But from time to time I was given briefs. After six months I earned my place and a computer in a creative department. I was still studying psychology at college, knowing the major was not right, but a college degree was. So I worked part-time for two years. I was lucky that a friend of a friend, Michael Heidtman, an American copywriter with 30 years of experience, came to live in Poland. Hanging around him was the best advertising and English school I could imagine. We spent hours talking about ideas. During vacations from studying I was interning at TBWA and Ogilvy in Warsaw. After graduating I got my first full-time job at Euro RSCG 4D. After more than one year I decided to look for a job abroad. In the meantime I was regularly reading the blog by Robin Stam—a very cool copywriter who liked my story and my book (portfolio). He showed it to his creative director at Duval Guillaume. Unfortunately his CD wasn't interested but his former art director, Yigit Unan, a Miami Ad School graduate and ex–Duval Guillaume employee, was. So Yigit suggested maybe we could become a team and look for a job together. As it was a time of financial crisis we could only find a job in Poland. We ended up at Brain, a local Polish agency. After one year working there we switched to Leo Burnett. Working with Yigit was like another ad school for me. We are not a team anymore, and for me it's time to apply for a job abroad. Because Polish advertising really sucks and my dreams won't come true here.

Someone once said, "An advertising career is not a sprint. It's a marathon." In my case it has been a long marathon, and I'm an ad turtle. Slowly getting closer to my dreams.

My advice: If you want a shorter way, don't start your ad career in Poland. Go to portfolio school.[15]

Anna Gadecka, copywriter, Leo Burnett, Warsaw, Poland, cargocollective.com/ adturtle

B2C—Business-to-Consumer, as opposed to B2B (Business-to-Business)

BDI—Brand Development Index

CDI—Category Development Index

CMS—Content Management System

CMYK—Cyan Magenta Yellow Black (*Black* is represented as *K* so it's not confused with *Blue*)

CPG—Consumer Packaged Goods

CPM—Cost Per Thousand (*M* stands for the Latin word for "thousand")

CPP—Cost Per Point

CRM—Customer Retention (or Relationship) Management

CTR—Click-Through Rate

DMA—Designated Market Areas (not to be confused with the DMA, which stands for Direct Marketing Association)

DVE—Digital Video Effects

FSI—Free-Standing Insert

GRP—Gross Rating Point

HD—High Definition

HTML—Hypertext Markup Language

HUT—Households Using Television

IGA—In-Game Advertising

IMC—Integrated Marketing Communications

ITV—Interactive TV

LTCV or LTV—Lifetime Customer Value

MIS—Marketing Information System

PLA—Program-Length Advertisement (infomercial)

PM—Push Money (also known as "spiff")

PMS—Pantone Matching System

POP—Point of Purchase (also called POS—Point of Sale)

PURL—Personalized Uniform Resource Locator (personalized domain name)

RFM—Recency, Frequency, Monetary

RGB—Red Green Blue

ROP—Run of Paper or Run on Press

ROS—Run of Station

RSS—Really Simple Syndication

SAU—Standard Advertising Unit

SEM—Search Engine Marketing

SEO—Search Engine Optimization

SRDS—Standard Rate and Date Service

SWOT analysis—Strengths, Weaknesses, Opportunities, and Threats

TAP—Total Audience Plan

This concept-driven ad from an art direction student at Miami Ad School helped land her a job at Mother in New York.

TVHH—Television Households

UPC—Universal Product Code

USP—Unique Selling Proposition (or sometimes Unique Story Proposition)

VALS—Values and Lifestyle System

VNR—Video News Release

VO—Voice-Over

How to Sell Your Work

In Chapter 1, we said one role of creatives is selling their ideas to the client. You could opt to just slide your ideas under the client's door and run away, hoping the client will like them. However, in selling your ideas, you're also selling yourself, ensuring gainful employment, and building some very valuable self-esteem. People learn a fear of public speaking in kindergarten. Most people, even gifted public speakers, never get over that naked fear of standing in front of an audience. The difference is that gifted public speakers have the ability to channel that fear into positive energy.

At the risk of sounding like an ad for Toastmasters: The ability to present your ideas in public is a skill you'll use all your life, whether you're an advertising executive or just offering a toast at a wedding. While you may dread presenting your work to your peers or outside reviewers, without solid presentation skills your best idea will die before it even gets past your creative director.

Here are 10 tips offered to students competing in the National Student Advertising Competition sponsored each year by the American Advertising Federation. While they apply to a high-level formal new-business pitch, most of the tips work for informal presentations as well.

It's a jungle up there.

REMINGTON
Nose-Hair Clipper

Keep it simple. The student who designed this billboard gets it! The symmetry between headline and visual is clear and simple.

1. **Start with an idea.** Tell how that idea relates to your strategy and tactical recommendations. Keep using that idea throughout your presentation, and come back to it at the end. Tell 'em what you're gonna tell 'em, sell 'em, and then tell 'em what you told 'em.

2. **If you have a theme, use it early and often.** Weave it through your presentation. If you use a stunt or a gimmick, make sure it fits. It should complement your theme and recommendations. Don't use a gimmick just to be different; rather, focus on the theme.

3. **Remember, the first minutes of your presentation are critical.** This is when you set the tone of your presentation. The introduction grabs attention. It should instantly engage the audience.

4. **Your insight of the target audience will drive your presentation.** It's very simple—who are you talking to/what will you tell them/how will you deliver the message/how do you know it will work?

5. **Don't memorize.** Know your material and speak from the heart, not from memory. And above all, don't read from note cards. If you need note cards, sneak a peek before you begin speaking.

6. **Eye contact is important.** Use "eye bursts," where you look at an individual audience member for two to three seconds at a time. Find the "head nodders"—people who are listening and agreeing with you. (These should be your nonpresenting teammates.) They'll give you confidence.

7. **Aim for a tone that's confident but humble.** In other words, be confident and enthusiastic but also self-effacing when necessary. Don't come across as a know-it-all. Refer to your research as the basis for your opinions rather than your superior intelligence. Don't be afraid to use a little humor, if it can be naturally worked into the presentation. You should not be deadly earnest or too flippant.

8. **Don't be a slave to your graphics or technology.** PowerPoint, Prezi, or Keynote should highlight the key concepts in your verbal presentation, but you still need to actually present the information. Don't read from your slides, and keep them simple. If you have a lot to say, use more slides. Never apologize for poor-quality visuals, video, or audio. All anyone will hear is that you didn't care enough to give it your best effort.

9. **Get technical help to set up.** If you're not confident of your technical ability, make sure you have someone who is an expert at setting up the equipment.

10. **Ask for the business.** You're not there to just entertain them. You're there to land the business—or win the competition.

How to Make It Memorable

You have to find the right blend of entertainment and serious business information. Here are some methods others have used to open up their presentations:

Tell a story. Every brand has a story. Every consumer has a profile. Every marketer has an inspiration. Discover the story behind the product and the people who buy it—or need to buy it—and use it to open your presentation.

Ask a question. One winning presentation opened with "Your house is burning down. Your family is safe, but you only have time to get one possession from your house. What would it be?" Or more generically, "What's the most important thing in your life?"

Words of Wisdom

"At the end of a presentation, it's not your brilliant strategy or clever ideas that win the business. It really depends on whether the client thinks you're the kind of people they want to hang around with."[17]

John Melamed, executive vice president, Cramer-Krasselt

Start with a video. If you use a video, it should be short and crisply edited, with a clear message. Remember, this sets the tone for the whole presentation.

Make a series of statements. Each team member states an opinion or a misconception about the client or their products. Follow with "That's what people told us . . . and this is how we plan to change their minds."

Bring your target audience to life. A day in the life. "Let me introduce you to . . . [name of people]." Or some other compelling way to draw the audience in.

This student portrayed a traditional symbol of Judaism in a monumental way. Many students put public service ads in their book, but few create something truly different. His efforts to build a portfolio that differentiated him from his competitors paid off handsomely when he landed a copywriting position right out of school.

How to Handle Questions

Sometimes the outcome of a presentation depends more on how you defend your work than on the quality of the work itself. Here are a few tips for dealing with questions. Remember, how you answer is just as important as what you say.

Each question is an opportunity. Don't take it as a criticism of your effort. Sometimes reviewers just want to see how you defend your work. If you get too defensive, vague, or impatient, your attitude may turn them off. (They are much more sensitive to this than you may realize.)

Answer the question! You should be able to explain calmly and confidently why you did what you did. Don't be a politician. (If you can't defend what you did, then you made the wrong decisions.) Prepare for them. Try to come up with the toughest possible questions.

Pay attention to your tone of voice. Just like your physical motions, your tone of voice says a lot about you. Be sure to answer questions in a strong, consistent tone. Don't act offended, impatient, or flustered.

Avoid wavering. Talking too softly, mumbling, or speaking too quickly won't win them over.

You are too close to your work. That's why it's hard for you to understand why someone doesn't get it. Think about the early phases of your planning. What

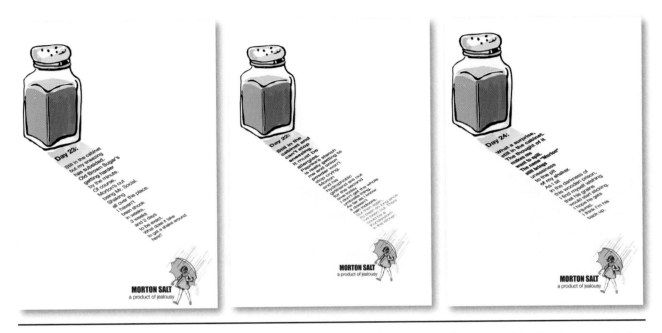

What can you say about Morton Salt that hasn't been said? This student used the point of view of the lonely pepper shaker that sits neglected on the shelf while the more popular Morton is always out and about.

questions did you ask yourself? Why did you do things that way? Those are some of the questions others will also have.

Get an outsider's opinion. Have them review your book and presentation and invite their questions and comments. Don't be surprised if people are not as crazy about your ideas as you are. Encourage constructive criticism. It's good practice for handling reviewers.

How to Think on Your Feet

Take a deep breath. Think for a second and then begin to answer. This will help calm your nerves and will give you the opportunity to "look before you leap" when it comes to answering important questions.

Repeat the question. You can always ask the client or reviewer to clarify a part of it. This gives you and your teammates more time to think about an answer.

Finish your answer. Don't taper off and leave a question unanswered. Your teammates will instinctively jump in to finish your sentence and try to bail you out.

Don't act surprised. If a question comes out of left field, try to retain your composure because it may seem very logical to the reviewer. For example, if someone asks you why you didn't do something, you could say, "We looked into that, but our research indicated that some other approaches would work better" or "We studied a lot of ways to do this and found this was the most cost-efficient way to achieve our objectives."

Forget "That's a good question." That's code for "We never thought of that and don't have the answer."

Words of Wisdom

"The secret is to keep listening to that wee, small voice—and don't ever be afraid of getting your hands dirty."[19]

Leo Burnett, founder,
Leo Burnett

A Peruvian creative team won a Young Lion at Cannes for this work. The ad simply and graphically depicts how helping a single young girl rise out poverty can positively impact her family for generations to come. They went on to win another Young Lion the following year.

Don't change the subject. Think for a second and then answer the question to the best of your ability. If you sense the reviewer is not satisfied, simply ask, "Did I answer your question?"

Don't argue. Don't cave in. You had reasons for making these decisions. The reviewers don't necessarily disagree, but they want to see how you defend your work.

How to Get That Next Great Job

Young creative people often ask about job hopping. They're worried that changing jobs too many times will limit their future employability. In many industries that's a concern. But in the ad business, jumping from agency to agency is the norm. However, honor any commitments you've made and try to stay at least one or two years before you start looking. Just don't burn any bridges when you leave. You might have the opportunity to come back to a former employer in a few years for even more money. Advertising is a small world, and the "get along" factor is almost as important as talent. In the end, you will be judged on how well coworkers, bosses, and especially clients like you. That may very well determine how much you're really worth. And remember—never stop working on your portfolio.

How to Get More Information

We've compiled a list of trade publications and creative magazines, books, and digital resources from websites to blogs to Twitter feeds. We hope they will help you understand more about the creative side of the business. Never forget—this is only the beginning of a lifetime of learning.

Trade Publications and Creative Magazines

- *Advertising Age*—for decades *Ad Age* has been *the* authoritative voice of the industry. If you read one magazine about advertising, this is it.

- *Adweek*—edited for ad agency executives with the inside stories on creativity, client–agency relationships, and successful global advertising strategies.

- *CMYK*—where aspiring creatives showcase their talents and where creative directors recruit students and recent graduates.

- *Communication Arts*—calls itself the world's most inspiring magazine, and who can argue with that, given that it's the first book nearly every creative looks to for ideas in concepts, design, and copywriting excellence for virtually every phase of our business?

- *Creativity*—a monthly magazine, published by *Ad Age,* covering all things creative in advertising and design.

Books

Back to Basics

Design, Form, and Chaos by Paul Rand

Eats, Shoots & Leaves: The Zero Tolerance Approach to Punctuation by Lynne Truss

Flow: The Psychology of Optimal Experience by Mihaly Csikszentmihalyi

Idea Industry: How to Crack the Advertising Career Code by Brett Robbs & Deborah Morrison

Creative Process

The Do-It-Yourself Lobotomy: Open Your Mind to Greater Creative Thinking by Tom Monahan

Hey Whipple, Squeeze This: A Guide to Creating Great Advertising by Luke Sullivan

How to Be an Explorer of the World: Portable Life Museum by Keri Smith

Unstuck: A Tool for Yourself, Your Team, and Your World by Keith Yamashita & Sandra Spataro

Controlling Your Career

The Adventures of Johnny Bunko: The Last Career Guide You'll Ever Need by Daniel Pink

How to Put Your Book Together and Get a Job in Advertising by Maxine Paetro

Pick Me: Breaking Into Advertising and Staying There by Nancy Vonk and Janet Kestin

Radical Careering: 100 Truths to Jumpstart Your Job, Your Career, and Your Life by Sally Hogshead

History

Ad Women: How They Impact What We Need, Want, and Buy by Juliann Sivulka

A History of Advertising by Stéphane Pincas & Mark Loiseau

Ogilvy on Advertising by David Ogilvy

Soap, Sex, and Cigarettes: A Cultural History of American Advertising by Juliann Sivulka

Marketing and Strategy

Brand Relevance: Making Competitors Irrelevant by David Aaker

Brand Sense: Sensory Secrets Behind the Stuff We Buy by Martin Lindstrom

Killing Giants: 10 Strategies to Topple the Goliath in Your Industry by Stephen Denny

Look at More: A Proven Approach to Innovation, Growth, and Change by Andy Stefanovich

Media Influence

Groundswell: Winning in a World Transformed by Social Technologies by Charlene Li & Josh Bernoff

Social Boom! How to Master Business Social Media . . . and Grind Your Competition Into the Dirt by Jeffery Gitomer

Users, Not Customers: Who Really Determines the Success of Your Business by Aaron Shapiro

ZMOT: Winning the Zero Moment of Truth by Jim Lecinski

Digital Resources

Branded Thinking

brandrepublic.com	@MediaPost
brandtags.net	@stuartenyt
digitalbuzzblog.com	@tastytruth
sethgodin.com	@trendwatching

Career Development

fastcompany.com	@bogusky
ihaveanidea.org	@the99percent
radicalcareering.com	@WFCD

Creative Inspiration

adverbox.com	@behance
howdesign.com	@BreakingCopy
mashable.com	@InspirationRoom
moderncopywriter.com	@leeclowsbeard

Get Smart

changethis.com	@BoingBoing
freakonomics.com	@CreativeReview
ted.com	@GOOD
visualthesaurus.com	@Mediabistro

Portfolio Schools

brainco.org
brandcenter.vcu.edu
creativecircus.edu
miamiadschool.com
portfoliocenter.edu

Who's Who?

Kate Lummus—Kate Lummus is an adventurous spirit. She interned on Capitol Hill in college and grew up to be a traveler, living on six continents before she hit high school. Today she considers herself a Texan living in New York. As an art director, Kate's a big believer in taking in everything she can get her hands on and head around. As for the ideas, Kate believes that while the brief tries to put things together, the ideas live in her head. "Somewhere," as she likes to say. She began her career at Atmosphere BBDO working on FedEx online and the merger of Cingular and AT&T. She moved on to Publicis Modem working on everything from luxury goods to packaged goods. And then onto McCann New York, where the chief creative officer, speaking of working with her, simply said, "I love Kate." Not letting any grass grow under her feet she's now at mcgarrybowen.[20]

Donna Speciale—Donna Speciale is regarded as one of the most outstanding thinkers in the media agency space. As president of investment and activation and agency operations at MediaVest, Speciale counted Coca-Cola, Kraft, Mars, Procter & Gamble, and Walmart among her clients and was named Advertising Women of New York's 2010 Advertising Woman of the Year. In 2012, she took the top ad sales post at Turner Broadcasting System's entertainment division. She exemplifies her own philosophy, "Those with the most agility and fearlessness win in the industry today."[21]

Mark Zuckerberg—Mark Zuckerberg cofounded Facebook with three Harvard classmates in 2004. Today advertising is about 83% of Facebook's revenue, though Zuckerberg says advertising revenue was never his goal. Rather, he says, Facebook as an expression of a users-first philosophy. "These days I think more and more people want to use services from companies that believe in something beyond simply maximizing profits."[22] In May 2012 Zuckerberg took the company, valued at $28 billion, public. Not only did he exceed Wall Street's expectations in value, but he arranged to keep a larger percentage of control in his public company than Bill Gates had when Microsoft went public. Not bad for a 28-year-old college dropout. Zuckerberg was born in 1984 and named *Time* magazine's "Person of the Year" in 2011. He is the youngest billionaire in the world, as well as the youngest attendee at the Davos, Switzerland, World Economic Forum in 2012.

Omar Sotomayor and Gastón Soto Denegri—Omar Sotomayor and Gastón Soto Denegri are two young Peruvian creatives skyrocketing to the top. Copywriter Sotomayor and art director Soto Denegri won the Young Lions Competition at Cannes two years in a row. In 2010 they won a Young Lion for their work for a nonprofit charity dedicated to helping raise girls out of poverty. You saw their work earlier in the chapter. Back then they were working at Circus in Lima, Peru. In 2011 they won their second Young Lion with a TV spot they concepted and created in 24 hours. Today the creative duo is in Chicago creating great work at Lápiz, Leo Burnett's Hispanic advertising agency.[23]

Words of Wisdom

Our parting thoughts come from Charles Hall, an African American copywriter who early in his career worked at Nike and later taught at VCU Brandcenter. While some of it applies specifically to people of color, it's good advice for anyone starting out:

to the blacks browns reds and yellows periwinkles teals and fuchsias

if you want to be in advertising, there is one thing to remember.

don't be afraid.

of hard work, rejection, racism, responsibility, sexism.

don't be afraid of being the only one in the room.

don't be afraid to ask questions. find answers. listen. hear. Trust.

don't be afraid to follow. don't be afraid to lead.

don't be afraid to learn. to grow. to mature. to change.

don't be afraid to try. to fail. to try again. fail again. try again and fail again.

don't be afraid to ask for help.

don't be afraid to be smart. clever. witty. funky. hard. street. elegant. beautiful. you.

don't be afraid to be fired.

don't be afraid when you hear the word nigger.

don't be afraid to remind them that right after the black jokes come the jewish jokes the polish jokes and the fat jokes.

don't be afraid to master the craft. to master the game.

don't be afraid when they don't understand your accent, dialect, or slang. your heroes, your sex symbols. your style. your music. your people. your culture. your you.

don't be afraid to take criticism.

don't be afraid to be wrong. to be right.

don't be afraid to speak your mind. stand up for what you believe and pay the consequences.

don't be afraid to be a team player.

don't be afraid to be the peon. the rookie. the junior. the helper. the pair of hands. the intern. the student.

don't be afraid to not be the victim. don't be afraid to not take it personally. don't be afraid to call a spade a spade.

don't be afraid to have a personality. an opinion. a point of view. a perspective. an objective. a positive attitude.

don't be afraid of those who are threatened by your presence. or feel you don't belong. or those who need you to fail for them to succeed.

don't be afraid to understand the difference between racism and insecurity. between racism and power. between sexism and chauvinism.

don't be afraid to forgive. to apologize. to be humble.

don't be afraid to surrender. to win. to lose. to fight.

don't be afraid of titles, awards. salaries. egos. offices. windows. ponytails. clothes. jewelry. degrees, backgrounds. lifestyles. cars. beach houses.

don't be afraid to compete.

don't be afraid of not being popular.

don't be afraid to work weekends. holidays. birthdays. sick days. personal days.

don't be afraid to work twice as hard. twice as long. twice as good.

don't be afraid to get more out of this business than this business ever intended on giving.

p.s. and under no circumstances whatsoever are you to be intimidated. because some will try.[24]

Exercises

With these final exercises we wish you well on your professional journey.

1. Creative Think Tank

- Find a group of fellow creatives and have a dedicated meeting time every week.

- Carve out two or three hours each week dedicated to going on a creative hunting expedition. Be committed to coming away with at least three new creative concepts, ideas, or campaigns that rock your world.

- Now use your weekly meeting as a creative think tank. Share the new ideas you find and critique each other's work. And if you can find a place dedicated to this process, leave things behind. Create an artifact room.

- Chances are you'll become friends and allies for life.

2. Improving on Schedule

- Find an industry mentor, someone you trust and who will be brutally honest.

- Make a commitment to seeing them regularly. No excuses.

- Show them new and revised work every time you meet. Listen to them. Trust them.

- One day, return the favor.

3. Do Nothing

- Do nothing related to advertising for an entire day.

- Do this with regularity, even if infrequently.

- Rest and replenish your creative spirit.

Visit www.sagepub.com/altstiel3e to access these additional learning tools

- Video Links
- Web Resources

- eFlashcards
- Web Quizzes

Copy Platform (Creative Strategy Statement)

Product (Service) _____

The Product (or Service)

A. Primary features/benefits in order of importance (remember to ask "So what?")

Features   Benefits

1. _____   1. _____

2. _____   2. _____

3. _____   3. _____

4. _____   4. _____

B. Exclusive or unique product (service) attributes

_____

C. Can product claims be substantiated?

_____

D. Is the parent company name important? _____ Why?

_____

E. Brand value: High status _____ Low status _____ No brand image _____

The Consumer

A. Demographics (age, sex, education, income, occupation, geographic distribution)

_____

_____

_____

B. Psychographics (lifestyle, attitude, personality traits, buying patterns)

_____

_____

_____

C. Needs fulfilled by buying this product or service

_____

_____

_____

The Marketplace

A. Major competitors/rank in market/market share

1. _____ / _____ / _____

2. _____ / _____ / _____

3. _____ / _____ / _____

B. Competitive advantage/disadvantage of product (service)

Competitor   Our advantage (disadvantage)

_____   _____

_____   _____

_____   _____

C. Position of product (service in market)
Parity product (no perceived competitive advantage) _____

_____

New product category (first of its kind) _____

_____

Significant improvement over similar products _____

_____

D. Pricing position (compared to competition)
Premium priced _____ Comparably priced _____ Low priced _____

Creative Strategy

A. The "One Thing": If you could say one thing about this product or service:

_____

_____

_____

B. Significant facts or statistics about the product, consumer, or market

_____

_____

_____

Copyediting and Proofreading Symbols

Begin paragraph	¶	Years ago we invested in a small Seattle-based coffee…
Set in italics		Isn't it interesting how the English countryside… (ital)
Set in caps		Try the hotpockets. they're breathtaking. (cap)
Set in lowercase		Is it an Evil Petting Zoo? (lc)
Insert period, comma		No, Mr. Powers, I expect you to…. ⊙ / ˀ
Insert question mark		Why won't you die. ^ ?
Insert apostrophe		It got weird, didn't it? ˀ
Insert hyphen		Do you like your quasifuturistic outfits? =
Insert quotes		When a problem comes along, you must zip it. ˇˀ / ˇˀ
Put in space		Are they angry seabass? #
Close up		Crikey! I've lost my mojo. ◡
Set in boldface		I'm from Holland. Isn't that weird? (bf)
Insert word		He kind of looks like baby. ^ a
Delete word		No, this is me in a a nutshell. ϱ
Delete and close up		Moove over rover. This chick is taking over.
Leave as it was		A trillion is more than a billion… stet
Transpose		I call it the Parsons Allen Project. (tr)
Spell out word		Who does number 2 work for? (sp)
Copy on next page		more
End of copy		### or —30—

Radio Production Terms

AFTRA American Federation of Television and Radio Artists, one of the two main unions for voice talent

ANNCR Announcer

Board Electronic control panel for recording, mixing, and editing

Boom mike Microphone on long extension, over announcer's head

Buyout Total payment to talent for one-time use, as opposed to residual payments

Cans Slang for announcer's headphones

Compression Electronically removing dead air between words

DAT Digital Audio Tape

Dead air No sound between words or sound effects

Demo Demonstration recording for reviewing or auditioning, not meant for airing

Donut Nonvocal segment of music or sound that allows an announcer to read copy over it

Double donut Usually a commercial with a musical intro, an announcer segment, a musical middle, an announcer segment, and a musical close

Fade Gradually reduce (fade out) or increase (fade up) volume

Flight Time frame that commercial runs

In Introduce music or effect

Out Music or effect is deleted abruptly

Nonlinear Segments recorded out of sequence and assembled digitally

Phone patch Review recording over phone lines instead of in the studio

PD Public domain (music with no royalty fees, as in classical music)

Punch in Insert re-recorded segment into commercial to replace a segment

P&W Pension and Welfare, additional payments made to SAG/AFTRA talent

Quarter track   Analog recording tape with 4 channels (2 each direction)

Residual   Payments made to talent after the initial run of the commercial

Reverb   Reverberation, an echo-like effect

SAG   Screen Actors Guild, one of the two main unions for voice talent

Sample   Digital recording and re-creation of music or sound effect

Segue   Gradually lead into a new segment of a commercial

SFX   Sound effects

Slice of life   Simulated real-world situation, usually using dialogue

Spot   Commercial

Spot market   A local media buy rather than network

Stage whisper   Whisper that's loud enough to be easily heard and understood

Stinger   Musical effect to provide emphasis, usually at the end of a jingle

Swell   Expansion of copy to fit a specific segment, for example translation of English to Spanish usually accounts for a 20% swell due to the increase in words

Tag   End of a commercial, usually with the name of store locations, hours, or other information

Talent   Announcer, singers, or musician in a commercial

Take   Reading of a segment of copy at one time; each reading is a take, with most commercials involving several takes

Talk back   The button an engineer or producer uses to communicate with talent in an isolated booth

Under   Reduce the volume of music or an effect so you can hear the announcer

Up   Raise the volume of music or an effect

Voice of God   Conversion with someone "off camera," usually with an effect such as an echo

White noise   Undefined noise such as static

TV and Video Production Terms

Accelerated montage: A sequence edited into progressively shorter shots to create a mood of tension and excitement.

Ambient light: The natural light surrounding the subject, usually understood to be soft.

Aspect ratio: The ratio of the width to the height of the film or television image. The formerly standard Academy aperture is 1.33:1. Wide-screen ratios vary. In Europe 1.66:1 is most common; in the United States, 1.85:1. Anamorphic processes such as CinemaScope and Panavision are even wider (2.00:1 to 2.55:1).

Asynchronous sound: Sound thatdoes not operate in unison with the image. Sound belonging to a particular scene thatis heard while the images of the previous scene are still on screen, or continue over a following scene. Also: Diegetic sound whose source cannot be seen on screen, or sound unintentionally out of sync with the image track.

Backlighting: The main source of light is behind the subject, silhouetting it, and directed toward the camera.

Bird's-eye shot(sometimes called an **Overhead shot**):Shot from directly overhead; that is, looking down on the subject.

Blue screen (also called **Green screen** or **Chroma key**): Shooting a subject in front of a blue or green background so that the image can be superimposed over another background. The camera can be adjusted not to pick up blue or green so, in effect, you have a blocked-out image on clear background.

Boom: A traveling arm for suspending a microphone above the actors and outside the frame. See also **Crane**.

Bridge: A passage linking two scenes either by continuing music across the transition or by beginning the sound (including dialogue or music) of the next scene over images of the previous scene (aka "sound advance").A very common phenomenon in contemporary cinema.

Bridging shot: A shot used to cover a jump in time or place or other discontinual changes.

Continuity editing: Technique whereby shots are arranged in sequence to create the illusion of a credible chronological narrative. Often contrasted with **Montage editing**.

Crane: A mechanical arm-like trolley used to move a camera through space above the ground or to position it at a place in the air. A **crane shot** allows the camera to vary distance, angle, and height during the shot (aka **Boom** shot).

Crosscutting: Intermingling the shots of two or more scenes to suggest **Parallel action**.

Cutaway: A shot inserted in a scene to show action at another location, usually brief, and most often used to cover breaks in the main take, as in television and documentary interviews. Also used to provide comment on the action, for example by cutting away from scenes of explicit sex or extreme violence.

Day for night: The practice of using filters to shoot night scenes during the day.

Depth of field: The range of distances from the camera at which the subject is acceptably sharp.

Detail shot: Usually more magnified than a close-up. A shot of a hand, an eye, a mouth, or a subject of similar detail.

Drive-by shot: View of person, object, or place from a camera located on a moving vehicle as it passes by.

Dub: [1] To rerecord dialogue in a language other than the original. [2] To record dialogue in a specially equipped studio after the film has been shot.

Dupe: [1] To print a duplicate negative from a positive print. Also, to print a duplicate reversal print. [2] A print made in this manner.

Establishing shot: Generally a long shot that shows the audience the general location of the scene that follows, often providing essential information and orienting the viewer.

Fast motion: Also called *accelerated motion.* The film is shot at less than 24 frames per second so that when it is projected at the normal speed actions appear to move much faster. The camera is undercranked. Often useful for comic effect.

Final cut: The film in its final state, as opposed to **Rough cut**.

Flashback: A scene or sequence (sometimes an entire film) that is inserted into a scene in "present" time and that deals with the past. The flashback is the past tense of film.

Flash forward: On the model of **Flashback**, scenes or shots of future time; the future tense of film.

Flash frame: A shot of only a few frames in duration, sometimes a single frame, which can just barely be perceived by the audience.

Focus pull: To pull focus during a shot in order to follow a subject as it moves away from or toward the camera.

Follow focus: To pull focus during a shot in order to follow a subject as it moves away from or toward the camera.

Follow shot: A tracking shot or zoom, which follows the subject as it moves.

Frame: [1] Any single image on the film. [2] The size and shape of the image on the film, or on the screen when projected. [3] The compositional unit of film design.

Freeze frame: A freeze shot, which is achieved by printing a single frame many times in succession to give the illusion of a still photograph when projected.

FX: Normal abbreviation of "effects." See **SFX**.

Gaffer: Chief electrician, responsible to the director of photography, who is responsible for all major electrical installations on the set, including lighting and power.

High key: A type of lighting arrangement in which the **Key light** is very bright, often producing shadows.

Intercutting: Same as **Parallel editing**;that is, the cutting between different narrative strands of a film intended to be taken as happening simultaneously.

Key light: The main light on a subject. Usually placed at a 45° angle to the camera-subject axis.

Mask: Shield placed in front of the camera lens to change the shape of the image. Often used as POV (point of view) shots (e.g., looking through binoculars or a keyhole).

Master shot: A long take of an entire scene, generally a relatively long shot that facilitates the assembly of component closer shots and details. The editor can always fall back on the master shot; consequently it is also called a *cover shot*.

Match cut: Cut in which the two shots joined are linked by visual, aural, or metaphorical parallelism. Famous example: At the end of *North by Northwest*, Cary Grant is pulling Eva MarieSaint up the cliff of Mount Rushmore; match cut to Grant pulling her up to a Pullman bunk. Do not confuse with *jump cut*, which usually happens within the same scene. In this case the framing within the same scene changes, dramatically jarring to the eye.

Montage editing: Technique of arranging shots in sequence to create connotations and associations rather than a standard chronologically unfolding narrative (see **Continuity editing**).

Parallel action(also called **parallel montage**):A device of narrative in which two scenes are observed in parallel by **Crosscutting**.

Parallel editing: Narrative construction **Crosscutting** between two or more lines of action that are supposed to be occurring simultaneously. Usually restricted to particular sequences in a film,**Crosscutting** can also occur between lines of action that are thematically related rather than simultaneous.

Postproduction: The increasingly complex stage in the production of a film thattakes place after shooting has been completed and involves editing, the addition of titles, and the creation of special effects and the final soundtrack, including dubbing and mixing.

Preproduction: Phase of film production following the securing of financial backing but preceding shooting. It includes work on the script, casting, hiring crews, finding locations, constructing sets, drawing up schedules, arranging catering, and so on.

Reaction shot: A shot that cuts away from the main scene or speaker in order to show a character's reaction to it.

Rough cut: The first assembly of a film, prepared by the editor from the selected takes, which are joined in the order planned in the script. Finer points of timing and montage are left to a later stage.

SFX: Abbreviation for special effects, which can be anything from optical to mechanical including audio and video.

Shooting ratio: The ratio between film actually exposed in the camera during shooting to film used in the final cut. A shooting ratio often to one or more is not uncommon.

Soft focus: Filters, Vaseline, or specially constructed lenses soften the delineation of lines and points, usually to create a romantic effect.

Subjective camera: A style that allows the viewer to observe events from the point of view of either a character or the persona of the author.

Swish pan (also called **flick pan, zip pan, whip pan**): A pan in which the intervening scene moves past too quickly to be observed. It approximates psychologically the action of the human eye as it moves from one subject to another.

Sweep in/out: Frame-by-frame revelation from blackout of complete image. More commonly called **Wipe in**. **Sweep out** is the opposite of **Sweep in**.

Synchronous sound: Sound whose source is visible in the frame of the image or whose source is understandable from the context of the image (e.g., source music).

Tracking shot: Generally, any shot in which the camera moves from one point to another either sideways, in, or out. The camera can be mounted on a set of wheels that move on tracks or on a rubber-tired dolly, or it can be handheld. Also called **Traveling shot**.

Wild sound: Sound recorded separately from images.

Digital Production Terms

Application programming interface (API): Documented interface that allows one software application to interact with another. For example, Twitter API.

Avatar: Image or username that represents a person online within forums and social networks.

BackType: Social media analytics company that helps measure social engagement.

Bit.ly: Free service that condenses long URLs to make them easier to share, such as on Twitter.

Collective intelligence: Information shared that emerges from the collaboration and competitions of many individuals and appears in consensus decisionmaking in social networks.

Content management system (CMS): A format to design and populate websites that allows creation of content without extensive knowledge of programming language. CMS can range from very simple to quite complex and from free open-source programs to very costly, depending on their capabilities.

Flash mob: A large group of people who assemble in a public place, perform an unusual and typically pointless act, then quickly disperse. Usually facilitated by social media, texts, or viral e-mails.

Forum (also known as a**message board**): An online discussion group.

Hashtag: A tag used on Twitter as a way to annotate a message. A word or phrase preceded by a #.

HootSuite: A web-based Twitter client that helps manage multiple Twitter profiles, pre-schedule tweets, and view metrics.

HTML (HyperText Markup Language): Programming language for webpages. HTML5 (under development in June 2012) offers potential for cross-platform mobile applications.

Inbound marketing: Focuses on getting found by customers. Related to **relationship marketing** and **permission marketing**, wherein customers seek out information rather than being contacted by an advertiser.

Lifecasting: Continual broadcast of events in a person's life through digital media.

Link building: An aspect of search engine optimization where website owners cooperate to add links to their sites from other sites to improve their search engine ranking. Blogging is a popular method of link building.

Mashup: Multiple layers of media from preexisting sources to create a new work.

Permission marketing(also known as **relationship marketing**): Allows the recipient of direct marketing messages to opt in to accept future e-mails or direct mail.

Podcast: Nonstreamed webcast, either audio or video, released episodically and often downloaded through an RSS.

PostRank: Monitors and collects social engagements related to content around the web.

Search engine optimization (SEO): The process of improving the volume or quality of traffic to a website from search engines via unpaid or organic search traffic.

Tag cloud: Visual depiction of user-generated tags, typically used to describe the content of websites.

TweetDeck: An application that connects users with contacts across Twitter, Facebook, Myspace, LinkedIn, and more.

Video blog: Produces regular video content often around the same theme on a daily or weekly basis, such as Wine Library TV.

Web analytics: Measurement, collection, analysis, and reporting of Internet data to aid understanding and optimization.

Webinar: Live meetings, training, or presentations on the Internet.

Yammer: A business communication tool that operates as an internal Twitter-like messaging system for employees within an organization. It provides real-time communication and helps reduce dependence on e-mail.

Zoho: A suite of online web applications geared toward business productivity and collaboration.

The Whole Book in One Page

- Find the central truth in a product. Discover the "One Thing" you can communicate. Look for that single adjective that defines a brand.

- Don't write to the masses. Talk to an individual. Find out how to satisfy his or her wants and needs.

- Learn to write structured, well-crafted body copy. People will read long copy if they are interested in the subject.

- Write hot. Edit cold. In other words, write with enthusiasm and let the words flow. Later, go back and edit ruthlessly. After you edit, cut another 20%–30%.

- Headlines can be the most important words of the ad. Do not write a weak headline and try to support it with a subhead.

- Learn to write theme lines. Really good taglines or slogans can make a product.

- Learn teamwork. Learn to collaborate. Not just with art directors, but also with account people and the client. Become valuable to the client, and you become valuable to the agency and the next agency.

- Think visually. Look for the visual-verbal connection. They work together—one does not describe the other.

- Learn everything you can about digital marketing and social media, but never forget the value of any marketing program, online or offline, is measured by return on investment.

- Engagement is the measure by which online and offline marketing will be measured. It's all about building relationships.

- Just because you *can* do it, doesn't mean you *should*. While rules and regulations can sometimes be bypassed, never forsake your own moral compass. Do the right thing, even if no one makes you.

- Think globally. Understanding of different cultures and customs is critical to creating advertising messages that resonate. This applies to your local community too.

- As the lines between online and offline marketing blur, you need to understand how to integrate marketing communication using different media and nontraditional methods.

- Keep it simple. That applies to copy and design. When you emphasize everything, you emphasize nothing. Stick to one basic idea and make it work.

- Think campaigns. Different elements that work individually and cumulatively to convey the message. Think of how you can extend and repeat campaign components.

- Learn how to present. Be confident, persuasive, logical. If you're naturally funny, use it. If you're not, don't try to be. Defend your opinions but know when to back down (see "Learn teamwork").

- Continually upgrade your portfolio. Don't put things in just because they were produced. Don't get sentimental. Weed out anything less than wonderful.

- Accept criticism and use it to improve. Develop a thick skin—creative directors, account people, clients, and your peers will think they have a better idea. Throw a tantrum and you won't sell the *next* idea either.

- Get involved in outside activities. Read, pay attention to pop culture, and take an interest in life outside of advertising and marketing.

- We'll end where we started—never stop learning!

Preface

1. E. B. Weiss, C. B. Larrabee, and F. C. Kendall, *The Handbook of Advertising* (New York: McGraw-Hill, 1938), p. 133.
2. Weiss, Larrabee, and Kendall, *The Handbook of Advertising*, p. vii.

Chapter 1

1. William Bernbach, *Bill Bernbach Said . . .* (New York: Doyle Dane Bernbach, 1989), p. 3.
2. Walter Isaacson, *Steve Jobs* (New York: Simon & Schuster, 2011), p. ix.
3. Quote from University of Texas at Austin, Department of Advertising, http://advertising.utexas.edu/research/quotes (accessed May 19, 2005).
4. MagnaGlobal 2011 Advertising Forecast, http://www.neoadvertising.com/ch/wp-content/uploads/2011/06/2011-MAGNAGLOBAL (accessed January 1, 2012).
5. Wayne Weitten, *Psychology Themes and Variations* (Belmont, CA: Thomson Wadsworth, 2005), pp. 255–256.
6. Mihaly Csikszentmihalyi, "Implications for a Systems Perspective for the Study of Creativity," in *Handbook of Creativity*, ed. Robert Sternberg (Cambridge, UK: Cambridge University Press, 1999), p. 314.
7. Mark Runco, "Creativity," *Annual Review of Psychology* (2004), p. 55.
8. Mark Runco, "Creativity," p. 658.
9. Daniel Pink, *A Whole New Mind: Why Right-Brainers Will Rule the Future* (New York: Penguin, 2006), p. 3.
10. Quote from Born to Motivate, http://www.borntomotivate.com/FamousQuoteCarlAlly.html (accessed May 19, 2005).
11. Quote in Angela Partington, ed., *The Oxford Dictionary of Quotations* (New York: Oxford University Press, 1992),p. 501.
12. Quote in Michael Jackman, ed., *Crown's Book of Political Quotations* (New York: Crown Publishing, 1982), p. 2.
13. Quote from University of Texas at Austin, Department of Advertising, http://www.advertising.utexas.edu/research/quotes/Q100.html#Advis (accessed May 19, 2005).
14. Steve Ohler, "Birth of a Network," April 2012.
15. Quote from University of Texas at Austin, Department of Advertising, http://www.advertising.utexas.edu/research/quotes/Q100.html#Advis (accessed May 19, 2005).
16. Emmie Nostitiz, "Gut Instinct," April 2012.
17. See "Maslow, Abraham Harold," in *Microsoft Encarta Online Encyclopedia* (2005), http://www.encarta.com (accessed May 19, 2005).
18. Leo Burnett, *100 Leos: Wit and Wisdom From Leo Burnett* (Chicago: NTC Business Press, 1995), p. 47.
19. Walter Isaacson, *Steve Jobs* (New York: Simon & Schuster, 2011), p. 56.
20. Walter Isaacson, *Steve Jobs*, p. xxi.

Chapter 2

1. Quote from the Clio Awards website, http://www.clioawards.com/html/wsj/spivak.html (accessed January 10, 2005).

2. Quoted in "Mary Wells Lawrence," *Vogue*, February 15, 1972.

3. Quoted in Glenn Griffin and Deborah Morrison, *The Creative Process Illustrated: How Advertising's Big Ideas Are Born* (Cincinnati: How, 2010), p. 24.

4. Quoted in Glenn Griffin and Deborah Morrison, *The Creative Process Illustrated*, p. 117.

5. Quote from the Clio Awards website, http://clioawards.com/html/wsj/dusenberrry.html (accessed December 20, 2004).

6. Quote from the Clio Awards website, http://clioawards.com/html/wsj/chiat.html (accessed December 20, 2004).

7. David Ogilvy, *Ogilvy on Advertising* (New York: Random House, 1985), p. 166.

8. Luke Sullivan, *Hey Whipple, Squeeze This: A Guide to Creating Great Ads* (New York: John Wiley & Sons, 1998), p. 35.

9. Quoted in Glenn Griffin and Deborah Morrison, *The Creative Process Illustrated*, p. 47.

10. Quoted in Nancy Vonk and Janet Kestin, *Pick Me: Breaking Into Advertising and Staying There: Hundreds of Lessons You Can't Learn in School* (Hoboken, NJ: John Wiley & Sons, 2005), p. 15.

11. Quoted in Luke Sullivan, *Hey Whipple, Squeeze This: A Guide to Creating Great Ads* (New York: John Wiley & Sons, 1998), p. 28.

12. Luke Sullivan, *Hey Whipple, Squeeze This: A Guide to Creating Great Ads*, p. 28.

13. Seth Godin, *Purple Cow: Transform Your Business by Being Remarkable* (New York: Penguin, 2003), p. 87.

14. Quoted in Alain Thys, "The Ten Truths of Branded Storytelling," *Future Lab*, July 26, 2006, http://blog.futurelab.net/2006/07/the_ten_truths_of_branded_stor.html (accessed December 9, 2008).

15. Quoted in Mark Di Somma Workshops, 2006, http://www.markdisomma.com/workshops.asp (accessed January 2, 2012).

16. Quoted in Tim Nudd, "Not Just a Tech Genius," *Adweek*, October 10, 2011, p. 37.

17. Laurence Vincent, *Legendary Brands: Unleashing the Power of Storytelling to Create a Winning Market Strategy* (Chicago: Dearborn, 2002), p. 70.

18. "Data Points Making the Brand," *Adweek*, October 24, 2011, p. 20.

19. Alain Thys, "The Ten Truths of Branded Storytelling," *Future Lab*, July 26, 2006, http://blog.futurelab.net/2006/07/the_ten_truths_of_branded_stor.html (accessed December 9, 2008).

20. George Felton, *Advertising: Concept and Copy* (Englewood Cliffs, NJ: Prentice Hall, 1994), p. 60.

21. Quoted in Glenn Griffin and Deborah Morrison, *The Creative Process Illustrated*, p. 113.

22. Quoted in Glenn Griffin and Deborah Morrison, *The Creative Process Illustrated*, p. 58.

23. Quoted in Bruce Bendinger, *The Copy Workbook* (Chicago: The Copy Workshop, 2002), p. 105.

24. Mario Granatur, "*Eva Luna*—A Nontraditional Approach to Engagement," May 2012.

25. Meghan Casserly, "The World's Happiest Brands," Forbes.com, November 11, 2011, http://money.msn.com/how-to-invest/the-worlds-happiest-brands (accessed December 20, 2011).

26. Ibid.

27. Matt Miller, "I Hate Advertising," April 2012.

28. Quoted in Branding Strategy Insider, "The Brand Management Checklist—Advanced," July 15, 2007, http://www.brandingstrategyinsider.com/2007/07/the-brand-manag.html (accessed December 8, 2008).

29. Quoted in Stefan Stroe, "Best & Worst Brand US Extensions . . . But What About Romanian Ones?" May 7, 2007, http://www.stefanstroe.ro/2007/03/07/best-worst-brand-US-extensions-but-what-about-romanian-ones/ (accessed December 8, 2008).

30. Quoted in "*Adweek*'s 2011 Brand Genius Awards," *Adweek*, October 24, 2011, p. 22.

Chapter 3

1. See the AAAA website at http://www.aaaa.org.

2. http://www.marketing powr.com/AboutAMA/Pages/StatementofEthics.aspx (accessed November 12, 2011).

3. AFCARS Report, June 2011, http://www./childwelfare.gov/pubs/factsheets/foster.pdf, (accessed June 7, 2012).

4. Peggy Conlon, "Adoption for Foster Care," April 2012.

5. Diane Richard, "Local Advertisers Turn to Arbitration to Resolve Disputes Over Ads," *Minneapolis-St. Paul City Business*, Vol. 15, No. 9 (August 1, 2007), p. 1.

6. Quoted in http://www.dizzydean.com/quotes.htm (accessed January 5, 2012).

7. Mike Insley and Harry Stanford, "Never Too Late," April 2012.

8. Quoted in http://www.brainyquotes.com/quotes/keywords/law.html (accessed January 6, 2012).

9. Robert Brauneis, "Copyrights and the World's Most Popular Song," October 24, 2010, http://papers.ssrn.com/so13/papers.cfn?abstract_id=1111624 (accessed January 4, 2012).

10. Quoted in Kim Hooper, "Writing by Day," http://day.kimhooperwrites.com/2011/09/12/from-the-experts-jim-durfee/ *(accessed February 13, 2012).*

11. David A. Weinstein, "Overlooking or Forgoing Federal Registration of a Trademark Can Be a Costly Mistake," *Advertising & Marketing Review,* November, 1, 2001, p. 5.

12. Walter Isaacson, *Steve Jobs* (New York: Simon & Schuster, 2011), pp. 419–420.

13. Quoted in William Arens, Michael Weigold, and Christian Arens, *Contemporary Advertising*, 12th ed. (New York: McGraw-Hill Irwin, 2009), p. 132.

Chapter 4

1. Eric Klinenberg, "The Solo Economy," *Fortune*, February 6, 2012, pp. 130–132.

2. Ibid.

3. Ibid., p. 131.

4. U.S. Census Bureau, http://www.census.gov/ (accessed February 21, 2012).

5. Marti Barletta, *PrimeTime Women* (Chicago: Kaplan, 2007), p. 10.

6. Marti Barletta, "Marti Barletta: Maddened by 'Mad Men': Decades Later, Markets Are Finally Coming to Understand Women's Buying Power," *Advertising Age,* July 28, 2008.

7. Hope Yen, "Interracial Marriage Hits New High: 1 in 12," *Appleton Post-Crescent*, February 16, 2012, p. 6.

8. Stone Brown, "African Americans Aren't Dark-Skinned Whites," http://www.diversity inc.com (accessed December 6, 2004).

9. Quoted in Stephen Donadio, ed., *The New York Public Library Book of Twentieth-Century American Quotations* (New York: Stonesong, 1992), p. 70.

10. Brown, "African Americans Aren't Dark-Skinned Whites."

11. "African-American/Black Market Profile," www.magazine.org/marketprofiles (accessed January 14, 2012).

12. "Hispanic Fact Pack," *Advertising Age*, July 25, 2011, p. 18.

13. Ibid., p. 3.

14. Leo Olper, personal interview, New York, January 13, 2012.

15. Ileana Aléman-Rickenbach, e-mail correspondence, July 13, 2004.

16. Ibid.

17. U.S. Census Bureau, http://www.census.gov/ (accessed February 15, 2012).

18. Ileana Aléman-Rickenbach, e-mail correspondence, July 13, 2004.

19. Ibid.

20. Ibid.

21. http://css.edu./user/dswenson, October 8, 2001 (accessed June 1, 2005).

22. "Hispanic & Latino Marketing US and Latam," http://www.hispania-accent.com/?page_id=25 (accessed March 4, 2012).

23. Ibid.

24. Stuart Feil, "The Best of Both Worlds," *Adweek,* March 12, 2012, p. H12.

25. Ibid.

26. "Data Points Tech Set," *Adweek,* March 12, 2012, p. 15.

27. "Hispanic Fact Pack," *Advertising Age*, July 25, 2011, p. 3.

28. Ibid., p. 36.

29. Quoted in Peter Ortiz, "Calling the Shots—in Spanish," *DiversityInc,* December 13, 2004.

30. "Hispanic Fact Pack," *Advertising Age*, July 25, 2011, p. 20.

31. http://she-conomy.com/report/facts-on-women/ (accessed February 23, 2012).

32. Brian Steinberg, "Nielsen: This Isn't Your Grandfather's Baby Boomer," *Advertising Age,* July 19, 2010.

33. Ibid.

34. Beth Snyder Bulik, "Boomers—Yes, Boomers—Spent the Most on Tech," *Advertising Age,* October 11, 2010.

35. Ibid.

36. Ibid.

37. Steinberg, "Nielsen: This Isn't Your Grandfather's Baby Boomer."

38. Ibid.

39. Judann Pollack, "The 15 Biggest Baby Boomer Brands," *Advertising Age,* March 1, 2010.

40. Witeck-Combs Communications and Harris Interactive, "Gay Consumers Brand Loyalty Linked to Corporate Philanthropy and Advertising," http://www.witeckcombs.com/news/releases/20020722_loyalty.pdf (accessed July 20, 2009).

41. Jean Grow, "The Gender of Branding: Antenarrative Resistance in Early Nike Women's Advertising," *Women's Studies in Communication,* Vol. 31, No. 3 (2008), pp. 310–343.

42. Kelly Brownell, "Marketing of Sugary Drinks to Kids and Teens: As Strong as Ever," *The Atlantic*, October 31 2011, http://www.theatlantic.com/health/archive/2011/10/marketing-of-sugary-drinks-to-kids-and-teens-as-strong-as-ever/247580/ (accessed February 18, 2012).

43. Bruce Horovitz, "Marketing to Kids Gets More Savvy With New Technologies," *USA Today*, August 15, 2011, http://www.usatoday.com/money/industries/retail/2011-07-27-new-technolgies-for-marketing-to-kids_n.htm (accessed June 8, 2012).

44. Sandra L. Calvert, "Children as Consumers: Advertising and Marketing," *Future of Children,* Vol. 18, No. 1, (2008), pp. 205–234.

45. Anna R. McAlister and T. Cornwell, "Children's Brand Symbolism Understanding: Links to Theory of Mind and Executive Functioning," *Psychology & Marketing,* Vol. 27, No. 3 (2010), pp. 203–228.

46. Calvert, "Children as Consumers: Advertising and Marketing."

47. McAlister and Cornwell, "Children's Brand Symbolism Understanding: Links to Theory of Mind and Executive Functioning."

48. Brownell, "Marketing of Sugary Drinks to Kids and Teens: As Strong as Ever."

49. Barletta, *PrimeTime Women.*

50. Sheri J. Broyles and Jean M. Grow, "Creative Women in Advertising Agencies: Why So Few 'Babes in Boyland,'" *Journal of Consumer Marketing,* Vol. 15, No. 1 (2008), pp. 4–6.

51. Stephanie Holland, She-conomy, http://she-conomy.com/report/facts-on-women/ (accessed February 23, 2012).

52. Amanda Stevens and Thomas Jordan, *PurseStrings* (HY Connect, 2011), p. 204.

53. Dawn L. Billings, "The Purchasing Power of Women," http://she-conomy. com/2012/02/19/the-purchasing-power-of-women-infographic/ (accessed February 23, 2012).

54. Ibid.

55. Cheryl C. Berman, Diane Fedewa, and Jeanie Caggiano, "Still Miss Understood: She's Not Buying Your Ads," *Advertising & Society Review,* Vol. 7, No. 2 (2006), muse.jhu.edu.

56. Tami Anderson and Elizabeth Howland, "7 Powerful Insights for Marketing to Women," http://www.startupnation.com/business-articles/1220/1/AT_Powerful-Insights-Marketing-Women. asp (accessed February 23, 2012).

57. Stevens and Jordan, *PurseStrings,* p. 46.

58. Ibid., pp. 186–201.

59. David Ogilvy, *Confessions of an Advertising Man* (New York: Ballantine, 1971), p. 84.

60. Sarah Kell, "Hungry for Work," April 2012.

61. Michael Hastings-Black, "Marketing Must Engage the Muslim Consumer," *Advertising Age,* November 10, 2008.

62. John Kuraoka, "How to Write Better Ads," http://www.kuraoka.com/how-to-write-better-ads.html (accessed May 25, 2005).

63. Ibid.

64. Bob Dylan, 1963, http://www.bobdylan.com/songs/the-times-they-are-a-changin (accessed February 25, 2012).

65. Anthony Vagnoni, "'Role Model' Jones, 59, Dies," *Advertising Age,* July 16, 2001, http://adage.com/article/news/role-model-jones-59-dies/54271/ (accessed January 18, 2012).

Chapter 5

1. Quoted in W. Glenn Griffin and Deborah Morrison, *The Creative Process Illustrated* (Cincinnati, OH: How, 2010), p. 48.

2. Millward Brown, *BrandZ™ Top 100 Most Valuable Global Brands* (New York, 2011).

3. Ibid.

4. Ibid.

5. Ibid.

6, Quoted in Jack Neff, "K-C: 'We Don't Believe in Digital Marketing . . . [But] Marketing in a Digital World,'" *Advertising Age,* March 21, 2012, p. 48, accessed June 12, 2012, http://adage .com/article/cmo-strategy/kimberly-clark-elevates-clive-sirkin-top-marketing-post/233451/?utm_ source=daily_email&utm_medium=newsletter&utm_campaign=adage.

7. Bradley Johnson, "Where's the Growth in Marketing? Follow the BRIC Road," *Advertising Age,* December 5, 2011, pp. 1, 8.

8. Millward Brown, *BrandZ™ Top 100 Most Valuable Global Brands.*

9. Quoted in Terri Morrison and Wayne A. Conaway, *Kiss, Bow or Shake Hands: Sales and Marketing* (New York: McGraw-Hill, 2012), p. 34.

10. Johnson, "Where's the Growth in Marketing? Follow the BRIC Road," *Advertising Age.*

11. Claudia Penteado, "Rock in Rio," *Advertising Age,* December 5, 2011, p. 12.

12. Johnson, "Where's the Growth in Marketing? Follow the BRIC Road," *Advertising Age.*

13. Morrison and Conaway, *Kiss, Bow or Shake Hands: Sales and Marketing,* p. 31.

14. Millward Brown, *BrandZ™ Top 100 Most Valuable Global Brands.*

15. Ibid.

16. Morrison and Conaway, *Kiss, Bow or Shake Hands: Sales and Marketing,* p. 158.

17. Morrison and Conaway, *Kiss, Bow or Shake Hands: Sales and Marketing,* p. 169.

18. Millward Brown, *BrandZ™ Top 100 Most Valuable Global Brands.*

19. Morrison and Conaway, *Kiss, Bow or Shake Hands: Sales and Marketing,* p. 93.

20. Neil Munshi, "Spain's Starring Role in Bollywood Movie a Boon to Tourism," *Advertising Age,* February 6, 2012, p. 6.

21. Johnson, "Where's the Growth in Marketing? Follow the BRIC Road," *Advertising Age.*

22. Morrison and Conaway, *Kiss, Bow or Shake Hands: Sales and Marketing,* p. 96.

23. Johnson, "Where's the Growth in Marketing? Follow the BRIC Road," *Advertising Age.*

24. Ibid.

25. Ibid.

26. Erin Regenwether, "Bonjour de Paris," April, 2012.

27. Ibid.

28. Neff, "K-C: 'We Don't Believe in Digital Marketing . . . [But] Marketing in a Digital World,'" *Advertising Age.*

29. "The Advertising Industry in Mexico Deserves to Know the Truth, Latin American Multichannel Advertising Council," October 12, 2011, accessed June 12, 2001, http://www.lamac .org/america-latina-ingles/releases/the-advertising-industry-in-mexico-deserves-to-know-the-truth.

30. Morrison and Conaway, *Kiss, Bow or Shake Hands: Sales and Marketing,* p. 151.

31. Alvaro Carvajal, "Mexico," *Advertising Age,* October 17, 2011, p. 8.

32. Stephan Mangham, "Indonesia," *Advertising Age,* October 17, 2011, p. 8.

33. Ibid.

34. Morrison and Conaway, *Kiss, Bow or Shake Hands: Sales and Marketing,* p. 104.

35. Buz Sawyer, "South Korea," *Advertising Age,* October 17, 2011, p. 8.

36. Ibid.

37. Morrison and Conaway, *Kiss, Bow or Shake Hands: Sales and Marketing,* p. 204.

38. Toygun Yilmazer, "Turkey," *Advertising Age,* October 17, 2011, p. 8.

39. Ibid.

40. Ibid.

41. Ibid.

42. Morrison and Conaway, *Kiss, Bow or Shake Hands: Sales and Marketing,* p. 223.

43. Millward Brown, *BrandZ™ Top 100 Most Valuable Global Brands.*

44. Thorsten Jux, "Adventure at the Touch of a Button," April 2012.

45. Marieke de Mooij, *Global Marketing and Advertising: Understanding Cultural Paradoxes* (Thousand Oaks, CA: Sage, 2010), p. 29.

46. Ibid., p. 8.

47. Ibid., pp. 34–35.

48. "Advertising: The Year's 10 Most Killer Pieces of Creative," *Advertising Age,* December 11, 2011, accessed February 12, 2012, http://adage.com/results?endeca=1&searchprop=AdAg eAll&return=endeca&search_offset=0&search_order_by=score&search_phrase=10+most+killer +peices+of+creative.

49. Ibid.

50. "The Five Best Global Ideas," *Advertising Age,* February 6, 2012, p. 6.

51. Ibid.

52. Kate MacArthur, "Kraft's Name Brings New Meaning to Snacking in Russia," *Advertising Age*, March 22, 2012, accessed February 20, 2012, http://adage.com/article/global-news/kraft-s-close-russian-translation-oral-sex/233459/.

53. Griffin and Morrison, *The Creative Process Illustrated,* pp. 45–48.

54. Laurel Wentz, "Brazilian Creative Renta Florio Joins U.S. Hispanic Shop Wing," *Advertising Age,* September 8, 2011, accessed March 28, 2012, http://adage.com/article/hispanic-marketing/brazil-creative-renata-florio-joins-u-s-hispanic-shop-wing/229669/.

55. "The Brand Union Names Juan Tan Creative Director, China," press release, The Brand Union, June 28, 2011, accessed March 25, 2012, http://www.thebrandunion.com/news/news_posts/2011/06/the-brand-union-names-juan-tan-as-creative-director-china/#news/news/posts/2011/06/the-brand-union-names-juan-tan-as-creative-director-china.

Chapter 6

1. Quote from the Clio Awards website, http://www.clioawards.com/html/wsj/spivak.html, 1996 (accessed January 10, 2005).

2. Quote from the Clio Awards website, http://www.clioawards.com/html/wsj/goodby.html, 1996 (accessed January 10, 2005).

3. Charlotte Moore, "In Service of Story," April 2012.

4. See "Allegedly Out-of-Date Comparative Advertising Triggers Lawsuit," August 14, 2003, on the By No Other website, http://www.bynoother.com/2003/08/comparative_adv.html (accessed June 3, 2005).

5. Daniel Pink, *A Whole New Mind: Why Right-Brainers Will Rule the Future* (New York: Riverhead Books, 2005), p. 50.

6. Pablo Castillo, " Truth or Legend," April 2012.

7. Luke Sullivan, *Hey Whipple, Squeeze This: A Guide to Creating Great Advertising* (New York: John Wiley & Sons, 1998), p. 52.

8. Paul Arden, *It's Not How Good You Are, It's How Good You Want to Be* (London: Phaidon, 2003), p. 80.

9. Leo Burnett, *100 LEO's, Wit & Wisdom from Leo Burnett* (Chicago: NTC Business Press, 1995), p. 52.

10. Sullivan, *Hey Whipple, Squeeze This*, p. 37.

11. Maureen Shirreff, interviewed by authors, February 2009.

12. Paul Arden, *It's Now How Good You Are, It's How Good You Want to Be*, p. 49.

13. Quoted from Clio Awards website, http://www.ciadvertising.org/sa/spring_04/adv382j/cristin44/home.html, 2004 (accessed December 20, 2004).

14. David Wallis, "The Breast of Advertising," *Adweek*, June 4, 2012, p. 20.

15. Ibid.

16. Ibid.

17. Quoted in Christin Burton, "The Life and Career of Carl Ally," March 31, 2004, http://www.ciadvertising.org/sa/spring_04/adv382j/cristin44/home.html, 2004 (accessed June 3, 2005).

18. Burnett, p. 7.

19. Quoted in Daniel Sacks, "The Future of Advertising," November 17, 2010, http://www.fastcompany.com/magazine/151/mayhem-on-madison-avenue.html (accessed January 10, 2012).

20. Christin Burton, "The Life and Career of Carl Ally", March 31, 2004, http://www.ciadvertising.org/sa/spring_04/adv382j/cristin44/home.html (accessed June 3, 2005).

21. http://www.amazonadv.com/ (accessed April 19, 2012).

Chapter 7

1. Paul Arden, *It's Not How Good You Are, It's How Good You Want to Be* (London: Phaidon, 2003), p. 78.

2. Quote from the Clio Awards website, http://www.clioawards.com/html/wsj/krone.html (accessed December 20, 2004).

3. Robin Williams, *The Non-Designer's Design Book: Design and Typographic Principles for the Visual Novice* (Berkeley, CA: Peachpit, 2004), p. 15.

4. Quote from the Clio Awards website, http://www.clioawards.com/html/wsj/spivak.html (accessed December 20, 2004).

5. Robin Williams, *The Non-Designer's Design Book,* p. 35.

6. Mooren Bofill, "Creative Passion," April 2012.

7. Quote from the Clio Awards website, http://www.clioawards.com/html/wsj/lois.html (accessed December 20, 2004).

8. Robin Williams, *The Non-Designer's Design Book,* p. 71.

9. Amy Attenberger, "Breaking the Cycle," April 2012.

10. Robin Landa, *Advertising by Design: Generating and Designing Creative Idea Across Media,* 2nd ed. (Hoboken, NJ: Wiley, 2010), p. 232.

11. Woody Pirtle, contribution to *Graphic Design: Inspirations and Innovations,* ed. Diana Martin (Cincinnati, OH: North Light, 1998), p. 50.

12. Robin Landa, *Advertising by Design,* p. 240.

13. Robin Landa, *Advertising by Design,* p. 232.

14. Quoted in Kim Hooper, *http://day.kimhooperwrites.com/2011/09/12/from-the-experts-jim-durfee (accessed June 15, 2012).*

15. "Top 100 People of the Century," *Advertising Age,* March 29, 1999, http://www.adage.com/century/people.html (accessed June 3, 2005).

16. Ibid.

17. Quoted in Jack H. Summerford, "Woody Pirtle: Completing the Circle," 2003, http://www.aiga.org/content.cfm/content?ContentAlias=woodypirtle (accessed June 3, 2005).

Chapter 8

1. Maxine Paetro, *How to Put Your Book Together and Get a Job in Advertising* (Chicago: The Copy Workshop, 2002), p. 7.

2. Thomas O'Guinn, Chris Allen, and Richard Semenik, *Advertising and Integrated Brand Promotion* (Mason, OH: South-Western, 2003), p. 50.

3. Quote from the Clio Award website, http://www.clioawards.com/html/wsj/dupuy.htm, 1996 (accessed December 20, 2004); Thomas O'Guinn, Chris Allen, and Richard Semenik, *Advertising and Integrated Brand Promotion,* p. 50.

4. Jim Albright, *Creating the Advertising Message* (Mountain View, CA: Mayfield, 1992), p. 49.

5. Quoted in Brainy Quotes, http://www.brainyquotes.com/quotes/authors/s/SteveJobs.html (accessed January 6, 2012)

6. Tom Monahan, "When an Ad Is Not a Campaign," *Communication Arts,* May/June 2000, http://ww.comarts.com/ca/colad/tomM_.31.html (accessed May 27, 2005).

7. See Nancy Gardner, "Celebrity Voice-Overs: That Not-Too Familiar Voice Could Be Selling You Something," Foster School of Business News Website, December 20, 2005, http://bschool.washington.edu/new/full_stories//voice-overs.html (accessed December 10, 2008).

8. Jeannie Caggiano, "Making Mayhem," April 2012.

9. Dan Augustine, "Midwest Ad Cat," April 2012.

10. Jim Albright, *Creating the Advertising Message,* p. 49.

11. Bob Garfield, "Top 100 Advertising Campaigns of the Century," *Advertising Age*, March 29, 1999, http://www.adage.com/century/campaigns.html (accessed May 27, 2005).

12. "The Young Influencers: Adweek Picks 20 Under 40 Who Are Wicked Smart and Rebooting Your World," *Adweek*, March 19, 2012, http://www.adweek.com/news/advertising-branding/young-influentials-138997 (accessed April 6, 2012).

Chapter 9

1. David Ogilvy, *Confessions of an Advertising Man* (New York: Ballantine Books, 1971), p. 92.

2. Morris Hite, *Adman: Morris Hite's Methods for Winning the Ad Game* (Dallas, TX: E-Heart Press, 1998), p. 33.

3. Quoted in Phillip Ward Burton, *Advertising Copywriting* (Lincolnwood, IL: NTC Business Books, 1991), p. 54.

4. Stuart Elliott, "Ads That Soothe When Banks Are Failing," *New York Times*, October 7, 2008.

5. George Felton, *Advertising: Concept and Copy* (Englewood Cliffs, NJ: Prentice-Hall, 1993), p. 93.

6. Quoted in Glenn Griffin and Deborah Morrison, *The Creative Process Illustrated: How Advertising's Big Ideas Are Born* (Cincinnati, OH: How, 2010), p. 128.

7. Jennifer Stopka, "Word Problems," April 2012.

8. Quoted in Denis Higgins, *The Art of Writing Advertising: Conversations With Masters of the Craft: William Bernbach, George Gribbin, David Ogilvy, Leo Burnett, Rosser Reeves* (New York: McGraw-Hill, 2003), p. 92.

9. Quoted in Kim Hooper, "Writing by Day," http://day.kimhooperwrites.com/2011/09/12/from-the-experts-jim-durfee/ (accessed February 10, 2012).

10. George Felton, *Advertising Copywriting*, p. 99.

11. "Top 10 Slogans of the Century," *Advertising Age*, March 29, 1999, http://www.adage.com/century/slogans/html (accessed June 15, 2005).

12. Dave Hanneken, "Blind Ignorance," March 29, 2012.

13. http://christinebronstein.com/post/698858138/why-a-band-of-wives (accessed April 19, 2012).

14. MacMillan Speaker Series, bio, www.macmillanspeakers.com/janemaas (accessed April 19, 2012).

Chapter 10

1. Quoted in Erik Clark, *The Want Makers: Inside the World of Advertising* (New York: Penguin Books, 1988),
p. 56.

2. John Caples, *Wall Street Journal* ad, 1978.

3. Designers and Art Directors Association of the United Kingdom, *The Copy Book* (Hove, UK: RotoVision SA, 2001), p. 120.

4. Jamie Shuttleworth, "Sharpie. Cap What's Inside," May 2012.

5. Seth Godin, *All Marketers Are Liars* (New York: Penguin Books, 2005), p. 9.

6. Godin, p. 810.

7. Godin, p. 122.

8. Godin, p. 89.

9. George Ault, "Breathing Room," April 2012.

10. Caples, *Wall Street Journal* ad, 1978.

11. Quoted in Denis Higgins, *The Art of Writing Advertising: Conversations with Masters of the Craft* (Lincolnwood, IL: NTC Business Books, 1990), p. 118.

12. Quoted in Kim Hooper, "Writing by Day," http://day.kimhooperwrites.com/2011/09/12/from-the-experts-jim-durfee/ (accessed February 10, 2012).

13. Quoted in Brainy Quotes, http://www.brainyquotes.com/quotes/keywords/advertising.html (accessed January 6, 2012).

14. Quoted in Randall Rothenberg, "The Advertising Century," *Advertising Age,* March 29, 1999, http://www.adage.com/century/Rothenberg.html (accessed June 27, 2005).

Chapter II

1. Quote from the Clio Awards website, http://www.cliowards.com/html/wsj/chiat.html (accessed December 20, 2004).

2. Quote from the Clio Awards website, http://www.clioawards.com/html/wsj.riney.html (accessed December 20, 2004).

3. Quoted in "Advertising & PIB: Kelly Awards," Magazine Publishers of America website, http://www.magazine.org/advertising_and_pib/kelly_awards/winners_and_finalists (accessed June 28, 2005).

4. Quote from the Clio Awards website, http://www.clioawards.com/html/wsj.spivak.html (accessed January 10, 2005).

5. Quote from the Clio Awards website, http://www.clioawards.com/html/wsj/mcelligott/html (accessed December 20, 2004).

6. Kate Harding-Jackson, "Advertising Found Me," April 2012.

7. Quote from the Clio Awards website, http://www.clioawards.com/html/wsj/spivak/html (accessed January 10, 2005).

8. David Burrows, "Insights Matter," April 2012.

9. "The Young Influentials: *Adweek* Picks 20 Under 40 Who Are Wicked Smart and Rebooting Your World," *Adweek*, March 19, 2012, http://www.adweek.com/news/advertising-branding/young-influentials-138997 (accessed April 6, 2012).

Chapter I2

1. Erin Griffith, "Streaming Music Has a Problem—It's a Huge Success," *Adweek*, January 9, 2012, p. 22.

2. Quoted in Griffith, p. 23.

3. Ibid.

4. Ibid.

5. George Belch and Michael Belch, *Advertising and Promotion: An Integrated Marketing Communications Perspective,* 9th ed. (New York: McGraw-Hill, 2011), p. 506.

6. Luke Sullivan, *Hey Whipple, Squeeze This: A Guide to Creating Great Ads* (New York: Wiley, 1998), p. 142.

7. Sullivan, p. 145.

8. Quoted in A. J. Jewler and B. L. Drewniany, *Creative Strategy in Advertising,* 7th ed. (Belmont, CA: Wadsworth, 2001), p. 168.

9. Sullivan, p. 132.

10. "Jeff Goodby's Creative Rules," *Advertising Age,* January 29, 2001, Center for Interactive Advertising, http://www.ciadvertising.org/student_account/spring_02/adv382j/eoff/ultimategoodby/creative.html (accessed July 6, 2005).

11. Bruce Bendinger, *The Copy Workshop Workbook* (Chicago: Copy Workshop, 2002), p. 279.

12. Quoted in Jewler and Drewniany, p. 160.

13. Quoted in Sullivan, p. 139.

14. Eric Collins, Larry Pipitone, and Joey Ellis, "Moving," May 2012.

15. Sullivan, p. 103.

16. See the AAAA website at http://www.aaaa.org.

17. Tim Nudd, "The 10 Best Commercials of 2011," November 28, 2011, http://www.adweek.com/news/advertising-branding/10-best-commercials-2011-136663 (accessed January 12, 2012).

18. David Ogilvy, *Confessions of an Advertising Man* (New York: Ballantine, 1971), p. 70.

19. Sullivan, p. 56.

20. David Ogilvy, *Ogilvy on Advertising* (New York: Random House, 1985), p. 111.

21. Phillip Ward Burton, *Advertising Copywriting* (Lincolnwood, IL: NTC Business Books, 1991), p. 258.

22. Adrian Alexander, "When Marketing Becomes Entertainment," April 2012.

23. http://www.3percentconf.com/index.php/mary-alderete (accessed April 19, 2012).

24. Quoted in Karen Lee, "The Lowdown on Lee Clow: Advertising's Chief Creative Maven of the Last Quarter Century," 2000, Center for Interactive Advertising, http://www.ciadvertising.org/student_account/fall_00/adv382j/klee/Lee_Clow/Lee_Clow.htm (accessed July 6, 2005).

25. http://www.3percentconf.com/index.php/jennifer-siebel-newsom (accessed April 19, 2012).

Chapter 13

1. Paula Bernstein, "Social, Mobile, Display, Search, Video . . . How Marketers Are Choosing Their Digital Colors," *Adweek*, May 14, 2012, p. D2.

2. Quoted in Danielle Sacks, "The Future of Advertising," Fast Company website, November 17, 2010, http://www.fastcompany.com/magazine/151/mayhem-on-madison-avenue.html (accessed February 13, 2012).

3. Helen Legatt, "Online Ad Spend to Exceed Newspaper, Magazine Spend Combined," Biz Report website, January 19, 2012, http://www.bizreport.com/2012/01/online-ad-spend-exceeds-newspaper-and-magazine-spends-combin.html# (accessed March 28, 2012).

4. Brian Quinton, "Widgets: They're Easy," *Direct*, January 2008, p. 35.

5. Jonathan Small, Branded Entertainment Mythbusters, Gigaom website, March 10, 2011, http://www.gigaom.com/video/branded-entertainment-mythbusters/ (accessed February 15, 2012).

6. Matthew Hill, "Fantastic Voyage to a Career in Online Advertising," April 2012.

7. Ibid.

8. Paula Bernstein, p. D2.

9. Quoted in Danielle Sacks.

10. Ibid.

11. Michal Charvát, "The Perfect Door Opener," April 2012.

12. Robert Klara, "*Adweek*'s 2011 Brand Genius Awards," *Adweek*, October 24, 2011, p. 26.

13. "First Mover: Simon Fleming-Wood," *Adweek*, February 6, 2012, p. 12

14. http://www.3percentconf.com/index.php/rebecca-rivers (accessed April 19, 2012).

Chapter 14

1. Quoted in Dan Frommer and Jen Ortiz, "The Future of Social Media Is . . . ," Business Insider website, November 13, 2011, http://www.businessinsider.com/future-of-social-media-2011-11#jeffrey-zeldman-designer-writer-and-publisher-5#ixzz1p5rpDykL (accessed March 15, 2012).

2. "Social Media Breaks Down Barriers for Shoppers," *Adweek*, March 12, 2012, p. 12.

3. Quoted Dan Frommer and Jen Ortiz, "The Future of Social Media Is . . ."

4. "5 Differences Between Social Media and Social Networking," Social Media Today website, May 4, 2010, http://socialmediatoday.com/SMC/194754 (accessed March 21, 2012)

5. Quoted in "Ford Launches Second Chapter of the Fiesta Project; Eight New Webisodes Hit YouTube for Ford Fiesta's 2011 Social Media Campaign," PR Newswire website, July 22, 2011, http://www.prnewswire.com/news-releases/ford-launches-second-chapter-of-the-fiesta-project-eight-new-webisodes-hit-youtube-for-ford-fiestas-2011-social-media-campaign-99009744.html (accessed March 15, 2012).

6. Quoted in "Top 20 Social Media Quotes of All Time," Anson Alexander blog, May 24, 2011, http:/ /www.ansonalex.com/technology/top-20-social-media-quotes-of-all-time/ (accessed February 21, 2012).

7. Jeff Lyon, "Viral Marketing," *Chicago Tribune Magazine*, August 5, 2007, p. 6.

8. Jeff Koyen, "Mouth Meets Mouse," *Adweek*, November 21, 2011, pp. W1–W9.

9. "The Best of Word of Mouth," *Adweek*, November 21, 2011, p. W12.

10. Todd Wasserman, "Is Talk Cheap? How Cheap?" *Brandweek*, June 29, 2008, http://www.brandweek.com/bw/content_display/news-and-features/crm/e3i3a6a726c3dd89a14be65cf4e81526914 (accessed December 28, 2008).

11. Ibid.

12. William Bernbach, *Bill Bernbach Said . . .* (New York: DDB Needham Worldwide, 1989), p. 15.

13. Jeff Koyen, "Mouth Meets Mouse," pp. W1–W9.

14. Ibid.

15. Ibid.

16. Quoted in "Top 20 Social Media Quotes of All Time."

17. Quoted in Brian Morrissey, "Clients Try to Manipulate 'Unpredictable' Viral Buzz," *Adweek*, March 19, 2007, http://www.adweek.com/aw/research/article_display.jsp?vnu_connect_id=1003559592 (accessed December 21, 2008).

18. Quoted in "Top 20 Social Media Quotes of All Time."

19. Jeff Koyen, "Mouth Meets Mouse," pp. W1–W9.

20. Zak Mroueh, "Can Advertising Make People Happy?" April 2012.

21. Tari Arbel, "Poll: Half of Americans Call Facebook a Fad," AP-CNBC, May 15, 2012, http://finance.yahoo.com/news/poll-half-americans-call-facebook-040555197.html (accessed May 24, 2012).

22. Alexei Oreskovic, "YouTube Hits 4 Billion Daily Video Views," Reuters website, January 23, 2012, http://www.reuters.com/article/2012/01/23/us-google-youtube-idUSTRE80M0TS20120123 (accessed March 17, 2012).

23. Gabriel Beltrone, "Instagrammers in Demand by Major Brands," *Adweek*, May 26, 2012, p. 19.

24. Josh Constine, "Pinterest Hits 10 Million U.S. Monthly Uniques Faster Than Any Standalone Site Ever," Techcrunch.com website, February 7, 2012, http://www.techcrunch.com/2012/02/07/pinterest-monthly-uniques (accessed March 17, 2012).

25. Quoted in "Top 20 Social Media Quotes of All Time."

26. "Hottest Digital," *Adweek*, December 5, 2011, p. 36.

27. Quoted in David Rowan, "Status Updates," *GQ*, January 2012, p. 140.

28. Katie Feola, "All Stars," *Adweek*, November 21, 2011, http://www.adweek.com/topic/media-all-stars-2011 (accessed April 12, 2012).

29. Kenneth Clow and Donald Baack, *Integrated Advertising, Promotion, and Marketing Communications*, 5th ed. (Upper Saddle River, NJ: Pearson, 2012), p. 245.

30. Ibid.

31. "T.G.I. Friday's Urges Facebook Fans to Buy Beers for Friends," *Direct,* October 2011, p. 60.

32. Daniel Farey-Jones, "Who Killed Deon?" Brand Republic website, January 11, 2012, http://www.brandrepublic.com/news/1111487/ (accessed January 11, 2012).

33. Kenneth Clow and Donald Baack, *Integrated Advertising, Promotion, and Marketing Communications*, p. 248.

34. Steve Hall, "Amex to Use Twitter Hashtags to Offer Merchant Discounts," Adrants website, March 7, 2012, http://www.adrants.com/2012/03/amex-to-use-twitter-hashtags-to-offer.ph, (accessed March 7, 2012).

35. Giselle Abramovich, "Social Media ROI Arrives, " Digiday website, April 3, 2012, http://www.digiday.com/brands/social-media-roi-arrives/ (accessed April 3, 2012).

36. Quoted in "Top 20 Social Media Quotes of All Time."

37. Christina Berk, "#McFail? McDonald's Twitter Campaign Gets Hijacked," CNBC website, January 25, 2012, http://www.cnbc.com/id/46132132/McFail_McDonald_s_Twitter_Campaign_Gets_Hijacked (accessed March 26, 2012).

38. Jeff Koyen, "Mouth Meets Mouse," pp. W1–W9.

39. "The Buzz," *Marketing News*, March 15, 2012, p. 5.

40. Mike Shields, "Report: Facebook Ad Performance Is Abysmal," *Adweek*, January 31, 2011, http://www.adweek.com/fdcp?1296573766575 (accessed April 3, 2012).

41. Ibid.

42. Larissa Harris, "Staying on Top of Social Media Trends," Talent Zoo website, April 25, 2011, http://www.talentzoo.com/news.php?articleID=10007&ref=articlerss (accessed March 15, 2012).

43. Ibid.

44. Quoted in "Top 20 Social Media Quotes of All Time."

45. Nicholas Mejia, "Rock On, "April 2012.

46. Steve Parker, "Google + Social Engagement Falls Short," Business 2 Community website, March 14, 2012, http://www.business2community.com/social-media/google-social-engagement-falls-short-infographic-0146331 (accessed March 17, 2012).

47. "Trends: Social Media Advertising," *Adweek*, October 12, 2011, p. 29.

48. "TR35 Young Innovator," Technology Review website (Massachusetts Institute of Technology), 2008, http://www.technologyreview.com/tr35/Profile.aspx?Cand=T&TRID=700 (accessed November 5, 2008).

49. "The Young Influentials: Adweek Picks 20 Under 40 Who Are Wicked Smart and Rebooting Your World," March 19, 2012, *Adweek*, http://www.adweek.com/news/advertising-branding/young-influentials-138997 (accessed March 22, 2012).

Chapter 15

1. Bob Stone and Ron Jacobs, *Successful Direct Marketing Methods*, 7th ed. (New York: McGraw-Hill, 2001), p. 5.

2. Direct Marketing Association, "Findings and Analysis From the DMA 2001–2002 Economic Impact Report" (press release), June 10, 2002, http://www.the-dma.org/cgi/disppressrelease?article=339 (accessed June 30, 2005).

3. Carol Krol, "Marketer's Secret Weapon: Direct Mail," *Direct Marketing News*, February 2011, p. 23.

4. Ibid.

5. Philip Ward-Burton, *Advertising Copywriting* (Lincolnwood, IL: NTC Business Books, 1991), p. 163.

6. Connie O'Kane, "Direct Mail With Promotional Products, Imprint" (publication of the Advertising Specialty Institute), available on Printable Promotions website, http://www.printablepromotions.com/Articles/DirectMail.htm (accessed June 30, 2005).

7. Quoted in Maxine Paetro, *How to Put Your Book Together and Get a Job in Advertising* (Chicago: The Copy Workshop, 2001), p. 189.

8. Grant Johnson, "Hey, (Your Name Here)! When Does Personalization Go Too Far?" *DIRECT* magazine, February 2008, p. 20.

9. Ibid.

10. Janet Champ, "Stand Up to Cancer," April 12, 2012.

11. Drayton Bird, *Commonsense Direct Marketing,* 3rd ed. (Lincolnwood, IL: NTC Business Books, 1994).

12. Quoted in Willam F. Arens, Michael F. Weigold, and Christian Arens, *Contemporary Advertising* (New York: McGraw-Hill Higher Education, 2009), p. 584.

13. Kenneth Clow and Donald Baack, *Integrated Advertising, Promotion and Marketing Communications*, 5th ed. (Upper Saddle River, NJ: Pearson Education, 2012), p. 248.

14. John Hayes, "Realize Email's Potential; in the 'Mocial' Era," 2011 Essential Guide—Email Marketing, supplement to *Direct Marketing News*, September 2011, p. 6.

15. Quoted in Dianna Dillworth, "Email, Social Media: Marriage or Divorce?" 2011 Essential Guide—Email Marketing, supplement to *Direct Marketing News*, September 2011, p. 6.

16. Teodorina Bazgu, "My Coffee Addiction," April 2012.

17. Michael Brush, "After iPhone and iPad, and iTV?," MSN Money, January 24, 2012, http://money.msn.com/investing/after-iphone-and-ipad-an-itv-brush.aspx (accessed January 24, 2012).

18. Christine Birkner, "Looking Back Means Looking Ahead," *Marketing News*, December 30, 2011, p. 11.

19. Quoted in Ki Mae Heussner, "Do Mobile Ads Still Suck?" *Adweek,* February 13, 2012, p. 30.

20. Ki Mae Huessner, "Do Mobile Ads Still Suck?" p. 31

21. "Data Points," *2011 Mobile Guide* Special Advertising Section, p. M14.

22. Tim Peterson, "Mobile Tagging Extends TV Ads for Brands," *Direct Marketing*, August 2011, p. 12.

23. Stuart Feil, "The Time for Tablets," *Adweek,* February 13, 2012, p. M1.

24. Stuart Feil, "The Time for Tablets," p. M5.

25. Quoted in Ki Mae Huessner, "Jason Spero: Mobile Evangelist," *Adweek,* February 13, 2012, p. 12.

26. Quoted in Drayton Bird, Wikipedia website, http://en.wikipedia.org/wiki/Drayton_Bird (accessed February 22, 2012).

27. Willam F. Arens, Michael F. Weigold, and Christian Arens, *Contemporary Advertising*, p. 584.

28. http://www.3percentconf.com/index.php/cindy-gallop (accessed April 27, 2012).

Chapter 16

1. Quoted in Luke Sullivan, *Hey Whipple, Squeeze This: A Guide to Creating Great Ads* (New York: John Wiley, 1998), p. 82.

2. Russ Lidstone, "Let's Colour," April 2012.

3. "McDonald's Boosts Billboard," *Direct* magazine, August 2011, p. 45.

4. Jay Conrad Levinson, *Guerilla Marketing Attack* (Boston: Houghton Mifflin, 1989), p. 109.

5. "Aflac Duck's Paddle to Stardom: Creativity on the Cheap," *Wall Street Journal*, July 30, 2004, p. B1.

6. Jay Conrad Levinson, *Guerilla Marketing Attack,* p. 146.

7. Luke Sullivan, *Hey Whipple,* p. 80.

8. Pete Harvey, "Meritocracy," April 2012.

9. George E. Belch and Michael A. Belch, "Sales Promotion," in *Advertising and Promotion: An Integrated Marketing Perspective*, 6th ed. (New York: McGraw-Hill, 2003), pp. 510–561.

10. "007: Licensed to Place Products," *Guardian* website, April 2, 2012, http://www.guardian.co.uk/film/shortcuts/2012/apr/02/james-bond-product-placement (accessed April 3, 2012).

11. FIND/SVP & Media Post.com (accessed December 15, 2008).

12. Tim Peterson, "Brands Blend In-Game Ads With Consoles," *Direct* magazine, October 2011, p. 14.

13. Ernest Cavalli, "Study: 82 Percent of Consumers Accept In-Game Ads," Game|Life website, June 17, 2008, http://blog.wired.com/games/2008/06/study-82-percen.html (accessed January 5, 2009).

14. Mike Shields, "When It Comes to Ads in Games, These Guys Aren't Playing Around," *Adweek*, June 18, 2012, p. 23.

15. Tricia Duryee, "Four Types of Advertising Are Emerging in Social Games, EA Says," April 4, 2012, http://www.allthingsd.com/20120404/theres-four-types-of-advertising-emerging-in-social-games-ea-says/ (accessed June 21, 2012).

16. Ibid.

17. "10 Most Recalled New 'Hybrid' Ads" Oct./Nov. 2008, Nielsen Wire website, December 10, 2008, http://www.nielsen.com/.../10-most -recalled-new hybrid-ads (accessed December 20, 2008).

18. David Hauslaib, "Hybrid Ads: The Only Commercials That Are Still Worth the Cash," October 24, 2008, http://www.jossip.com/hybrid-ads-the-only-commercials-worth-the-cash (assessed December 20, 2008).

19. Paul Arden, *It's Not How Good You Are, It's How Good You Want to Be* (London: Phaidon, 2003), p. 30.

20. Sarah Lacy, "Foursquare Closes $50M at $600M Valuation," Tech Crunch website, June 24, 2011, http://techcrunch.com/2011/06/24/foursquare-closes-50m-at-a600m-valuation/ (accessed March 8, 2012).

21. "The Young Influentials: *Adweek* Picks 20 Under 40 Who Are Wicked Smart and Rebooting Your World," *Adweek*, March 19, 2012, http://www.adweek.com/news/advertising-branding/young-influentials-138997 (accessed April 6, 2012).

Chapter 17

1. Luke Sullivan, *Hey Whipple, Squeeze This: A Guide to Creating Great Ads* (New York: Wiley, 1998), p. 83.

2. Ibid.

3. Colle + McVoy website, http://www.collemcvoy.com/?q=Winfield+Solutions+Work (accessed February 19, 2012).

4. Tim Peterson, "B-to-G Marketers Shift Focus to Digital and Social Channels," *DM News*, August 2011, p. 35.

5. Ibid.

6. Seth Godin, *Purple Cow: Transform Your Business by Being Remarkable* (New York: Penguin, 2002), p. 87.

7. Chris Chariton, "Marketing Thought Leaders," AMA Access website, November 10, 2011, http://www.marketingpower.com/ResourceLibrary/Pages/newsletters/mtl/2011/seven_digital_trends_marketers_should_know.aspx (accessed December 12, 2011).

8. Jeff Wolf, "Creative Pants," May 2012.

9. Chariton, "Marketing Thought Leaders."

10. Casey Hibbard, "How Social Media Helped Cisco Shave $100,000 Off a Product Launch," Social Media Examiner website, August 30, 2010, http:www.socialmediaexaminer.com/cisco-social-media-product-launch (accessed February 20, 2012).

11. Hibbard, "How Social Media Helped Cisco Shave $100,000 Off a Product Launch."

12. Rob Morrice, "Business Technology Shall Inherit the Earth," March 2012.

13. sheilakloefkorn.com (accessed March 22, 2012).

Chapter 18

1. Quoted in Maxine Paetro, *How to Put Your Book Together and Get a Job in Advertising* (Chicago: Copy Workshop, 2002), p. 152.

2. Jancy (Janet Kestin and Nancy Vonk), "Ask Jancy," August 19, 2011, http://ihaveanidea.org/askjancy/2011/08/19/how-can-i-make-the-most-of-my-job-seeking-time/ (accessed June 28, 2012).

3. Ellen Steinberg, interviewed by authors, May 2007.

4. Joyce King Thomas, interviewed by authors, June 2007.

5. Quoted in Paetro, *How to Put Your Book Together and Get a Job in Advertising*, pp. 185–186.

6. Paul Arden, *It's Not How Good You Are, It's How Good You Want to Be* (London: Phaidon, 2003), p. 30.

7. Quoted in David Rowan, "Status Updates," *GQ*, January 2012, p. 140.

8. Margaret Johnson, "Google TV-Ivan Cobenk," May 2012.

9. Sheri J. Broyles and Jean M. Grow, "Creative Women in Advertising Agencies: Why So Few 'Babes in Boyland,'" *Journal of Consumer Marketing* 15, No. 1 (2008), pp. 4–6.

10. Quoted in Chris Ellis, "The Power of Local," *Adweek*, October 19, 2011, p. C1.

11. Broyles and Grow, "Creative Women in Advertising Agencies," pp. 4–6.

12. Interview series, April–June 2007.

13. Quoted in Kim Hooper, "From the Experts: Jim Durfee," September 12, 2011, http://day.kimhooperwrites.com/2011/09/12/from-the-experts-jim-durfee/ (accessed February 12, 2012).

14. Interview series, April–June 2007.

15. Judy John, interviewed by authors, July 2007.

16. Anna Gadecka, "Breaking the Family Tradition," April 2012.

17. John Melamed, presentation, Marquette University, Milwaukee, WI, February 10, 2004.

18. Arden, *It's Not How Good You Are*, p. 68.

19. Leo Burnett, "Keep Listening to That Wee, Small Voice," talk to the Chicago Copywriters Club, October 4, 1960.

20. W. Glenn Griffin and Deborah Morrison, *The Creative Process Illustrated: How Advertising's Big Ideas Are Born* (Cincinnati, OH: How Books, 2010), pp. 111–113.

21. Quoted in Chris Ellis, "The Power of Local," *Adweek*, October 19, 2011, p. C1.

22. Cotton Delo, "Facebook Files for IPO; Reveals $1 Billion in 2011 Profit Advertising Is 83% of Facebook's Revenue," *Advertising Age*, February 1, 2012.

23. Marco, "Cannes Advertising Festival Starts with Young Lions Winners," *Fast Media* magazine, June 21, 2010.

24. Quoted in Paetro, *How to Put Your Book Together and Get a Job in Advertising*, p. 156.

Tom Altstiel (M.A., University of Illinois at Urbana-Champaign) is owner/partner of Prom Krog Altstiel, Inc. (PKA Marketing), an integrated marketing communications service provider. Altstiel is responsible for developing creative strategy and tactics, print and broadcast copywriting, Web development and content, online video, client service and new business development. Since 1999, Altstiel has been an adjunct instructor at Marquette University, teaching Copywriting, Advanced Copywriting, Principles of Advertising, and Campaigns. He has won more than 250 local, regional and national creative awards and has served on several judging panels for national award competitions. Altstiel received the Dean's Award for Outstanding Part Time Faculty for the College of Communication at Marquette.

Jean Grow (Ph.D., University of Wisconsin-Madison; M.A., University of Wisconsin-Stevens Point; B.F.A., The School of the Art Institute of Chicago) is an Associate Professor of Advertising at Marquette University. Grow has received a number of teaching awards including third place in AEJMC's 2002 Promising Professors Competition. She has worked with such clients as Coca-Cola, USA, Kellogg USA, and Kimberly-Clark. She is former Director of Marketing for Apple Studios and heads her own advertising consulting firm, Grow Creative Resources. Her articles have appeared in the following journals: *Women's Studies in Communication*; *Qualitative Health Research*; *Journal of Consumer Marketing*; *Journal of Business Ethics*; *Journal of Communication Inquiry*; and *Journal of Advertising Education*.

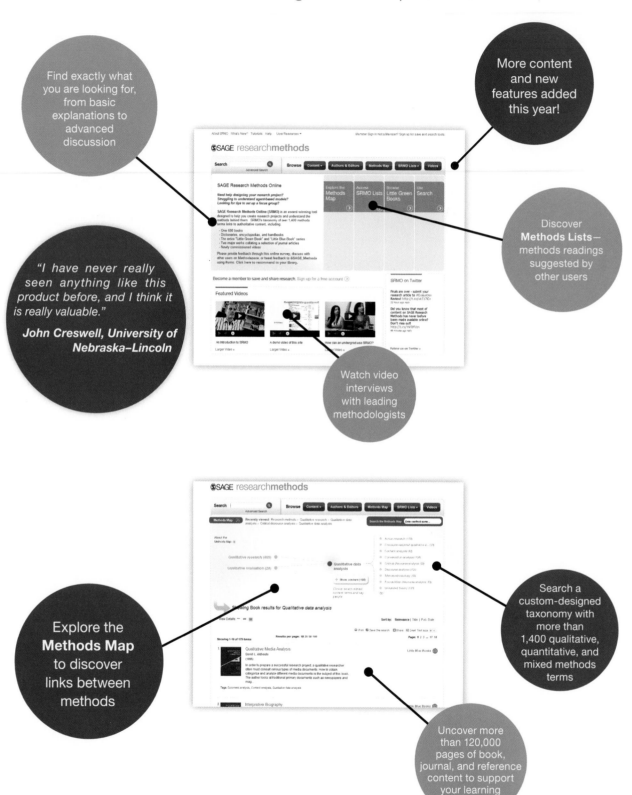

SAGE researchmethods

The essential online tool for researchers from the world's leading methods publisher

Find exactly what you are looking for, from basic explanations to advanced discussion

More content and new features added this year!

Discover **Methods Lists**— methods readings suggested by other users

"I have never really seen anything like this product before, and I think it is really valuable."

John Creswell, University of Nebraska–Lincoln

Watch video interviews with leading methodologists

Explore the **Methods Map** to discover links between methods

Search a custom-designed taxonomy with more than 1,400 qualitative, quantitative, and mixed methods terms

Uncover more than 120,000 pages of book, journal, and reference content to support your learning

Find out more at
www.sageresearchmethods.com